Siting Postcoloniality

Sinotheory A series edited by Carlos Rojas and Eileen Cheng-yin Chow

Edited by Pheng Cheah and Caroline S. Hau

Siting Postcoloniality

Critical Perspectives from the East Asian Sinosphere

Duke University Press
Durham and London 2022

© 2022 Duke University Press
All rights reserved
Designed by Aimee C. Harrison
Typeset in Minion Pro, Helvetica Neue, and SangBleu Versailles by
Westchester Publishing Services

Library of Congress Cataloging-in-Publication Data
Names: Cheah, Pheng, editor. | Hau, Caroline S., [date] editor.
Title: Siting postcolonality : critical perspectives from the East Asian
Sinosphere / Pheng Cheah and Caroline S. Hau, eds.
Other titles: Sinotheory.
Description: Durham : Duke University Press, 2022. |
Series: Sinotheory | Includes bibliographical references and index.
Identifiers: LCCN 2022027013 (print)
LCCN 2022027014 (ebook)
ISBN 9781478016687 (hardcover)
ISBN 9781478019312 (paperback)
ISBN 9781478023951 (ebook)
Subjects: LCSH: Postcolonialism—China. | Postcolonialism—Southeast
Asia. | Postcolonialism—East Asia. | China—Relations—Southeast Asia. |
Southeast Asia—Relations—China. | China—Relations—East Asia. |
East Asia—Relations—China. | BISAC: LITERARY CRITICISM / Semiotics &
Theory | HISTORY / Asia / General
Classification: LCC DS740.2 .S585 2023 (print) | LCC DS740.2 (ebook)
DDC 950.4—dc23/eng/20220816
LC record available at https://lccn.loc.gov/2022027013
LC ebook record available at https://lccn.loc.gov/2022027014

Cover art: Collage of protest banner and photograph of imperial
lion sculpture in Forbidden City, Beijing. Source: Pixabay.

Contents

vii   **Series Editor's Preface**   Carlos Rojas

xi   **Acknowledgments**

1   **Introduction: Situations and Limits of Postcolonial Theory**
       Pheng Cheah

Part I   Framing the Postcolonial

33   1   **Mythmaking: The Nomos of Postcoloniality**
           Robert J. C. Young

53   2   **On Twenty-First-Century Postcolonialism**
           Dai Jinhua, translated by Erebus Wong and Lisa Rofel

Part II   Chinese Socialist Postcoloniality

71   3   **Who Owns Social Justice? Permanent Revolution, the Chinese Gorky, and the Postcolonial**
           Wendy Larson

90   4   **De-Sovietization and Internationalism: The People's Republic of China's Alternative Modernity Project**
           Pang Laikwan

Part III   Hong Kong Postcoloniality among the British, Japanese, and Chinese Empires

109   5   **From Manchukuo to Hong Kong: Postcolonizing Asian Colonial Experiences**
            Lo Kwai-Cheung

127   6   **Decolonization? What Decolonization? Hong Kong's Political Transition**
            Lui Tai-lok

148	7	Locating Anglophone Writing in Sinophone Hong Kong
		Elaine Yee Lin Ho

Part IV   Taiwan Postcoloniality between Japanese and Chinese Colonialisms

171	8	The Slippage between Empires: The Production of the Colonized Subject in Taiwan
		Lin Pei-yin
191	9	Questions of Postcolonial Agency: Two Film Examples from Taiwan
		Liao Ping-hui

Part V   Diasporas in East and Southeast Asian Postcoloniality

213	10	Sinophone Geopoetics: From Postcolonialism to Postloyalism
		David Der-wei Wang
232	11	Multiple Colonialisms and Their Philippine Legacies
		Caroline S. Hau
250	12	Diasporic Worldliness in Postcolonial Globalization
		Pheng Cheah

277	References
313	Contributors
315	Index

Carlos Rojas   Series Editor's Preface

First published in 1978, Edward Said's groundbreaking book *Orientalism* examines the intertwined vectors of power and knowledge that developed under Western imperialism in and around the region known as the "Orient." Although this study helped catalyze the modern discipline of postcolonial studies, which has been used to examine a wide range of imperial formations around the world, Said himself notes that his focus in this volume is more specifically on the "Anglo-French-American experience of the Arabs and Islam, which for almost a thousand years together stood for the Orient" (1978, 17).

Coincidentally, it was also in 1978, the same year Said published *Orientalism*, that Deng Xiaoping launched the Reform and Opening Up Campaign, which similarly helped catalyze a wide-ranging set of economic and political transformations in China. After nearly three decades of Mao-style communism, the nation's strategic shift to a hybrid system of "socialism with Chinese characteristics" yielded an extended period of rapid economic growth that ultimately helped transform the relatively poor country into the world's second-largest economy. During the first decade of this post-Mao political and economic transformation, meanwhile, a newly strengthened China reached important agreements with the governments of Britain and Portugal (in 1984 and 1987, respectively) to have the colonies of Hong Kong and Macau transferred to Chinese control. When these territorial transfers were carried out in 1997 and 1999, respectively, they marked not only the formal end of the once-vast British and Portuguese Empires but also an important watershed moment in China's reassessment of its own history under colonialism (or, as Chinese historians often describe it, the nation's "semifeudal, semicolonial" past).

While this post-Mao realignment of colonial legacies was unfolding in China, Hong Kong, and Macau, an indirect result of China's post-1978 political liberalization and economic expansion was simultaneously playing out across the Taiwan Strait. After having been occupied (either in part or in toto) since the seventeenth century by the Dutch, the Spanish, and the Qing, Taiwan had been handed over to the Japanese in 1895 following China's defeat at the end of the First Sino-Japanese War and remained a Japanese colony for the next fifty years. In 1945, after Japan's defeat at the end of World War II, Taiwan was handed over to the Republic of China, but after China's Nationalists were defeated by the Communists four years later, the entire government of the Republic of China relocated to Taipei, where it immediately implemented a martial law regime that would remain in place for nearly four decades. During this post-1949 period, the governments based in Beijing and Taipei maintained a delicate geopolitical balancing act, whereby they both agreed that there was only one "China," while each claiming to be the nation's legitimate leader. Once Taiwan's martial law regime was finally lifted in 1987, meanwhile, it became possible for locals to revisit a set of previously proscribed historical topics—such as the "2.28" government-initiated massacre in 1947, which occurred as the island was transitioning from its former status as a colonial possession under the Japanese to a quasi-colonial possession under the Nationalists from the Chinese mainland.

Just as Said's *Orientalism* helped encourage a general reassessment of European colonial legacies, these post-1978 developments in Greater China helped draw attention to the distinctive sociopolitical formations that had developed under the region's overlapping colonial and quasi-colonial regimes—including European imperialism, Japanese imperialism, and even the imperial dimensions of China's traditional dynastic structure as well as some of its post-1911 incarnations. In addition to Hong Kong's and Macau's long-term colonization by the British and the Portuguese, and Taiwan's historical palimpsest of colonization by multiple different powers, other colonial formations in the region include European nations' extraterritorial control over parts of some Chinese port cities in the nineteenth and early twentieth centuries, the Japanese puppet state of Manchukuo (in what is currently northeastern China) between 1932 and 1945, overlapping colonial regimes in sinophone regions of Southeast Asia, and the quasi-colonial status of some of the border regions of the Chinese empire itself.

In *Siting Postcoloniality*, Pheng Cheah, Caroline Hau, and their contributors explore the sociopolitical, ideological, and cultural dimensions of colonialism and its legacies within a Sinitic geocultural context. The volume's twelve chapters examine postcolonialism from different conceptual or thematic perspectives, while also considering the specific conditions in various "sites" in the Sinosphere—including Hong Kong, Taiwan, Manchukuo, and different regions in Southeast Asia. As such, the volume has important implications for our understanding of the Sinosphere's colonial and postcolonial pasts, presents, and potential futures—a topic that is particularly relevant at the present moment, as China uses its economic, political, and military heft to expand its influence not only over the various border zones/regions/nations over which it claims sovereignty but also (and particularly through its massive new Belt and Road transnational infrastructure initiative) over many countries throughout the world, especially in the Global South.

Acknowledgments

This volume originates from a conference held at the University of Hong Kong on June 25–27, 2015, co-organized by Pheng Cheah and Elaine Yee Lin Ho. Thanks to the Faculty of Arts and the Schools of English and Chinese at the University of Hong Kong and the Institute of East Asian Studies at the University of California, Berkeley, for funding support for the conference.

Pheng Cheah thanks Prasenjit Duara, Edward Friedman, Bryna Goodman, Caroline Hau, He Jianye, Rebecca Karl, Jon von Kowallis, Lydia Liu, Carlos Rojas, and Geoff Wade for their indispensable help in discussing Chinese imperialism and experiences of colonialism and for suggesting bibliographical materials and sending him electronic files of texts otherwise inaccessible because of library closures. Their generosity indicates that intellectual community is possible during a pandemic.

Pheng Cheah   Introduction

Situations and Limits of Postcolonial Theory

Sites of Colonialism and Postcoloniality

The field of postcolonial theory and literary studies has been the subject of vigorous debate and contention since its emergence four decades ago, if one dates this with the publication of Edward Said's *Orientalism* (1978). Numerous introductory surveys, monographs, and edited volumes have explored its intellectual historical sources and subjected its central premises and concepts to questioning (R. Young 2001, 2004; Gandhi 1998; Moore-Gilbert 1997; Loomba 1998; Ahmad [1992] 2008; Chibber 2013b). However, none of these studies have examined a foundational limitation of the field: the historico-geographically determined conceptual matrix that tacitly ties postcolonial studies to certain experiences of *Western* colonialism and their enduring legacies in Asia and Africa (and, to a lesser extent, Latin America).

This limitation is justified on the grounds of Western colonialism's historically unprecedented expansiveness, its capacity for incorporating all corners of the globe into modern capitalism's web of domination. As Robert Young, a contributor to this volume, puts it in his authoritative historical survey of the field, the history of Western colonialism

> was extraordinary in its global dimension, not only in relation to the comprehensiveness of colonization by the time of the high imperial period in the late nineteenth century, but also because

the effect of the globalization of western imperial power was to fuse many societies with different historical traditions into a history which ... obliged them to follow the same economic path. The entire world now operates within the economic system primarily developed and controlled by the west, and it is the continued dominance of the west, in terms of political, economic, military and cultural power, that gives this history a continuing significance. (2001, 5)[1]

In the vocabulary of world-systems sociology, colonialism incorporated zones outside the European world-system and extended it to create the truly global modern world-system. "Eventually by the end of the nineteenth century and the beginning of the twentieth, *the entire globe, even those regions that had never been part even of the external arena of the capitalist world-economy, were pulled inside*" (Wallerstein 1989, 129; emphasis added).

The postcolonial condition is strictly post-late-nineteenth-century Western colonialism. From a political perspective, it is concerned with the colonial power relations of Western states in a post-Westphalian interstate system and the external places to which the territorial nation-state form was subsequently transplanted through their coerced incorporation into the capitalist world-system. The postcolonial episteme was formed by abstracting from the cultural analysis of specific sites: British India, British and French colonialism in the Middle East, the French Maghreb, and the British and French Caribbean. Colonialism in these locations drew in varying degrees on the discourse of the civilizing mission. Because postcolonial theory originated from literary studies, it was concerned with how colonial discourse shaped canonical European literature. But these analyses were based on a broader argument about the fundamental role of discursive representation in imperialist political expansion and colonial governance: the axiomatic equation of cognitive and political authority. Edward Said argued that Orientalist discourse instituted an insurmountable ontological division between the West and the non-West. As a form of expert knowledge, it was an exercise of intellectual mastery that legitimized the non-West's political subjugation. Orientalism did not merely rationalize colonial domination but stimulated the West's will to colonial power through advance justification (Said 1978, 39). Non-Western peoples should be colonized because their true interests were served when governed by "a race that knows them and what is good for them better than they could possibly know themselves" (Lord Balfour, quoted in Said 1978, 35).

Said's diagnosis of Orientalism as the conceptual logic and discursive-representational system of colonialism tout court is exemplary (see R. Young

2001, 18). Colonial discourse, it was argued, not only made colonizing subjects arrogantly confident about their world-historical election as saviors of the non-Western world but also created compliant colonized subjects. Effective colonial government required the production of scholarly knowledge about colonized populations. Colonized subjects were created by internalizing this knowledge through "the epistemic violence of imperialism" (Spivak 1988, 287): colonial education, the administration of law, public health, and so on. In a similar vein, Homi Bhabha (1994) argued that colonial discourse employed racial and cultural stereotypes that established incommensurable differences between the colonizer and colonized while its pedagogical project reinforced these differences by requiring the colonized to mimic the colonizer's culture as an unreachable ideal.

This representationalist understanding of power emphasized the cultural dimension of political and economic relations: discursive, psychical, and ideational mechanisms secured the oppression and exploitation of colonized peoples. Colonial representational systems were so pervasive that it mattered little whether the colonized populations were savages consigned to the dark prehistory of humanity or had grand civilizations that required rescue and preservation from the degraded present. The colonized needed to be brought into Western modernity and were constructed as subjects of lack and inferiority that assented to being civilized and educated. This sense of lack continues to scar postcolonial peoples after decolonization. Said suggested that the enduring power of Orientalist knowledge leads to the modern Orient's willing participation in its own Orientalization (Said 1978, 325). Gayatri Chakravorty Spivak (1988) argued that the violent exclusions of colonial culture continue into the present. It intersects with indigenous patriarchy and Indian class and caste hierarchies to ideologically produce the postcolonial bourgeois national subject who, by masquerading as "the people" and effacing the superexploited female subaltern from phenomenality, serves global capitalism.

Postcolonial studies' ethico-political vocation was to analyze colonial cultural hegemony and its legacy in the formation of postcolonial nationalism, neocolonialism, and contemporary globalization, focusing in particular on moments of opposition and resistance and the possibilities of strategic subversion in the colonial archive, literary texts, and cultural processes. The postcolonial critique of nationalism also led to an interest in processes of cultural transnationalism, diasporic movement, and globalization, often understood under the sign of hybridization, as means of undermining the territorial authority of the postcolonial nation-state.

The culturalist focus of postcolonial studies was subjected to critique from the moment of its academic institutionalization, especially by Marxist critics. Benita Parry (2004) argued that postcolonial theory was an offshoot of the poststructuralist linguistic turn and conflated the textual and the social. Its skepticism of universal narratives of legitimation led it to distance itself from the Marxist critical legacy, which informed anticolonial national liberation struggles. Its focus on resistance within signifying processes was an "exorbitation of discourse." When coupled with an "incuriosity about enabling socio-economic and political institutions and other forms of social praxis," this textual idealism obscured the concrete agency of colonized and postcolonial subjects (Parry 2004, 26). Indeed, despite postcolonial theory's radical rhetoric, its lack of a historical-materialist dimension resulted in a performative contradiction. Without a careful analysis of the connection between colonialism and global capitalism and an awareness of how the problems of postcolonial societies have been shaped by class divisions, postcolonial theory could only mystify the postcolonial world. Instead of being a concrete historical term, *the postcolonial* designated a general condition of subversiveness, a radical attitude, and even an empty signifier of difference from the hegemonic world order (Lazarus 2011, 17). Indeed, it has been scathingly argued that the ascendancy of postcolonial studies is a direct reflection of global capitalism in the 1980s, which produced postcolonial intellectuals employed by prestigious Western universities as unwitting ideologists who mystified the world capitalist economy (Dirlik 1998).

Another strand of criticism focused on postcolonial theory's spatiotemporal limits. It has been criticized for its inattention to experiences of Western colonialism beyond its implicit geographical purview and for its backward-looking temporal preoccupation with the legacy of the colonial past. Consequently, it has failed to analyze contemporary struggles for freedom in formerly colonized places that may no longer operate according to a colonial discursive logic and its postcolonial negation. For example, postcolonial theory has not focused on Southeast Asia because the surge of capitalist industrial modernization in much of the region led to an interest in economic growth in the present and future instead of an obsession with colonial history's aftermath (Chua 2008). Contemporary political movements such as the Arab Spring may indicate the exhaustion of the colonial/postcolonial episteme because they constitute a new future-oriented planetwide liberation geography that has transcended the binary between the West and the rest of the world (Dabashi 2012). The decolonial critique of postcolonial theory not only objects to the lack of attention given to Latin America but argues that the colonizer-colonized model ignores the persistence of radical indigenous traditions and fails to account for the mixed indigenous-settler culture that developed in Latin America, which is distinct from North American settler culture (Mignolo 2000, 2007).

The problems delineated by these critiques have a common root. Postcolonial theory accords primacy to discourse in colonial power relations—Orientalism's subjectifying power, the epistemic violence of imperialism, or the psychical scars caused by colonial pedagogy—because it takes the civilizing mission as the paradigm of colonial power and generalizes the experiences of British and French colonialism, where the civilizing mission was most pronounced, into analytical categories for understanding postcoloniality. It also focuses on parts of the postcolonial world that are less developed because "development" and "modernization" are easily characterized as contemporary forms of the civilizing mission. This is the unspoken spatiotemporal matrix of postcolonial studies. The shortcomings of such a framework are apparent in the tedious mechanical application of Orientalism as an accusatory appellation or pathological diagnostic for contemporary cultural forms (for example, world literature, advanced technology) when Orientalism may have only a weak connection to power relations in postcolonial and postsocialist globalization.

History of Sino-Postcoloniality: "Chinese" "Colonial" Experiences

This collection's primary aim is to "reopen the box" of the postcolonial episteme and reevaluate its theoretical claims by focusing on a largely ignored site outside its geographico-temporal frame: the Sinosphere, defined as the region of East and Southeast Asia that has been significantly shaped by relations with various dynasties of the Middle Kingdom and the republican and communist regimes of modern China.[2] By definition, postcoloniality involves changes in global power relations in the wake of colonialism. Any account that does not consider the Sinosphere is necessarily distorted because the region's complicated experiences of colonialism have decisive consequences for the contemporary world order.

One can construct a conventional edifying narrative of colonial oppression, liberation, and postcolonial nation building. First, although mainland China was never formally colonized, it was a victim of Western colonial depredation. The collective sense of humiliation inflicted by the "unequal treaties" that concluded the Opium Wars stimulated modern Chinese nationalism. This national shame led to the anti-imperialist stance of the People's

Republic of China (PRC), which, in combination with the discourse of socialist internationalism, has resulted in the PRC's self-representation as the champion of all oppressed nations in the ongoing struggle against Western imperialism. As stated in its constitution's preamble, "China consistently opposes imperialism, hegemonism and colonialism, works to strengthen unity with the people of other countries, supports the oppressed nations and the developing countries in their just struggle to win and preserve national independence and develop their national economies."[3] In this spirit it has assumed unofficial leadership of third world countries and promoted South-South multilateral relations based on principles of equality and mutual benefit as a supportive observer of the Non-Aligned Movement.

Second, Western incursion in the mainland marked the beginning of the end of the Sinosphere-grounded tribute and trade system in Asia and created the conditions that brought Chinese subjects under the rule of European colonial regimes in the rest of the world.[4] The legalization of Chinese emigration to all parts of the British Empire by the Convention of Beijing (October 24, 1860), which followed the sacking of the Summer Palace by European forces, opened the floodgates for mass migration from China through the British and Portuguese colonies of Hong Kong and Macau and various treaty ports to other colonial dominions, especially those in Southeast Asia: British Malaya, the Spanish Philippines, the Dutch East Indies, and French Indochina.[5] The aim was to supply British and other colonies with cheap Chinese labor. Migration plugged China into the web of European overseas territories and created a condition of global interconnectedness. It established a network of overseas Chinese communities that would accumulate considerable wealth by strategically negotiating between multiple colonial regimes. This is the primal scene, so to speak, of one branch of the Sinophone that David Wang's chapter explores. This network was an important source of patriotic financial support for the republican nationalist revolution against the Qing empire and Western imperialism (Karl 2002) and the early phase of the socialist revolution; a source of knowledge and investment for China's economic modernization from the late Qing period onward; and a preexisting circuit for the PRC to tap for its Belt and Road Initiative. Third, postsocialist China is the only former colonized power that has emerged as a global hegemon that has decisively changed the world-system. Hence, recent theoretical attempts to dislodge the world-system from its North Atlantic center have argued for its recentering in China, with the broader goal of elaborating a polycentric world-system or a series of overlapping world-systems (Frank 1998; Arrighi 2009).

However, Chinese experiences of colonialism do not fit the straightforward Western colonizer versus non-Western colonized binary or the progression from colonial bondage to political freedom. First, although the brunt of the hardship inflicted by Western colonialism was borne by the masses, the violated political authority in question was not that of a nation-state but the Qing empire, the last in a long line of Middle Kingdom imperial dynasties. The Qing dynasty expanded the Middle Kingdom's territorial boundaries to its historically largest expanse through conquest, ruled its borderlands, and exerted control over its East and Southeast Asian neighbors through tribute and trade relations. Moreover, it was a foreign empire, the descendants of northern nomadic Manchu tribes that ruled over a Han majority and a multitude of ethnic minorities from 1644 to 1912. The modern Chinese national awakening was not primarily directed against Western colonialism but against the effete Qing empire, whose corrupt incompetence had caused China's degeneration into the "Sick Man of East Asia" and made it vulnerable to Western incursion. As Rebecca Karl observes, unlike the Philippine revolutions against Spain and the United States with which they identified, Chinese revolutionary intellectuals "reformulated the seventeenth-century Manchu conquest of the Ming dynasty as a modern colonial conquest of China and proposed revolution as the way to remedy this 'colonial' situation" (2002, 85).

Second, the topos of Qing imperialism raises the question of older forms of imperialism before nineteenth-century European territorial imperialism. For example, were the tributary relations between the Middle Kingdom and its neighbors colonial? Considered within the *longue durée*, Hong Kong and Taiwan (the subjects of parts III and IV of this book), territories the Qing empire ceded to Britain in 1842 and 1860 after the First and Second Opium Wars and to Japan in 1895 after the First Sino-Japanese War, were incorporated into the Middle Kingdom by imperial invasion. The area that is currently Guangdong and Hong Kong became part of Han territory after the defeat of the kingdom of Nanyue around 112 BC. Taiwan's annexation is recent: the Qing empire conquered this holdout of Ming dynasty loyalists during the Kangxi emperor's reign in 1683. These power relations were part of world-systems that preceded and were purportedly destroyed by the modern world-system created by European colonialism. However, they may have persisted into the early twentieth century. As late as 1904, Liang Qichao characterized earlier centuries of Chinese migration to Southeast Asia as a colonial enterprise: "In the hundred or more countries in the Southern seas [*hai yi nan* 海以南], the majority of the population are descendants of the Yellow Emperor. Whether from a geographical or historical perspective, they are the natural colonies of our race [*wo zu zhi zhimindi* 我族之殖民地]" (Liang 1999, 1368).[6]

Finally, the fact that mainland China was not formally colonized suggests that it was only minimally subjected to the cultural violence of the Western civilizing mission. The influence of Western ideas from the late nineteenth to early twentieth century was mediated through translation and transculturation, much of it through Japanese thought. This puts into question postcolonial theory's privileging of discursive subjectification in securing consent to colonialism. Modern China's strongest relationship of political and cultural tutelage is arguably not with the West but instead with the Soviet Union. It may be here that China's postcoloniality is more fruitfully explored (see Pang, Larson, Part II of this volume).

Simply put, the multivalent complexity of colonial and postcolonial relations in the Sinosphere problematizes two fundamental axioms of postcolonial studies: the correlation of West and non-West with the opposition of colonizer and colonized and the power of colonial discourse as an ideology and technology of subjectification. Because this volume focuses on the Sinosphere from the twentieth century to the present, I will provide a selective digest of scholarship about its colonial experiences because of their legacy for the postcolonial era.

Although this lies beyond the scope of this volume, it is important to note that in the premodern period, the Middle Kingdom was the political, economic, and cultural center of East Asia and extended its influence into Southeast Asia by virtue of ritual relations of trade and tribute (*gong* 貢), expressed in diplomatic exchanges through the classical Chinese language shared with Japan, Korea, and Vietnam.[7] These tribute relations were consolidated by a Confucian moral-political model of administration. They intersected with trade relations and were facilitated by the "soft power" of intellectual, literary, religious, and cultural influence (Bary 1988). Despite their asymmetrical character, neither the Middle Kingdom's diplomatic relations with foreign kingdoms nor its land-based imperial expansion have been conventionally characterized in academic discourse as colonial because colonialism was associated with nineteenth- and twentieth-century European and American conquest and control of overseas territories for the purposes of exploiting their natural resources and human labor to benefit Western industrial capitalist economies (Schneider 2020, 317). Qing documents referred to European colonies in South and Southeast Asia as *shudi* 属地 or *shuguo* 属国, the dynastic terms for "inner territory" and "vassal" (Okamoto 2019a, 16; 2019b, 225), and nineteenth-century missionaries in China used *shudifang* (属地方)

to translate the term *colony* (Liu 2004, 254n33). The concepts "colonization" (*zhimin* 殖民) and "colony" (*zhimindi* 殖民地), essential terms in modern Chinese nationalist discourse used primarily to refer to modern Western and Japanese colonialism, entered Chinese thought only in the 1890s through neologisms adapted from Japanese publications read by students and intellectuals during their sojourns in Japan (Pan 2013). Hence, Liang's description of the Chinese diaspora in Southeast Asia in the Ming and Qing period as colonizers is anachronistic. They were not colonial settlers in the Western sense: migrants who exploited their destination countries at the behest of their dynastic states to the advantage of their economies.

Some recent Ming and Qing historians have, however, attempted to define *colonialism* more broadly to encompass premodern Chinese imperialism. They have provocatively argued that the Ming empire engaged in colonizing activity. In addition to trade-related tribute diplomatic missions in Southeast Asia, the Ming state also incorporated Yunnan, annexed Dai Viet territory as a Ming province between 1407 and 1428, and undertook military excursions in maritime Southeast Asia.[8] The wave of large-scale migration of Chinese to Southeast Asia in this period gave rise to hybrid Sino-Southeast Asian societies (Wade 2008, 628). It is, however, erroneous to characterize such societies via a Eurocentric analogy with European colonialism in the Americas, the Caribbean, Africa, and Australasia as colonial settler societies because they were largely unconnected to the Ming state.[9] As Geoff Wade notes, the eunuch-led voyages of this period "constituted only a maritime proto-colonialism as there was no real rule over a people or territory" but merely "rule over nodes and networks" for short-term economic advantage (2005, 55). In contrast, the invasions and occupations of Dai Viet and Yunnan justified by the Ming dynasty's Heavenly Mandate (*tianming* 天命) to rule the Middle Kingdom and everything under heaven anticipate features found in high European colonialism: policies of divide and rule and indirect rule through local elites (Wade 2006, 88–89, 91–92).

In a similar vein, US proponents of New Qing History or the Altaic school have suggested that Qing territorial expansions into Yunnan, Guizhou, Xinjiang, Tibet, southern China, and Taiwan were colonial in character. Peter Perdue (2009, 92) has argued that the Manchu conquest of China in the seventeenth century and the subsequent Qing expansion into central Eurasia and incorporation of Mongolia, Xinjiang, and Taiwan fits Jürgen Osterhammel's (1997) expanded psychological definition of colonialism as a relation of political domination between an indigenous majority and an invading foreign minority whereby the colonizers, who are convinced of their superiority and ruling mandate, govern by pursuing metropolitan interests (Perdue 2009, 92). Like British India, the Qing state also practiced indirect rule in these territories: the Altaic system involved the administrative co-optation of local elites while maintaining a hierarchical separation of Han and Manchu society through the banner system (Perdue 2009, 96). Of special significance for this volume, historians studying Qing travel writings and the journals of officials in Yunnan, Guizhou, and Taiwan have emphasized the recurrence of tropes that represent local ethnicities as primitive barbarians requiring cultural assimilation (Hostetler 2001; Rowe 2001; Teng 2004). These representations, it is argued, constitute a Confucianist civilizing discourse similar to European colonialism's civilizing mission. Although its civilizing project privileged Confucian culture, the Qing empire's Altaic ruling style suggests that it is fundamentally different from earlier Sinocentric Chinese empires and more closely related to the post-Timurid empires of Central, West, and South Asia (Perdue 2005, 542).

The heated response to New Qing History, especially from PRC scholars, indicates that these arguments have important political implications.[10] If the Qing empire is an alien colonizer instead of the legitimate successor of the unification programs of earlier Sinitic dynasties, the modern Chinese nation-state's territorial integrity becomes problematic (Perdue 1998, 255–56). And if the Sinocentric PRC regime is not a successor of the Qing state, then its sovereign claims over Qing-incorporated territories like Tibet and Taiwan are illegitimate (Schneider 2020, 325). With respect to Taiwan, the PRC's pledge to fulfill "the historical task of the complete reunification of the motherland" (Garcia and Tian 2021) is colonial in character. Eo ipso the inaugural Kuomintang (KMT) regime of the Republic of China (ROC) in Taiwan was also a colonial regime. The ROC's colonial origins have been ameliorated by its democratic political history, which has seen KMT governments voted out of power and has led to the constitutional enshrinement of Taiwan's non-Sinitic aboriginal peoples, its true indigenes or natives, as *yuan zhumin* (原住民). Taiwan's public culture has also attempted to document and preserve aboriginal cultural heritage and to promote contemporary aboriginal cultural production (see Lin, this volume). Such gestures are reminiscent of the reconciliation measures of Anglo settler colonial nations like Australia, Canada, and New Zealand.

The advent of Western colonialism in China did not create a situation that fit better with the presuppositions of postcolonial studies. Using Orientalist discourse analysis to study the Macartney Embassy of 1793 and the political impact of the Opium Wars on China, James Hevia (1995, 55) argued that the

Qing court regarded the first British mission as a cosmologically based tribute ritual between a supreme ruler (*huangdi* 皇帝) and a lesser foreign king (*fanwang* 藩王) instead of a relation between two equal national sovereigns operating within a post-Westphalian interstate system. The British in turn viewed the Qing emperor through Orientalist fantasies. The Opium Wars catalyzed a concerted pedagogical project to civilize China and discipline the Qing regime into a Westernized modern political entity that could engage in proper diplomatic intercourse with Western nation-states and be the signatory to treaties that conceded to foreign demands for territory, indemnity, economic privileges, and settlement and extraterritorial rights. This pedagogical discipline was a form of colonization. Hence, "China was not outside of the 'real' colonial world. Rather, it was a variation on forms that were both present and incomplete in Africa, South America, and South and Southeast Asia" (Hevia 2003, 26).

However, the target of this discipline was the Qing empire rather than the Chinese nation-people, which was in a nascent state of emergence, and this meant that Orientalism's penetration of any collective Chinese psyche was extremely limited. Because China was not formally colonized, there was no colonial education system to "create" á la Thomas Macaulay ([1835] 1995, 430) "a class of persons Chinese in blood and color, but English in taste, in opinions, in morals and in intellect." That occurred only for elite Chinese subjects of British Hong Kong and "the Queen's Chinese" of Malaya, the upper echelon of the diaspora with access to anglophone colonial culture. As Prasenjit Duara observes, "The absence of institutionalized colonialism in most of China . . . meant that colonial ideology was not entrenched among both colonizer and colonized in the same way as it was in India and other directly colonized countries. . . . [There was no] urgent need to root out imperialist ideology in the very self-perception of a people" (1997, 224).

Moreover, as Bryna Goodman and David Goodman (2012, 1–2) point out, "the diversity of . . . colonial arrangements [in China] defies systematic characterization": they ranged from actual colonies (British Hong Kong, Portuguese Macau, Japanese Taiwan) and territories leased to Russia, Britain, Germany, and France, where Chinese sovereignty was suspended, to treaty ports with foreign settlements governed by extraterritorial law and areas of foreign residence that facilitated imperialist interests without full colonization, as well as coastal and inland zones of foreign colonial influence adjacent to European colonies. This complex and uneven field of multiple and varied colonialisms enabled a proliferation of manifold agencies among the colonized Chinese, who gained advantages by negotiating between different colonial zones and Chinese-controlled territory in order to economically exploit other Chinese or to further the emerging nationalist movement.

Legalization of Chinese emigration to the British Empire created a different complexity in Southeast Asia, where the Chinese diaspora functioned as middlemen between European colonial regimes and indigenous populations and migrants of various ethnicities. Early twentieth-century Chinese nationalist intellectuals and contemporary Sinophone theory have mistakenly described such Chinese diaspora as settler colonialists. In actuality, they functioned within agricultural and resource-extractive colonial economies where they exploited Chinese and non-Chinese laborers alike. They were also oppressed by the colonial state, which dictated their comprador role even as it stigmatized them as exploiters of natives and migrants through racial ideology and divide-and-rule strategies.

The establishment of the nominally independent state of Manchukuo (1932) as a component of Japanese imperialism in China constitutes a different experience from European colonialism. Duara (2003) has provocatively suggested that it marks the ascendancy of a new form of colonialism in the modern world-system. Its two main features are imperial control without direct colonization, involving massive economic investment and infrastructure development, and the ideology of pan-Asian unity (see Lo, chapter 5). According to Duara, this modulation in Japanese imperialism was a response to the March 1, 1919, Korean uprising against the repressiveness of Japanese colonial occupation. Meant as an exemplar of Japanese industrial capitalism, Manchuria was established as an autarchic unit with modern industry and public infrastructure and was part of the yen bloc. This broke with older patterns of colonial domination in which a small Westernized industrial sector emerged alongside a traditional agricultural sector with little transfer of technology and negligible economic integration of colony and metropolis (Duara 2003, 68). Whereas European imperialism emphasized the inferiority of non-Western peoples, Japanese imperialism sought cooperation through a statist discourse of pan-Asianism, which espoused the formal equality of Asian peoples as members of a shared civilization requiring protection from Western imperialism (62–63). At the same time, Japan, the innately superior nation, would lead and unite all Asian peoples into a Greater East Asia Co-Prosperity Sphere. In its concretization as colonial violence, Japan's racist self-perception as an elect nation gave the lie to the idea of inter-Asian equality. However, Duara argues that Manchukuo left a lasting legacy in contemporary East Asia: "the East Asian modern," in which modern social, political, and economic institutions were indigenized by means of an ideology of cultural authenticity. This paradigm is a precondition of the model of East Asian state-led capitalist development in the former colonies of Taiwan and South Korea and has influenced the PRC's postsocialist economic development. More broadly, the motifs of an authentic Asian culture requiring cultivation and Asian solidarity are important to modern Chinese and PRC nationalism and to postcolonial Asia.

The preceding overview of "Chinese" experiences of "colonialism" shows the term's semantic flexibility and referential elasticity. In its broadest definition, colonialism is a power structure in which a nation or people exists in a relation of political or economic subordination to another. In Chinese experiences, the line between colonizer and colonized is often indeterminate. Chinese are victims as well as perpetrators of colonialism, sometimes simultaneously. The colonial hierarchy is also not always based on the (Orientalist) difference between East and West. Japanese colonialism relied on an ideology of civilizational similarity. Colonialism's target also depends on the specific relation: it is variously the Qing state, the Han people, peripheral regions of China and their non-Han ethnicities, the Chinese diaspora, indigenous Southeast Asians, and the modern nation of China. Moreover, what is *China*? The two-character expression Zhina 支那 originally derived from an early Sanskrit transcription of Qin 秦, the dynastic name that foreigners used as a toponym for the Middle Kingdom, and can be found in Chinese Buddhist writings and Tang poetry (Fogel 2012, 8–9, discussing Aoki Masaru). However, as Lydia Liu has noted, the more proximate source of the expression's use as a self-appellation in late nineteenth- and early twentieth-century China is a Japanese transliteration (Shina 支那) of the European term *China*, which was reimported to China by Qing students studying in Meiji Japan. Late-Qing nationalist intellectuals like Liang Qichao 梁启超 and Zhang Taiyan 章太炎 were concerned about the term's referent: China was a name imposed by colonial relations with foreigners and not an organic self-identity (L. Liu 2004, 76–79).

Nowhere is *colonialism*'s referential elasticity more apparent than in the differences between Sun Yat-sen's and Mao Zedong's uses of the term. Sun (1924, 1975) used the term to refer to China's oppression by Western powers and Japan. Since this oppression was primarily economic and did not involve political occupation, China appeared to be a semicolony, which Sun understood to mean having a higher degree of freedom than a colony.[11] To provoke shame and self-loathing as stimuli of patriotic passion, he argued that China's degradation makes it inferior to a full colony. Although Chinese deride Koreans and Annamese for being "slaves without a country [*wangguonu* 亡国奴],"

Introduction   13

a colonized nation is better off than China because it may receive aid from its master in times of crisis (Sun 1975, 38). In contrast, unequal treaties reduce China to a colony of all great powers, who, not being its colonial masters, are not obligated to provide relief. Hence, China is a hypocolony (*ci zhimindi* 次殖民地), a neologism derived from the term used in chemistry to refer to lower-grade compounds (39).

Sun acknowledged China's imperial past as the omnipotent power in Asia around which a tributary world-system was centered to emphasize the extent of its degradation. But he distinguished Chinese imperialism from European colonialism using the traditional *wen/wu* (文/武) dichotomy, creatively interpreted as a civilization/barbarism opposition. Chinese imperialism "used peaceful means to influence others and what was called 'the royal way' to bring weaker and smaller nations under her rule [*changyong wangdao qu shoufu ge ruoxiao minzu* 常用王道去收服各弱小民族]" (67). He tendentiously suggested that small Southeast Asian countries were willing to be annexed by the Ming empire or felt honored to be a tributary state because they admired Chinese culture (91). In contrast, European colonialism is conquest by brutal means (*yeman shouduan* 野蛮手段) (67), the brute force (*wuli* 武力) of "the way of might [*badao* 霸道]" (7).[12]

Although Sun does not call the Manchu occupation of China colonial, the Qing empire is the colonizer par excellence. Far more pernicious than Western and Japanese colonialism, its policies of epistemic violence were technologies of subjectification that obscured the Chinese national spirit for almost three hundred years to the point of obliteration. Sun drew an analogy between the Manchu denationalization of China and the Japanese empire's educational project of Japanizing Korea so that Koreans would no longer recognize their identity as a formerly independent nation. The Kangxi emperor initiated a similar program of intellectual subjugation to quell anti-Manchu revolution. He co-opted former Ming-dynasty literati by instituting an examination system for bureaucratic advancement, thereby making it impossible for the national spirit or revolutionary ideas to be expressed in scholarly writings (58). Literature expressing nationalist sentiment was banned (*wenziyu* 文字狱), while pro-Manchu literature extolling the foreign Qing emperor's Heavenly Mandate was widely disseminated (64, 60). The Qianlong emperor destroyed literati national consciousness by erasing all distinction between Hans and Manchus: he prohibited these terms and revised Chinese history by deleting mention of Song-Mongol and Ming-Manchu conflict and banning histories of foreign invaders, the Manchus, Xiongnus, and Tartars (60). Thus deprived of literary phenomenality, the national spirit survived only through the coded transmissions of secret societies and the fragmented oral narratives of homeless *jianghu* (江湖) wanderers and the lowest social strata (58).

Since nationalism is the driving principle of a country's progress and a people's survival (*guojiatu fada he zhongzutu shengcun* 国家图发达和种族图生存), Sun argued that the Qing eradication of Chinese national consciousness was the root cause of China's vulnerability to Western and Japanese colonial encroachment (55). Moreover, the Qing state was powerless to resist colonial demands and lost many territories and tributary countries such as Korea, Taiwan, the Pescadores, Annam, and Burma to foreign powers (33–34). The revolutionary overthrow of the Qing empire was therefore imperative. The immediate effectiveness of this cure is seen in the fact that foreign powers relinquished the idea of partitioning China after the 1911 revolution. But China's weakness had a deeper historical cause. Its imperialist legacy espoused cosmopolitan tolerance of other cultures. This was beneficial to conquered peoples but gradually eroded Chinese national consciousness to the point that the people welcomed a Manchu ruler and were eager to be "Manchu-ized" as part of the Chinese division of the Manchu army (68–70).

Sun's pathological diagnosis of colonialism is a technology of subjectification that counters the Qing lobotomization of the Chinese national spirit by reviving national consciousness. In a quasi-Schmittian turn of phrase, Sun suggests that the self-conscious recognition of the threat of *national* extinction, when understood as leading to clan extinction, becomes a unifying force and the occasion for sacrifice for the national good: "We could use the clan's fear of extinction [*miezu* 灭族] to unite our race easily and quickly and form a nation [*guozu* 国族] of great power" (117). The nation is the upscaling of the familial clan. Despite Sun's insistence on the national spirit's existence before Qing occupation, the Chinese nation is a modern collectivity generated from the process of anti-Qing revolution and the response to colonial economic exploitation and political oppression. Sun's Han-centric Chinese nation is created through a performative-constative ruse—the conjuration of a new collectivity that is declared to have existed since time immemorial and merely requires reawakening. Sun conceded that "we have never had national unity" (113). Indeed, China has always been an empire that governed territories with Sinitic and non-Sinitic ethnolinguistic groups. It is doubtful that the alienated territories he regarded as part of China or as tributaries attracted to its cultural grandeur viewed themselves thus.

The colonizer is a fluid position in the process of national subjectification via the diagnostic technology of colonial oppression. It is made determinate by and changes with specific historical conditions. Each determination of the colonizer leads to a corresponding change in the national subject's character. Mao, for whom the colonizer is foreign capitalism, approached imperialism through the lens of a situationally modified Marxism-Leninism and linked it to foreign capitalism's retardation of the development of Chinese capitalism. Although the imperialist penetration of China undermined its feudal economy and stimulated capitalist development, it also had an obstructive dimension. The end of imperialist invasion "is to transform China into their own semi-colony or colony," and it employs "military, political, economic and cultural means of oppression" to achieve this, including "collusion with ... Chinese feudal forces to arrest the development of Chinese capitalism" (Mao [1939] 1965b, 310).

Mao is confident in the Chinese nation's inevitable victory over imperialism, which he argued was based on the historical ability of "all the nationalities of China" to resist foreign oppression ([1939] 1965b, 306). Modern China is principally driven by the contradiction between imperialism and the Chinese nation, which is intertwined with the contradiction between feudalism and the Chinese masses. For imperialist rule is propped up by the feudal landlord class and a newly created comprador merchant-usurer class in the network of trading ports and areas of foreign influence. Hence, the Qing empire has been replaced by "the warlord-bureaucrat rule of the landlord class and then the joint dictatorship of the landlord class and the big bourgeoisie" (311–12). Accordingly, the national subject is a revolutionary mass subject uniting China's nationalities, and its enemies are the bourgeoisie of imperialist countries and the Chinese landlord class. But the enemy changes with the historical situation. After Japan's invasion of China, it is Japanese imperialism and Chinese traitors and reactionaries. During the first phase of the Chinese Civil War, it is the reactionary bourgeoisie of the KMT regime that has betrayed the revolution by forming an alliance with the landlord class and collaborating with imperialists (315).

Especially noteworthy here is China's changing relation with the Soviet Union (see Pang, chapter 4). Although Mao insisted on the Chinese Revolution's specificity, he also emphasized the importance of the Soviet Union's tutelary guidance: "The experience of the civil war in the Soviet Union directed by Lenin and Stalin has a world-wide significance. All Communist Parties, including the Chinese Communist Party, regard this experience and its theoretical summing-up by Lenin and Stalin as their guide" ([1936] 1965a, 194–95). However, after the Sino-Soviet split, Mao accused the Soviet Union of "great-power chauvinism" and of collaborating with US imperialism to divide the world into their colonial possessions. As a 1964 *People's Daily* editorial puts it:

Under th[e] signboard [of peaceful coexistence] the Khruschov [sic] clique has itself abandoned proletarian internationalism and is seeking a partnership with U.S. imperialism for the partition of the world; moreover, it wants the fraternal socialist countries to serve its own private interests and not to oppose imperialism or to support the revolutions of the oppressed peoples and nations, and it wants them to accept its political and military control and be its virtual dependencies and colonies. Furthermore, [it] . . . wants all the oppressed peoples and nations to serve its private interests and abandon their revolutionary struggles, so as not to disturb its sweet dream of partnership with imperialism for the division of the world, and instead submit to enslavement and oppression by imperialism and its lackeys. (Editorial Departments of *Jen Min Jih Po* [People's Daily] and *Hung Ch'i* [Red Flag] 1964, 81–82)

In response to the invasion of Czechoslovakia, the Soviet proclamation of its right to intervene in any communist country to stop counterrevolution (the Brezhnev Doctrine, 1968), and the Sino-Soviet border war of 1969, the PRC accused the Soviet Union of "social imperialism," imperialism disguised as socialist solidarity (Schram 1977, 461–62). Because the latter was now viewed as the strongest imperialist threat, the PRC entered into a détente with the United States in the post–Vietnam War era to limit Soviet influence. Although the Soviet Union's fall and US support for the 1989 Democracy Movement made the United States the primary imperialist adversary, the PRC's ambivalent relation with the United States has remained intact.

Postcoloniality as a Nontotalizable Field of Immanence

In modern Chinese history, the self-conscious recognition of and protest against colonial oppression is a technology for stimulating national consciousness and mobilizing support for nationalist revolution and resistance. With the achievement of sovereign independence, the diagnosis of colonialism and imperialism can also function as a state ideology. Sinitic experiences of postcoloniality are framed by three modulations in the world-system: the New International Economic Order inaugurated within the political framework of the American informal empire; the alteration of the bipolar structure of the Cold War occasioned by the Sino-Soviet rift, which destroyed the unity of the communist world; and the PRC's ascendancy as an economic superpower from the late twentieth century onward.

Like Japanese imperialism in Manchukuo, US informal imperialism during the Cold War years is the exercise of control without direct colonial occupation. To contain the spread of communism, the New Deal political principle celebrating the virtues of productive efficiency that was initially exported to build the industrial economies of occupied Germany and Japan was extended to the free world through foreign aid and private capital investment (Maier 1978). The developmentalist regimes of South Korea, Taiwan, Hong Kong, and Singapore willingly adopted this politics of productivity. Rapid growth through intraregional trade and export-oriented industrialization resulted in the miraculous rise of the East and Southeast Asian dragon and tiger economies, thematized as the "Asian model of capitalist development" (Sugihara 2019, 85–86).

This laid the groundwork for the PRC's rise as a postsocialist hegemon. When the PRC reformed its economy, it was integrated into the global economic system via the manufacturing and industrial complexes of the Pearl and Yangtze River Deltas (Sugihara 2019, 92–93). It is too early to say whether the PRC's emergence on the global political stage and its Belt and Road Initiative (BRI) have decentered the Pax Americana world-system. However, its break from its earlier Soviet tutelage and its emergence as the leader of the third world are arguably postcolonial in character. At the same time, the PRC's assertion of sovereignty over Hong Kong and Taiwan and its flexing of economic power through the BRI have been viewed as forms of colonialism. In the former, a postcolonial gesture of reclaiming colonized territories has stimulated Taiwanese national and Hong Kong local consciousnesses and social movements for political freedom.

Although it lies beyond the scope of this volume, which focuses on the aftermath of modern Western and Japanese colonialism in the Sinosphere and responses to it, the cases of Tibet and Xinjiang are fascinating examples of the complex constellation of the historical legacy of dynastic imperialism with contemporary Chinese colonialism in postsocialist globalization. As late as the early nineteenth century, Xinjiang, Tibet, and Mongolia were viewed by the Qing court as *fanbu* 藩部, borderlands in the northwest that were not provinces of the Qing empire because they were neither Confucian nor Sinitic. By the late nineteenth century, they had metamorphosed into *shudi*, which, unlike *shuguo*, or vassal countries lying outside China proper, were part of China's inner territories. They are on the way to becoming colonies in the modern sense and subsequently, with the adoption of the modern concept of territory (*lingtu* 领土), the subjects of Chinese national territorial sovereign claims (Okamoto 2019a). The PRC's current stance on Tibet and Xinjiang draws on this history of dynastic imperialism and territorial sovereignty. Cultural and religious oppression and political violence in Xinjiang and Tibet are euphemistically called "Sinicization" and justified as patriotism (*Economist* 2021a). Referring to Xi Jinping's invocation of the Silk Road as a precursor of the BRI's ideological project of promoting intercivilizational exchanges to facilitate human development and world peace, Prasenjit Duara (2019, 16–17) suggests that the BRI combines neotraditional soft power with the modern PRC state's expansionist political and economic ambitions, that is, a hybridization of ancient tributary relations with modern colonialism. We see a similar mining of dynastic imperialist archives in Xi Jinping's recent identification with the Qianlong emperor. This identification teems with historical irony. The same emperor whom the father of modern China, Sun Yat-sen, had reviled for erasing Han-Manchu distinctions and destroying national consciousness is now reimagined as a builder of the Chinese nation who pacified and expeditiously governed Xinjiang and Tibet and unified the multiethnic Chinese nation (*Economist* 2021b). These invocations of the Silk Road and Qing imperial heroism are instructive examples of the constellation of dynastic imperialism and contemporary PRC statist colonialism within its perceived sovereign territorial space and beyond. This is a novel modality of postcolonial power relations that requires further analysis in understanding the PRC as a contemporary colonial power.

To reiterate, the complexity of experiences of colonialism and postcoloniality in the Sinosphere challenges fundamental tenets of postcolonial theory. We can add two further shortcomings to the simplistic dichotomy between Western colonizer and non-Western colonized and the overemphasis on Orientalist discourse's disciplinary power. First, the mechanical application of Orientalist discourse analysis exaggerates the continuing hold of Western colonialism over the present. Rapid economic growth in East and Southeast Asia and corresponding changes in the international division of labor coupled with the relative decline of developed Western economies challenge the presupposition of cultural inferiority vis-à-vis Western modernity. Contemporary PRC triumphalism is not necessarily a mimetic rivalry with the West as former colonizer. Second, the PRC's position as a global hegemon is arguably secured at the infrastructural and ideological levels by networks and cultural resources that predate Western colonialism.

These far-reaching changes in the global political-economic landscape lead to the redistribution of cultural hegemonies and the rise of new hierarchies in East-West, North-South, and South-South relations. This raises with renewed urgency the question of culture's relation to political and economic forces, which has also been the concern of materialist critiques of postcolonial theory. However, Sinosphere situations also problematize the implicit teleological fixation of such critiques. The historical-materialist emphasis on oppositional praxis requires identifying a righteous political subject of resistance that will eventually triumph against (neo)colonial forces. But such a subject cannot be fixed in the Sinosphere. The Chinese nation and diaspora have occupied the positions of colonized and colonizer, and the PRC has modulated from the leader of third world anti-imperialist struggles to a hegemon accused of colonialism.

This indeterminacy issues from the historical instability of power relations, and any adequate understanding of postcoloniality must account for it. Colonialism's noematic structure (to abuse a Husserlian term) is a relation where a nation uses the natural resources and human capacities of another people for its political and economic ends to the other's disadvantage, thereby constituting an encroachment on sovereign self-determination. Colonialism has conventionally been linked to nineteenth-century global capitalist exploitation. *Neocolonialism* retains the principle of sovereignty by stressing that the encroachment is primarily economic. The expanded psychological definition of colonialism as a *rationalized* form of collective domination (Osterhammel 1997) emphasizes colonialism's subjective basis: it is subordination of one sovereign *subject* by another sovereign subject. This subjectivist understanding of colonialism is seductive because it allows us to engage in moralistic pathologization of a sovereign power, isolate the period of its dominance, and suggest a cure for the disease.

However, the examples of Manchukuo and American imperialism and, more broadly, neocolonialism illustrate that the technologies sustaining colonialism are detachable and adaptable in situations sans colonial occupation or after decolonization to achieve similar ends where direct colonial rule is politically and economically inefficient or no longer ideologically justifiable. Mechanisms of premodern or early modern non-Western imperialism such as tribute relations can likewise be detached for use in a later historical period. Their mobility makes it difficult to clearly delimit epochal breaks between China's imperial past, modern Western colonialism, and postcoloniality. Moreover, although we conventionally view these technologies as the tools of collective subjects, they are processes that produce sovereign and subordinate subjects. These processes are dynamic and reversible depending on changing circumstances. In the 1911 revolution, the self-awareness of Han victimage from the Qing occupation and the Western and Japanese colonization of China induced a modern national consciousness that recognized, in its violation, its capacity for self-determination. It projected national sovereignty back into ancient history in order to reclaim it. In its short history, the imperialist powers denounced by the PRC have drastically changed, and it has adapted such technologies to produce colonial effects in the contemporary world. Although Hong Kong and Taiwan are not preexisting nations with international legal recognition, colonizing technologies have induced a sense of peoplehood and the desire for self-determination. Indeed, Hong Kong concerns about local cultural autonomy and the project of building Taiwan culture recall Sun's critique of the corrosive impact of Manchu epistemic violence on Chinese national identity.

In his analysis of the ascendancy of governmental power in Western modernity, Michel Foucault argued that unlike juridical subjects, who can be ruled by legal commands because their actions are knowable by the sovereign, homo economicus requires different political treatment because he or she functions according to contingent, unpredictable processes that cannot be fully comprehended and that work optimally by being left alone. Hence, homo economicus inhabits an indefinite, nontotalizable field of immanence, which can only be governmentally regulated (Foucault 2008, 277–83). This is a useful analogy for understanding the global field of colonial power relations and their constitutive technologies. The racist ideological justification of colonialism is morally reprehensible and clearly indefensible. But regardless of the extent of public enlightenment, collective entities will always attempt to use others to pursue self-interested ends. The pragmatic-realist technologies they deploy are shaped by conjunctural forces and are infinitely adaptable and reversible. The sovereign identity of actors—a people's self-identity and whether it is oppressed by other nations or oppresses other peoples or subgroups within the nation—is continuously shaped by the expedient use of such technologies. These instruments do not play (*jouer*) like a morality play with its lesson of poetic justice. Western colonialism made the Sinosphere part of a global field of immanence. Postcoloniality is the ongoing condition where actors adaptively deploy cultural, political, and economic technologies to reverse power relations to their advantage without possessing omniscience over the field. Hence, instead of judging the morality of sovereign actors according to the telos of national or revolutionary justice, each situation needs to be analyzed in terms of its oppressive distribution of power and the available strategies for altering this distribution.

Organization of the Book

This book interrogates the closure of Western colonialism/postcoloniality's conceptual matrix from the perspective of various locations in Sinitic East and Southeast Asia. Organized in five parts, it moves from theoretical considerations about the postcolonial; to socialist China's attempts to break with Soviet cultural hegemony; to Hong Kong's complex range of colonial experiences under the British, the Japanese, and mainland China after 1997; to the postcoloniality of Taiwan as it negotiates the legacy of Japanese colonial rule and fraught historical and contemporary relations with KMT and PRC official nationalism; and, finally, to comparisons with diasporic experiences of multiple colonialisms in the Philippines and Sinophone Malaysia.

The chapters in part I critique the axiom of temporal progression in postcolonial studies exemplified by the *post-* prefix. Taking as his point of departure Carl Schmitt's account of the emergence in 1919 of an Anglo-Saxon global order centered around the United States that displaced the nomos of Europe and its colonial territories, Robert Young argues that modern world orders are nomoi of coloniality because of their constitutive connection to colonialism. Raising the question of whether we can speak of a new nomos of postcoloniality, he cautions us against viewing postcoloniality as a triumphant progression from subjugation to liberation. Such mythical linear narratives are similar to colonial myths of the discovery and civilizing of the world. A critical study of colonial and postcolonial history should attend to the multiplicity of spaces and times. Dai Jinhua's chapter sounds a similar note about the dangers of narrating a break with colonial political-economic formations. She argues that postcolonial theory is an expression of the post–Cold War conjuncture that draws on the oppositional discourse of national liberation to code Cold War bipolar structures (socialist vs. capitalist, undeveloped South vs. developed North) as a cultural binary between the formerly colonized East and the West. However, it lost its political basis and connection to effective social practice in capitalist globalization, and its focus on cultural imperialism symptomatically obscures concrete third world problems. Dai asks, Does China's rise in the post–post–Cold War conjuncture lead to a new critical subject position with alternative political possibilities, or is it a different model of destruction? The book's later chapters on the impact of the PRC's rise on Hong Kong and Taiwan pick up these questions about postsocialist China.

Part II is concerned with cultural struggles that are markedly different from the struggle against Orientalism: the PRC's attempt to break away from

Soviet political-economic models and cultural forms and its relevance to postcolonial studies. Following the collapse of the Soviet Union, some scholars of Eastern Europe and Eurasia have used a postcolonial framework to understand Russian imperialism. The PRC's de-Sovietization is the pioneering example of a postcolonial break with the Soviet empire. Wendy Larson argues that the Chinese conceptualization of permanent revolution anticipates postcolonial debates about the political import of cultural critique. In revising Leon Trotsky's concept, Mao argued that China's semicolonial status meant that the Chinese Revolution needed to rely on the politicization of subjectivity to mobilize the peasant masses. In this context, leftist writers adapted Maxim Gorky's socialist-realist theory of character type into a cultural guide for revolutionary conduct. She cautions us that this voluntarist-subjectivist view of revolutionary justice led to the coercive production of revolutionary subjectivity. Pang Laikwan argues that the PRC's efforts at de-Sovietization in the 1950s–1960s were an attempt to change the socialist world order by recentering it in the PRC as the leader of Asian, African, and Latin American peoples in the battle against Soviet and US imperialism. The project's basis in racial discourse is similar to Japan's World War II pan-Asianist discourse, which sought to unify Asia against Western imperialism. Pang argues that unlike the alternative modernity celebrated in subaltern studies, this is a hierarchical statist project. Its linear narrative of progress needs to be critically historicized to open up different spatiotemporal configurations from below.

Parts III and IV focus on Hong Kong and Taiwan, respectively, former colonial territories of Britain and Japan. These chapters explore two related topoi: negotiations with multiple and overlapping colonial pasts and concern about the PRC's assertion of sovereignty, which encroaches on local Hong Kong governance and Taiwanese national self-determination and has stimulated forms of agency that strategically draw on colonial culture, sometimes to the point of nostalgia for the colonial era.

The chapters on Hong Kong examine the ambivalent legacies of Hong Kong's British and Japanese colonial past and its post-handover repositioning in a drastically changed global economic landscape. Developing Prasenjit Duara's work on Japanese imperialism and Manchukuo, Lo Kwai-Cheung argues that Japanese policies in Manchuria are postcolonial because they liberated Manchuria from European colonialism and established a modern multinational client state. Aspects of this developmental state have influenced later state practices: the PRC's governance of non-Han nationalities and the control of client states by the United States and the USSR through economic modernization and support for local authoritarian rule. Post–World War II

British colonialism adopted similar ideas of local self-government, using economic liberalism to create healthy economic growth to prevent the spread of communism. Postcolonial Hong Kong civil society has internalized the British image of benevolent colonialism. Its principle of local self-government has become the basis for democratic demands in the onslaught of contemporary PRC nationalization. The latter is ironically viewed as colonial, while the colonial past has nostalgically become the marker of postcolonial freedom.

In contrast, Lui Tai-lok argues that the handover was not a genuine decolonization and that the problematic character of Hong Kong's demand for political autonomy stems from structural contradictions in the One Country, Two Systems (OCTS) arrangement. Despite its nationalist rhetoric, the PRC was pragmatically motivated in its plan to maintain a prosperous capitalist Hong Kong that would facilitate China's economic modernization. Hence, unlike the founding constitutions of decolonized territories, which specify the chain and division of political power, Hong Kong was constitutionally designated a special administrative region (SAR) under PRC sovereignty with loose political arrangements that preserved its colonial political-legal superstructure. This gave Hong Kong the *illusion* of autonomy with the promise of future political democratization. The PRC's accelerated takeoff and integration into the global capitalist system has made Hong Kong's development dependent on China's growth. The destabilizing consequences of PRC capital and human inflows have exposed the structural contradictions of OCTS's pragmatic-economistic framework. The SAR government's political legitimacy has declined, and the PRC has responded to civil-society protests such as the Umbrella Movement by passing the authoritarian National Security Law of June 2020.

Elaine Yee Lin Ho explores the postcolonial agency of anglophone Hong Kong literature. Echoing Lui, she suggests that the handover is not emancipatory but places Hong Kong in a difficult position between a British colonial past and a PRC "colonial" present. Anglophone Hong Kong literature offers an alternative telling of the Hong Kong story that linguistically performs the subversion of overlapping colonialisms through hybrid language that simultaneously provincializes English and estranges Cantonese. This linguistic subversion resonates with the Sinophone decentering of mainland Chinese.

The chapters on Taiwan explore how postcolonial Taiwan draws on resources from the Japanese colonial period and how the triangular relations among Taiwan, Japan, and mainland China problematize postcolonial theory's understanding of resistance as a Manichean struggle between the West and its colonized others. Lin Pei-Yin examines how Taiwan postcolonial identity is generated from a slippage between the Japanese and Han Chinese empires. She traces the main phases of its formation—as the subjective correlate of demands for local self-governance in the Japanese colonial era, a response to the Han imaginary of KMT official nationalism, the search for tribal indigeneity to decenter Han hegemony, and a postmodern identity without ethnic history or cultural tradition. Lin suggests that Taiwan is heuristically useful for helping us understand the postcolonial not as a temporal period but as an ongoing construction of subjectivity from negotiations between hegemonic cultures.

Liao Ping-hui explores Taiwan postcolonial agency in the period of socioeconomic and political insecurity that characterizes the transition to the twenty-first century by focusing on the rise of new Buddhist sects in the 1980s. These religious cults alleviate the anxieties of the hegemonic class concerning the end of Taiwan's economic miracle in the era of the PRC's ascendancy by promising revitalization through ritual sacrifice and purification. Through an analysis of *Great Buddha Plus (+)* and *The Bold, the Corrupt, and the Beautiful*, two 2017 films that thematize the hidden violence and hypocrisy of Buddhist cultism, Liao foregrounds the vulnerability of the lower strata of postcolonial Taiwan society. Echoing Pang's point about alternative modernities from below, Liao suggests that postcolonial agency must be mass based and avoid co-option by hegemonic forces.

Diaspora is an important topic in postcolonial theory because migrants from former colonies remind Western nations of their imperial sins, and migrant experiences of inequality expose structural racism. Diasporic attachments also resist metropolitan narratives of national belonging. The chapters in the book's final section question the conventional postcolonial understanding of diaspora. Diasporic flows from China extend the field of multiple colonialisms beyond East Asia to Southeast Asia either by connecting the Chinese diaspora from different colonies of the same European empire into a transcolonial network or by traversing the dominions of different empires. These flows also connect them to other diasporas. They engender forms of agency that are more complex than the Manichean opposition favored by much of postcolonial studies. Chinese diasporas simultaneously are exploited by colonial regimes and also are beneficiaries that exploit others. They are economically powerful but politically vulnerable citizens of postcolonial nations and have fraught relations to the cultures of their ancestral homeland and their adopted countries. Diasporas can also resist colonialism in their own country or sustain national development by drawing on resources afforded by another colonial regime or postsocialist globalization.

David Der-wei Wang questions the adaptation of postcolonial theory in Sinophone studies by rejecting characterizations of China as a colonial power and of the Chinese diaspora as settler colonialists. Expanding the focus beyond China's immediate hinterland of Hong Kong and Taiwan to Malaysia, a former British colony with a sizable Chinese population, Wang argues that such Chinese subjects should be characterized as *postloyalist*. Their relations to Chinese culture and colonial culture are not those of simple resistance or acquiescence to colonial power but the complex weaving of multiple temporalities. Like the Chinese of Hong Kong and Taiwan, Malaysian Chinese have maintained their Chinese identities but problematically, alongside an uneasy sense of local belonging. The works of the Mahua writer Ng Kim Chew synchronize multiple temporalities by expressing an impossible dream of left political allegiance with a postsocialist motherland and the insecurity of not belonging in contemporary Malaysia.

Caroline S. Hau examines the agency of the Filipino diaspora in decolonization and postcolonial nation building through a study of Nick Joaquin's *The Woman Who Had Two Navels* ([1961] 1991). She argues that the novel's Hong Kong setting has a twofold significance. First, it connected the Philippines to the rest of Asia and was an enabling refuge for Filipino anticolonial, pan-Asianist, and socialist activities and networks. The *ilustrado* elite drew on this cosmopolitan network and the resources afforded by a history of multiple colonialisms (Spanish, Japanese, US) in anticolonial struggles. For example, unlike the indigenous elite of British India, the *ilustrado* could create knowledge about the Philippines for anticolonial use because of the lack of an extensive Spanish tradition of Orientalist knowledge. Second, it suggests that the spirit of revolution now resides outside the Philippines, which has become a failed developmental state under American governance. Overseas Filipino workers, whose remittances have been the main driver of economic development, have assumed the mantle of revolutionary promise, although this form of development holds both possibilities and dangers.

My contribution returns to the question of temporality by examining the inadequacy of influential theories of diasporic temporality (Homi Bhabha, Paul Gilroy) in postcolonial studies. I argue that temporality must be understood at a deeper level than representations of historical progress used to legitimize colonial and postcolonial regimes. A temporal order is a concrete regime that organizes experiences of time to facilitate capitalist accumulation. It is created by material technologies (such as the international division of labor) that produce corresponding subjects. Through a study of four anglophone bildungsromans by Hanif Kureishi, K. S. Maniam, Mohsin Hamid, and

Tash Aw, I contrast the Malaysian Chinese diasporic subject in postsocialist China with South Asian diasporic subjects in Britain and Malaysia in the 1970s and the United States in the 2000s. The impossibility of cosmopolitan *Bildung* for a diasporic subject on the subordinate side of the international division of labor reveals the limits of the North Atlantic diasporic model. The Chinese diasporic subject who is alienated in the metropolis of a PRC-centered world-system and can neither identify with his ancestral culture nor be at home in Malaysian public culture finds refuge from global capitalist modernity's temporal order by returning to the time of our first coming into the world. Remembering this time enables the envisioning of new worldings.

In summary, this book delimits the closure of the Western colonial/postcolonial episteme by elaborating on four themes. First, it suggests that fundamental changes in the world-system put into question the cultural supremacy of Western modernity, the reach of its civilizing mission, and the importance of Orientalist discourses of difference. These changes are the emergence of Asian solidarity in the wake of Japanese colonialism's use of Asian civilizational discourse to emphasize commonality between Japan and other Asian peoples (Pang, Lo); the rise of the socialist bloc; global financialization under the framework of US empire from the Cold War onward and the subsequent transformation of Cold War bipolarity by the Sino-Soviet rift (Dai, Larson, Pang, Hau); and the alteration of the Pax Americana world order by the PRC's rise and its exertion of cultural, political, and economic power (Dai, Lo, Lui, Cheah). Taken together, these chapters remedy a much-noted weakness of postcolonial studies by providing a thorough analysis of key features of global capitalism. Second, negotiations with the legacies of multiple and overlapping colonialisms in interconnected East and Southeast Asia engender complex forms of agency (Lo, Lui, Ho, Lin, Liao, Hau, Wang). Third, the historically changing identities of colonizer and colonized, exemplified by the ambivalent position of the Chinese diaspora and the colonial character of PRC sovereign claims over Hong Kong and Taiwan, problematize the colonizer/colonized binary and the conception of Manichean oppositional struggle (Lin, Ho, Wang). Finally, the book replaces the understanding of colonialism and postcoloniality in terms of linear temporal progression marked by clear breaks between epochs and political orders with more complex accounts of temporality (Dai, Young, Pang, Wang, Cheah).

While many of the book's chapters are analyses of literary, film, and cultural texts, their foregrounding of decisive changes in the global political-economic landscape corrects the overly culturalist focus of postcolonial studies. At the same time, they also reject the implicit teleological fixation of materialist critiques of postcolonial studies by problematizing conceptions of Manichaean oppositionality and temporal progression. Although the book focuses on Sinitic East Asian sites, its intellectual perspective is structurally open-ended and contains an implied exhortation to test its provisional conclusions with examples from other postcolonial sites.

Notes

1. Ania Loomba (1998, xiii) also stresses European colonialism's geographic extensiveness, noting that it covered 84.6 percent of the globe's land surface by the 1930s.
2. Tani Barlow noted in 1993 that "postcolonial critiques work by analogy from India and West Asia, regions that were outright European possessions," and that China had been ignored (254).
3. Constitution of the People's Republic of China (amended March 14, 2004), http://www.npc.gov.cn/zgrdw/englishnpc/Constitution/2007-11/15/content_1372962.htm.
4. This tribute system ended with the First Sino-Japanese War (1894–95), which destroyed Qing pretensions to suzerainty over Korea.
5. Qing laws prohibiting emigration were not officially rescinded until 1893. Between the 1850s and 1939, over six million moved from Hong Kong. From the 1870s onward, the primary destinations were Singapore and the Malay states, and by the turn of the century, over 100,000 people were leaving Hong Kong and Amoy annually for Nanyang (Skeldon 1996, 438).
6. These "Chinese colonialists" included the Ming-era pirate Liang Daoming, who ruled Palembang (part of Sriwijaya) with the recognition of the Ming court and the protection of Zheng He's fleet, and Zheng Zhao, or King Taksin, founder of the short-lived Thonburi dynasty in Siam (1767–82).
7. For a concise account of the related ideas of *gong* and *li* (禮, ritual/ceremony), especially in the Qing empire, see Perdue (2009, 86–88) and Hevia (1995, 9–25, 116–33). On the connection among tribute, international trade, and geopolitics in East Asia, see Hamashita (2008) and Nakajima (2018).
8. On the colonial character of the Ming dynasty's tributary relations with Southeast Asia, see Dreyer (2007) and Wade (2005, 2006, 2008). What is now Yunnan and parts of Guangxi and Guizhou were Sino-Southeast Asian borderlands whose Tai polities also paid tribute to Burma, Siam, and Tai polities outside China (Giersch 2006).
9. Although Shu-mei Shih doesn't go back to the Ming period, one of the main limbs of her theory of the Sinophone is this "rough parallel" (2011, 713).
10. For useful reviews of the political stakes of New Qing History, see Cams (2016), Schneider (2020), and Jenco and Chappell (2020).

11 Sun's use of the term is neither Leninist—for Vladimir Lenin (1987, 230–31), "semi-colonial countries like Persia, China and Turkey" designated "a transitional form" to being fully colonized—nor the later twentieth-century Marxist use of the term to refer to underdeveloped countries that were dominated by more advanced countries.

12 Sun equates colonialism with modern Western imperialism, defined as "the policy of aggression upon other countries by means of political force [yong zhengzhi li qu qinlüe bie guo 用政治力去侵略别国]" ([1924] 1975, 79).

# Part I

Framing the Postcolonial

Robert J. C. Young

Mythmaking

Au bout du petit matin . . .
Va-t'en, lui disais-je, gueule de flic, gueule de vache, va-t'en
je déteste les larbins de l'ordre et les hannetons de l'espérance.
Va-t'en mauvais gri-gri, punaise de moinillon.
—AIMÉ CÉSAIRE, *Cahier d'un retour au pays natal*
(1947 Bordas version)

At the brink of dawn . . .
Get lost I said you cop face, you pig face, get lost, I hate
the flunkies of order and the cockchafers of hope.
Go away bad grigri bedbug of a little monk.
—AIMÉ CÉSAIRE, *Notebook of a Return to My Native Land*

Aimé Césaire's *Cahier d'un retour au pays natal*, without doubt the most extraordinary and intellectually complex anticolonial poem ever written, and probably the twentieth-century poem most often translated from French into English, was first published in Paris in the journal *Volontés* in August 1939, with a dramatically different opening: "Au bout du petit matin bourgeonnant d'anses frêles les Antilles qui ont faim, les Antilles grêlées de petite vérole, les Antilles dynamitées d'alcool, échouées dans la boue de cette baie, dans la poussière de cette ville sinistrement échouées" (Césaire 1939, 23).[1]

Publication in August 1939 was hardly an auspicious moment to achieve maximum impact. Undeterred by World War II, however, in April 1942 Césaire published a separate, highly politicized anticolonial poem, "En guise de manifeste littéraire" ("By Way of a Literary Manifesto"; Césaire 1942) in his journal *Tropiques*, published in Martinique, that would later be integrated into the *Cahier*; the first book edition was then published in Havana in 1943 in a Spanish translation, *Retorno al país natal*, by the writer-anthropologist Lydia Cabrera. With the war over, Césaire brought out a French edition in book form—twice, in changing versions. New York had been the international center of surrealist activity during the war, and it was there that the first French edition was published by Brentano's bookshop in January 1947, with a facing English translation by the writer Lionel Abel and the surrealist-expressionist poet Yvan Goll that has never been republished. The poem itself was presented under the title *Memorandum on My Martinique / Cahier d'un retour au pays natal* (Césaire 1947). In late March 1947, the poem was issued again in a different version by Bordas in Paris—the version, never translated, that was learned and cited by Frantz Fanon, who reputedly knew this *Cahier* by heart. It was then republished in a last, substantially re-revised version in Paris again by *Présence Africaine* in 1956, in the version by which the poem has been known ever since. Since 1956 there have been six more English translations. While Césaire was developing and refashioning his poem according to his changing aesthetic and political priorities—in 1947 he transformed the whole poem into a surrealist topography, and in 1956 he swapped some of its arresting surrealism for a more up-front Marxism—he was also developing another well-known text, later to be known as the *Discours sur le colonialism* (*Discourse on Colonialism*). A first version of this was originally published as an article in 1948, entitled "L'impossible contact"; a second, a thin pamphlet of sixty pages entitled *Discours sur le colonialisme*, was published in 1950 by Réclame, a publisher with links to the PCF (Parti Communiste Française); and then a third, the extended and once again revised version we read today as the *Discours sur le colonialisme*, was published by *Présence Africaine* in Paris in 1955 (Césaire, 1948, 1950, 1955).

All these different versions of the *Cahier* and the *Discours* were distinct products of their historical moments and embody Césaire's changing but very distinct aesthetic responses and political perspectives. Several scholars have unpicked and compared at length the complex rewritings of the texts. Typically, however, we read such texts ahistorically, as if there were a single version, usually the last. Even the date of the *Discours* is often cited by anglophone writers as 1955, because if you looked at the credits page in the Monthly Review translation, for many decades it cited the copyright of the 1955 French edition from which it was translated (Césaire 2000). Césaire's intervention is thus offered anachronistically, so that, for example, it looks as if his equation of fascism with colonialism was already anticipated by Hannah Arendt in *The Origins of Totalitarianism* in 1951.

As it happens, Arendt herself considerably revised her thesis about this connection as the Cold War developed: by the time she published *The Origins of Totalitarianism* in 1951, she had softened the connection between fascism and European race imperialism in order to accommodate the Soviet Union in her critique of totalitarianism: whatever you might say about the Soviet Union, its antiracism was exemplary from a policy point of view. In her desire to include the Soviets, Arendt came to downplay the importance of race, the core of European imperialism as well as fascism. As with Césaire's text, most readers read the last version. As scholars, if we have access to the original materials, we can, of course, register that texts such as Césaire's, or even Arendt's, were shifting formations that cannot be anchored to a single edition; that historically different readers were and will be responding to different versions of texts at different times; and that we need to consider them in all the added complexity and intricacy of their distinct varieties across punctuated, crisscrossing historical moments. History in some sense is only a larger translation of this kind of multifaceted voluminous structure, yet we often persist in trying to read it as if it were a single text, like the narrative of a nation, when in fact its plots are far more layered, variegated, and random than any literary text, which has by definition already organized its components, even if it sometimes stutters into being in different versions, as in the case of Césaire's texts. Colonial and postcolonial histories in particular constitute fluctuating, clashing rhythms of space-times with different curving layers simultaneously reacting to and against each other, rather than evolving as part of a single narrative. There is no synchronous now across postcolonial histories or times; they march always out of joint across the body of the earth. How can we conceptualize such histories to acknowledge the kind of unstable multiplicity evident in Césaire's *Cahier*—or rather *Cahiers*?

The temporal and spatial densities and convolutions of history—its asynchronous distended multiplicities, the vast manifold of determined, disparate, and random events occurring across different frictional temporalities—have always been a problem for the writing of history in general and therefore for the concept of postcoloniality in particular. As soon as the term *postcolonial* came into currency, the question of what the *post* in the postcolonial represented was the subject of endless articles, the most tiresome of which attempted to make a distinction between the meanings of *postcolonial* written as one word and written with a hyphen. No wonder it took some time for those in other disciplines to take it all seriously. That discussion is now thankfully largely forgotten—who cares about the meaningless hyphen?—but it did have a significant underlying point, which lies in the question of the divergent temporalities of the postcolonial. That problem has not gone away; indeed, it has been revived by the theorists of decoloniality with their important emphasis on "the colonial difference" (Grosfoguel 2002). Can the various, intersecting historical epochs of colonialism be subsumed under a single term? Does the postcolonial describe some general historical condition of modernity or mark particular historical eras across certain regions of the world? Can the historical differences of geographies be subsumed under one narrative time? Or should the differences within postcoloniality be separated out into different volumes of space-time? History, like the novel, indeed far more so, must necessarily take the form of chronotopes, for its differences are not only of time but simultaneously of the vast distended geographic spaces of the world. If so, does that then leave it uniform enough to be amenable to a general theoretical description? What could a history look like that allows for the discordant differentiations of space and times? How could we conceptualize such a thing?

Proposing Pivot Points in History

In a remarkable essay, "Poésie et connaissance" (Poetry and knowledge), published in three versions between 1944 and 1947, Césaire made the following Nietzschean assertion:

1850—La revanche de Dionysos sur Apollon.
1850—Le grand saut dans le vide poétique. (Césaire 2013a, 1378)[2]

According to Césaire, engineering a sublime reduction of the complexity of history to a proto-Foucauldian epistemic shift, 1850 was the moment when France pivoted from prose to poetry by means of an inventive, imaginative Baudelairean leap away from revolutionary activity into the poetic void, the moment when political change (such as that of 1848) was translated into conceptual transformation, often identified with Charles Baudelaire's own characterization of the contemporary era with the new but ever-enduring word *modernity*—the era of "the transitory, the fugitive, the contingent" (Baudelaire 1964, 13). And with the coming of Baudelaire's fortuitous modernity, of a history deconstructed, discomposed, discombobulated, came the new tradition of strange, ultimately protosurrealist French poetry with a line that would run to Césaire himself. Behind Césaire's historicization of this revolutionary moment in French culture lay not only Friedrich Nietzsche but also Oswald Spengler's *The Decline of the West* (1918–22), a book whose significance for anticolonial thinkers, like the work of Nietzsche, has been largely underestimated. In offering an early critique of the Eurocentric linear narrative of history dominated by the story of progressive European expansion, Spengler (1918–22) offered a decline-and-fall template for the *Untergang*, or "going under," of modern Europe that was of obvious interest to those activists struggling against European imperialism around the world. Césaire rewrites Spengler's division of the three phases or forms of civilization (Apollonian or classical, Magian or Semitic, and finally Faustian or western European from the tenth century on) into more explicitly Nietzschean terms: Apollonian (or Western) followed by Dionysian, or universal. Nietzsche for Césaire, as for the young Fanon, offered a critique of European civilization that allowed for a will to power that would emerge, leap, soar out of the colonial void to invent new forms of dithyrambic existence.

The desire to offer a moment, a particular historical year, as a pivot point in the narrative of the history of the world is a long-standing trope and inevitably a seductive one. It creates a perspective that shifts from the metonymic time of antiquarian history to what Nietzsche called *monumental time*, a time that englobes smaller histories within its vast, capacious hold, creating exalted entities that span centuries, that seeks to give history its own meaning and unfolding direction. Baudelaire's characterization of 1850 as the beginning of modernity, here also defined by Césaire as a prospective global power reversal with the undoing of Apollonian European civilization, is popular with cultural historians, even if they do not usually include Césaire's own particular anticolonial perspective within their analyses.

In 1950, a hundred years after the Baudelaire/Césaire fulcrum, and the same year as the *Discours sur le colonialisme* was first published under that title, another work of monumental history pursuing a dialogue with Nietzsche appeared, this time in Cologne, which provided a rather different characterization of defining moments in European and global history, Carl Schmitt's *Der Nomos der Erde im Völkerrecht des Jus Publicum Europaeum*, or *The Nomos of the Earth, in the International Law of the Jus Publicum Europaeum* (Schmitt 1950, 2003; Shapiro 2012). Distinct as it certainly was, *The Nomos of the Earth* has nevertheless recently been allied in broad terms with Césaire's era of postcoloniality. Could there be a nomos of postcoloniality?

1492, 1942

Schmitt's controversial work, written in the early 1940s during World War II, argues that the European basis of international order that had been developed since the sixteenth century had come to an end in 1919.[3] As he puts it in a well-known passage from the preface:

> The traditional Eurocentric order of international law is foundering today, as is the old *nomos* of the earth. This order arose from a legendary and unforeseen discovery of a new world, from an unrepeatable historical event. Only in fantastic parallels can one imagine a modern recurrence, such as men on their way to the moon discovering a new and hitherto unknown planet that could be exploited freely and utilized effectively to relieve their struggles on earth. The question of a new *nomos* of the earth will not be answered with such fantasies, any more than it will be with further scientific discoveries. Human thinking again must be directed to the elemental orders of its terrestrial being here and now. We seek to understand the normative order of the earth. (Schmitt 2003, 39)

As Schmitt puts it, up to 1492, the peoples living on the two landmasses of the earth had been existing discretely since the beginning of time, each with their own cultures and histories, each totally oblivious of the other, which in the era of globalization is an extraordinary thought. It is almost impossible for us today to imagine what it was like for those on both continents to discover that there were people, cities, and lands altogether elsewhere, in places that only the then ultramodern, revolutionary technology of the *caravela*, the first sailing ship that could navigate the oceans rather than simply sail along coastlines, invented by the Portuguese around 1490, could reach. While we routinely decry the old idea of the European "discovery" of America, we forget what an epochal event the news of there being another continent must have been, not only to Europeans but also to Native American peoples. The closing of the earth, and the arrival of globalization—there being nowhere left that was in any way "undiscovered"—marked, according to Schmitt, the end of one era and the beginning of the modern age.

For Schmitt, the European sighting of the New World was revolutionary because it fundamentally altered the political geography of Europe with regard to the perception of land and space: the world beyond Europe was not perceived as an encounter with a new enemy or enemies but as the discovery of free space, to which the prime basis of European law, landownership, was almost immediately applied—but in a particular way. According to Schmitt, "the discovery of the new world" for Europeans led, soon after 1492, to the development of what he calls a new conceptual mode of *global linear thinking* in which the first lines of division and distribution were drawn. So in 1494 Pope Alexander VI published the edict *Inter caetera divinae*, which established a line that ran from the North to the South Pole, a hundred miles west of the meridian of the Azores and Cape Verde. In the same year, with the Treaty of Tordesillas signed between the Spanish and Portuguese, another line was drawn approximately through the middle of the Atlantic Ocean, "in which the two Catholic powers agreed that all newly discovered territories west of the line would belong to Spain and those east of the line to Portugal. This line was called a "partition del mar océano" (an ocean sea partition). Since Spain and Portugal were also already rivals for the Spice Islands of the Moluccas in the East, by the Treaty of Saragossa of 1526, "a *raya* [line] was drawn through the Pacific Ocean, at first along what is now the 135th meridian, i.e., through eastern Siberia, Japan, and the middle of Australia" (Schmitt 2003, 89). In an extraordinary moment of sixteenth-century fantastic thinking, the world was thus literally divided up between them—presumably, at that time, without Australia, since no European would catch a glimpse of it before 1606, when it was sighted by the Dutch navigator and colonial governor Willem Janszoon. Schmitt, however, strategically overlooks the role of the Dutch in his selective account of the establishment of European global colonial power.

In the narrative of *The Nomos of the Earth*, it was not too long before Spanish-Portuguese global domination began to break down as the hegemony of the first duo of European colonial superpowers receded before a second, that of France and England, who themselves established a different order, known as the *amity lines*. While the *rayas* were "internal divisions between two land-appropriating Christian princes within the framework of one and the same special order" (Schmitt 2003, 92) the amity lines that were developed in the seventeenth century operated according to a completely different principle pertinent to a secular world in which the power structure of the Roman Church had been remodeled into that of the modern Westphalian state. Instead of propagating Catholicism and incorporating the New World into the Old, the principle of the amity lines was that "treaties, peace, and friendship applied only to Europe, to the Old World, to the area on this side of the line" (92). "The line" ran roughly "along a degree of longitude drawn in the Atlantic Ocean through the Canary Islands" to the west and along the equator to the south. On the European side of this line, seafarers were forbidden to attack the ships of other European powers (93). "At this 'line,' Europe ended and the 'New World' began" (93). This arrangement allowed privateers and pirates to operate as informal agents of the king of France or England. Beyond these lines, there were no legal limits, and only the law of the strongest applied. As Schmitt describes it, mutual enmity between European powers was thus distinguished from absolute enmity with respect to non-European powers, limiting war within Europe to conflict between European sovereign states and at the same time preventing their mutual total destruction.

The appropriation of global space, meanwhile, was organized on the basis of an international system of mutual recognition that assured nonintervention in each other's territories, which were defined in legal terms as simultaneously inside and outside the borders of the colonizing state. This European system of a global international order separating Europe and the non-European world began to break down in the nineteenth century, according to Schmitt, with the declaration of the Monroe Doctrine by the United States in 1823, which divided the world into two autonomous spheres of influence, one of them non-European, which Schmitt considered first impinged on Europe itself in the Berlin Conference of 1884–85; it ended in 1919 with the Treaty of Versailles when the New World itself, by which he meant the United States, became the arbiter of a new Anglo-Saxon global order that was no longer exclusively European. The American mode of informal imperialism was consolidated by an unlimited claim to a "right of intervention" and supported by the concept of a just war that was written into the war-guilt clause (no. 231) of the Treaty of Versailles (Schmitt 2003, 13; Kervégan 1999). This accused Germany of having waged a criminal war, initiating a legal category that continues to this day to provide the legal basis for wars of "humanitarian intervention" (Schmitt 2011; C. Brown 2007). Schmitt blamed this change from the earlier European nondiscriminating concept of war in international law to one that criminalized the losing side on the British: for him, the British always remained outside the continental European consensus and had in fact been steadily creating a different and antagonistic system of international law; it was they who, during the nineteenth century, had effectively been enforcing the Monroe Doctrine, whose principles were finally imposed at Versailles over the earlier long-standing European nomos (Derman 2011).

In recent years, Schmitt's analysis has caught the attention of postcolonial geographers and historians, who have highlighted that he offers one of the few pre-twenty-first-century accounts of European history in which the European colonization of the world plays a central, rather than marginal, role. By focusing on the nomos, that is, the political and legal order that governed the behavior of the kings, princes, popes, and states of Europe, and by pointing to its beginnings in 1492 with the European discovery—to Europeans—of the continent they called America, commentators have emphasized the determining role that European colonialism, and colonial difference, played in Schmitt's historico-geographico-legal narrative (Kalyvas 2018; Kistner 2020; Koskenniemi 2017).[4] This is certainly of interest with respect to Schmitt's work, and to the historiography of international law, even if Schmitt's account is not generally accepted in the latter domain. But how useful is it as an analysis of European colonialism from a contemporary postcolonial perspective? Does it mean that we should place Schmitt beside "an unlikely company of anticolonial and postcolonial thinkers," as Andreas Kalyvas suggests, and indeed corroborates by pointing to Schmitt's recent invocation by figures such as Walter Mignolo and Achille Mbembe? (Kalyvas 2018, 36; Mignolo 2011, 27–33; Mbembe 2017, 59–61). One commentator has even compared Schmitt to Edward Said (Legg 2011, 107). There are three considerations in relation to Schmitt as a theorist of European coloniality that need to be kept in mind when invoking his work: the historical context in which he wrote, his own positionality and interests in the narrative that he constructs, and the effect of his political theology on the form that he proposes for it. Such considerations do not generally feature among these commentators, whose critical comments largely involve contemporary critical perspectives such as "the glaring absence of the indigenous and the colonized" (Kalyvas 2018, 48). Observations such as Ulrike Kistner's, "Much as Schmitt critically exposes the colonial underbelly of the Eurocentric order, he does not grant anticolonialism a politically constitutive role" (2020, 276), imply that the primary aim of Schmitt's project is to reveal and unmask the importance of colonialism for "the Eurocentric order," making the fact that he does not also endorse the importance of anticolonial movements an anomaly. It is certainly the case that Schmitt proposed the centrality of the colonies in his argument that before 1885 "the whole spatial structure of the earth in European international law was *based on the distinctive territorial status of colonial overseas lands*" (Schmitt 2003, 221). Interesting and significant though this may be, it also needs to be recalled that this claim was not arrived at after sifting the historical evidence in a detached non-Eurocentric scholarly way but was created to fulfill specific political and ideological objectives.

The Juridical Legitimation of State Land Grabs

Schmitt stresses that the European world order was based on spatiality, by which he means its relation to the concept of the land, not on the modern idea of the state. We might more accurately call this "sedentary spatiality" or even "settler spatiality": law, he writes, owes its origin and its authenticity to its relation to the land through its physical occupation, its tilling and cultivation, and the creation of tangible barriers around property. It does not matter whether this occupation was of previously "free" land or whether it takes the form of a succession, or even of appropriation by force. "In every case, land-appropriation, both internally and externally, is the primary legal title that underlies all subsequent law. Territorial law and territorial succession, militia and the national guard presuppose land-appropriation" (Schmitt 2003, 46).

Schmitt, as Bruno Bosteels remarks, elevates land appropriation to "the originary event of all human history" (2005, 296). This authentic, primary, and even primal relation to the land, Schmitt claims, gets lost with the rise of internationalism from the 1884–85 Berlin Conference onward and its formalization with the Treaty of Versailles. Commentators repeat Schmitt's geopolitical narrative of the loss of spatiality without necessarily asking why he should so identify with this concept, why he should see the right to the soil as the absolute foundation of Europe's legal system and hence the primary basis for its conceptualization of international law. Schmitt's emphasis on the importance of land, on "das Erde," correlates directly with the eco-colonial narrative of blood and soil, intrinsically connected to the earth, that formed a significant part of Nazi political ideology, and one means of contrasting Germanic spatiality with the claimed rootlessness of Jewish peoples: as Oliver Simons points out, "it was, in [Schmitt's] estimation, above all the Jews who had detached themselves from space" (Simons 2017, 802; see also Palaver 1996, 114–15).

When we recall that Schmitt wrote his text between 1942 and 1945, and began developing his ideas of spatiality from 1939, it becomes clearer that his interest in colonialism, and the different historical forms of colonial taking-possession, presumes a particular perspective. Schmitt's direct involvement as a Nazi *Kronjurist* associated with Hans Frank and Hermann Göring, and editor of the *Deutsche Juristen-Zeitung*, ended in December 1936 after he was attacked in the ss journal *Das Schwarze Korps* on the grounds of his opportunism, and because he never conceptualized the state in the fundamental form central to Nazi ideology, that of a *Volksgemeinschaft* (racial community) (Bendersky 1983, 219–42).[5] As a response to his downfall, Schmitt withdrew from public life and moved his research into the realm of international law, which he considered would be less conspicuous. In 1939, a few weeks after the German invasion of Czechoslovakia, however, Schmitt began to articulate his version of Karl Haushofer's *Raumtheorie*, or space theory: the fundamental concept, as he would argue in *The Nomos of the Earth*, that forms the basis of the development of European international law (Bendersky 1983, 250–61; Minca and Rowan 2016). By 1941, with Germany in full occupation of much of Europe, Schmitt connected the *Grossraum* (*Großraum*) of *Mitteleuropa* with what he envisaged as a new Germanic political sphere of influence, which he compared to that of the Americas promulgated by the Monroe Doctrine, an idea that was quickly taken up by Adolf Hitler himself (Schwab 1994).

Schmitt's biographer Joseph Bendersky notes that "to write about international law without acknowledging recent developments proved to be an impossible task for someone whose basic tendency was always to analyze political and legal questions in the light of a concrete situation" (1983, 250).[6] We should therefore interpret *The Nomos of the Earth* in the light of the concrete situation that pertained at the time of its composition. The book was begun at the very time in which Nazi Germany itself, inspired by the geopolitical ideas of Halford J. Mackinder, Friedrich Ratzel, Friedrich Naumann, and above all Karl Haushofer, was expanding its borders by invading its European neighbors to claim and occupy the land and territory of most of Europe and beyond, from France in the west, to Greece in the south, to large parts of the Soviet Union in the east. It's in this context that Schmitt's interest in colonialism should be understood, given that it was, as John Blanco and Ivonne del Valle put it, "first and foremost a lawmaking act based on land seizure and coercive entitlement, which had historically served as the basis of European law" (2014, 3). Unlike the maritime empires of Spain, Portugal, Britain, and France, Nazi Germany, stripped of its short-lived overseas colonies in 1919, was pursuing a very different form of expansion, land empire, a form of imperialism that Schmitt does not discuss in terms of imperialism as such but that forms the basis of the whole argument of the *Nomos*. Indeed, the entire trajectory of Schmitt's work itself has been described as "his attempts to retheorize *empire* (first as *Reich* and *Grossraum*, and then as nomos), the process of *imperial mimesis*, and the structure of the *imperial imaginary*, that is, the spatiotemporal imagination that shadows any imperial project" (Hell 2009, 284). Nazi ideology in fact abjured imperialism as a concept because the latter is founded on a claimed universalism—the universality of the rule of different races and peoples, as in the case of the British or Roman Empires—whereas Nazi theory saw Germanic territorial expansion across Eastern Europe as a form of settler colonialism in which all the indigenous people would be expelled or exterminated. In its ideal form, there would be no colonialism at all because the indigenous people would have been eliminated, and the land occupied and settled would have been incorporated into the Greater German Reich. In practice, no country expanding its borders has altogether achieved this elimination, even if several have imagined it, and no term therefore exists to describe its precise form (Guettel 2013). A cumbersome descriptive term might be "settler land appropriation with indigenous population erasure." Schmitt's focus on land appropriation as a form of proximate spatiality cannot be thought, therefore, without its relation to the *Geopolitik* of National Socialism and the logic of contemporary events (Barnes and Minca 2013). From 1938 onward, either through treaties and agreements such as the Munich Agreement and the Molotov-Ribbentrop Pact or through direct invasion, Germany annexed and incorporated into Germany proper, or rather the new Großdeutsches Reich, territories from, or the territory of, Austria, Belgium, the Czechoslovak Republic, France, Lithuania, Luxembourg, Poland, and Slovenia, while the following countries (or parts of them) were occupied and administered on a colonial basis: Denmark, France, Greece, Hungary, the Netherlands, Norway, and the Soviet Union, with some, such as Denmark, the Netherlands, and Norway, designated to be incorporated eventually into the Großdeutsches Reich. The long-standing strategy of lebensraum, first formulated by Ratzel in his *Politische Geographie* (1897), was developed by Hitler as the *Drang nach Osten* ("Drive to the East") plan for the colonization of Eastern Europe by German settlers, with the indigenous Slavic *Untermenschen* ("subhuman" inferior races) population envisaged as being assigned as *Ostarbeiter*, or slave labor, expelled, exterminated, or dying from starvation. The practice of this policy primarily took the form of settler colonialism in populated areas: many of the former *Auslandsdeutsche Volksdeutsche* were resettled all across the appropriated territories in the emptied houses of the expelled local inhabitants (Giaccaria and Minca 2016).

After the dissipation of the nomos of European order from 1884–85 onward, the Greater Germanic thousand-year Reich, in this narrative, was dismantling the existing state system of Europe by creating a German *Mitteleuropa* that would return Europe to its true center. Schmitt's fulminations against what he regarded as the disaster of the Versailles Conference exactly replicated the position of Hitler, who made it his life's mission to destroy its legacy. Schmitt's argument, in which Versailles forms a tragic fulcrum, was therefore centered on Nazi grievances and possibly, in its first conceptualizations, overtly directed toward accommodating Nazi policy. In his January 30, 1941, Berlin Sports Palace speech, Hitler proclaimed, "The year 1941 will be, I am convinced, the historical year of a great European New Order [*die Neuordnung Europas*]," a reorganization of Europe comparable to that of 1648 or 1815, in which Germany would become the dominant power of the whole continent, no longer reduced to playing a role in the "balance of power" game within Europe historically orchestrated, Hitler claimed, by the English.[7] If Schmitt places colonialism as central, therefore, it seems likely that it was at least originally because he was concerned to justify Nazi colonialism and its land appropriation as Germany expanded across Europe—not because he was concerned, as if from a proto-postcolonial perspective, to emphasize the centrality of colonialism in the history of Europe as such. Such a perspective would fit with Schmitt's singular lack of interest in *The Nomos of the Earth* for anything to do with the peoples being colonized. Although, unlike most imperialists, he openly concedes that the practices of European discovery were technically illegal, it is only to offer a higher justification for European land appropriation: "From the standpoint of the discovered, discovery as such was never legal. Neither Columbus nor any other discoverer appeared with an entry visa issued by the discovered princes. Discoveries were made without prior permission of the discovered. Thus, legal title to discoveries lay in a higher legitimacy. They could be made only by peoples intellectually and historically advanced enough to apprehend the discovered by superior knowledge and consciousness" (Schmitt 2003, 131–32).

If Versailles had produced a new global dynamic in which the New World, that is, the United States, had become a dominant player, in the Nazi formulation, after Germany had consolidated itself in Europe, subsequent war with the United States would lead to German world domination. Although Schmitt left no explicit evidence with respect to how *The Nomos of the Earth* was originally conceived and envisaged, it is not hard for it to be reimagined to fit other historical outcomes than that which did finally ensue, such as the victory of the Axis powers anticipated in the Germany of the early 1940s. The book, however, was not published until after the defeat of Germany in 1945: the result is that the geopolitical identification with spatiality becomes more abstracted, historicized, set in the past, and the narrative turns from being a triumphal narrative of recuperation and restoration to the continued tragic Spenglerian decline of the West in the idiom of twentieth-century Germanic mourning literature. Schmitt's thoughts in 1950 regarding a new world order deliberately omit the relevant international events of Bretton Woods or the founding of the United Nations.

Any centrality that European colonialism may play in Schmitt's narrative, therefore, was not simply an acknowledgment of the role that colonialism played in the formation of European law: it also happens to offer the legal basis for Nazi claims for the right of conquest of the smaller, less populated, or "lower" nations configured around Germany. Schmitt's emphasis on colonialism, in other words, was less a non-Eurocentric perspective on history than a German-centric, self-interested corollary to Nazi expansion, which explains why the framework in which he projects it serves primarily to develop the basis of Europe as the center of global power—he has minimal interest in the colonized lands, their inhabitants, or their cultures. The colonies simply provide a conceptual frame for the claimed historical constitution of "the European spirit" through which he claims mutually binding rules were established that regulated the conduct of war and instituted the basis of international law (Schmitt 1990, 37).

If Schmitt's project analyzed and extended Nazi geopolitical dreams and mythmaking, we should also ask how far the history formulated in *The Nomos of the Earth* is itself a piece of mythmaking. Although Schmitt incorporates colonialism as the excluded-included element in the formation of the European international legal system, it is noticeable that in taking it back to the fifteenth century, he speaks of it as if it already constituted an acknowledged, established "European" system that operated by mutual consent across the continent. In fact, no such system or consensus existed, and it is doubtful whether people at that time even thought of Europe as a holistic entity. Even the idea of Christendom was not universally understood across Europe's different languages, kingdoms, and empires as anything like "Europe," since for one it also included the Byzantine Empire to the east. Anything like a pan-Christian identity faded rapidly with the rise of Protestantism after the publication of Martin Luther's *Ninety-Five Theses* in 1517, just twenty-five years after Christopher Columbus's voyage. The result was that the various empires, kingdoms, and powers of Europe broke into the savage infighting of religious conflicts, rebellions, and counterattacks, which ended with the devastating Thirty Years' War. The first real moment of something like a European consensus came with the Peace of Westphalia of 1648, which began the breakup of papal power and dynastic empires in favor of states and nation-states. But unlike the Treaty of Tordesillas of 1494, Westphalia was largely concerned with decolonizing the Spanish provinces of northern Europe, with acknowledging the sovereignty of the Dutch Republic and Switzerland, with establishing religious tolerance at the level of the state, and with readjusting the internal dynamics of the complex Holy Roman Empire: its relation to the rest of the world was minimal. Whether or not (according to the arguments between historians) it established notions of sovereignty, Westphalia did establish sovereign responsibility for subjects and wars. But even then it did not form a European consensus as such. Although the various treaties involved delegations and representations from sixteen European states (including Spain, France, and Sweden), sixty-six imperial states of the Holy Roman Empire, as well as various special interest groups, it did not include all "European" countries—for example, Great Britain. A truly European consensus of the major powers would not come until the Congress of Vienna of 1814–15, and even after that there were plenty of wars within Europe, leading up to the Great War. Schmitt's idea of Europe imagined in terms of a European consensus is a retrospective projection, created in order to align with the future of the Greater Germany as *Mitteleuropa*. The claims of commentators, for example, that "the extra-European world came to provide a spatial correlate to the juridical state of exception, i.e., as the anchor and guarantor of the Eurocentric interstate system and international legal order" (Blanco and del Valle 2014, 3), take Schmitt's assertions far too much for granted. There was no European "anchor and guarantor of the Eurocentric interstate system." Indeed, there was no European interstate system, Eurocentric or not. Nor was there peace in Europe. Schmitt's nomos was a myth of his own creation.

Schmitt's European historical trajectory of the development of international law, in which civility and state borders within Europe were achieved through division from the colonial world, was indeed quite deliberately mythic, since the book begins with his identification of the mythic origins of law.[8] His narrative continues in the same mode. While two countries such as Spain and Portugal might have formally agreed on global divisions for their empires, this was not something that was respected as a European consensus—far from it, in fact. The Dutch or the British devoted much of their energy to attacking and eventually appropriating Spanish and Portuguese colonies; in both cases, though more so with respect to the Dutch, this was simply a part of intra-European rebellion and war. European international law did not emerge fully formed like Venus from the sea with the Treaty of Tordesillas but was rather the result of hundreds of years of a complex multiplicity of interstate treaties, alliances, and, as with Westphalia or Vienna, resolutions to internal European wars. Schmitt was not writing a history of Europe but a history of international law as a European creation: his *longue durée* narrative created the form that he was describing and claimed to have existed. However, it existed not at any empirical positivistic level but only as a legend, as the spiritual entity evoked in *The Nomos of the Earth*.

Contrary to Schmitt's claims, there was no historical European consensus that was respected by all parties. If Europe did provide the foundation of international law, it was through a slowly developing, complex, and accumulating scaffolding of individual treaties, practices, and agreements among individual states, corporations, institutions, professions, and the like. The very fact that it can be argued that the Treaties of Westphalia did not initiate sovereignty shows the fragility of what was actually involved in even one of the most significant moments of the historical creation of European international law. Instead of Schmitt's antipositivistic mythmaking, for an accurate history of European international law, its formation, and its relation to colonialism, we need to turn to Anthony Anghie's magisterial historical account in *Imperialism, Sovereignty and the Making of International Law* (2005).

Legend: History as Mythmaking

To consider this point at a more theoretical level, we can turn to a book published just four years before *The Nomos of the Earth*, written by a former compatriot of Schmitt's who had been dismissed by the Nazis from his professorship of Romance philology at the University of Marburg in 1935: *Mimesis*, by Erich Auerbach (1946, 1957). In the famous introductory chapter, "Odysseus' Scar," having quickly established his fundamental comparative dichotomy that will guide him through his material of texts that offer self-evident meaning or those that demand interpretation, between the *Odyssey* and the Bible, Auerbach proceeds to make a further distinction between them in terms of their presentation of reality, one that he develops in terms of the concepts of myth or legend versus history. He writes:

> It is easy to separate the historical from the legendary in general. Their structure is different. Even where the legendary does not immediately betray itself by elements of the miraculous, by the repetition of well-known standard motives, typical patterns and themes, through neglect of clear details of time and place, and the like, it is generally quickly recognizable by its composition. It runs far too smoothly. All cross-currents, all friction, all that is casual, secondary to the main events and themes, everything unresolved, truncated, and uncertain, which confuses the clear progress of the action and the simple orientation of the actors, has disappeared. The historical event which we witness, or learn from the testimony of those who witnessed it, runs much more variously, contradictorily, and confusedly; not until it has produced results in a definite domain are we able, with their help, to classify it to a certain extent; and how often the order to which we think we have attained becomes doubtful again, how often we ask ourselves if the data before us have not led us to a far too simple classification of the original event—legend arranges its material in a simple and straightforward way; it detaches it from its contemporary historical context, so that the latter will not confuse it; it knows only clearly outlined men who act from few and simple motives and the continuity of whose feelings and actions remains uninterrupted. (1957, 19)

In Auerbach's terms, Schmitt attempts the creation of a legend rather than a history; *The Nomos of the Earth* should not be mistaken for history. His book shares the quality of the Bible in ranging through the domains of, in Auerbach's words, "legend, historical reporting, and interpretative historical theology" (21). This last phrase comes closest to what Schmitt offers us in *The Nomos of the Earth*: an interpretive, historical political theology. Schmitt is not concerned with "the confused, contradictory multiplicity of events, the psychological and factual cross-purposes, which true history reveals," but rather offers us a narrative characterized by a "smoothing down and harmonizing of events" (Auerbach 1957, 20), whose complex trajectory is simplified to produce a single theological narrative. What we are offered is a Heideggerian regression to a founding moment of truth, where the law, like language in Martin Heidegger, is attached to and stems from its ontological origin in the earth, which makes all subsequent history a gradual falling away from this originary foundation—in Schmitt's narrative, to the low point of the Treaty of Versailles. The low point, of course, according to Schmitt, for Europe, but this argument is an ingenious attempt to convert what was in fact a low point for Germany into a European experience. From Schmitt's German perspective of the early 1940s, Germany had literally become Europe: with Nazi expansion across all of Europe, Germany could be said to have consolidated its claim to have created a new European *Großraum*. In focusing exclusively on Versailles and ignoring the Treaty of Sèvres, which followed in 1920, or the Treaty of Lausanne of 1923, which drew and then redrew the colonial carve-ups following the German and Ottoman defeat, Schmitt shows that his interest in the colonies was entirely instrumental, in other words, that he was interested in them only insofar as they related to the internal history of his idea of a European spatiality that was in his own time in the process of being renewed through Nazi colonization.[9]

Bruno Bosteels (2005, 302) has pointed to "the tenuousness of the suture between the ontological and the historical" in *The Nomos of the Earth*. Schmitt's *Nomos* amounts to a kind of retrospective utopic translation of the mess and contradictions of history, its various cross-currents, its antagonisms, its confusions, unresolved, truncated, and uncertain, specially reengineered and fabricated for his own particular purposes. For an example of how such myths about the past are created, take the "doctrine of discovery," to which Schmitt refers as if indeed it was a doctrine. But the doctrine of discovery was also a retrospective myth, created by the *Johnson v. M'Intosh* case in the US Supreme Court in 1823, where Chief Justice John Marshall settled a land title claim by invoking the European claim to sovereignty over indigenous lands during the so-called Age of Discovery (Banner 2005; Dunbar-Ortiz 2014; Miller et al. 2010). Like Schmitt, Marshall himself had a vested interest in its creation: he stood to lose a huge portion of his own lands if he ruled in favor of Native title; he therefore self-servingly claimed that there had been "universal recognition" of this doctrine, an assertion that legal historians have subsequently shown to be false. There was in fact no such doctrine; if there was any sort of concept involved, it included a range of different practices, such as the right of the explorer to negotiate with indigenous peoples as if on behalf of the king. This single example shows clearly how attempts to codify, or unify, international legal or quasi-legal arrangements that developed over hundreds of years in very different theaters can form retrospective consolidations where historical practice is transformed into legend or myth—and a claim to a universally recognized historic statute in international law.

The complexity of historical realities, however, means that, as Auerbach observes, "to write history is so difficult that most historians are forced to make concessions to the technique of legend" (1957, 20). Every history simplifies events, motives, and consequences in a way that, if you drill down further, can always be complicated. Conventionally, myths and legends spring up from below, but they can also be created from above, particularly for ideological and political purposes: when a twentieth-century writer attempts to turn history into a legend, it will always form part of a political agenda, as it did for Schmitt.

Any history that claims a formation, an arc, a narrative, a consistent principle, thread, or spirit that can be traced across the *longue durée* of centuries of human time will inevitably take the form of a myth, will succumb to the desire to create meaning out of history through a metahistory, to find shape, patterns, and progressive or sometimes regressive movement among the confusions of its unfoldings. Yet all modes of writing history, even if focusing on a microhistorical moment, will each in their own way involve the same forms of narratological creation that emerge with the erasure of historical multiplicity, history's contradictions, and subaltern formations, its differentiated, disordered temporalities and events. History by definition must, as Ernest Renan (1887, 286) suggested for the nation, involve forgetting as well as remembering: to remember, we have to forget—as the British today forget the British invasions of Argentina in 1805 and 1806, or the French their invasions of Mexico in 1838 and 1862. We should be wary of invoking Schmitt without qualification in any attempt to define a new nomos of postcoloniality, that emergence of a contemporary historical narrative that despite its diverse temporalities, its uneven modalities, began with the first modern colonial rebellion of 1776. Schmitt's account of European history and the development of international law was framed and conditioned by a Nazi ideology of a pan-Germanic Europe. At the same time, however, such distancing of Schmitt alone is too comfortable, if it implies a total disassociation of Nazi political ideology from that of the other imperial powers. As Césaire, Arendt, Simone Weil, and others pointed out, fascism was simply European colonialism brought home to Europe. While there were differences in degree and in method, there was also an uncomfortable underlying correspondence, above all in the utilization of the concept of race. Race ideology in Nazi Germany took the particular form of anti-Semitism as the most virulent aspect of its broader hostility toward Eastern European *Untermenschen* peoples, but that extreme racism, coldly put into practice, was founded on the established, then normative Western scientific, medical, and anthropological discourse of racial difference, of beliefs in racial superiority and racial inferiority, the fundamental ideology of imperialism. Despite writing anti-Semitic articles, Schmitt himself did not place race at the center of *The Nomos of the Earth*. Yet the colony itself, as Kalyvas asserts, was indeed his "master concept" (2018, 35): the German jurist openly acknowledged the importance of European colonialism because he wished to position contemporary German land imperialism at the center of that tradition. Schmitt's is not a critical account of that tradition, nor does it involve anticolonial critique—it rather forms a theory of prospective colonialism. *The Nomos of the Earth*, however mythic its narrative, however adapted and then readapted to its particular political circumstances, is first and foremost a painful testimony to the historical reality of colonialism and its ideology in the twentieth century. If we can imagine a nomos of postcoloniality, as a new political myth, it is only because *The Nomos of the Earth* remains a callous, cruel testament to coloniality itself.

Notes

1 "At the end of first light burgeoning with frail coves the hungry Antilles, the Antilles pitted with smallpox, the Antilles dynamited by alcohol, stranded in the mud of this bay, in the dust of this town sinisterly stranded" (Césaire 2013b, 2–3).
2 "1850—The revenge of Dionysus on Apollo. / 1850—The great leap into the poetic void." (Césaire 1990, xliv).
3 This section contains some material also included in the preface to the fifteenth-anniversary edition of my *Postcolonialism: An Historical Introduction* (2016).
4 Julia Lossau (2011) offers a more skeptical assessment.
5 For Schmitt's relation to the Third Reich and the legal system under the Nazis, see also Ohana (2019), Smeltzer (2018), and Suuronen (2020).
6 See Schmitt's own historical analysis of *Hamlet* "from out of its concrete situation" (2009, 5).

7 As recorded by the BBC; translation available at "Adolf Hitler: Speech at the Berlin Sports Palace (January 30, 1941)," Jewish Virtual Library, https://www.jewishvirtuallibrary.org/hitler-speech-at-the-berlin-sports-palace-january-30-1941.
8 On the status of myth in Schmitt's *Nomos*, see Aravamudan (2005).
9 Schmitt (1990, 38) does mention Lausanne in "The Plight of European Jurisprudence."

Dai Jinhua

TRANSLATED BY
EREBUS WONG AND LISA ROFEL

On Twenty-First-Century Postcolonialism

Limited Independence

In December 2013 former South African president Nelson Mandela passed away. The mourning from around the world sounded like an echo of a vanished refrain from the remote twentieth century, a finale after the end. With the termination of white supremacist rule in South Africa in 1994, it appeared as if a heavy curtain on five hundred years of brutal imperialism and racist colonialism had finally come down. Mandela's death further sealed the end of imperialism, even though South Africa was still in turmoil, still torn by conflicts after the disintegration of extreme racism and colonial rule. In 2013 another biographical movie came out, *Mandela: Long Walk to Freedom*. (dir. Justin Chadwick). Once again, it narrated the glorious life of this great warrior of peace. In similar historiographies Mandela is portrayed as having fought peacefully, using his forty years of imprisonment to finally turn the scales of power upside down.

In fact, from the remnants of post–Cold War historiography, this one is the most important and the most—if not the only—legitimate narrative of the war-trodden twentieth century. From Mahatma Gandhi to Martin Luther King to Nelson Mandela, the dominant narrative is about a peaceful struggle of nonviolence and noncooperation that eventually brought an end to colonial rule, achieving the status of "national hero" and "father of the country" for these great historical figures. Mandela's passing seemed a perfect culmination to the era of resistance against imperialism and racist colonialism. Nevertheless, both before and after his death, there persisted "untimely" whispers. In the Sinophone world, these are treated as "revelations" and "scandals": his short-lived membership in the South Africa Communist Party, his discourse on Mao Zedong's armed struggle, his admiration for China's revolutionary path, Umkhonto we Sizwe, and the bomb attack that led to his imprisonment.[1] Although these are actually simple, clear facts, they are marked by deep historical traces. In contrast, during the peaceful transition of power, as well as before and after Mandela's election, and naturally around his death, there was a plethora of reportage, compilations, and informal commentary about the last period of his imprisonment, when negotiations took place in the jail, and about the actions and roles of the variety of people involved.

Nevertheless, an event that set in motion these protracted—and ultimately successful—secret negotiations has been lost, like a needle falling through the narrative fissures. Interestingly, this lost saga was in fact an open secret. This "secret history" was reported in Robert Harvey's *The Fall of Apartheid: The Inside Story from Smuts to Mbeki* (2011) and adapted into the film *Endgame* (dir. Pete Travis, 2009). According to this story, as early as the late 1980s, the African National Congress leaders in exile had secretly contacted the South African white supremacist regime and started negotiations. Intriguingly, the agent who mediated the contact and the negotiations was not a politician but a representative of British mining companies. The negotiations thus took place in a private mansion in the United Kingdom. These long, drawn-out negotiations were not only the first contact between the African National Congress and the South African white racist regime after decades of bloody confrontation but also the ultimate, substantive resolution of South African politics.

This behind-the-scenes story seems to be a mere anecdote, a brief episode. However, worth pondering is how to pry open the identity of the key person: the representative of British mining companies, as well as the venue of the secret negotiations. The film and the original work do not reveal the pertinent answer to this riddle in the grand reunion at the end. But obviously in the final consensus the interests of British mining companies were to be guaranteed or safeguarded as an additional condition. A small corner of contemporary South African history actually reveals a universal and central fact of former colonies before and after they emerged as nation-states: other than a few born in the fire of bloody revolution and war, the vast majority of new nations, to a different extent and through various negotiations and compromises, gained their independence by ceding economic sovereignty and interests to former colonizers. Needless to say, former colonizers permitted limited independence on the precondition that their economic interests be protected to the greatest extent, thereby extracting enormous gains from former colonies by cutting management and governance costs. These political and economic facts are missing in the recapitulated post–Cold War narratives about the great peace warriors of the twentieth century. They are also rarely broached as premises in the postwar branch of critical theory known as postcolonial discourse or in third world studies broadly conceived.

No doubt, postcolonial theory came into being as a cultural legacy of national liberation movements, echoing the vast prestige and momentum of independent nation-states in formerly colonized regions. Borrowing from Jean Baudrillard (1975), one could say that postcolonial discourse, in a certain sense, successfully established a new binary opposition: colonized/decolonized, colonial/postcolonial. A prevalent discourse is as follows: during World War II, especially on the battlegrounds of Europe, people from the former colonies fought bravely and made a significant contribution to the victory of the Allies against the Axis powers. As a consequence, national independence in Asia, Africa, and Latin America was the bargaining chip former colonizers had to turn over afterward. This kind of narrative may have exposed one aspect of historical truth. However, it has also covered up the grand scale of scenes of bloody war and revolution in the global history of decolonization. If former colonizers finally surrendered (in part) their scepter, this was because the vast majority had no choice, since they suffered a crushing defeat and were forced to pull out. In fact, for many former European colonizers, the independence movements on the three continents are an open wound, a trauma perhaps not yet fully healed even to this day.

Cold War Superpowers, Third World Nonalignment, and the New Colonialism

However, what I want to add as a supplement is another differential structure and coordinate parameter that has been blurred or even concealed in this new binary opposition of colonized/decolonized, colonial/postcolonial. That is the Cold War structure of two confrontational superpowers. After the war the formation of the socialist bloc, headed by the Soviet Union (USSR), for the first time on a world scale delineated a realm of power equal to that of Euro-America. The successes of the Russian Revolution and especially the Chinese Revolution became alternative models for establishing independence and sovereignty, and an independent economy and industrial system.

As everyone knows, this is the reason many newly established African nations bore the name of People's Republic. In fact, these nation-states across the three continents, especially in Asia and Africa, which had arisen out of national liberation movements, became equivocal "fragile zones" (Spanier 1983) between the two confrontational blocs. In the rather long period of the Cold War, they became valuable objects over which the two superpowers competed.

Precisely against this backdrop, the United States, in response to the Cuban Revolution, Chile's socialist regime, and the Nicaraguan Revolution, consolidated its presence in its "backyard" of Latin America through military intervention, assassination, and a coup d'état orchestrated by the Central Intelligence Agency. It thereby militarized Latin America with the pretext of helping it to modernize at the lowest institutional cost. In Africa the USSR exported revolution by supporting antigovernment military forces, thereby militarizing the continent against former European colonial powers. In counterpoint, the United States meanwhile made use of peacekeeping forces and nongovernmental organizations financed by large foundations as a way to openly export its ideology and modernization program. As for the regions that served as lifelines of energy and transport, the United States did not hesitate to take extreme measures, including military action. In Asia, torn apart by the great schism of the Cold War, in addition to the persistent "border wars" of the region (Korea, Vietnam, and then the whole of Indochina), there were military and ideological confrontations between countries and regions along the front lines of the Cold War. Exactly along these front lines, the "four little dragons" created economic miracles under non-Western but also nondemocratic regimes.

This seems to be a suitable case in point of subject-object theory. The processes of objectification by the United States and the USSR greatly consolidated the formation of new international subjects and mutual recognition among the regions of and countries in Asia, Africa, and Latin America. The Bandung Conference, held by twenty-nine Asian and African countries in 1955, was called on the precondition of excluding colonizers and former colonial countries for the first time. Under the banner of nonalignment, it demonstrated an entirely new type of international alliance. The convening of the Bandung Conference along with its resolutions, as well as the regionalized movements (Latin American resistance movements, pan-African movements) that resisted the imperialist superpowers before and after Bandung, thrust onto the international stage an ordinal number excluded by the binary code of the so-called principle of difference: namely, the third (world). If we grant that the prominence of the third world was a product of the Cold War structure, the self-consciousness of the third world along with its diverse, authentic appeals for political alliance tore apart the Cold War binary with an actual tripartite structure.

Interestingly, the rise of the Non-Aligned Movement and the third world redrew the world map in the true sense of the word. Under new parameters, this rise thrust forward political issues like national sovereignty. At the same time, it revealed the invisible writing underneath: what replaced the old colonial structure was a new colonialism, or the political-economic reality known as globalization. On the one hand, through negotiation, strategic risk, and compromise, new nations emerged. On the other hand, they are a far cry from being genuine sovereign states, as they are thoroughly dependent on the economic structure of the colonial metropole. And even though they acquired full political sovereignty, these postcolonial nations are still under the yoke of a monolithic, unified economic structure shaped by colonial rule. Or they are in a state of destitution, lacking the necessary capital and resources to initiate industrialization and economic reconstruction. This is the important subtext of "fomenting revolution elsewhere" in the glorious or should we say tragic denouement of Che Guevara, the red legend of the twentieth century.

In other words, after World War II the world order seemed to have been thoroughly overhauled. In fact, thanks to the rise and total domination of finance capital and the capital monopoly of new technologies such as the green revolution—which is actually irrelevant and even contrary to ecological issues—the entire third world/former colonies and semicolonized regions were integrated into and reconstructed as production zones for cheap goods (the world factory) and fields of monoculture or cash crops. On the premise of a global economy with regional divisions of labor, Western Europe and North America outsourced industry and a portion of the proletariat offshore and on this basis turned themselves into a postindustrial, postmodern consumer society.[2] Therefore, the topic of the third world corresponds to the Cold War structure of confrontation between East and West, written as a North-South opposition of rich and poor countries. This opposition clarifies that the astronomical debt carried by the South has usually been imposed by former colonial powers. Such is the direct and bitter economic and political reality of the third world. Perhaps it is unnecessary to further elaborate that the Cold War confrontation of East/West and the global wealth inequality of North/South do not so much offer a complete diagram of the second half of the twentieth century by way of the four compass points but rather indicate different closed systems of difference and academic disciplines. The keywords of the former are socialism (communism) versus capitalism, represented in the post–Cold War era as dictatorship versus democracy—political and ideological terms. The latter is about the first and second worlds versus the third, developed versus developing countries, rich versus poor countries. These are economic or sociological discourses. In this coordinate field of differential dimensions, postcolonial theory seems to return us to another facet of the East/West coordinate; namely, on the Eurocentric world map initiated with modern history, the "East" of formerly colonized countries and regions is facing the "West" of Europe (Western Europe and North America). Needless to say, in this "new" East/West formulation, history, culture, and geography appear to be narrated anew. Yet World War II and the Cold War still serve as their enunciatory folds. Such is the underlying motivation internal to the West for the publication of books like *The Chrysanthemum and the Sword* (Benedict 1946) and the rise of regional studies in the United States.

What I would emphasize here is the significance of the Cold War as the "fold" of postcolonial narrative in its nearly literal meaning. In doing so, not only do I attempt to draw attention to this history, which has been deliberately obliterated and buried in oblivion, but I also point out that its basic parameters are exactly its strong political and economic character. I have repeatedly argued (Dai 2018) that the emergence of the "cultural" in postwar US-European social fields and the humanistic sciences (the counterculture movement, cultural studies, cultural politics, or cultural revolution) may have been a critique and refusal of Soviet-style dogmatic political economy or economic determinism. However, the strength and vitality of the cultural was no doubt dependent on the global political structure of the US-USSR confrontation and the (more than) two economic systems based in (more than) two categories of difference. In other words, it is owing to the pervasive diffusion of Cold War political culture and the politicized (and even militarized) representation of third world economic questions that the critical issues of cultural politics have unique significance and vitality in social practice within the United States and Europe. Therefore, despite disparities in terms of demands, enunciatory subject positions, and disciplinary and discursive fields, postcolonial discourse or postcolonialism no doubt has a potential or direct affiliation and dialogic relationship with Immanuel Wallerstein's theory of the modern world-system, Samir Amin's dependence theory, and other postwar social and political-economic critical theories (Wallerstein 2004; Wallerstein 2011; Amin 1974; Amin 2014; Amin 2019).

Capitalist Globalization and Postcolonial Theory

With the termination of the Cold War and the arrival of the post–post–Cold War, a rapidly changing world has transformed the actual structure and coordinates on which Euro-American critical theory was once mapped. The world has entered the era of capitalist globalization in the truest sense. First, there is no longer an outside or alternative to capitalism. Second, we no longer see variant forms of capitalism within the Euro-American world. Not only has the particular Cold War–era political culture vanished but also the real space for political practices of global critique and resistance. Indeed, not long after the Cold War, forces opposing capitalist globalization reassembled, from the Seattle antiglobalization protest and the World Social Forum to the Occupy Wall Street movement. However, resistance movements of this sort were not merely insufficient to counter the surge of global capital. They furthermore could not really converge into a new resistant force because, except for having the same enemy, they could not reach consensus on a constructive solution or point to a way out. "One No, Many Yeses," as they say (Bray 2013; van Gelder 2011). Similarly, owing to the failure or refusal to respond to the question of what the new historical subject is and whether we should be naming, summoning, or shaping such a subject, the ideological struggle between the (New) Left and Right within Euro-America, once different from the opposition of US versus USSR and capitalism versus socialism, found its political coordinates and orientation shattered and obscured in the new global discursive context. Nowadays, cultural theory, including postcolonial discourse, has lost its political basis in reality, becoming debilitated and even losing its momentum as effective social practice. The problematics of cultural politics have begun to show their limits and even their phantasmatic nature.

At the same time, what erupted at the end of the Cold War was a global flow (of capital, population, and ideology) at an unprecedented scale and magnitude. This enormous tidal flow may be forcefully integrating global capital. But it is also destroying international society or transnational alliances formed during the Cold War. Along with the USSR, what have vanished as "names disappearing from the map" are not only the former socialist bloc and capitalist camps, which have disintegrated, but also the Non-Aligned Movement, which had once assembled a third world identity, as well as the pan-Latin American and pan-African movements that were part of the forces of countersystem struggle.[3] Now the nation-state has once again become a suspicious, fragile, but seemingly irreplaceable unit of international ideology. In contrast to the closing of European wounds with the integration of

Europe into the European Union after the Cold War, we witness the ups and downs of separatism and frequent conflicts here and there in the world, especially among former socialist countries. As for the postcolonial narrative, the colonial/postcolonial binary has begun to obscure its critique, reflection, and confrontation with imperialist colonial history, becoming a rhetoric that functions well in quite distinctive discursive contexts and enunciatory positions.

It is well known that although postcolonialism originated in the anticolonial struggle in the third world/former colonized countries—for example, the social practices and works of Frantz Fanon and scholars in India—as a critical theory and an ism it was born in North American universities and produced by and from the viewpoint of scholars of English-American (and Asian American) literature who were from the third world (mainly from Asia). Thus, from the beginning it has exhibited reversals, displacements, and paradoxes of subject-object positionalities in multiple senses. As far as its birthplace within the North American academy is concerned, it is first of all an insightful rediscovery of colonial culture and narrative in the history of European/English American literature. It discovered and revealed that the construction of the Euro-American imperialist Subject requires the objectification and subhumanity or nonhumanity of the former colonies and the third world as its Other. From an entirely new standpoint, it repeatedly shredded the apparent naturalization of Euro-American colonizers' role as Subject. It opened a brilliant chapter in the critique of cultural imperialism and modernism. Rediscovering and giving voice to the Other in Euro-American classical literature and occupying and appropriating this particular object position achieved a new subject position of speaking from the third world. Needless to say, rather than emphasize the fact of a subject position for the formerly colonized, I am arguing that in the era of globalization we find the creation and acquisition of a new subject position of cultural diaspora. This theoretical achievement highlights the so-called reverse journey by postcolonial theorists into the "heart of darkness" in the age of globalization. The particularity of a cultural diasporic subject position further highlights the complex reality of identity.

Postcolonialism, as a new critical theory from the West, was widely disseminated to non-Western, formerly colonized regions by means of the growing hegemony of English and the status of the United States as a major hub and exporter of theory after World War II. This situation triggered new sociocultural problems, an exchange of subject-object positions, and various paradoxes. There is no doubt that postcolonial arguments, responding to the universality and profundity of colonial cultures (following from their sociopolitical-economic colonial structures), exposed and reflected on pervasive cultural imperialism and occasionally served as a pointed warning against the "self-Orientalism" prominent in the interflow of international cultures. Nevertheless, for most third world countries, the most urgent actual problem has always been political and economic modernization (or we could call it Westernization)—political sovereignty, national self-determination, industrialization, monetary sovereignty, and so forth. Fredric Jameson (1986) asserted that third world writers were still writing fables in a "Sherwood Anderson" manner. Even though his suggestion was heavily questioned and criticized, it is indeed true that the representation or reflection of reality by third world writers and artists, with all the vigor and fervor of a life-and-death struggle, was usually produced in a displaced or totally different postcolonial discursive context from that which they were describing.

In most third world societies, including their cultural reality, postcolonial theory has not caught up with the actuality of neocolonialism. Moreover, the coordinate of "race" highlighted in postcolonialism is not an anguish felt as constantly or keenly as class and gender. Working with imported theories, local third world scholars hold a peculiar doubled position of subject-object, speaking the language of "the Other" but also holding a self-referential enunciatory position. Even more profound than this peculiar cultural experience of receiving third world discourses from the West is the following: in the real context of capitalist globalization with no alternative, many Western colonial thoughts and ideas packaged as "universal values" and carried by colonialism's violent coercions have become internalized or even rewritten as one's own cultural resources through the long historical process that includes anticolonial struggles and the establishment of modern nation-states. It is no doubt the best example of appropriation in postcolonial theory. My favorite expression is "the Other is not far away but deep inside ourselves." Such is the universal cultural reality of the third world and former colonies and also an appropriate description of their political and economic realities.

Here, what is important is not that after centuries of capitalism there is no longer any pure local culture or third world authentic cultural "self." Not only have imperialism and colonialism violently destroyed the social structure and soil the local culture depended on to exist. They also created an epistemic gap between traditional culture and modern society. Postcolonial theory has sharpened and will continue to spark the cultural awareness of third world/non-Western countries. But following on critique, finding a creative, realistic program of action is another kind of social predicament. On the one hand, it is difficult to directly revive diverse, rich traditional resources. Therefore, the "modernization of traditional culture" becomes a self-contradictory sociocultural issue that is urgent but difficult to put into practice. On the other hand, cultural particularism often becomes the slogan of political conservatism, serving third world political elites who sustain their rule in the name of tradition and national culture, whereas the suspicious, pervasive Western ideas often become a strategic banner of local resistance. The latter, as a pragmatic double-edged sword, also reconstitutes through real resistance a cultural "internal exile" indebted to colonial history, even becoming a new political colonization.

Nowadays, in the middle of the second decade of the twenty-first century, we bring up again postcolonial problematics to look at the reality of today's cataclysmic world. We can say that South Africa terminated white rule, but in fact that was a lingering, oscillating echo and a late conclusion to colonial/racist history. Interestingly, colonial/postcolonial discourse has not faded away. To the contrary, it has emerged as a recurring world thesis in the new century. Doubtless, it corresponds to the contest of financial capital fighting to construct a new empire of capital for plunder, to the open and submerged currency wars or resource wars, and to the widening wealth gap internationally and within nations in a divided world. In most cases, *colonization* is used more as a rhetorical term. Borrowing from the brutal and bloody history of colonialism, it connotes the level of barbarism and cruelty of global exploitation and oppression against the poor in the post–Cold War era when the international and domestic power of checks and balances has disappeared. People, including myself, often use the term *internal colonization* to describe how brutal the progression of capitalism in China has been at the turn of the century. However, it is not so much a reference to colonial history as a trope dissociated from the memory of colonial history.

At the turn of the century, the concentration of public wealth in the hands of a few has taken place not only between the geographic and political center and the periphery but also between the urban and the rural, between coastal regions and the hinterland, and in core cities—once the backbone of medium and large state-owned enterprises, the pillars of society. Under the unequal structure of an urban-rural dyadic system, rural youths pour into the cities into sweatshops known as world factories. They have in fact become the direct creators of the surplus value necessary for the primitive accumulation of capital. However, it is the former state-owned-factory workers who have fallen to the bottom of society, into despair and helplessness. Circulating across the vast land of China, more than 200 million peasant workers have in reality become the primitive proletarian army. Their circumstances are occasionally visible in reportage, literary writing, cinema, and television because their suffering (their "problems") can be interpreted through the logic of modernization.

But those off-duty [*xiagang*] (laid-off) workers have long been in a nameless and aphasic state as there is no counterpart in the takeoff of modernity in Euro-American history. In 2011 and 2014, they finally made their first appearance in two low-budget art films. *The Piano in a Factory* was directed by Zhang Meng (2011); *Red Amnesia* was directed by Wang Xiaoshuai (2014).

Although *The Piano in a Factory* did poorly at the box office in a film market in China dominated by big capital, it was through this family tragicomedy that the brutal expropriation during 1995–97 made its first appearance in the prudent discourses of sociologists and scholars of contemporary history. Even more interestingly, it is not a reality exclusive to the third world or emerging countries like BRICS (Brazil, Russia, India, China, South Africa) but is universal to worker communities in former industrial cities during the process of outsourcing industry from advanced industrialized nations to third world countries in the post–Cold War era. Also with profound implications, apart from this tragedy performed in comic form, any attempt to understand clearly similar sufferings is nowhere to be found, whether in writing, documentary, or discourse. If this is a universal scene of internal colonization happening in the former metropoles and (semi)colonies alike, then its proper reference is the historical progress of modernity or, bluntly, the logic of capital rather than the logic of colonization.

In analogous examples, *colonization* as rhetoric still contains social critical force. As a social trope, it highlights the atrocities of exploitation. However, this is not the whole or even major usage of *colonization* as a trope in the twenty-first century. It may be said that after the post–Cold War, the rapid and drastic process of globalization has unfolded the world as "masterless space," "masterless time," and "masterless land."[4] The world has once again moved into an era of global competition for hegemony. *Colonization*, then, has become a term applied by global left-wing critique and movements to describe the global flow of capital from different locations and its destructive impact on and aftermath in local economies, production, and livelihood (first of all in the third world, or we could say developing countries).

This use of the term *colonization* is similar to the barricades rebels built on the streets of Paris in 1968 that were not so much fortifications as symbolic constructions. Long gone are the narrow streets and alleys from the time of the Paris Commune. The barricade no longer has any function of military defense or occupation. It is rather an appropriation of historical memory. Once a barricade is constructed, the rebels' opponents on the other side can be defined as tyrant, royalist, and executioner. The memory carried by the barricade can confer righteousness on the insurgents and condemn the opponents to the category of the unjust. The rhetorical yet ahistorical usage of *colonization* can also emphasize how formidable, vicious, and unjust enemies/foreigners are and remind us that the history of capitalism reeks of blood. However, at the same time, it might obscure our recognition and understanding of the condition of global capitalism after the post–Cold War and cover over the underlying historical context from which the current reality is fabricated. Most dangerously, colonization as social designation or imagination must directly or implicitly carry or construct a national or even racial identity politics, an identity position preconditioned by absolute difference.

As already mentioned, with the end of the Cold War, what has developed along with global capital flow is a widening social division and unequal distribution of wealth. As Li Meng (2015) says, "At the end of the last century, radicalism received a hard blow. Since the seventeenth century, the Left has never been weaker. Society is at its most unequal since World War II, yet the people are more willing to put up with it than ever before." Here I do not plan to argue with Li Meng in detail. I quote this statement to delineate a certain perspective on reality: the intensification of social inequality. People's so-called tolerance of it is directly related to the steep decline in the power of the global Left, its power to explain social reality and its ability to mobilize. People "put up with" this inequality because they choose to deny the Left's explanation of the cause of social inequality and, most important, the left-wing program of social equality and justice. Doubtless, they do not really bear with this ever more dire inequality. In fact, a growing despair and helplessness is spreading among the global middle class (especially among millennials). Therefore, we witness different social groups repeatedly meeting and gathering in street struggles, social movements, or violent conflicts occasioned by random social incidents: namely, the continuously enlarging social bottom (the economic outcasts) and the middle-class youth who have become angry and hopeless in the face of the steady closing off of paths to social mobility.

We may for the moment set aside discussion of the form and nature of social movements and social resistance at the turn of the twenty-first century (for example, features such as internet mobilization, conscious or unconscious semiotic performance, borrowing from popular culture texts, instant transmission of countless images and videos, and so on). A prominent change in social movements from the second half of the twentieth century is the debilitation—even the loss—of the Left's power of social interpretation and mobilization. As a result, right-wing narratives, often right-wing populisms, appropriate social sufferings, inequality, injustice, the helplessness and hopelessness of the lower classes and youth, and even the critical rhetoric of colonialism from the global Left. Purged of the coordinate of class and a critique of capitalism, these social narratives and mobilization count on religious fundamentalism of various sorts, blunt or implicit nationalism, and racism. This is the paradox of the twenty-first century: on the side of "radical" political conservatism, we find a peculiar social effect from the rhetorical usage of *colonization*. Emotional mobilization by populism of this sort expunges the parameters of capital and class. Domestic and international population/labor flows (of the upper and lower classes, but first of all the lower classes) in the era of globalization become the scapegoat for "local" social problems and sufferings. The fundamental rhetoric of us/them necessary for political mobilization is converted into local people/foreigners, our race/the other. When the expansion of transnational flows of capital and labor becomes equivalent to colonialism in this imagination, the historical facts of colonialism such as military invasion, political domination, and economic exploitation become invisible. At the same time, this conservative imagination further uses the sufferings and menace of current reality to obstruct local memories of imperialism and colonialism. It not only successfully creates a social imagination of pathos but also rewrites or, better, creates a new structure of feeling.

The twenty-first-century world situation has once again incorporated a "postcolonial" discursive field into the global political-economic fabric. From the Rwandan genocide to the 9/11 terrorist attack, from the Tea Party to ISIS (Islamic State of Iraq and Syria) and the rise of various right-wing and extreme-right political forces, there is no doubt an echo of colonial history and imperialist atrocity. Moreover, after the world finally closed the colonial chapter of history, the exacerbation of inequality in the global political economy nonetheless occurs through a pattern reminiscent of the former colonial system. Is this, once again, postcolonial? Or neocolonial? A historical stage of capitalist imperialism or a universal logic?

The US-China Struggle

Doubtless, the highlighting of colonial and postcolonial issues in the world, especially in East Asia, is related to the global race for hegemony, the integration of Europe, and the rise of China after the issuance of the euro in 1999. One could say that the 2008 financial crisis led to the rise of China becoming a prominent, attention-grabbing global reality. In the following years, Chinese capital and industry marched into the Asian periphery and then into Africa. In recent years we have the Shanghai free-trade-zone initiative, the unrolling of One Belt, One Road[5] in the world (though with a lot of setbacks), and the establishment of the Asian Infrastructure Investment Bank, which has triggered increasingly vociferous discourses from both the Left and the Right, such as "Chinese imperialism," "Chinese colonialism," and "China as threat" (strangely accompanied by "China on the verge of collapse").

One of the prominent transformations after the Cold War has been the integration of Europe by the winner (Western Europe), with the material economy of the former Soviet and Eastern European socialist nations as its trophies, which enabled that integration. Moreover, the rise of the euro impelled Europe's endeavor to get a piece of the action in the global financial empire monopolized by the United States and US dollar, starting a new round of competition between the old and new continents, which seems to be tearing apart the former Cold War alliance. Thus, the rise of China is one of the important marks of what I call "after the post–Cold War."

Rather interestingly, the Wall Street financial crisis that swept across Europe and then affected the rest of the world is both the background and the stage of as well as providing the significance for the rise of China. On one hand, China's relatively closed currency policy protected it from major trouble. Moreover, its relatively undervalued assets became a global attraction. On the other hand, the astronomical wealth of the real economy accumulated during the socialist era was at that time still in a process of capitalization. The vitality of the Chinese economy for capital, with the latter's vastness and depth, makes China the frontier of global capitalism and even its savior.

In less than a decade, the global expansion of the Chinese economy has given rise to talk of a US-China struggle for hegemony followed by multiple intensified tensions surrounding China. As for the theory of Chinese colonialism/imperialism, it rhetorically highlights, as already mentioned, the speed and scale of Chinese economic growth and its global expansion, as well as the impact and influence of Chinese capital and products on the world economy. Apart from this, however, it fails to raise and even conceals a related major question, one that should stimulate thought: Has China today achieved a political and economic status comparable to that of the former USSR so as to be powerful enough to be an empire that can contend with the United States?

We may say that a US-China confrontation has become a fact. However, it does not contain the ideological opposition of the Cold War. Does China, then, in relation to the United States, represent a different type of capitalism or its potential? The reverse of that argument would be, if China has become a global empire, then why is it still listed as a BRICS emerging economy, a newly rising nation, and a developing country? Do the precedents of periodic setbacks to and even disintegration of the momentum of BRICS emerging economies support the various versions of the China-on-the-verge-of-collapse theory? If the US-China confrontation is an established fact, then how do we choose a position in theory and practice that is a critique of and resistance to the multiple hegemonies of capitalism and imperialism? With globalization after the post–Cold War era, are different forms of capitalism still possible? Does this even make any sense? Does opposition to China's hegemony signify a deceleration in the decline of US global dominance, even a fortification of the US hegemonic position? How does the rise of China accelerate the crisis and collapse of capitalism? Or does it create new momentum and new possibilities for global capitalism?

Searching for New Coordinates

For me, a highly realistic and ethical problem is, What is the position for a social critic facing the world today? Facing the reality of global capitalism with no alternative, should we just choose to take the "better" side? Or should we refuse to take sides and insist on critique? If critique inside and outside academia is still possible, what is the meaning of critique in practice? In other words, should the social critic take responsibility for a new construction? A related question is, For the third world, is the rise of China exacerbating the disaster? Creating a new disaster? Or a new possibility (as a new model, or the creation of a new power fissure as a rival to the United States)? In the history of capitalism over the past several centuries, the rise of China is the only non-European example. Does the rise of China still represent an alternative path? Does "China's path" today imply the significance of the Chinese Revolution or its betrayal? To what extent did the twentieth-century international Communist movements achieve an alternative path of modernization (and therefore decolonization)? I have no definitive answers to these questions. No answer, not because of my Chinese identity, but rather because, in the face of this era of global capitalism and of multiple crises surrounding China, I am searching for new coordinates, new language, and new possibilities for theory and practice. Today what is highly intrinsic to the issues of the colonial, postcolonial, and neocolonial is not only the structure and reality of financial capitalism but also the fact that the environmental and energy crises point to the historical end of capitalism.

Notes

1. Umkhonto we Sizwe was the armed wing of the African National Congress, which Mandela cofounded.
2. The Soviet regime established a system of "international division of labor" pivoted around nation-state interests within its new empire. The difference is that the plan and orientation of socialist nations, including the USSR, except East Germany, was the acceleration of industrialization (militarization for the arms race) and "modernization."
3. *Names Disappearing from the Map* is the Chinese title of a 2003 Russian film *Koktebel* (Коктебель, dir. Boris Khlebnikov and Alexey Popogrebsky).
4. From the title of part 3 in the third volume, *Twilight Watch* (2004), of the Russian novelist Sergey Lukianenko's trilogy of fantasy novels.
5. Subsequently known in English as the Belt and Road Initiative.

Part II

Chinese Socialist Postcoloniality

Wendy Larson

Who Owns Social Justice?

Cultural studies as a field, which displaced a textually oriented new criticism, was founded on the idea that the study of culture could and should be important for social justice. In addition to pedagogy, research in humanistic areas was supposed to be part of a larger conversation of the well-educated about social, historical, and cultural aspects of the social sciences, natural sciences, and professions, as well as art, literature, and other humanities. The careful unraveling of naturalized and universalized Eurocentrism and the thinking through of other previously unquestioned perspectives—such as the valorization of the human being—are projects that were developed through and included in the reformation of humanistic studies through cultural studies. Much of this socially relevant humanities work drew on Marxist theory, particularly that of the Frankfurt school and Antonio Gramsci (1891–1937). Deploying Marxist lenses of ideological exposure, class analysis, and social justice, humanities researchers developed new insights and pedagogical strategies. Postcolonial studies, with its emphasis on cultural and social imperialism, universalized modern structures, unrecognized hierarchies, and damage to or obliteration of non-Western cultural practices, developed in this context and drew on some of these insights and strategies.

With the fall of the Berlin Wall, the dismantling of the Soviet bloc, and the creep of capitalism into the heart of former socialist countries such as China, the belief that cultural studies and its pedagogy might further social justice has diminished. Without a direct connection to political policy makers, let alone to the material developments of technology and science, the field that became known as critical theory rested uneasily on the value of changing minds via humanistic pedagogy: reading, writing, and discussion. Humanities professors who relied on the sequence of "teach—learn—change society for the better" and connecting to the ideals of academic Marxism have resorted to schooling themselves in economics and other social sciences, hoping that the injection of these disciplines into the humanities will provide a clear bridge to action. They have had to consider the possibility that their labor may be an ineffective catalyst for change and that to recognize the location of humanities work within the Marxist superstructure seemed to always imply a secondary status.

By virtue of its far-reaching critique of Western imperialism, postcolonial studies until recently has been somewhat sheltered from attacks that argue that academic humanities are of limited political relevance. Teaching students and readers about the damaging cultural and social changes that were part of colonial invasion suggests a moral reckoning, even if there still is no direct route from this analysis to social transformation. In other words, since it was connected to recognizing and understanding systematic oppression, bias, and stereotyping in the "real world," postcolonial studies—even with a focus on literary analysis—seemed more material than many other humanistic endeavors.

Yet eventually criticisms that were directed at the humanities from both within and without landed hard on postcolonial studies, intersecting with an earlier debate within the field on the blind spots of Marxist approaches (Huggan 2008; Lindner 2010). Recently, scholars including Benita Parry (2004), Neil Lazarus (1999), Arif Dirlik (1998), and Aijaz Ahmad ([1992] 2008) have accused postcolonial studies of playing with texts and rejecting materialist understandings of historical processes that could lead to change. Is such work, Graham Huggan (2008) asks, better left to the social sciences, which are well equipped to understand and address the historical, social, and economic conditions of postcolonialism and to propose policy solutions, than to literary scholars, a question taken up by many others?[1] As Dai Jinhua suggests in her chapter, the fact that the old colonial structure never fully disappeared but was replaced by the economic dependency of formerly colonized regions on the colonial metropole shows that there may be no simple way to address the problems raised within the field of postcolonial studies. Ironically, although a broad Marxist context of social justice helped form the postcolonial studies critique, the literary emphasis of some work resulted in an attack from precisely the same quarters. Most recently, Vivek Chibber has launched a critique of the humanities bias of postcolonial studies, criticizing the field's avoidance of class analysis in favor of a culturalist emphasis on identity, discourse, and symbols:

> Postcolonial theory has made real gains in certain domains, especially in mainstreaming literature from the global South. In the 1980s and 90s it played an important role in keeping alive the idea of anti-colonialism and anti-imperialism; and it has made the problem of Eurocentrism a watchword among progressive intellectuals. But these achievements have come with a steep price tag. It seems bizarre, at a time like this, to find ourselves stuck with a theory that made its name by dismantling some of the conceptual pillars that can help us understand the political conjuncture, and to devise effective strategy. . . . Postcolonial theorists have wasted much effort tilting against windmills of their own creation, and so have licensed a massive resurgence of nativism and Orientalism. It is not just that they emphasize the local over the universal. Their valorization of the local, obsession with cultural particularities, and insistence on culture as the wellspring of agency has licensed the exoticism that the left once abhorred in colonial depictions of the non-West.[2] (Chibber 2014)

In chapter 2 of this volume, Dai Jinhua, like Chibber, also argues that cultural politics, including postcolonial discourse, have lost their political basis in reality.

According to Chibber (2006, 2013b, 2014), postcolonial studies and in particular the Subaltern Studies Group embody the fundamental contradiction I have described: a focus on texts, discourse, or other humanistic and cultural concerns strays from class analysis and more generally a materialist approach. As such, it is difficult to reconcile with the promotion of social justice and may even work against it. The debate has amplified divisions among those who work with texts or aesthetics, creating a hierarchy that places political and economic study above literature, art, and culture. Hence, cultural studies, bent on solidifying its social relevance, generally has rejected elite writers or artists and focused on popular culture, imagined as at least closer to the authentic voice of the masses.

For literature professors who want their work to be politically important—whether within postcolonial studies or another area—academic Marxist theory has both promoted aspiration toward social transformation and thrown up logistical roadblocks to its realization. It is not surprising, therefore, that internal fatigue within cultural studies has resulted in a resurgence of interest in a new formalist approach of close reading. Even so, so powerful is the hope for overt political relevance that the contextualization of such work within the framework of social justice persists. For example, Caroline Levine (2006, 2015) elevates the study of structural elements within literature and other forms of culture while maintaining a Marxist emphasis on social justice. She goes so far as to defend her version of formalism by directly stating that "the primary goal of this formalism is radical social change" (2015, 18).

Considering China's deep engagement with Marxism, it is not surprising to observe similar topics in the past century of Chinese intellectual practice. Figuring out exactly what humanities intellectuals were supposed to be doing often became contentious, with ideological campaigns that were open not only to the sincere but also to the manipulative. In this chapter I investigate literary and cultural research and pedagogy in twentieth-century China, with reference to the environment of Marxist and Maoist theory and to related concerns in postcolonial studies. First, I consider the concept of permanent revolution, which was invoked in its preliminary conceptual forms by Karl Marx (1818–83), Vladimir Lenin (1870–1924), Leon Trotsky (1879–1940), and Joseph Stalin (1878–1953). A short examination of the discussion reveals the concept's important role in mediating the concept of how change could occur: Do material conditions absolutely determine the possibilities for change, or can certain stages of development be accelerated through political mandate? In the late 1950s, several years after the victorious Chinese Communist Party established a government under the banner of socialism and communism, Mao Zedong (1893–1976) mentioned permanent revolution (*buduan geming* 不断革命) in a speech on January 28, 1958. Mao distinguished his use of the term from that of Trotsky, leading some to translate the term as Mao uses it as "continuous revolution" (Dittmer 1987); to some extent, for Mao, permanent or continuous revolution was a state of mind associated with "correct thinking/knowledge" (*zhengque sixiang* 正确思想) or proper subjectivity.

The development of proper subjectivity as the linchpin of humanities work was one solution to the logistical problems raised by the study of culture within Marxist theory. If, after all, a "genuine theory of *praxis* must stress, as Marx did, the intrinsic bond between consciousness and productive activity," then consciousness, and its corollary subjectivity, needs to be formed correctly (Dupré 1980, 112). In China, Maxim Gorky (1868–1936) eventually became a figurehead for the valorization of proper subjectivity and thought. In the second part of this chapter, I argue that the reconfigured and reinterpreted Chinese Gorky functioned like a springboard, assisting writers who located themselves within May Fourth humanistic traditions to embrace Marxist determinism while simultaneously separating literature from other humanities areas and enhancing its relationship with political work. The Chinese interpretation of Gorky's literature of "blood and tears" helped bring literature down from the intellectual stratosphere, drawing it closer to the material base. Gorky lay at the heart of the 1935–36 debate between future literary commissar Zhou Yang 周扬 (1908–89) and writer/theorist Hu Feng 胡风 (1902–85), which centered on the necessity and role of the typical character. The mid-1930s debate in China transformed Gorky into a powerful revolutionary tool, paving the way for the creation of the Chinese Gorky, who contributed to the recontextualization of literature and literary studies while helping writers and literary scholars develop a vanguard revolutionary position (Larson 2016; Qiu 1997).

My overall focus on the interpretive and didactic work of literary scholars and the way it relates to political ideology and change is a vast twentieth-century concern that has run through Marxist theory, postcolonial theory, and literary theory in general. Is it possible to think of literary studies as socially effective in some way, without falling prey to the conceptual trap I described earlier? Can we pay attention to the way in which literature as an aesthetic form works to influence minds, societies, and histories, while simultaneously avoiding the dangers of determinism and coercive didacticism? My conclusion is that although we may all agree that culture is influential, our hopes that we can powerfully craft social justice through our work have pushed us too far in arguing for the direct political efficacy of literature, literary theory, and literary pedagogy. In the third section, I read Chibber's critique of humanistic postcolonial studies by way of inquiring as to whether we can avoid the pitfalls that turned late 1950s Chinese discourse of the postrevolutionary, or permanent revolution, into a punitive projection of correct knowledge.

Permanent Revolution and Social Change

By the time Mao Zedong laid out and affirmed his own definition of *permanent revolution* in the late 1950s, the term had been molded by a perplexing hundred-year history. Since Marx's early use of the term in 1843 in "On the Jewish Question," students of Marxism have debated exactly what Marx, Friedrich Engels, and others meant by the term (Day and Gaido 2009; Dunn and Radice 2006; Lih 2012; Marx [1844] 1978; van Ree 2013). As Michael Löwy (1981) explains, there are three parts to the problem: the possibility of proletarian revolution in industrially undeveloped countries, the uninterrupted transition from democratic to socialist revolution, and the global spread of socialism. The most pressing issue centers on whether Marx used the notion of permanent revolution (*die Revolution in Permanenz*) (Löwy 1981) to broach the possibility that in certain cases communism could be achieved without a society passing through the advanced industrialization that capitalist development provided. The extent to which Marx, Engels, and later Marxist theorists found this scenario plausible, the role of material development as the basis of historical materialism and revolutionary change, and the possibility that Marx and Engels slid into idealism in their exuberance to move revolutionary transformation forward mark the outlines of the issue.

Two schools of thought represent the poles of this debate (van Ree 2013). The first maintains that Marx and Engels believed the proletarian revolution would arrive only when capitalism reached an advanced level, at which moment its internal contradictions would foment rebellion. Under this scenario, industrialization must be well developed, and the industrial proletariat must be a majority of the population. The stages of development, which can be lengthy, must be fully engaged, and there can be no shortcuts. The second, to which most academic researchers of early communism subscribe, contends that Marx and Engels recognized the possibility of proletarian revolution in areas of relatively backward circumstances (such as those of France and Germany in the mid-1800s). In this interpretation, although a fixed succession of long stages may be the normal route to communism, a shortcut is available under exceptional conditions, which allow for a shift from the deterministic route through economic stages toward a journey driven more by thought and politics. Although many recognize this strand of thought in early work by Marx and Engels, some go even further, arguing that these foundational theorists came to the conclusion that this route is in fact not a shortcut but rather the normal way that modern revolutions will take place, awarding the notion of permanent revolution a more central and dominant role. As Erik van Ree (2013) explains, this seemingly contradictory set of ideas about how the proletarian revolution will come about introduces a paradox into Marxist revolutionary doctrine.

Over the second half of the nineteenth century, the failure of socialist revolution in industrially advanced nations, as well as the difficulty of predicting if, when, and how the revolution would occur in countries with vastly different levels of development and populations, engendered significant debate. By 1895 Engels saw that capitalism in continental Europe was far from reaching its zenith, leading him to slightly move away from the concept of permanent revolution or, in other words, the possibility of skipping over, truncating, or shrinking the capitalist stage. Although Karl Kautsky (1854–1935), Rosa

Luxemburg (1871–1919), Alexander Parvus (1867–1924), David Ryazanov (1870–1938), and Franz Mehring (1846–1919) rejected the idea of a rapid transition to socialist revolution in Russia, they nonetheless adhered to the idea of permanent revolution or uninterrupted revolution: "In 1905, the language of permanence was used as a way of presenting this advice [that the proletariat keep up its revolutionary pressure in victory or defeat] about the best way to conduct a democratic revolution" (Lih 2012, 446). After 1905 Lenin argued that skipping over the capitalist stage would result in a revolution whose economic and social content was bourgeois. Rather than going along with Marx's assignment of revolutionary leadership to the petty bourgeoisie, Lenin identified the proletariat as the leader, and socialist rule as a collaboration between the proletariat and the peasantry (Davidshofer 2014; Skilling 1961).

Interpreted as a moderate line between "leftists" who argued for immediate or rapid transition into the dictatorship of the proletariat and "rightists" who insisted on full capitalistic development first, Lenin's concept of uninterrupted revolution was quickly countered by Trotsky. Trotsky argued that the peasantry could be nothing more than an ally to the proletariat, affirmed that conditions in Russia after 1917 were ripe for socialist revolution, and claimed that in some undeveloped countries, the proletariat may assume power without the nation passing through a capitalist stage (Skilling 1961; Trotsky 1970). Although many believe the doctrinal difference between Lenin and Trotsky to be minimal, under the Stalinist regime it was enhanced and codified: "Taking advantage of the subtle original shades of difference between Lenin and Trotsky on the forthcoming Russian revolution, Stalin elevated this distinction into a dogma of orthodoxy in the interpretation of future revolution. Henceforward to advocate a direct transition to socialism without a prior democratic transitional stage was fraught with danger" (Skilling 1961, 18).

The concept of permanent revolution was discussed in the early days of the Chinese Communist Party, with the question of whether China should devote itself to the development of a nationalist revolution (the "democratic transition stage" referred to above) or try to move directly into socialism being central to the debate (Xue, Xin, and Pan 1984). Ultimately, the struggle against semicolonialism, or the control of Chinese territory by foreign nations, took precedence over the socialist revolution. The Second National Congress of the Chinese Communist Party in 1922 stipulated that the socialist revolution would be a second phase that would "immediately" (*jike* 即刻) follow (Xue, Xin, and Pan 1984, 108–9). The debate was crucial throughout the 1920s, when the issue of cooperation or merging between the Communist and Nationalist Parties was under heavy discussion. The twin dangers of being too far to the left (that is, overpromoting the proletarian revolution and fighting cooperation with the Nationalists) and being too far to the right (demanding the necessity of a prior national revolution, recognizing the Nationalist Party as its leader, and giving up on the simultaneous work of fostering the proletarian revolution) were "errors" documented at the Fourth National Congress of 1925 (113–14). One solution to the divide was to recognize the "natural affinity" of peasants with the proletariat and the proletarian revolutionary goals of overturning capitalism in both national and global arenas, an approach that reaffirmed the importance of peasant revolution in China, where 80 percent of the population were peasants, and more generally in East Asia. Of course, the hostility of Marx, Lenin, and Stalin toward peasants; Trotsky's criticism that China had abandoned the proletariat; and the "semifeudal" status of peasant society made this solution more problematic. And yet the active support of this peasantry was necessary if the proletariat were to be successful in the national revolution (Kelliher 1994; Peng 1980; F. Li and Peng 1974; F. Wang 1980; Xue, Xin, and Pan 1984).

The debate about which group was the "natural" leader of the Chinese revolution, what the relationship between China and the Soviet Union really was, and who was and was not a Trotskyite involved many communist intellectuals, including Chen Duxiu 陈独秀 (1879–1942), Peng Shuzhi 彭述之 (1896–1983), and Qu Qiubai 瞿秋白 (1899–1935), and raged over the first half of the twentieth century, until the victory of the Communist Party in 1949 (Kelliher 1994; F. Li and Peng 1974; F. Wang 1980). When Mao explained his ideas about the Chinese approach to revolutionary theory in "The Chinese Revolution and the Chinese Communist Party" (中国革命与中国共产党; [1939] 1965b) and "On New Democracy" (新民主主义论; [1940] 1967), he adopted the two-stage notion of revolution that would take China through first a democratic stage and then a socialist stage, both with Chinese characteristics, clearly rejecting the theory of a single revolution.[3] Yet in his January 28, 1958, speech to the Supreme State Conference, Mao stated, "I advocate the theory of the permanent revolution. You must not think that this is Trotsky's theory of the permanent revolution" (quoted in Schram 1971, 222).

In the two main passages on permanent revolution that Mao put forward in 1958, he not only distanced himself from Trotsky but also affirmed a dialectical process between authorities and local conditions. While mentioning the industrial backwardness of China, the necessary economic construction, and the relatively long duration over which changes could take place, Mao complicated his concept of permanent revolution by stating, "Our revolution is like fighting a war. After winning one battle, we must immediately put forward new tasks. In this way we can maintain the revolutionary enthusiasm of the cadres and the masses, and diminish their self-satisfaction, since they have no time to be satisfied with themselves even if they wanted to; new tasks keep pressing in, and everyone devotes his mind to the question of how to fulfill the new tasks" (quoted in Schram 1971, 227). He insisted on the integration of politics into all technological, economic, and industrial work. And, finally, Mao specified:

> After the people have come to have their own political power, the relationship between this political power and the people is basically a relationship among the people, and the method employed is not forcible repression, but persuasion. . . . After the transition period has come to an end, and classes have been completely abolished, then, as far as conditions within the country are concerned, politics will consist entirely of relationships among the people. At that time, ideological and political struggle among man and man, as well as revolution, will definitely still continue to exist, and moreover cannot fail to exist. (quoted in Schram 1971, 228)

Mao reaffirmed his confidence in "revolution by stages" at the 1958 Wuhan Plenum and later that year advocated recognition of the "sprouts of socialism" even under backward conditions.

Terms such as *skipping, acceleration, telescoping,* and *rapid,* all used in reference to the nuances of permanent revolution, point to issues of pace and duration, which are essentially temporal concerns. These time-based concepts combine with discussions about "equilibrium" and "disequilibrium"—notions of stability and change during times of transformation—as well as recognition of the importance of human subjectivity, within which emotional values such as "enthusiasm," "complacency," and "self-satisfaction," along with the function of "persuasion," speak to the balancing act that constitutes progress under the conditions of revolution. Mao both affirmed the idea of permanent revolution as a way to maintain the enthusiasm of cadres and the masses and simultaneously connected it to "more, faster, better, and more economical" (*duo kuai hao sheng* 多快好省) (quoted in Schram 1971, 237–38). The interrelated elements of permanent revolution, voluntarism, and mass mobilization become key elements of Mao's vision of socialism (T. Chen 2012; Larson 2010; Meisner 1982, 1999). The emphasis on human consciousness, subjectivity, will, and the power of the mind became more important as Mao broke with the Soviet Union, by 1961–62 describing the difference between the socialism of the USSR and that of China as an "emphasis on technologies and cadres over politics and masses" (T. Chen 2012, 167).

In the next section, I bring issues involved in the relationship among culture, thought, and social justice to the field of literary studies by taking a look at the transformation of Maxim Gorky from a writer concerned with many aspects of life to an indicator of the temporally forward position of politics that developed under Maoism. Via the theory of typicality in socialist realism, the Chinese Gorky came to represent the emblematic crafting of subjectivity that embodied the unity of the aesthetic and the real. There were two parts to this extensive construction: a strategic movement of literature closer to the base, and an opening that allowed literary workers to become more revolutionary or to guide the movement of history.

The Chinese Gorky and the Theory of Typicality

When Maxim Gorky's work was first introduced in China, it was appreciated not so much for its role in carving out the relationship between culture and politics but rather for its deeply humanistic perspective. Gorky's work was influential among students and intellectuals in the 1920s, and he was well known among May Fourth writers such as Ding Ling 丁玲 (1904–86) and Shen Congwen 沈从文 (1902–88) (Kinkley 1990). His essays from his later years were widely read, even more than his fiction, and Gorky, called "unsurpassable" by the literary giants Lu Xun 鲁迅 (1881–1936) and Guo Moruo 郭沫若 (1892–1978), quickly became the most influential foreign literary theorist in China (Liu Z. 2012, 102). One of the most enthusiastic, prolific, and influential translators and interlocutors of Gorky was Qu Qiubai, who worked as a correspondent in Moscow and took on the role of propaganda director for the Chinese Communist Party in the 1920s but was removed from leadership in 1930 (Knight 2005; Liu Z. 2012). Liu Zhongwang (2012) argues that it was Qu Qiubai who most extensively and persuasively molded Gorky as the carrier of the Soviet Union's socialist realism template, emphasizing the Russian writer as an exemplar of revolutionary writing whose personal struggle out of misery into the new happy era stood as proof of the ability of literature, if managed according to the theories of socialist realism, to influence and even direct social change. As China's political situation worsened during the first half of the 1930s, the dominant understanding of Gorky—which was limited by the translations available—tended to emphasize his affiliation with revolutionary literature. More broadly, the focus became the relationship between politics and literature, art, and culture in general.

In his work on romanticism in China, Yu Zhaoping (2011) cogently argues that Gorky provided May Fourth writers with a model of transition that showed how it was possible to move from being a romantic writer to becoming a political writer. Both Gorky's impoverished past and his search for humanistic truth were relevant. As Yu notes, Gorky emphasized the "real" and stated that literature injects thought with flesh and blood, endowing it with persuasive powers (Yu 2011; see also Wang J. 2005). In the introduction to *On Literature* ("How I Studied"), Gorky wrote:

> In the opinion of certain critics my romanticism was a reflection of idealism in my philosophy. I think that appraisal wrong. Philosophical idealism teaches that man, animals and all man-created things are under the sway of "ideas." . . . For me there are no ideas that exist outside of man; for me it is man and only man that is the creator of all things and all ideas; it is he that is the miracle-worker and the future lord of all Nature's forces. What is most beautiful in this world of ours has been created by man's labour, by his clever hands; all our thoughts and ideas spring from the process of labour, and this is something the history of art, science and technology convinces us of. (1973a, 66)

In "Soviet Intellectuals," Gorky exhorted writers to learn "if not everything, at least as much as possible about the astronomer and the mechanic, the biologist and the tailor, the engineer and the shepherd, and so on," implying a connection between literature and physical labor (despite a well-documented scorn for the Russian peasantry) (Gorky 1939, 191; Ivanov 1994). In promoting "labor as a creative act," Gorky directly identified creativity with physical labor (1973b, 254). At the same time, as Yu details, Gorky's work provided a model of one kind of romanticism—political romanticism—that was highly influential in pushing some May Fourth writers to become politicized writers who ascribed to the theory of socialist realism that unfolded in the Soviet Union during the early 1930s. The implication that socialist realism could capture the real elevated it in relation to romanticism, but Gorky's political-romantic model, infused with flesh, blood, and spirit as opposed to decadence, came to represent a form of progressive literary effort that was closely tied to the material world of labor, class struggle, and revolutionary change. Discussing Zhou Yang's understanding and promotion of Gorky as a model, Yu Zhaoping explains:

> Zhou Yang pointed to the essential difference between Gorky's romanticism and the old romanticism. Basically, although the old romanticism as represented by the aesthetic romanticism of Rousseau emphasized a critique of the alienation of reality, it nonetheless used the return to natural

human nature and the methods of medieval times to carry out its resistance. Or it unfolded by means of the ascendance of concepts of individual subjectivity such as aesthetic discernment, religion, symbolism, and so on, through which the individual could transcend reality, moving from having limitations to transcending them. Considering the political struggles just underway, and the armed struggles to win national power and the complete liberation of the proletariat, these aesthetic tendencies were simply too abstract and ethereal, too far removed from the actual struggle. So what was needed was not a Rousseau-style aesthetic romanticism, but Gorky's political romanticism. (2011, 161)

Thus, Gorky's literature and theories offered Chinese writers a powerful connection to the very physical and material fight, and a way to distance their efforts from abstract aestheticizing approaches.

Gorky and his association with socialist realism were discussed in the 1935–36 debate on "type" between Zhou Yang and Hu Feng. Broadly speaking, the theory of typicality was one result of the attempt of leftist intellectuals to develop a theory of culture that corresponded to their Marxist principles, at that time theorized through socialist realism. The synthesis of typicality within a character's personality, along with the organization of that character within a social environment that clearly showed the relative political position of the group, indicated the writer's correct grasp of the direction of history. Such a construction provided a comprehensive moral, political, and social model to readers. Characters with the correct political beliefs and behavior were also innately good. In his study of Hu Feng and Lu Ling 路翎 (1923–94), Kirk Denton argues that Zhou Yang and Hu Feng both promoted the theory of typicality in realist literature, although Zhou's idea was narrower: "Zhou believed a character should be a common denominator of the class to which he belongs. Hu Feng, perhaps influenced by Hegel through the Hungarian Marxist critic Georg Lukács (whom Hu Feng viewed as a rebel), saw the hero of a fictional work as a microcosm of larger social forces and thus representative of the zeitgeist" (1998, 83). Quoting Engels, Zhou Yang in his "Thoughts on Realism" argued that creating types "entails extracting from a certain social group the most characteristic traits, habits, tastes, aspirations, actions, speech, and so forth and embodying these in a character" while simultaneously maintaining a distinct personality (Denton 1996, 342).[4] Implicitly siding with Mark Rozental (1906–75) over Isaac Nusinov (1889–1950) in the Soviet debate of 1933–34, Zhou also emphasized the writer's proper worldview. Hu Feng opposed this emphasis on worldview, arguing that writers' ability to collect their impressions and experiences and mold them into a universal literature depended on their subjective power.[5]

In this debate Gorky was further pushed into becoming a symbol for the mandatory guidance of culture by correct political positioning. The creative reading of Gorky's understanding of typicality in China also threw aside earlier interest in the social role of literature, also a concern of the leftist literary camp. As Zhang Tiexian explains, "Gorky believed that literature was the 'textbook of life,' and writers were then the teachers of life. . . . Gorky emphasized a writer's world view and social position. He felt that working in literature was simply a method of serving the vast majority of people, not a job that meant searching for individual fame" (1958, 8).

Although Gorky's work was plagued by the tension between romanticism and realism—which meant that determining whether any textual character was real or realistic, or whether any fictional textual work possessed "realness," was an issue for Gorky—in Chinese revolutionary romanticism, his socialist hero nonetheless became a beacon of the correct direction of time, or the future as imagined through present policies (Borras 1967; L. Yang 1996). In the late 1950s and into the 1960s, Gorky's work was anthologized in literary textbooks, which illustrated its importance in providing a seamless connection among society, the writer, and the teacher and in pulling the reader into a concrete culture that provides clues for thought and behavior. In two collections chosen by Zhou Yang to be used as textbooks in colleges and universities in the 1960s, *Wenxue gailun* 文学概论 (Introduction to literature) and *Wenxue de jiben yuanli* 文学的基本原理 (The basic principles of literature). Gorky's work was referenced more often than that of any other single author except major revolutionary thinkers such as Marx and Lenin (Liu Z. 2012; Zhi 2008).

Postcolonialism, the Humanities, and Social Justice

Vivek Chibber's *Postcolonial Theory and the Specter of Capitalism* (2013b) focuses on historians rather than literary or cultural scholars and thus may seem a poor choice to help us understand the historical dilemmas of literary and cultural studies. However, Chibber argues that two leading postcolonial studies scholars, Partha Chatterjee and Dipesh Chakrabarty, both rest their claims for an authentically different modernity in the East on cultural difference. He interprets this approach as a denial of universal needs or interests across cultural boundaries:

> In the West, we are told, political psychology revolves around secular conceptions of the individual and his rights; whereas in the East, agency is motivated by the concept of duty, or obligation, making the actor's basic orientation religious, not secular. To expect that political modernization in the postcolonial world will follow a course similar to that in the West is therefore mistaken. . . . The fact that laboring groups in the East are not motivated by the same commitments as those in the West is symptomatic of the distinctive modernity that capital wrought as it left European shores. It was a modernity that witnessed the implantation of modern political institutions, and even the language of modern politics, but these, say the Subalternists, were foisted atop a culture in which the basic elements of political identity remained unchanged. Western theories fail to comprehend its distinctiveness, because they assume that capital did in fact carry out its universalizing mission. (Chibber 2013b, 153; see also Chakrabarty 1989; and Chatterjee 1984)

In arguing that the psychological orientation of Bengali or Indian peasants is different from that of Westerners with "bourgeois consciousness," postcolonial theorists concluded that "universalizing theories of class or class conflict must collapse as they travel eastward into the colonial world" (Chibber 2013b, 179). According to Chibber, this is a serious mistake:

> The main such worry [leveled at materialist theories of agency] is that reference to material interests or rationality ignores the cultural embeddedness of social agents—that it treats agency as asocial or even hedonist. I show that these concerns are unfounded. Recognizing the structuring role of interests does not require that we ignore the importance of culture and the abiding role of norms or ideology in shaping agency. It is just that such a theory refuses to allow that agents' socialization *entirely constitutes* their practical reasoning. Agents have the ability to reflect upon their norms and, when these norms threaten or undermine their well-being, to reject them. So the appreciation of certain universal interests among social actors does not require that we deny them their culture, but it does demand that we not treat them as cultural automata. (2013b, 178–79)

Chibber accurately identifies the important role that many postcolonial critics assign to culture, and their offer of the "heavily socialized, culturally constructed agent as an antidote to the parochialism of Western theories" (193). Yet he rejects the idea that cultural difference is the only route to agency, or that rationality requires agents to be placed outside their cultures, instead arguing that as a source of agency, culture has limits. Agents have varying ability to modify or even reject their habits and traditions if they believe such cultural norms go against their well-being, according to Chibber, who also argues that "capitalism is not only compatible with social difference, but systematically produces it" (243). As he further explains in an interview from 2013 (Chibber 2013a), although capital's universalization will put into effect some cultural change, ending noncapitalist practices such as praying at work, others, such as wearing colorful clothes, consulting astrologers, or using ancient marriage rituals, can easily continue under capitalism.

The question that Chibber (2013a) provocatively raises is whether it is logical to imagine that deep cultural difference can combat the spread of capitalism and the partial universalization of cultural norms that accompanies it: "There are some aspects of our human nature that are not culturally constructed: they are shaped by culture, but not created by it. My view is that even though there are enormous cultural differences between people in the East and the West, there's also a core set of concerns that people have in common . . . a concern for a degree of autonomy and self-determination; there's a concern for those practices that directly pertain to your welfare. This isn't much, but you'd be amazed how far it gets you in explaining really important historical transformations." Confusing this question is the issue of what is included in the cultural, from seemingly superficial differences in, for example, cuisine or clothing to unique temporal and spatial practices. The complexity of what counts as culture, how culture is sustained and transmitted, how community is created, and how culture works to create a sense of an authentically lived life are given short shrift in Chibber's discussion. So exactly what is modified as capital universalizes, and what can be continued as part of a vital past, is unclear.

Nonetheless, Chibber's criticism of the cultural turn in postcolonial studies helps us think through both the way in which cultural difference is related to political practice and the assumptions about culture that are part of the research and teaching of humanities professors. My brief inquiry into the idea of permanent revolution, the Chinese Gorky, and theories of typicality has delved into a series of related problems. The idea of permanent revolution, or the possibility of reaching communism without "stopping" for a lengthy duration within the stages of industrialization and capitalization, suggests that over the first hundred years of dialectical materialism, many imagined that social change could result from evolving thought and ideas as well as from material development. If that is true, the role played by cultural and literary pedagogy and research is important and relevant. Such a perspective lay behind the field of cultural studies, in which social justice became a research goal. Along these lines, the domestic construction of the Chinese Gorky was a great benefit for Chinese writers and theorists, encouraging them, first, to imagine that their work was closer than other intellectual efforts to the material base and, second, to accept the direction of history that was prescribed by Maoist revolutionary perspectives. Once the door to revolutionary sensibility was opened and the correct subjectivity determined, the meaning and goal of cultural work were clear. The theory of typicality, overall concerned with codifying the relationship between the aesthetic and the real, embodied the psychological and temporal aspects of this approach. Within literature, the progressive fictional character could be identified by his or her represented subjectivity, which would then lead to language and actions that would push the revolution forward. The emphasis on correct subjectivity applied not only to writers but also to theorists, teachers, and researchers. And yet, as we have seen, within this comprehensive organization of cultural work, problems immediately began to appear. Central to these was the question of which fictional characters were sufficiently revolutionary and which writers had the correct subjectivity: Who, in other words, owned social justice?

Chibber accuses postcolonial studies of overestimating the power of cultural norms and consequently of inflating the ability of culturally different societies to produce an alternative modernity that resists the universalization of capitalism. If we accept the limitations of cultural work that Chibber suggests, on what edifice does the study of culture rely? Even among those who disagree with Chibber that postcolonial studies has reproduced the Orientalism it purports to attack, there are many plaintive wails about the failure of the broader field of cultural studies to dismantle the structure of disciplinary power in the university and to fight hierarchy, let alone to further social justice (Macek 2001). One of the founders of cultural studies, Lawrence Grossberg, eventually asked why the field had become so boring, answering his own question with an analysis of the movement of cultural studies away from elite culture into popular culture, where the meaning of any cultural product or artifact had to be sought in the sensibility and identity of the audience (Cornut-Gentille D'Arcy and Grossberg 2010; Grossberg 2006; Grossberg, Nelson, and Treichler 1991). What Grossberg recognized as problematic is the same turn toward subjectivity and sensibility that became part of socialist realism and revolutionary romanticism, which could suggest that the demand for political efficacy in cultural work has been misguided. Others bitterly admit the failures of the field of cultural studies, echoing Chibber's critique of postcolonial studies:

Judged in terms of the movement's constitutive counter-disciplinary and political aspirations, cultural studies' impact on the American university has been decidedly less than revolutionary. Instead of subverting disciplinary boundaries, the rise of cultural studies has merely rendered them somewhat more permeable. Instead of radically transforming the nature of scholarly inquiry in the humanities and social sciences, it has often merely sparked border skirmishes and jurisdictional disputes of various kinds between warring departments. Instead of addressing "the genuine controversies of a given culture," writers associated with cultural studies have frequently exhibited a profound lack of political judgment by carrying on about the oppositionality implicit in the gesture of ripping one's jeans and waxing eloquent about Madonna's threat to dominant order. . . . Instead of producing "resisting intellectuals," cultural studies has more commonly produced academized scholars whose chief concern is professional advancement not social change. Rather than providing hegemonic leadership within movements of the oppressed, it has more often than not indulged in the sort of fruitless, self-important "literary" politics that Marx once attacked in the work of the "critical critics." (Macek 2001)

Postcolonial studies emerged within the same human rights environment that produced feminist studies, ethnic studies, and more. Although new fields had bones to pick with the blind spots of Marxist theory in terms of race and gender, they benefited from the century-long leftist focus on social justice that had been developed in Marxist approaches. Yet even with their connection to blood, sweat, tears, and labor, liberatory humanistic studies have had a hard time shaking themselves loose from the internal contradictions that plagued the subservient position of teaching and research of the humanities within Marxist theory.

Chibber attacks postcolonial studies for its textual bias and for its agenda of searching for an alternative modernity, based on a cultural specificity and difference, that can fight the grand narrative of capitalism. And yet he points out that rejecting the radical political potential of the cultural does not mean that culture is not important. This statement would seem to imply that the study of culture also can be important. But important for whom, and for what? As nineteenth- and twentieth-century attempts to locate within Marxist guidelines a powerful position from which to study culture suggest, every path toward enhancing relevance and forcing humanistic study to become a tool for social justice has led to problems. The most obvious of these is the construction of a covertly idealistic imaginary that grants to cultural study and, by extension, to education and thought powerful transformative abilities in the material world, displacing a materialist focus on labor and class. Another is the enhancement of understanding subjectivity and thought as a focus of literary research, which then is uncritically imagined as contributing to social justice. And a third deals with an array of coercive strategies designed to produce the subjectivities necessary for a specific understanding of the past, the present, and the future. Certainly, an interest in hegemony, legacy, opposition, and resistance has been part of leftist literary studies for much longer than postcolonial studies has been in existence, and a critique of these tendencies can be applied to many areas. As I have tried to show in this chapter, the emphasis on a direct route from the study of humanities to social justice produces an overly homogenizing account of the many different roles that cultural study can play.

Notes

1 Huggan (2008) separates postcolonial studies into waves, with the first wave solidly located in the humanities, the second wave a breezy attack on the first from the perspective of a supposedly more correct historico-materialist angle, and then a staunch defense of literature's ability to change and decolonize minds.

2 Chibber further explains his theory in his monograph *Postcolonial Theory and the Specter of Capital* (2013b) and in the article "On the Decline of Class Analysis in South Asian Studies" (2006), where he argues that "whereas Marxism was motivated by a bedrock materialism and universalist assumptions about human needs and interests, the Orientalist tradition was resolutely *culturalist* in approach—meaning not just that it focused on the production of culture, but on culture as the *source* of the institutional and structural differences of these areas from the West" (2006, 365–66).

3 By this point, Mao was taking sides in a debate already won by Stalin (Skilling 1961). As Pang Laikwan shows in chapter 4 of this book, an enduring problem in China was figuring out how to develop a Chinese national form, especially under the powerful influence of Soviet cultural models.

4 Zhou Yang's article was published in the journal *Wenxue* (文学) in January 1936; this translation is by Catherine Pease Campbell. While having some overlap with the sociological concept of the ideal type as developed by Max Weber (see Swedberg 2017) in the recognition of overarching historical trends and the attempt to grasp basic human tendencies at any given time (as in, for Weber, the Protestant ethic), the socialist literary concept of type is the identification of personal qualities typical of a certain social group (Eliaeson 2000).

5 The theory of the type or typicality has been taken up extensively by Peter Button (2009), who argues that it originated in China with Lu Xun 鲁迅 in "The True Story of Ah Q" (阿Q 正传, [1921–22] 2008) a decade before socialist realism adopted it and that this concept, which was part of the bildungsroman, was an essential part of the modern construction of the agency-infused, cognitively aware, free human subject. The relationship between the real and the aesthetic—as exemplified through the type—lay at the core of this subject, Button argues.

Pang Laikwan

4

De-Sovietization and Internationalism

China is usually not considered a postcolonial country. But this chapter tries to illustrate how its de-Sovietization efforts in the 1950s and 1960s could be relevant to larger postcolonial discussions. This chapter places the socialist nationalism of the young People's Republic of China (PRC) within a larger Cold War context and discusses how the construction of a distinct Chinese nationalism and internationalism was central to its socialist nation-building efforts. While Wendy Larson in her chapter traces the enormous influences of Soviet political theories in China, here I explore how the PRC also struggled to get rid of the socialist master and to develop its own national form and pride. Unfortunately, by disavowing the Soviet imperialist system, China's de-Sovietization project ended up developing its own version of socialist hierarchy, and the Soviet imperialism was denied only to be latently reaffirmed in a new form of Maoist internationalism. The PRC struggled to establish its state sovereignty by flirting with nationalism and internationalism, and its autonomy was intimately attached to hegemony. This investigation provides a historical narrative to illustrate how difficult it is to avoid the model of totality in imagining national sovereignty in a really existing socialist context. In fact, postsocialist, postcolonial, and postimperial overtones constantly intersect and communicate in the complex imaginary of the Soviet and ex-Soviet spaces (Tlostanova 2012, 141). The PRC in the 1950s was also caught in and struggled with many systems of world hierarchies. Trying to gain its autonomy from the Soviet Union, the PRC adopted a similar permanent-revolution discourse to export its influences to other parts of the world, therefore weaving a new Maoist world order where Beijing replaces Moscow as the center. As such, this investigation of China's nationalist-internationalist continuum also brings us back to the urgent question about the teleology of modernity and reminds us of the unfinished project of postcolonialism, which should be a genuine spatialization of temporality instead of simply the replacement of one regime with another.

De-Sovietization

The Communist Party of the Soviet Union (CPSU) considered the exportation of revolution one of its main duties from the 1920s onward, justifying its direct intervention in other countries. Moscow Sun Yat-sen University was set up in 1925 through the collaboration of the CPSU and the Kuomintang (KMT), China's ruling party at the time, to train Chinese revolutionaries in the Soviet style. Although the KMT retreated in 1927 after the alliance between the KMT and the Chinese Communist Party (CCP) broke up, the university operated until 1930 and trained many future leaders of the CCP.[1] All kinds of Soviet influences were prominent in the Central Soviet Areas in the 1920s and later in Yan'an, and Maxim Gorky's works were standard texts in the Lu Xun Academy (Chen Yong 1979; see also Larson's chapter in this volume). Of course, the relationship between the Soviet Union and China, or all other existing socialist states at that time, cannot be quickly generalized as colonial. The socialist international bond was supposedly reciprocal, so that the relationships among all socialist states were not bounded by their universal loyalty to the Soviet Union; rather, as the Soviet Union claimed, they formed friendships and lent mutual aid to each other.

In fact, the early 1950s could be seen as a honeymoon period between the PRC and the USSR, as the young Chinese state saw the Soviet Union as its role model on all fronts (Bernstein and Li 2010). At the very outset of the establishment of the PRC, Mao Zedong in his famous speech "About the People's Democratic Dictatorship" (1949) had already announced that the CPSU was the best teacher of the Chinese and that we had to learn everything from it. Politically, the PRC fashioned its state building after the Soviet Union's, importing the former's political structure and ideology almost wholesale and rephrasing the Marxist concept of the "dictatorship of the proletariat" into the "people's democratic dictatorship," to be written into the PRC's constitution (Meisner 1999, 46). Economically, a planned economy was adopted. Giving national priority to the development of heavy industry, the PRC also vigorously emphasized agricultural collectivism (Seow 2014). Culturally, socialist realism became the national artistic principle, emphasizing the role of propaganda played by the arts. Ballet was introduced and actively promoted, while Soviet films were shown all over China (T. Chen 2009). The Soviet Union's curriculum also began to dominate China's own education reform (Pepper 1996). The young PRC also adopted most of the Soviet Union's practices in diplomacy but soon found this adoption more difficult than those in other realms, because the autonomy of the PRC was actually at stake.

The situation began to change in the mid-1950s. Indeed, de-Sovietization efforts and sentiments could be observed in many socialist states in the 1950s. On the one hand, the death of Joseph Stalin created much instability in the Soviet bloc, but, on the other hand, it also relaxed some of the former stringent political control around the satellite countries. Poland and Hungary witnessed powerful popular uprisings in 1956 as a result. There was a rise of nationalism in both countries, and the protests were also responses to their incompetent socialist leadership (Lendvai 2008, 37–43; Machcewicz 2009, 173). The Prague Spring in Czechoslovakia in 1968, in contrast, resulted from a long period of intellectual and political incubation, with a Czech intelligentsia and socialist party hoping to develop a more democratic system while preserving its socialist character (Kusin 1971). Indeed, de-Sovietization policies in the socialist bloc were also motivated by the dynamics within the CPSU, as Nikita Khrushchev took up the top party leadership and adopted de-Sovietization as a part of his comprehensive de-Stalinization process (Kalinovsky 2018). Overall, de-Sovietization was a highly sensitive and uneven process across the wide socialist bloc. The struggles for cultural and political independence from the Soviet Union were probably most apparent and spectacular in China, largely because it was a movement led not by the people but by a rival socialist party that wanted to claim equal power.

In addition to Mao's persistent anxiety about the chauvinism of the Soviet Union, a number of things happened in the second half of the 1950s that prompted the PRC to disengage with its "Big Communist Brother." First, Khrushchev's 1956 speech against Stalin's cult of personality shocked the entire CCP upper echelon (Leese 2011, 27–46). To prevent China from running into the sorry state of affairs caused by the leader's cult as seen in the Soviet Union, Mao and his comrades took this chance to review many Soviet policies implemented in China. The anti-Stalinist revolt in Poland and Hungary also prompted the Chinese government to consider how much the Soviet model might be hegemonic and could endanger the stability of individual socialist states. With Mao's increasing distrust of Khrushchev, efforts were made to develop the PRC's own governance methods and principles. For example, in his 1956 speech "On the Ten Major Relationships" (论十大关系 *Lun shida guanxi*), Mao already questioned the PRC fashioning its state building completely on the Soviet Union (Mao [1956a] 1977).

Mao emphasized that the Chinese people had to admit that they were inferior to the Soviet Union in terms of industrialization and revolutionary experiences, but the Chinese people should also try their best to become otherwise. According to Maurice Meisner, "On the Ten Major Relationships," was "cryptically worded but clearly called for an abandonment of Soviet-type five-year plans and outlined a radically different strategy" (1999, 169). Mao's rereading of the Soviet *Political Economy* textbook was also a clear effort on his part to thoroughly review the "correctness" of the Soviet ideology in the specific context of the PRC (Mao [1961–62] 1974).

It was clear to the PRC leaders that the Soviet Union's influences on China had operated on both the institutional level and the psychological level, and a whole generation of Chinese youth in the 1950s viewed the Soviet Union as their ideal. They learned the language, read the literature, and went to Moscow for supposedly the best education. As He Donghui describes the Chinese cultural world of the 1950s, "No existing literary works by domestic writers were good enough for the young. A new model of more progressive culture had to be imported—in this case, from the Soviet Union—for the cultural reconstruction of the new China" (2010, 397). The state selected some of the most promising artists and cultural workers to study in the Soviet Union; they included music performers and composers like Yin Chengzong 殷承宗 and Wu Zujiang 吴祖强, dancers and choreographers like Bai Suxiang 白淑湘 and Jiang Zuhui 蒋祖会, and filmmakers such as Xie Fei 谢飞 and Wang Di 王迪. Artist Luo Gongliu 罗工柳 (1999, 46–47) reflected that he was given a very good stipend and much freedom in St. Petersburg to study with different master painters, and he spent much of his time in major museums copying the original masterpieces.

Most of these young intellectuals were sent to the Soviet Union in the mid-1950s when the two countries were still on good terms. But when they came back to China a few years later, they quickly sensed how the pro-Soviet attitude was silently changing, and they were asked to develop something more uniquely Chinese to correct the previous cultural imperialism. They would become the major cultural and social engineers to engage in the new "National Form" (民族形式 *minzu xingshi* or 民族风格 *minzu fengge*) campaign, and they developed all kinds of national styles and expressions that were supposedly both Chinese and modern.

The slogan of National Form or National Character was first raised by the party during the Second Sino-Japanese War (Shi 2008). It was part of the wartime propaganda, driven also by the CCP's urgent need to seek local support after its settlement in Yan'an.[2] The National Form campaign resurged in the late 1950s (Clausen 1998). A very important source that informed the Chinese communists in the development of National Form was indeed the Soviet policy of "national in form, socialist in content." The idea was first articulated in the Soviet Union in the 1920s as a set of instructions on how the new regime would instill its views in non-Russians by communicating with them in terms they could understand. In the early 1920s, Vladimir Lenin first called for a massive set of efforts to examine all cultures in the Soviet Union, identifying the good cultures of the different Soviet nationalities and combining them to form the new Soviet multinational culture. In 1925 Stalin formulated the idea of "national in form, socialist in content" to assure the Asiatic republics of the Soviet Union that the new proletarian culture would not need to change the existing national cultures but rather only gave them a new content (Tagangaeva 2017, 397). In a way, the slogan was meant to provide some protection to the national cultures, convincing all the nationals that minority cultures and local customs would be respected in the new republic. But entering the Stalinist period, the unclear meaning of the "national form" became the main subject of academic and aesthetic discussions related to the development of the unified national forms of art of Soviet peoples, thereby marginalizing discussions on art in national republics.

The case in the PRC was strikingly similar. Selectively following the Soviet Union's national-cultures policies, the PRC National Form campaign also began as a socialist effort to integrate the many cultures of the ethnic minorities. It was meant to be inclusive, trying to bring all the nations together to build the new state. John Fitzgerald (1995, 77) claims that both the KMT and the CCP built their state by beckoning to the many people in the existing nations and inviting them to join the new state under the discourse of nationalism. But the CCP launched fierce antiregionalist campaigns and suppressions around the country in the 1950s to differentiate the docile culture, which should be assimilated, from the resilient culture, which must be destroyed. State sovereignty was based on the Han culture, with minority cultures as the internal alternatives to support and enrich the national culture. This Han-centered national-character movement quickly overtook not only the regional cultures but also the Soviet influences and became hegemonic.

Overall, we can understand this de-Sovietization as a quasi-postcolonial project, but it is far from a project of emancipation. The PRC's de-Sovietization was a set of highly controlled efforts engineered from the top down, very different from many other bottom-up postcolonial efforts happening around the world that asserted the autonomy of a people from colonial control. It was the PRC state that maneuvered the public sentiment and sensibility to shift back to Chinese tastes, and it was not a difficult task, indeed, as most of the ordinary people found the Soviet styles foreign and alienating (Pang 2017, 162–71). A more relevant point of comparison is the relation between culture and politics. Indeed, a major contribution of postcolonial theories is their emphasis on the mutual conditioning of culture and politics. As Allen Chun (2012) reminds us, postcolonial theories do not apply to colonial practices only; they can also help us understand many different types and structures of cultural differences. Emphasizing the symbolic dynamics of difference, postcolonial theories call attention to subjectivity and magnify the role of culture. The young PRC also realized the same tendency. But it was a political decision of the state to introduce political changes by cultural maneuvering: for China to be politically independent from the Soviet Union, China had to develop its own national culture and rid itself of Soviet influence. Culture was incorporated into all kinds of statecraft under a Maoist cosmology in which everything was connected. The Maoist modernity project was both material and cultural, and the two were considered constituent of each other.[3]

Stuart Schram reminds us that Mao was always very conscious of the importance of the national "style." As Mao said in 1959, "There are some things which need not have any national style, such as trains, airplanes and big guns. Politics and art should have a national style" (quoted in Schram 1989, 135). Maoist China took both politics and the arts very seriously, and the two were treated almost as one. In addition to Mao's true artistic talent and deep affection for the arts, we can find an army of intellectuals in the upper Maoist echelon ready to defend the meanings of the arts and beauty along with the grandeur of the new republic. From Hu Feng 胡风 to Guo Moruo 郭沫若, and from He Qifang 何其芳 to Wang Zhaowen 王朝闻, they might be political enemies at times, and they were willing to forgo their beliefs under pressure to different degrees, but they all promoted the political meanings of the arts in Maoist China, forming a strong aesthetic establishment to articulate the splendor and glory of the new nation. Propaganda activities were considered highly important by the PRC regime, not only because the party relied heavily on culture to carry out political duties, but also because it was sincerely believed that a new China was already built and therefore demanded a new form of aesthetic organization and judgment. De-Sovietization was considered the necessary step for China to become independent.

Entering the 1960s, the PRC increasingly saw the Soviet Union as the most threatening enemy. In 1958, in the name of protecting China's sovereignty, Mao had already rejected the Soviet Union's request for the permanent stationing of Soviet forces in Luda (Dairen and Port Arthur) in the northeast, the establishment of a joint Pacific fleet under Soviet command, and the establishment of a powerful longwave radio station for naval communication in China under Soviet control (*China Review* 2001). All the Soviet experts were ordered to leave the country in 1960, and war efforts were directed as much against the Soviet Union as against the United States. The Cultural Revolution marked the complete split between China and the Soviet Union. In the Ninth People's Congress of the PRC in 1969, the Soviet Union was finally denounced as conducting socialist imperialism (社会帝国主义 *shehui diguo zhuyi*), parallel to the capitalist imperialism practiced by the United States. This kind of ideological work prepared and legitimized the PRC to enter the war-preparation phase, also giving the state the pretext to rebuild itself after three years of near anarchy practiced in the name of the Cultural Revolution. The PRC's identification of the Soviet Union as the prime national enemy was the result of both the CCP's sober evaluation of the current international relationship and its own legitimacy crisis.

Chinese Internationalism

But I must emphasize here that accompanying and legitimizing China's de-Sovietization was not only nationalism but also internationalism, which would most profoundly challenge China's state-building efforts as a postcolonial project. There had already been a rich history of liberal internationalism in the republican period, when journalists, feminists, and even laborers actively created and engaged in international liaisons and tried to form different kinds of world community (Benton 2007; Edwards 2010; Weston 2010). But instead of taking place primarily outside the state, as civil activities had in the republican period, socialist internationalism was exercised by the CCP as an official political ideology. Increasingly emphasizing the PRC's autonomous sovereignty, this de-Sovietization also morphed to become a new socialist world order in which China replaced the Soviet Union as a world center.

The theoretical base of Soviet internationalism is the Marxist conviction that it is economic class, not nationality or cultural identity, that is the main structural force dividing people in capitalist society, so that transnational class struggles, rather than national and ethnic wars, are assigned the role of organizing anticapitalist coalitions. To develop a proletarian internationalism that would ultimately bring humankind to communism, the CPSU supported revolutionary activities in many places from the 1920s on, to the extent that the new states formed under the assistance of the Soviet Union would become dependent on the Soviet Union (Chari and Verdery 2009). However, as already mentioned, Lenin also supported the right of nations to self-determination, under the conviction that national self-determination was also against imperialism, and these nations must restrain their intervention in other countries (see Lenin 1972). When Stalin came to power, the national interests of the Soviet Union were given priority over international collaboration. Stalin (1954, 356) advocated the notion of the "socialist nation," which refers to the new Soviet Union, in contrast with the other "bourgeois nations," which were condemned to wither away. With this new socialist nation in place, the idea of sovereignty was privileged over internationalism. But Stalin did not call the socialist network into question; what the new sovereign discourse took away was the egalitarian dimension of relationships among the socialist states, and Moscow continued to occupy the position of supreme power.

As one would expect, the Soviet Union's position at the center of the concentric circles and its demand for the loyalty and mimicry of other socialist nations increasingly alienated other socialist countries. While socialist international bonds are supposedly reciprocal, internationalism also became an excuse for the Soviet Union to exert control over many other countries. The Chinese Marxists, like their Eastern European counterparts, were confronted with novel problems concerning the relevance of the principle of sovereignty in an exclusively socialist interstate system. This socialist internationalism also prompted China to consider its independence from the Soviet Union. Through this internationalism the PRC reinstated the supremacy of national sovereignty against the Soviet Union's domination.

After World War II, Stalin decided to restore formal sovereignty to many Eastern European countries, owing partly to the nationalist sentiments that were widespread in these countries after the war and partly to the Soviet Union's need to protect its "world image" as a champion of self-determination (Jones 1990, 51–52). But the Soviet Union advocated the idea of "limited sovereignty" to describe the fraternal diplomatic relations with other socialist countries, in part to maintain Moscow's dominating power over the Soviet bloc. This idea attracted much dissatisfaction among other socialist countries. Although the Sino-Soviet relation did not sour until the late 1950s, we might say that de-Sovietization was already taking place in the PRC in the mid-1950s. In fact, such efforts could be found across the entire Soviet bloc. Unique to the PRC was the construction of its own internationalism with Beijing as the center. Both the Soviet Union and the PRC manipulated ideologies of sovereignty and internationalism to maintain their influence in the new socialist alliances (Chen Yong 1979, 43).

The three-worlds structure that placed China as the leader of the third world was first officially announced in 1974 in the United Nations, but related diplomacy and ideologies were already developed around and after the Bandung Conference in 1955, when China tried to shift its diplomatic emphasis to the other developing countries to counter both the United States and the Soviet Union. In the Bandung Conference, the PRC raised the official discourse of "South-South Cooperation," which promoted and promised solidarity among the global oppressed, thus initiating its own third world alliance. On the verge of war with the Soviet Union in the late 1960s, the PRC advanced most fiercely the importance of sovereignty against the Soviet Union's "socialist fraternity." The CCP criticized the limited-sovereignty idea, stating that it only demonstrated the Soviet Union's imperialist ambition in trying to turn the other socialist countries into suppliers of raw materials and markets for goods. "What exactly does the theory of 'limited sovereignty' mean? It means that the sovereignty exercised by the Soviet revisionist social-imperialists is 'unlimited'" (Qi 1969, 21).

Obviously, the world of enemies also included the United States. Mao ([1963] 1994, 509) proclaimed that all people in Asia, Africa, and Latin America were against US imperialism, and China's internationalism was established in particular on the opposition against this largest evil power. Underneath this universal political solidarity is the doctrine of state sovereignty, in which each country and people can make their own decisions and decide their future. In a meeting with the prime minister of the newly independent Laos in 1958, Mao made it clear that while the PRC would do everything it could to support the political struggles of different people, it would not intervene in their internal politics, and neither would it promote socialism and Maoism in these countries. It would be up to individual countries to decide their own policies (Mao [1956b] 1994, 244).

China became the center of a new Maoist international alliance by providing material and spiritual support to other countries. The PRC offered food and money to many independent and decolonizing Asian, African, and Latin American countries, and it also connected to the oppressed people in Western countries, such as Afro-Americans (Lovell 2019; Cook 2014). The internationalist mentalities and policies of the PRC also won the sincere friendship of major intellectual figures in the West, ranging from W. E. B. Du Bois in the United States (Frazier 2014, 37–79) to Julia Kristeva in France (Kristeva 1986). Indeed, communists around the world traveled to China from the 1950s to the 1970s to acquire political training, to travel around the country to be impressed by the model factories and agricultural collectives, and to meet the Chinese leaders. As Matthew Rothwell (2013, 46) reminds us, the personal stories of these travelers in China formed the basis for the creation of a counternarrative to the dominant Soviet narratives when they went back to their communities. They helped to construct the Chinese revolution as the best model of world revolution, hoping to reproduce the Chinese revolution in their countries in a new future. These Maoist intellectuals considered themselves both instructors and messengers, providing the masses with the political enlightenment they needed to become revolutionary.

An unfortunate development accompanying this de-Sovietization both in China and in some other places was the promotion of the Mao cult around 1959. Maoism was understood as a powerful revolutionary ideology that could replace the already corrupted Stalinism. Maoism was understood in China as specifically Chinese, as the uniquely Chinese path to communism and the end of this Chinese project (Leese 2011, 72–73). But outside China, leftist groups around the world also adopted Maoism as their own revolutionary path. From faraway places in Latin America and Africa to neighboring countries such as Thailand, the Philippines, Malaysia, and Singapore, Maoist groups were formed out of the members' sincere identification with Maoism, as well as the material support the PRC provided. Ironically, the active investigation of the detrimental effects of the leader's cult in the Soviet Union that the PRC had launched a few years earlier led to its own promotion of the Mao cult. Although the Mao cult was not a direct copy of the Stalin cult, they both unleashed an insurmountable volume of destructive energies, mocking the PRC's painstaking efforts of de-Sovietization.

Many international Maoists were particularly impressed by Mao's denial of Maoism as a set of universal doctrines. Instead, Mao advised that people should develop their political tactics based on their own national experiences. Kanu Sanyal, a main leader of India's Maoist Naxalite movement, for example, recounted how excited he was to meet Mao in person in 1967. Sanyal vividly remembers, "Mao's advice was: Forget everything you have learnt here in China. Once back in Naxalbari, formulate your own revolutionary strategies, keeping in mind the ground realities over there" (quoted in Paul 2014, 130). For many left-wing dissidents around the world, Mao's sincere belief in praxis and self-mastery made Maoism much more attractive than Stalinism, and the revolutionary dimension of this internationalism also effectively hid much of China's own national agenda in this Beijing-centered international coalition.

Gerald Horne (2004) explained how Japanese propaganda manipulated the widespread racism in British and American society to justify its war in World War II, promoting its wars in Asia as part of its international anti-imperialist efforts, claiming that these wars were meant to rescue those colonial subjects from British and American suppressions. The PRC utilized similar tactics, widely reporting on, and condemning, the racism in the United States and Western countries to illustrate how corrupt the West was and how Maoist China was on the side of the global oppressed. In turn, domestic propaganda was also used internationally to promote Maoism in other countries, through state-sponsored journals and posters exported to many parts of the world. Many local leftists actively introduced and distributed Maoist materials to readers in their own countries, creating a global network of Maoist propaganda (K. Zhang and Xie 2019). Some of the domestic propaganda, which reduced the complexity of world politics into simple racial oppression, also became effective propaganda of Maoist internationalism.

The Maoist internationalist coalition was racially defined, with international solidarity composed of racialized people from Asia, Africa, and Latin America (*ya-fei-la* 亚非拉). They were represented by different skin colors, with clear differentiation that supported the validity of racial identity, also indirectly legitimizing the nationalist discourse based on the Chinese race. A racially based national sovereignty facilitated the PRC's superimposition of biology and politics, constructing a nationalism based on blood. If we look closer at these depictions in visual propaganda, these *ya-fei-la* figures are also very standardized. They are often depicted in chains or shackles, or with weapons in hand (Du 2016). Or they are greeted by Mao, who is always in the center, as individuals in ethnic clothing with varying skin hues look up to him admiringly.[4] Oppression and race are directly linked, but social inequality only happens in other places, not China.

Although the needs of individual countries and groups of people were identified and targeted for different kinds of aid, the global Maoism campaign was based on a sweeping generalization about their commonality. During the Maoist era, its powerful propaganda apparatus catered to conflicting demands: under the overall principles of socialist realism, artists could depict only the positive aspects of society, but the idea of incessant struggle was also central to the CCP ideology at that time (Mao [1957] 1977). To solve this conflict, propaganda artists seem to be obsessed with two themes: Chinese fighting with mother nature to increase productivity, and the racial oppressions and struggles in some foreign land. In fact, the PRC's internationalist legacy is still widely respected today partly because many people of color could find themselves visually represented in the Maoist propaganda material (Fennell 2013; West 2014). Frank Dikötter goes so far as to assert that "in its propaganda about revolution, China placed itself on the top of a global racial hierarchy, leading the 'coloured peoples' on the bottom towards liberation" (2015, 126). The homogeneity of Africa and Africans' loyal friendship to China were particularly important in the PRC's diplomatic efforts when many of these countries undertook their decolonization struggles in the 1960s.

On the diplomatic level, the PRC's support of these colonial struggles would turn the former colonies into "China's friends," and the PRC's material aid in these wars would be transformed into actual power in the international system. But on a propaganda level, race is foregrounded to highlight racial discrimination in foreign lands and the Maoist utopia where political solidarity transcends race. Racism is therefore an essential, and also highly subtle, component in the projection of global solidarity in China: the essential differences between Han Chinese and other races must be visualized in order to highlight China as the utopian land without racism. This (anti)racist discourse was a phantasmagoria, as very few non-Chinese were living in China at that time, and most people had never come across a person of different skin color in their lives. The ways the propaganda posters visualize, and stereotype, people of different colors being united under Mao's leadership make the world accessible to the Chinese people but purely on an imaginative level.

Alternative Modernities

What I have illustrated here is clearly not a discussion of the relation between the postcolonial and the postsocialist as found in some recent East-Central European studies (Cervinkova 2012). China was still steeped in socialism when it morphed from student to competitor of the Soviet Union. Instead, I am interested in the structure of modernity's impulses and the desire for autonomy found in China's de-Sovietization, which in turn can bring us back to some core problematics of postcolonialism.

While I have emphasized political alliances and revolutionary ideologies, it is also important to be aware of the underlying economic thinking. As already shown, the PRC's de-Sovietization and internationalism were both driven by a mode of catching up and surpassing that is typical of all modernization projects (Mingjiang Li 2012, 56). Most of the party leaders, such as Liu Shaoqi 刘少奇 and Deng Xiaoping 邓小平, were also active advocates in this regard (Dittmer 1998, 184). Mao might have been keener on realizing, or exploiting, the people's potentialities to engage in the continuous revolution than on developing a politically stable modern state. But we can say that development is the most important and unchallenged part of the PRC's official ideology. In fact, around the world, the socialist economic logic tends to commit more to industrial development than to the creation of a socialist world, focusing only on productivity and frowning on all those who ask critical questions (Bauman 1976, 55–57). The political ideology of internationalism might be based on permanent revolution, but it was also accompanied by an economic thinking that tended to stress self-sufficiency, emphasizing a closed economy over international trade and privileging those investments that could directly increase the output of commodities, with revenues reinvested in national industries (Fallenbuchl 1970). The PRC's First Five-Year Plan could be understood accordingly as practically minded overall; its principal aim was to revitalize China's dismal economy and establish the foundation for the nation's socialist industrialization.

But the subsequent Second Five-Year Plan, under the presumption of the great success of the First Five-Year Plan, became much more progressive, setting unachievable targets with the objective of creating the conditions for the Chinese people to transition to a communist society. Most important, it was also a nationalist project. Many people criticize the Great Leap Forward as politically delirious, but the mania was also caused by the strong desire for national independence from both the Soviet Union and the United States economically and politically. The PRC strongly believed that in the US-dominated world order that marginalized all socialist countries, there was no other means than to rely on its own primitive capital accumulation for the Chinese people to jump-start the country's development. Historians also demonstrate that while the CCP vigorously promoted the goal of the Great Leap Forward to surpass Great Britain and catch up with the United States, Mao was more concerned about catching up with and surpassing the Soviet Union, with the aim of demonstrating that China's economic development model was superior to that of the Soviet Union (Shen and Xia 2011). In the end, the PRC was not able to provide a radically different imagination of the future.

As Slavoj Žižek has reminded us, "We should not forget that the first half of the twentieth century was marked by two big projects which fit this notion of 'alternate modernity' perfectly: Fascism and Communism.... And was not the rapid industrialization of the Soviet Union in the late 1920s and 1930s also an attempt at a modernization different from the Western-capitalist one?" (2009, 34). Along the same logic, I would like to emphasize that in the name of de-Sovietization, China's nationalism and internationalism also did not differ much from the Soviet practices in terms of their common desire for modernization. They both suffered from the same naivete of being entrapped in the modernity discourse in the very act of resisting it. The Chinese endeavors might be slightly more perplexing than the Soviet Union's campaign because the former resisted both the modernity of the West and of the Soviet Union, which already claimed itself as an alternative modernity. But by disavowing the Soviet model, the "unique" Chinese path of modernization submitted itself further to the development discourse of the grand modernity project. Constantly engaging with the pursuit of "Chinese characteristics," the PRC was in fact the most enthusiastic supporter of modernization as a universal concept, stripping itself of any critical space to imagine its own different future.

Postcolonialism has also been criticized as exhibiting a similar penchant. Some postcolonialist critics have advanced the idea of "alternative modernities" to demonstrate that there can be different models of modernity and that we should not universalize modernity based only on European/Western experiences (Gaonkar 2001). While the concept of alternative modernities has galvanized some academic echoes, particularly among those critics interested in decentralizing or provincializing the Eurocentric modernization discourse, some critics find the concept problematic and ineffective as a critical discourse to truly engage with our global modernity fashioned by capitalism and Western imperialism. For example, Fredric Jameson (2002, 1–13) argues that instead of promoting alternative modernities to create the impression that we can escape from modernity, we should take modernity more seriously, exploring and articulating its structure and contradictions. As shown in the global Maoism project that was meant to be an alternative to the Soviet world order, the new networks that were built were also based on a rigid order with a specific core and hierarchy, and it is unclear how global Maoism was structurally different from the Soviet world-system.

On another occasion, Harry Harootunian (2010) also criticizes the fact that the postcolonial "alternative modernities" discourse privileges and essentializes cultural differences while ignoring temporal differences. Using the 1930s and 1940s "Overcoming Modernity" discussions in Japan as a distant example, Harootunian reminds us that emphasizing cultural differences would never enable the critics to see the actual complexity of time that the modernity discourse worked to suppress. By emphasizing "overcoming," the

Japanese thinkers only reinforced the logic of "catching up," thereby eliminating the possibility of the coexistence of different temporalities in the present. Harootunian criticizes that many postcolonial discourses, treading a path similar to the Japanese "Overcoming Modernity" project, transform the material and contested site of subaltern enunciation into the fixed space of an alternative modernity, turning us away from taking seriously the very forms of unevenness that had marked the colonial experience and still persist as historical residues in the new decolonized present. The postcolonial discourse might try to break down the emulation theory of models and copies inherent in modernity, but most of the critics end up reinforcing the original temporality supported by the logic of capital accumulation (Harootunian 2010, 378). Both the Japanese philosophers in the 1930s and some contemporary postcolonial critics might only have endorsed the modernity discourse that should be discredited in the first place.

I agree with Jameson and Harootunian that we need to be careful not to fall into the same teleology of development by claiming to provide different paths to the same end of modernity. The most important contribution of postcolonialism, I would argue, is the challenges it poses to our normative space-time configuration, challenges that invite us to spatialize our temporality and temporalize our spatiality. The question is how to utilize a different spatial practice to realize a new temporal mentality and therefore radically change our imagination of the future and modernity. A more radical form of postcolonialism would demand a rethinking of the real outside the constitution of modern categories, so that we can take transformation and becoming more seriously (Grossberg 1996, 179–80). If the PRC was going to redevelop a new world order, there remains the question of whether it has offered any challenges to the original development discourse within Western modernity, which China inherited through the filter of Soviet statism. Put another way, did the different acts of "displacing" modernity, from the Soviet challenges to Western liberalism to the Chinese challenges to Soviet hegemony, ever produce a radically new modernity?

Geopolitically, the PRC had to assert itself as a unified modern nation-state against its external enemies and internal critics and ethnic minorities. But in relocating itself to the center of a new world-system, the PRC did not project any new revolutionary narrative that was really different from the Soviet Union's. Its anxious claim of "being different" was deployed only to prove its capacity as a modern nation. Benefiting from the postcolonial criticism just described, I am more interested in the cultivation of different modes of temporal consciousness that the PRC should have provided but failed to. Many critics have pointed out that postcolonialism and modernity could be rival projects, because colonialism and imperialism have been supported by a linear historical epistemology predetermining the positions of individual nation-states along the modernity scale, against which postcolonialism issued its challenge. We are increasingly aware that postcolonialism is not just a project of spatial differences emphasizing the coexistence of different worlds; rather, these worlds are locked in intense power struggles and hierarchical relations. Postcolonialism could be an effective theoretical tool to raise and politicize our temporal awareness of this structure, because this structure is based largely on the discourse of modernization that has directly informed and propelled coloniality and postcoloniality. Providing a new spatial consciousness, postcolonialism, as Dipesh Chakrabarty (2000, 42–46) emphasizes, should primarily be a historicizing effort. If we are able to rediscover new subaltern pasts, we can open up new ways to see history, while at the same time conceptualizing new spatial relations.

China's de-Sovietization was understood as the necessary path for China in order to achieve the autonomy of the Chinese state. But the imagination of an alternative modernity is achieved through an uncritical endorsement of an authentic past and fetishized present, without providing us with a truly different way to imagine our common future. De-Sovietization becomes complicitous with the hegemony of the communist party-state, and it legitimized a blueprint for the PRC to engage in the development of a new world order in which China is at the center. The idea of development implies a fixed temporality of progression, which tends to go on forever, demanding the people's incessant contribution and justifying their exploitation. I am interested in exploring how postcolonialism might liberate us from such historical imaginations. At a time when the current PRC state justifies all its policies, however problematic domestically and diplomatically, based on the aim of achieving national strength and pride, it is of even more urgency to historicize the development of this form of national sovereignty and global leadership.

Notes

The research contained in this chapter is partly funded by a GRF grant, no. CUHK 14607021, offered by Hong Kong's Research Grant Council.

1 As Sheng Yue 盛岳 (2004, 69) recounts, other than standard subjects such as history and philosophy, the curriculum also included "Party's Construction" and "Soviet Construction," meant to offer the Soviet experiences as models to be transplanted to China.

2 Besieged by the Nationalist government, the CCP in 1935 was forced to leave its base in Jiangxi to engage in the famous "Long March," which ended in Yan'an, a remote and poor rural area in Shaanxi province. There the CCP established its new "Soviet area" comprising areas in the three provinces of Shaanxi, Gansu, and Ningxia.
3 For example, not only did the Great Leap Forward campaign cover industrial and agricultural production, but cultural workers were also encouraged to produce as many works as possible.
4 Jin Shangyi 靳尚谊 and Wu Birui's 伍必瑞 1960 painting *Our Friends All Over the World* (我们的朋友遍天下) is such an example.

Part III

Hong Kong Postcoloniality among the British, Japanese, and Chinese Empires

From Manchukuo to Hong Kong

Postcolonial theory is often charged with being disconnected from the historical phenomena and real practices in different colonial situations, though it can be productive in offering some epistemological reflexivity on the discursive formation and hegemonic state building in relation to the colonial legacy. This chapter begins with the verb *to postcolonize* as a way to understand some Asian colonial experiences in specific historical periods. Such an understanding is mainly grasped through the perspective of governance. To postcolonize, of course, is not to decolonize but rather to colonize in a relatively different way in light of the changing sociopolitical circumstances. A different kind of colonialism or imperialism began in the 1930s in East Asia, though such "new imperialism," as Prasenjit Duara (2006) describes it, is not confined to only one geographic region. In comparison to the "old imperialism" of the traditional European powers, like the British imperialism of free trade, this new "imperialism [was beginning in the 1930s and continuing into the Cold War] exhibited in the foreign affairs of the United States, the Soviet Union, and Japan [as well as Germany, although Nazi racism was defeated in World War II], rather than in those of the older European colonial powers" (48). The main features of this new imperialism include maintaining the legal status of sovereign nation-states for their colonies or spheres of influence; making considerable economic investment in these client states, which have been conceived as part of the strategic plan for the imperialist power to compete for global supremacy; embracing anticolonial ideologies; and initiating the modernization of institutions and identities in these controlled regions.

However, the old-new differentiation is more a question of historical periodization than of rigid categorization, since the "old" imperialist powers also adopted new strategies in their occupied areas in the midst of decolonizing currents after World War I in order to strengthen their economic-political foothold and even enhance their hegemonic position. The really old imperialism mainly refers to the period from the sixteenth century to the eighteenth century when European maritime powers, such as Spain, Portugal, Great Britain, and France, built their overseas empires in the Americas, the West and East Indies, and Asia, along with the Netherlands' territorial holdings in coastal Africa and Asia—in contrast to the intensive "new" rivalries among the great powers between the mid-1870s and 1914, manifesting in the severe competition for occupation principally in Africa, Asia, and the Pacific rather than the Americas. The term *new imperialism* is still frequently invoked in the contemporary era to designate a present situation that is qualitatively different from the one analyzed by the classical Marxist view, characterized by hegemonic competition for markets and territories by industrialized and relatively equal states, or the one described in dependency theory, in which the hierarchy between a few rich imperialist nations and a majority of poor, dependent ones is perpetuated by the progressive polarization of wealth and power. While postimperialist theorists offer an interpretation of a world where imperialism has already been substituted by a global capitalist system in which the national states have lost much influence and power (Hardt and Negri 2001), many others believe that the new imperialism "might now be taking on a rather different allure" (D. Harvey 2003, 7). But we should be vigilant in calling any imperialism new, since there are always many elements of continuity with the old imperialism in the new order. In this chapter I locate the cases of Manchukuo and Hong Kong in the historical context of the new twentieth-century mode of the "postcolonizing" project in order to understand the complex relations and entanglement of these mandates with their foreign governing powers and explore how very different outcomes can be produced with changing historical circumstances.

What change was brought about by the postcolonizing process that took place in the post–World War I period? Was change better than not changing? Was the change specific to the place? Did it benefit the colonized people? Did the change of situation bring change to the structure or system? Close to the end of World War I, US president Woodrow Wilson presented a program of fourteen points in 1918 to deal with the territorial issues among the combatant nations and to propose general principles for a peaceful world by promoting adjustment of colonial claims based on the principles of self-determination. The fourteen-point proposal was the basis of the principles of the League of Nations guaranteeing the political independence and territorial integrity of great and small states. Even though Wilson used military force in suppressing the recalcitrant Central American nations around the time when the fourteen points were proposed, the Wilsonian principle of national self-determination prevailed, and the rhetoric was supported, or at least accepted, by many imperialist states.[1] Hence, new rhetoric and strategy were needed to justify the continuation of imperialism. The impact of the self-determination principle was far from benign. It actually evolved into a new rationale for military intervention and the expansion of imperialist power, while the new system of colonial domination was accompanied by the notion of mandate and the concept of pan-nationalism.

Mandates were administratively different from colonies, according to the covenant of the League of Nations in the post-1918 world order, since money and resources extracted from a mandate should be used for its local benefit rather than just for mandatory power. In other words, the mandatory powers, the principal World War I victors who took over the territories (i.e., the mandates) that were once under the control of the defeated nations, were obliged to work for the well-being and development of the peoples placed under their tutelage, though the mandatory powers were equally concerned about their own long-term diplomatic, strategic, and economic interests. Hence, it is still legitimate for a mandatory power to develop its mandate for its own strategic and economic advantages. In 1939 "the Japanese began construction of naval and air facilities in their mandates in Micronesia, and it was from these bases that attacks were launched against American territories in the Pacific in December 1941" (Duus 1996, 56). At the same time, it is assumed that a mandatory power is an advanced nation, while a mandate is a backward one, a dichotomy or bias that has not changed.

While the notion of mandate was appropriated to soften imperialism in light of the emerging liberal concept of national self-determination, the idea of pan-nationalism was meant to reconcile the ethnic identification with the nation-state. Pan-nationalism indeed was a weird twin of nineteenth-century European nationalism, emphasizing cultural, linguistic, and racial affinity across political borders to feed the ambitions of the great powers. While the classic notion of nationalism emphasizes one ethnicity, culture, and language, pan-nationalism speaks of ethnically or culturally related peoples and defines a nation as a cluster of these supposedly related ethnic or cultural groups.

The ideology of pan-nationalism proposed a commonality and solidarity of "equals" (in contrast with the advanced-backward dichotomy in the concept of mandate) in the face of alien invasion and domination. That someone must be a leader even among equals legitimizes a new form of domination. While the notion of Asianism means many different, if not conflicting, things to different people, the Japanese discourse of pan-Asianism and vision of the Greater East Asia Co-Prosperity Sphere in the 1930s, though anti-imperialist in tone, supported its new phase of expansion, when old imperialism increasingly became illegitimate and competition among nation-states manifested through forms of nationalism.

Although pan-Asianism has been seen as Japan's cover for militarist expansionism and a tool for legitimizing its hegemony and colonial rule, it is less an ideology that has a consistent vision and narrative than a disposition, a temperament, or a mood that runs through Japan's modern history.[2] Precisely because of its inconsistency, pan-Asianism can embody nationalism, statism, expansionism, and even left-wing internationalism. In the pan-Asianists' discourse, Western civilization is materialistic, militant, rational, aggressive, and decadent, in opposition to the spiritual, peaceful, natural, and ethical qualities of Asian civilization, thereby duplicating the binary-opposition structure that prevails in the Western mode of thought. If Western imperial nations have justified their conquest as a civilizing mission based on Christianity and the Enlightenment and argued that to be a nation was to belong to a higher order of civilization, Japanese pan-Asianism was also portrayed as a civilizational discourse denouncing the materialism and destructiveness of Western civilization (Duara 2001). Japan claims its inheritance of the leadership of Asian civilization on the basis of its success in mastering Western civilization. Civilization in the era of nation-states both serves and transcends the territorial nation—transcends because it may allow a critique of the nation and produce a loyalty problem dividing those committed to the nation and those committed to civilization.

Japan committed itself to launching the mission of harmonizing and synthesizing Eastern and Western civilizations. The discourse of Eastern civilization, whether viewed as superior to the Western one or as necessary to redeem the West, also flourished in China as intellectual and cultural movements in the early twentieth century. Republican China used the civilizational discourse to counter European materialist and imperialist civilization as well as to create a trans-Chinese, Asianist ideology in order to secure the loyalty of the ethnic minorities who occupied the vast hinterland over which the new Chinese nation-state attempted to exercise its sovereignty. The Japanese pan-Asianist discourse did inspire novel transnational fantasies and hopes of a romanticized Asian solidarity among colonized and oppressed peoples not only in East Asia but also in peripheral Southeast Asia. While sharing colonial experiences and transnational anticolonial discourse, the pan-Asianism that emanated from the Southeast Asian countries, such as the Philippines, Malaysia, and Vietnam, was distinct from that of the Sinic East Asian "center" of pan-Asianism. Though the traveling political activists and revolutionaries were bound up with nation-making projects, they created human networks and interconnections through transborder movements of people and ideas as a constitutive part of the formation of territorial nation-states (Hau and Tejapira 2011; CuUnjieng Aboitiz 2020).

In contrast to the pan-Asian solidarities among nationalist revolutionaries that are not necessarily forged by complementary and intersecting ideologies, the state-led Asianist narratives are far more conceptually oriented. The common themes propagandized by the Japanese discourse of pan-Asianism include cultural unity, the same script (*kanji*), racial kinship and a common language (*dōbun dōshu* 同文同種), yellow race (*ōshoku jinshu* 黄色人種), a common destiny (*unmei kyōdōtai* 運命共同体), the struggle against Western imperialism and Westernization, and Asian solidarity and equality, as well as efforts to overcome modernity with moral virtues of community (*seimeiteki kyōdōtai* 生命的共同体), familism (*kazokushugi* 家族主義), and agrarian commune (*nōson kyōdotai* 農村共同体). Asianist discourse in the early Meiji era of the late 1800s aimed at securing national independence, advocating Japan-Qing cooperation (*Nisshin teikei* 日清提携), and reviving Asia (*shin-A* 新亜). In the early 1900s, Japanese pan-Asian agitators were ambitious to overthrow the ancient regimes in Korea and China. Japan gained strong self-confidence after its victory in the Russo-Japanese War of 1904–5 and had become a recognized member of the great powers (*rekkyō* 列強). After World War I, the Japanese state followed the American model to advocate its own Asian Monroe Doctrine by stressing that the fate of Asia must be decided by Asians in order to keep the West out of Asia. Japan's definition of Asia was enlarged to include India and western Asia. In the 1920s pan-Asianism evolved into rhetoric aimed at legitimizing Japanese colonial rule over Asia. Finally, in the 1930s–1940s, the discourse mutated into an extended nationalism, serving Japanese hegemony in Asia (Saaler 2007).

In contrast to the European imperialist powers, Japan appointed itself to carry out the mission to modernize East Asia and to protect its Asian neighbors from Western encroachment by extending its control over them. Its colonial pattern expressed itself as a reunion with its Asian kin, very different from the European model of reproducing difference between the colonizer and the colonized. Imagining sameness through cultural and racial unity rather than otherness as the European mode of colonization, Japan built its empire by conquest through "territorial osmosis" (Park 2000), which makes full use of geographic and racial contiguity to realize imperialist ambitions in an incremental process. For example, Japan saw the occupation of Korea, after the integration of Taiwan, as the first step toward the colonization of Manchuria (first the Liaodong Peninsula under the Guandong Lease, then Jiandao, the area of Manchuria bordering Korea), China proper, and then Indochina, India, and ultimately all parts of Asia along with the Pacific Islands, through the concept of cultural-racial unity and the construction of an organic body called the Asian community. Compared with European colonialism, which was mostly driven by economic motives, Japanese colonizers were "greatly concerned with their country's immediate strategic interests" (Gann 1984, 499), envisaging the necessity to create vast defensive networks thrust outward through military campaigns from Korea to Manchuria, from Manchuria deep into China, from the concentric chains of Pacific Island bases to the Greater East Asian Co-Prosperity Sphere, in order to protect the heartland of empire, their island home, in pursuit of total security. The Japanese were convinced that potential or actual threats from Western powers could be met only by maintaining geopolitical control over the contiguous terrains, making Japan militarily invulnerable against external attack and independent of foreign supply of vital strategic imports. Pan-Asianism also developed into a criticism of Eurocentric modernization (overcoming modernity, or *kindai no chōkoku* 近代の超克) by promoting a return to certain essentialist Asian cultures and values that mirrored the efforts at defining a unique but fixed Japanese identity. As Pang Laikwan argues in her chapter, with the notion of "overcoming," Japanese only saw the West as the primal enemy and indeed reinforced the mechanism of catching up with the West in the linear history of modernization, while entirely ignoring the coevalness of other temporalities in Asia. As a result, its pan-Asianism was never successful in assimilating other Asians and even its own overseas imperial subjects to the Japanese way. Having been discriminated against by Western countries even though it had emerged as one of the imperialist powers, Japan attempted to reconfigure a different international system in order to supplant the "liberal" economic order under Anglo-American hegemony by creating a self-sufficient regional economic bloc through which the world's resources could be redistributed to give a greater share to non-Western nations. Decoupling from the Western-dominated system seems to have been easier in the early twentieth century when capitalist globalization was still in its initial stage.

Manchukuo

Manchukuo (1932–45) was a product of this new Japanese colonial plan. Pan-Asianism, multinationalism, and anticolonial ideologies were all embraced in Manchukuo to justify Japanese domination, further complicating the intertwined relationship between imperialism and nationalism. In terms of Asian experiences since the nineteenth century, nationalism is inseparable from imperialism and social Darwinism (the life-and-death struggle to eat or be eaten). Along its developmental process, the nation-state was converted into imperialism abroad because nationalism was both the goal and the means of competition for global resources and superiority among nation-states. Internally, nationalism was also a kind of colonial project in the sense that the ideology permitted the nation-state to explore and mobilize national resources, eliminate local differences, co-opt the proletarian class, demand national loyalty to suppress different and dissenting voices, and discipline the population for national competition, with vague promises of popular sovereignty and national glory.

To strategically incorporate such newly ruled land into the regional economic formation as a means to help the imperial power compete for global supremacy, Japan followed the principles of mandate and pan-nationalism and made considerable investments in Manchukuo, exploiting the place and brutalizing its people while promoting the modernization of its institutions and identity formation. Shin'ichi Yamamuro (2006) labels Manchuria under Japanese rule a "chimera," a mythical beast with a lion's head, a sheep's body, and the tail of a serpent that designates the illusion repeatedly created in Japanese minds by propaganda of the image of a harmonious, equalitarian, and self-governing multiethnic society, in contrast to the reality of brutal discrimination, humiliation, and oppression suffered by Chinese, Korean, and Manchu residents.[3] The inherent contradictions and flawed nature of this polity can be attributed to the fragile alliance between the Kwantung Army (Kantōgun 関東軍) and the Japanese settlers, in which both groups held fundamentally different goals for Manchuria. Rather than "liberating" Manchuria from European colonial practices, Japanese control over the place was actually not much different from European practices. Yamamuro has even gone so far to call Manchukuo "an Auschwitz state or a concentration-camp state, more than just a puppet state" (2006, 4). Its thirteen-year history as a fabricated haven driven by ideals and illusions has brought disaster to different racial groups agonized by human rights abuses and coercive exploitation. In place of the promised prosperity came starvation, forced labor, confiscation of land, and horrifying human abuse and experimentation.

Japan's "postcolonial" project in Manchukuo in terms of its modern process of state making and nation building did inspire other new nation-states, such as China, that looked to expand their territorial sovereignty claims over regions and groups with weak links to the central government. While communist China officially rejected and condemned the Japanese colonial strategies in Manchukuo, China's increasingly oppressive governance of its non-Han nationalities may generate impressions of their illicit similarity. The global circulations of modern ideas are mediated by regional historical and cultural interactions in East Asia. But the dissemination was not conducted on an open, equal basis. It had been carried out through specific forms of power relations in a world-system of unequal nation-states characterized by a hierarchy of core nations and peripheral states. Such inequality in the global flows of modern ideas, when arriving at the early twentieth-century East Asia, was also similarly expressed in the dominance of hegemonic Japanese terminologies and its reconfigurations of classical Chinese vocabularies in the modern Chinese and Korean languages (L. Liu 1995). However, the hierarchical dissemination of modern ideas could get complicated in the relationships among the imperial Japanese, semicolonial Chinese, and colonial Koreans in that era. Although the intra–East Asian cultural and intellectual contact network was made uneven and ambiguous by Japan's dual position as imperialist power and gateway to modern Western ideas, Chinese and Korean engagements with (re)imported Japanese ideas did not essentially display any subaltern indebtedness but rather often evinced fundamental ambivalence. Although the intra–East Asian cultural entanglements were subjected to the asymmetrical relations of domination and subordination in the Japanese Empire, the intellectual "contact nebulae" or networks of cultural interaction developed well in advance of official mandates or top-down cultural directives from the state (Thornber 2009).

The promises of the Manchukuo project were to liberate East Asia from the control of Western powers, accomplish autonomy and self-defense, gain mutual respect for sovereign independence, and promote economic development and prosperity. Historical facts may prove that they were not all empty rhetorical gestures, even though the harsh reality of life imposed on the Han Chinese (including many sinicized ethnic Manchu) by the Japanese imperial apparatus cannot be ignored. The efforts made by the Japanese imperialists in Manchuria from the late nineteenth century to the 1940s did turn the place into a multinational, multiethnic melting pot (Mitter 2005). A population census of Harbin, one of the major cities in Manchukuo, compiled by the new government in 1933, demonstrated the bewildering ethnic diversity, which included Chinese, Taiwanese, Russians, Japanese (from Japan proper, *naichi*, or inner land), Koreans, British, Americans, Germans, French, Italians, Poles, Jews, Greeks, Dutch, Turks, Austrians, Hungarians, Danes, Latvians, Portuguese, Czechs, Armenians, Belgians, Serbs, Swedes, Romanians, Swiss, and Indians, as well as Manchu, Mongols, and the Tungusic tribes. In comparison to European colonial policies, the Japanese one was more oriented toward economic development in its conquered lands. In the 1920s, even before Japan launched its comprehensive invasion, 85 percent of the total Japanese foreign investment was in China, and 80 percent of such investment was in Manchuria. Since the Japanese were not able to assimilate the Chinese into the Japanese nation (like what they did to Koreans and Taiwanese), pan-Asianist discourse was needed to express the Asian alliance (under Japanese leadership) to fight against Western imperialism and to form a self-sufficient economic bloc.

Manchukuo was created as a modern developmental state and later became the most industrialized region in Asia outside Japan. Japanese investment there grew to about 6 billion yen between 1932 and 1941, with fixed capital rising from 1.2 billion yen in 1930 to 8.6 billion yen in 1940 (L. Young 1998, 183). By 1945 Japanese investment in Manchukuo exceeded its combined total investment in Korea, Taiwan, and the rest of China. Industrial production tripled between 1933 and 1942. The rapid increase in industrial employment also attracted a lot of Chinese migrant workers (Duara 2006, 59). The Han Chinese had emigrated to the place in large waves, which was often described as the world's largest population movement by that time. The average yearly flow of Chinese from inland China into Manchukuo in the early twentieth century was estimated at 500,000 to 2 million, like "the roar of [a] human Niagara pouring into empty Chinese lands dominated by alien powers" (Chang 1936, 1). The banking system was reformed, and the new currency of Manchukuo was made equivalent to the Japanese yen, forming the trading sphere known as the yen bloc. Some investment had also been made in certain areas of the social infrastructure, like public health and the education system. The united military and capitalist joint force dreamed of the new nation as salvation in a time of economic crisis, given that Japan's own economy was deadlocked in the wake of obstacles posed by the domestic and global markets. Economic development in Manchukuo became the panacea for the age of uncertainty, a possible lifeline for a Japanese nation set adrift in the stormy waters of the global economy. At the same time, the brutality of the Kwantung Army in Manchukuo, which was beyond the full control of Tokyo, paralleled the rapid development there.

Manchukuo in the context of the new Japanese colonial policy fluctuated between a nominally independent nation-state and a dependent state, or even a younger brother, in the language of the Japanese "family state." For instance, Pu Yi, the emperor of Manchukuo, was called the younger half brother of the Japanese emperor Hirohito. Chinese officials were used at all levels in Manchukuo, but they were all supervised by Japanese officials. Local communal societies were formed to represent all major races: Japanese, Manchus, Mongols, Hui Muslims, Koreans, and the majority Han Chinese (now called Manchurians).[4] They functioned as a self-surveillance system (this system would be appropriated and applied by Japan during the occupation of Hong Kong). In this Japan-controlled Manchukuo, there also emerged some social religious movements that refused to acknowledge allegiance to any nation-state. These Chinese sectarian or redemptive societies worshipped Buddhist, Daoist, and folk deities and launched the mission of universalism and moral self-transformation and self-cultivation (such as practicing charity, cultivating close moral and spiritual introspection, exercising a strict disciplinary regimen, and abstaining from drugs, meat, alcohol, and the like) to supplement and correct the material civilization of the West with the spiritual civilization of the East. Because these movements' transnational spiritualism defied territorial loyalty, the Kuomintang Nationalist regime always wanted to outlaw and persecute these redemptive societies, but Japan in the 1930s manipulated these societies to advance its imperialist interests. For the first time, the Manchukuo regime was more tolerant and even welcoming of redemptive societies, which could pursue their transterritorial, nonnational, or even antinational socioreligious goals without fear of suppression (Duara 2003, 103–4). Other interesting records (including cinema, literature, and other sociocultural activities) reveal how the multiethnic peoples reacted to, adapted to, and even shaped the Japanese governance in Manchukuo, which, in line with the metaphor of the chimera, was a composite beast in its incorporation of fantasies and works of imagination (Lahusen 2000; Sewell 2004; Agnew 2013).

From the Chinese nationalist perspective, Manchukuo has been characterized as a puppet state of Japan (using the Chinese moralistic term of Wei-Man, literally "bogus state of Manchuria") and de facto colony, although the

Japanese labored mightily to convince themselves and others of the truth of Manchukuo's independent status. But what cannot be put aside is the implication of Manchukuo for our understanding of the "postcolonial" situation, particularly with its double process of economic investment and exploitative control.

Hong Kong

The Manchukuo model was not applied to Hong Kong since the Japanese occupation of the city was relatively short (1941–45), although, like Manchuria, Hong Kong was also controlled directly by the Japanese military. Historically, the Hong Kong model under British colonial rule (i.e., relatively indirect rule, absorbing the local elites into the governing body and maintaining only a small colonial polity) had been used as a reference for Japan to govern Taiwan. In the end, however, Japan converted Taiwan into a "province," part of its "inland" rather than a periphery or a client state, as part of its global strategic plan (Hamashita 1997, 124). Only in the later years of the Meiji era did the Hong Kong model serve as a good example for the Japanese Empire to construct its foreign governance.

In the late Edo period, Japan already used Hong Kong as a source of foreign ideas and commodities, as well as a place for collecting intelligence about China. Hong Kong as a transit place for migrant workers to the West and Hong Kong's extensive networks with Southeast Asia (Nan'yō 南洋, or the South Seas) were also exemplary for Japan as the latter sought to expand its trading paths and system. During the Anglo-Japanese alliance (1902–23), Japan's navy regularly visited Hong Kong's port, and the Japanese military had seen Hong Kong as a key contesting site for its competition in the Pacific. However, when the Pacific War broke out, Japan did not consider this British colony strategically important to fulfill its dream of the Greater East Asia Co-Prosperity Sphere. The main objective of the Japanese invasion and occupation of the port city was to block the transportation of strategic goods to the Chinese government in the mainland (Han 1981).

The significant transformation of traditional colonialism in Hong Kong into a well-developed capitalist society would have a lot to do with the specific conditions of the Cold War, under which the world order was determined by the rivalry between two superpowers and their camps and by their competition for control of the decolonizing nations. The common strategies used by the United States and the Soviet Union to control their client states consisted of fostering modernization, subsidizing their economies, and subjecting them to military constraint, as well as providing paternalistic enlightenment, offering limited self-determination, and even supporting undemocratic authoritarian ruling structures. In other words, the developmental imperialism example of Manchukuo survived into the Cold War even after the collapse of the Japanese Empire, though it has been recast in the rhetoric of modernization and economic growth, especially in the "free world," in which the imperial nature of the United States was masked by a democratic facade. Therefore, the Manchukuo model can still be used to understand from a different angle Hong Kong's "postcolonized" experiences from the 1950s onward.

It is true that the Japanese actually lacked a concrete plan for ruling their captured places as part of their empire. The governing body of the newly occupied territories only followed some general guidelines, and many decisions were made with inadequate information since the Japanese government was divided up into certain semi-independent bureaucratic structures that resulted in checks and balances on the unrestricted use of power. As policy was decided by the Tokyo War Cabinet, it was the bureaucracy, primarily the army and sometimes the navy, that took up the task of implementation. While the governing structures of the captured regions realized that their rule had to be flexible in order to win the sympathy of the occupied people and unite the entirety of the Japanese Empire, different considerations, particularly the impending war effort, rendered such policy flexibility very limited in scale.

The purpose of invading Hong Kong was primarily military, and not much concrete result was achieved in the short period of the occupation. In the stringent war situation, the Japanese Army even found Hong Kong a burden since the place offered very few raw materials or natural resources that could be exploited for war mobilization, and the population was too large and posed a serious food-shortage problem and threat to law and order. However, the impact of the rhetoric and practices of the Japanese during its occupation of Hong Kong had far-reaching consequences for British policies and attitudes in the colony during the postwar period (Duara 2012, 201).

Although the Japanese rhetoric of the equality of Asians was always negated in practice by Japanese racist policies, the spectacular defeat of Britain and other Western powers in Asia by Japan destroyed the myth of white superiority in many Asian minds. One dramatic episode during the occupation had the Japanese military forcing British men to pull rickshaws carrying Chinese and Indians (Duara 2012, 202). Moreover, the Japanese invasion of Hong Kong followed the practice in Manchukuo and other colonies. After weeks of senseless atrocities and rape by Japanese troops, the military government invited local elites and middle classes to work with them under the slogan of reformist pan-Asianism. Influential Chinese who had been representatives of the community for a long time were used to working under a colonial regime. Although they had very little power in the government during the Japanese occupation, they functioned as a pacifying force vis-à-vis the population. A number of historical studies prove that the Japanese did manage to establish a viable bureaucratic administrative system in captured Hong Kong even as the life of ordinary people became unbearable (Snow 2003; Xie 1995; Ye 1982). The Japanese included many Chinese and other Asians in all levels of government and social institutions. While the ideological appeal of pan-Asianism remained suspicious in Asians' hearts, the restructuring of the governance did overturn the European-dominated order. In the pre-Japanese invasion period, the British had run the entire administration with very few Chinese as members in the executive and legislative councils. In contrast, the Japanese military government drew many more Chinese into their bureaucratic machine than the British had. The use of natives as figureheads had been a common practice in Japanese colonies such as Taiwan and Korea.

Although the sympathy, if any, that the Japanese gained among the Chinese in removing their British colonial masters was quickly worn out by their brutal rule and replaced by fear and hatred of the Japanese soldiers (as Hong Kong was under military rule and mainly run by the military police corps Kempeitai), the wartime propaganda against European racism and the subsequent worldwide movement of decolonization made it more difficult for the British to continue their racist policies and institutions in the postwar era. The British made postwar reforms in Hong Kong: for instance, Asians were no longer banned from living on the Peak, mixed marriages were legalized, Chinese were recruited to the police force, some Urban Council members were elected rather than appointed and given more power over public works, and self-governing organizations such as neighborhood welfare groups (which resembled the self-government system during the Japanese occupation) were allowed to form as an answer to growing awareness of the colonial state's social responsibilities. The British made some adjustments in their colonial policy after the war as they increasingly began to rely on American strategic concerns to protect their own interests.

During the Japanese occupation, Hong Kong Island, Kowloon, and the New Territories were divided into several districts, each headed by a District Affairs Bureau, and the districts were subdivided into wards. In general, a ward consisted of thirty families, and a ward leader was elected. The wards were seen by the Japanese rulers as grassroots organizations, and their function of teaching people to respect the law was widely publicized in the press (Han 1981, 13). The ward system was not a Japanese invention but derived from the Chinese *baojia* system that was also practiced in Japan as *tonarigumi* (隣組; neighborhood associations). Through supervision of the wards, the District Affairs Bureau from top to bottom carried out the census, rationed daily necessities, repatriated the excess population, and organized defense and health campaigns. As the ward system embraced all levels of society and controlled all aspects of life for the people, the Japanese bureaucracy could effectively take two censuses—in September 1943 and May 1944—during their short occupation. The Japanese also enforced population-wide free inoculation campaigns three times a year, something the British had never been able to do in the past. After the 1967 riots, the system of district offices was introduced in Hong Kong, which was probably a late lesson learned from the Japanese.

The remarkable success and effectiveness of the Japanese bureaucracy, however, did not actually earn it a lot of credit with the people of Hong Kong since the Japanese government in its short period of rule did very little to alleviate the harsh conditions experienced by the people, and life was much more difficult under Japanese occupation than it had been under European rule. The lingering popular memories of Hong Kong people, undoubtedly selective and rather fragmentary by nature, include positive comments about and longings for British colonialism but not the Japanese occupation.

While sociopolitical lessons might have been learned by the British following their defeat by the Japanese military, their arrogant attitude and sense of white supremacy did not change drastically. As Hong Kong British expatriate elites in the postwar era still saw themselves as a superior race and lived apart from the local Chinese, why did the local colonial government increasingly develop a stronger commitment to the local interest of the city in the following decades, to the extent of sometimes defying, and struggling against, the metropolitan authorities in London?

The contextual reason would be the impact of global decolonization and the effects of the Cold War, as has repeatedly been argued. Also, the colony's healthy and steady economic development (which requires some degree of local control and self-government) would benefit both the imperial metropole and the peripheral dependency. But to say that the Hong Kong postcolonized experience and history are all about enhancing local interest may be somewhat misleading, as it would be hard to understand why the expatriate colonial bureaucrats would care about the local interest, given their sense of racial superiority. Perhaps it was a contradictory amalgamation of local commitment, ideational pressure exerted by the global decolonization trend, and limited universal enlightenment.

It is doubtful that these colonial bureaucrats would have a universalist civic consciousness or any sense of moral responsibility beyond their racial-national identity. And it would be even more uncertain that they would have the willingness to engage with the locals, let alone be open and self-reflexive with respect to the equal validity of other cultures, other values, and other mores. Although the British colonial bureaucrats may not have had a vision of a global political consciousness, the Cold War situation combined the colonial doctrine of laissez-faire free economy with the capitalist ideology of freedom and prosperity as strong weapons to fight against communism. In contrast, the economic-growth trajectories of Japan, South Korea, Taiwan, and Singapore could not have happened without American patronage, which afforded these anticommunist Asian allies the advantages of technology acquisition and upgrades, protectionist policies, and access to the US market for their export-oriented economies. Meanwhile, the British colonial bureaucrats were also pressured to conform to the emerging standards and norms set by some global organizations and international conventions after the war. The United States endeavored to end trade-war practices that had developed during the Great Depression, with open-door policy objectives underpinning American international commercial strategy. The International Monetary Fund, the International Bank for Reconstruction and Development, and the General Agreement on Tariffs and Trade were the main means to these ends. And these were the international institutions that the United States created and planned to unilaterally manage. Building the blocks of such postwar architecture was meant to facilitate and sustain the rise of US hegemony, in addition to explicitly staving off global conflicts triggered by zero-sum economic contests that brewed into trade barriers, nationalist rivalries, and security threats. The Cold War era has been called the age of ultraimperialism or postimperialism (Parrini 1993) in the sense that the United States maintained cooperation among industrialized nations through the International Monetary Fund, the International Bank for Reconstruction and Development, and the General Agreement on Tariffs and Trade to prevent the imperialist striving for monopolistic control of investment outlets, export markets, and low-cost supplies of raw materials. The ultraimperial-cooperation cartel among the capitalist states was also a response to the threat of revolutions or national liberation struggles in the decolonizing world.

The human freedom and economic growth enjoyed by colonized people in Hong Kong were maximized by the specific historical circumstances rather than by the grace of the colonial system. The Cold War enabled the dual movement between the self-regulating market and state intervention and effectively enhanced the state as the agent of redistribution and regulation of resources to ensure a relatively egalitarian society not just in Hong Kong but also in other parts of East Asia (like South Korea and Taiwan).

The Hong Kong of the postwar 1950s did not have a well-defined position in any political sense. Britain once wanted to give up this crown colony because of its indefensibility (and the heavy burden of the refugee problem), and communist China had showed no sign of taking it back even as China emphasized its territorial sovereignty and was at war with the United States in Korea at the time. The United States used Hong Kong to contain China, to gather intelligence, and to launch overt propaganda campaigns and other covert operations. China kept Hong Kong as an opening or window to the outside world (especially after its split with the USSR) and a wedge against the British-American alliance in order to alienate their relations (Mark 2004). Postwar Hong Kong found itself navigating the push and pull of containment and opening by the great powers with some successful leverage or balancing, serving as the Cold War battleground for political and ideological warfare.

The absence of a strong and pressing Chinese nationalist movement in Hong Kong provided friendly circumstances for the colonial bureaucrats to follow international standards and realize the ambiguous goals of a new colonialism designed to benefit both metropole and colony. Economic development and the ideology of the free market proved to be the best way for Hong Kong to remain neutral by staying out of the Cold War battles and to deter the growth of ethnic nationalism in alliance with communism. As part of investment outlets for surplus capital, the colonial state was also active in building infrastructure, providing public housing (to sustain capitalist growth and maintain a cheap labor force), and protecting local businesses (from metropolitan and international financial restrictions) in order to ensure economic competitiveness. There was a shift in the balance of power in the 1950s–1960s between Hong Kong and London precisely because of the economic status of the colony. For example, the huge size of Hong Kong's sterling assets, because of its colonial status, actually meant that the colonial city was able to "strike back" at its imperial master by negotiating to diversify official reserves (Schenk 2004, 2010).

Hong Kong locals, from the merchant class to the working plebeians, collaborated with this colonial system since most of them did not want the return of Chinese sovereignty under the aegis of the Chinese Communist Party. And they did not put pressure on the colonial authority by asking for more welfare and democracy, not even democracy in the sense of more bargaining power, more protection over their working conditions.

What changed the postcolonized experiences in Hong Kong? To a large extent, the British regime had successfully depicted itself as a benevolent and enlightened colonizer. Although British colonial rule did not allow democracy, and Hong Kong's present demands for democracy could not be simply attributed to its lingering nostalgia for the benevolent colonial rule, the colonial experience may have better prepared Hong Kong to demand democracy. The colonial past is an inevitable presence in the assertion of Hong Kong's autonomy against Beijing's control as a distinct feature of Hong Kong difference.

The postcolonized experiences of Hong Kong may make the city more reluctant to accept the current wave of Chinese nationalization, a rigid Chinese national sovereignty against the divided sovereignty between UK and Hong Kong local elites. What Hong Kong people mainly identify with in their postcolonized experiences is probably the increasing commitment to local interests. Different from British colonial officials, the special administrative region officials, in Hong Kong people's view, serve primarily Beijing's interests. It is now the People's Republic of China, a potential contender with the United States for global hegemony, that appears more as a metropole colonizing power, especially in the acute, impending, and possibly epochal change in the international political structure. Another revealing dimension of nationalism (in this context the Chinese one) is that nation building itself is a colonial activity. Coloniality in nation building is most visible when the nation-state denies its subjects popular sovereignty and citizenship rights while imposing on them unconditional obligations of loyalty and service to the abstract notions of nationhood embodied by the state.

Notes

1 As a "man of high ideals whose devotion to the cause of peace was unwavering" (Bacevich 2002, 115), Wilson sent US troops to Haiti, the Dominican Republic, and Mexico to shape democracy there and teach them to elect good politicians. "In the president's own view, all these actions were well intentioned" (116).
2 Takeuchi Yoshimi argues that "Asianism is a 'mood' present all around, and the ideas that run through Japan's modern history are founded on this 'mood'" (quoted in G. Sun 2000, 29).
3 Following the monster metaphors of Leviathan and behemoth used to symbolize the artificial nature of the state in history, Yamamuro borrows the beast

chimera from Greek mythology for its three distinctive corporeal parts to characterize the Kwantung Army (the head of a lion), the state of the emperor system (the sheep), and the Chinese emperor and modern China (the tail) as the political combination of Manchukuo.

4   When Japan created Manchukuo, the majority of its population was Han Chinese (about 30 million). The Manchu, from whom the name Manchukuo was derived, were actually few in number or had been greatly assimilated into the majority Han Chinese. The Japanese population in Manchuria at the end of the Japanese Empire was estimated to be 1.5 million, which was relatively insignificant as a percentage of the total population.

Decolonization? What Decolonization?

The Die Was Cast

To a large extent, the die was cast when Huang Hua, the permanent representative to the United Nations from the People's Republic of China (PRC), secured the endorsement of his request to remove Hong Kong and Macau from the list of colonial territories under the terms of reference of the Special Committee on Decolonization in early 1972. Both the United Kingdom and the United States, at that time busy with working out their new diplomatic relationship with the PRC, did not raise any objection.[1] The removal of Hong Kong and Macau from the list of colonies implied that the settlement of the political future of these British and Portuguese colonies fell within the sovereign right of China, and thus the committee's declaration of the granting of independence to colonial territories and people was not applicable to them. With the United Kingdom's and United States' understanding, Hong Kong's future was not supposed to be a question of decolonization; it would be China's call about when it would be appropriate to prepare for Hong Kong's return.

I underline the acceptance of China's position on Hong Kong by the United Kingdom and United States because their implicit acceptance was part of the political maneuvering in the context of international politics at that conjuncture. Instead of the isolation and sometimes even open hostility it faced in the 1950s and 1960s,

China was approached with flexibility. Such strategic diplomatic moves happened at a time when the Maoist line still prevailed. When Mao Zedong passed away, the remaining Maoist clique was removed from power, and the Chinese Communist Party (CCP) announced the ending of the Cultural Revolution, China was further brought into closer contact with non-Soviet societies. Indeed, with the launching of economic reform and the resultant reopening of China in 1978, this socialist country was incorporated into a reconstituting world economy. Such was the macro setting of a repositioning of China that forms the backdrop for our understanding of the talks about Hong Kong's future in the 1980s and the design of the One Country, Two Systems (OCTS) blueprint for the establishment of the Hong Kong Special Administrative Region (SAR) after July 1, 1997. The discourses adopted by different concerned parties arising from this macro setting shaped the political and socioeconomic transitions of Hong Kong in the forty years that followed the mention of the colony's political status during a governor's visit to Beijing in 1979.

This chapter is an attempt to examine Hong Kong's political and socioeconomic transitions in the light of a discourse of economism. Hong Kong's return to China was always phrased as "an economic question." Mortgage arrangements beyond 1997 triggered the talks, initiated by the British, on how to "blur" the issues about Hong Kong's uncertain future. China accepted Hong Kong's special status, at least partially, because of strategic economic considerations. Hong Kong's hope of maintaining the status quo was based on its economic value and a projection of China's commitment to marketization. The OCTS was expected to keep capitalist Hong Kong and socialist China apart so that the former would have "a high degree of autonomy" (One Country Two Systems Economic Research Institute 1992, 6). But it was marketization and economic liberalization, and the resultant flows of capital and people, that gradually posed a serious challenge to the original blueprint. At the same time, the avoidance of politics in sorting out Hong Kong's future, an approach adopted by the concerned parties during the negotiations, was found problematic. The SAR could not be effectively governed simply on the basis of a political structure largely inherited from the colonial past. The long-suppressed agenda for political development was brought to the forefront of current contentions. The discourse of economism was not able to contain demands for political changes, and post-1997 Hong Kong found herself dealing with challenging questions that the OCTS blueprint had not prepared for.

"Longer-Term Consideration"

There has always been a sense of uncertainty in Hong Kong's political status. The ninety-nine-year lease of the New Territories (whereas Hong Kong Island and Kowloon, the other two major geographic components of colonial Hong Kong, were ceded to Britain as a result of the signing of unequal treaties in 1842 and 1860, respectively) implied the existence of an expiry date for this former British colony. For this reason the British colony was described as a "borrowed place living on borrowed time" (Hughes 1976, 13). Toward the end of World War II, there were concerns about whether it should be returned to the Nationalist government of China or to Britain when the Japanese surrendered. The intervention by the United States upset Chiang Kai-shek's plan of resuming sovereignty over Hong Kong, and the British continued to govern the colony (Louis 1997, 1055). But very soon uncertainty arose because of the civil war in China. When the Communists' victory was in sight and the PRC would soon be established in late 1949, instead of upholding national integrity, the People's Army stopped making further advances on October 17, 1949 (Louis 1997, 1082), and the new government seemed to have put the issue of Hong Kong's colonial status quo aside, at least for the moment.

It was suggested that, at that moment, the CCP wanted to focus on internal nation building, avoiding the creation of tension and disagreement with countries like the United Kingdom and United States (Louis 1997, 1083). The decision was primarily driven by political and diplomatic considerations in the context of an international political environment that was hostile toward the spread of communism (Li H. 1997, 47). Pragmatism prevailed. In the years to follow, China began to recognize the functions of such a status quo—Hong Kong became a "window" for maintaining contact outside of the Soviet bloc and a source of economic benefits. The approach to Hong Kong was summarized as a matter "for longer-term consideration and fully utilizing the advantages offered by Hong Kong" (*changqi dasuan, chongfen liyong* 長期打算, 充份利用) (Huang W. 1997, 3). The outbreak of the Korean War further strengthened the maintenance of the status quo from both sides of the political rivalry. And things stayed that way from the 1950s onward. Even in the mid-1960s, which witnessed a spillover of political radicalism from the Cultural Revolution in the mainland to Hong Kong, with open confrontations between the colonial regime and pro-Beijing political forces during the 1967 riots, the political status of the colony was kept intact. Huang Hua's success in removing Hong Kong and Macau from the list of colonies seemed to have further reinforced such a state of development: as long as China and Britain found the status quo beneficial, and the people living in the colony were happy too, the question concerning Hong Kong's future could be set aside. The clock ticked; year after year, the end date of 1997 approached. Yet, interestingly, the "precarious balance" (M. Chan 1994) between China and Britain with Hong Kong in between seemed to function well after the 1967 riots in Hong Kong. The pragmatic approach adopted by China continued to prevail despite turbulent politics in its own domestic environment. Meanwhile, the governorship of Murray MacLehose (1971–82) was well received by the locals. Ian Scott (1989, 127–70) described the colony in the 1970s as "autonomous Hong Kong"—enjoying "the relative autonomy of the bureaucratic elite both from other elites and from the British and Chinese governments" (165). Ironically, it was in such an atmosphere—when Hong Kong was largely left on its own and began to explore its newly found identity (Baker 1983)—that the question of its political future was raised.

When "the Time Is Ripe"

Upon receiving an invitation to visit China in December 1978, which was seen as a friendly gesture, Governor MacLehose sought London's guidance. His arguments, together with those put forward by Percy Cradock, the ambassador in Beijing, for taking this opportunity to raise the question concerning land leases in the New Territories were deliberated. The Foreign and Commonwealth Office noted:

> The lease [of the New Territories] is due to expire in 1997, and until now property leases in the New Territories have always specified that year as their terminal date. This is bound to become a very serious deterrent to new investment as time goes on. The Governor's assessment, with which I agree, is that confidence will begin to erode quite quickly in the early-to-mid-1980s if nothing is done to remove the significance of the 1997 deadline in a way which is consistent with the Chinese position that the future of Hong Kong is a problem to be settled when "the time is ripe." A possible solution, which ought not to cause the Chinese too many difficulties, would be to convert the existing leases into ones whose length is "undetermined," and would thus bring the legal position into line with the political realities.[2]

The strategy was to blur the 1997 deadline (Tsang 1997, 84), replacing the expiry date with the phrase "as long as British administration continues."[3]

MacLehose believed "the invitation came at a time when we were already considering how to deal with a problem which is not yet acute, but which could become so over the next few years."[4] He raised the question concerning land leases when he met Vice Premier Deng Xiaoping. The outcomes were mixed. MacLehose paraphrased Deng's statement as saying that the investors in Hong Kong should "put their hearts at ease" (Chung 2001, 31).

What had not been made public were three important points. First, Deng coupled Hong Kong with Taiwan in the way he saw the longer-term solution to resolve their political status. Second, he objected to the phrase "as long as British administration continues." Third, he mentioned his concept of Hong Kong's future with "a specially guaranteed status under Chinese sovereignty and new (undefined) political arrangements."[5] It was suggested that "Hong Kong mov[e] to a special status under which, while continuing to function as a capitalist economy, it would be subject to Chinese sovereignty."[6]

As the question of Hong Kong's future evolved, MacLehose further noted, "The Chinese seem to be envisaging a capitalist society in Hong Kong which they themselves direct.... They may well see the special economic zone at Shum Chum [Shenzhen] as a place where capitalists, both Chinese and foreign, will learn that they can operate successfully under Chinese rule. It may take time before they realize that, for many years to come at least, essential elements of a successfully capitalist Hong Kong will be UK management and UK law and a currency separate to China's, and the confidence of investors that all these will continue."[7]

Furthermore, as recorded in the notes of a meeting between the UK secretary of state and MacLehose, the governor pointed out that the Chinese were beginning to recognize the short-term issues over land leases. Bankers' practice of granting fifteen-year mortgages implied that 1982 would be a significant year.[8]

At that time, many saw it as a good opportunity to push for a deal for Hong Kong's future. China was eager to secure support from Hong Kong, as a window to the world and a source of investment, to kick-start economic reform, after just recovering from the painful Cultural Revolution. Such conditions allowed the colony to have some leverage, and so the British posed the question of Hong Kong's future (Huang W. 1997, 3). Not very long after the meeting between MacLehose and Deng, China started its preparations in 1981 for a plan for Hong Kong's future too (Huang W. 1997, 6). The stage was set for the formal talks in 1982.

The End of "Borrowed Time"

Prime Minister Margaret Thatcher's visit to Beijing in 1982 ushered in the formal and open diplomatic talks between the Chinese and UK governments over Hong Kong's political future. The stormy meeting between Thatcher and Deng concluded with the clear signal that China stood firm on the issue of sovereignty. From then on, the 1997 question was more about the terms of reversion in the course of leading to Britain's withdrawal than about the choice among different political options (e.g., retaining British administration after 1997). China took the initiative in releasing, unilaterally, its twelve-point outline (adapted from its plan for unification of Taiwan) for the OCTS approach to Hong Kong's future in July 1983. Meanwhile, diplomatic talks between Britain and China were deadlocked. Hong Kong's future was left uncertain. As a result, the Hong Kong dollar collapsed in September, and people's confidence crumpled.

Given that a large share of the colony's population was composed of refugees and (legal and illegal) migrants from China who had direct or indirect experience of political campaigns after the Communist Revolution in 1949, such public response was understandable. The hint that Hong Kong would return to China in 1997, if not earlier, triggered fear and anxiety. In this regard, the prospect of having some kind of agreement between China and Britain on the colony's immediate and more distant future was a relief—at least the status quo would be maintained for the time being. The Joint Declaration of the Government of the United Kingdom of Great Britain and the Government of the People's Republic of China on the Question of Hong Kong, contrary to China's repeated attempts to deny the validity of the unequal treaties of the nineteenth century, formally recognized the British colonial government's effective rule over Hong Kong, at least up to June 30, 1997. At the same time, it was also formally stated that Hong Kong would return to China, and the colonial rule would be terminated on July 1.

A Political Compromise

The main concern of the negotiations between China and Britain in the early 1980s was working out an arrangement that the two concerned nations, as well as Hong Kong, would find "acceptable." Of course, the meaning of *acceptable* was contentious, and even today this continues to be a subject of heated argument. Yet, disagreement and argument notwithstanding, Hong Kong was given a framework to work out its future, according to the Joint

Declaration: "The Hong Kong SAR will enjoy a high degree of autonomy, except in foreign and defence affairs" and "The current social and economic systems in Hong Kong will remain unchanged, and so will the life-style" (One Country Two Systems Economic Research Institute 1992, 90). Though the meaning of "a high degree of autonomy" had not been clearly spelled out (Gittings 2013, 55), these promises constituted the key ingredients of the OCTS.

The political design of the OCTS was never an outcome of a consensus among all the concerned parties. China, Britain, and Hong Kong each respectively had their own agenda and priorities. For China, bringing Hong Kong's colonial status to an end was, at least partly, a question of national pride and dignity. Beijing leaders were ready to accommodate a capitalist Hong Kong in the Chinese socialist system in order to pacify the fear of the local people and respond to the skepticism of the international community. At the same time, there were pragmatic calculations that a prosperous Hong Kong would be most functional to China's project of Four Modernizations, the continuation of its economic reform, and the acquisition of the technical and managerial know-hows of the outside world via the colony. The maintenance of prosperity and stability in Hong Kong was not merely a concern of the local population; it was also China's key consideration. The purpose was not to liberate the colony. Hong Kong was valuable because it was a prosperous capitalist economy.

On the British side, handing over its colony to a socialist regime was a matter of controversy in the 1980s. Working out a resolution that could accommodate China's position and also guarantee the colony that its existing socioeconomic institutions would be disturbed as little as possible was a challenge. An agreement based on guarantees made by China in front of the international community looked respectable.

In the eyes of Hong Kong's people, who were not given the opportunity to have their representative join the negotiations, the offering of OCTS meant that at least there was no imminent threat that the colony would immediately revert to China. The promise of retaining free-market capitalism and some of the key features of the colonial system (e.g., the rule of law) seemed reassuring. How the future would evolve remained uncertain, but the intention was to maintain the status quo.

At the macro level, it was a political compromise among China, Britain, and Hong Kong. At the micro level, it was a political compromise among different social classes. Beijing's focus was on building a united front by actively rallying the support of the capitalist class of Hong Kong (Xu Jiatun 1993, 121).

This was partly out of fear of capital flight. It was also partly embedded in the notion of OCTS: the framework was designed to accommodate Hong Kong's capitalist economic system within China's socialism, and this could not be done without the capitalists' participation. Indeed, the nationalist capitalist class (i.e., the Chinese capitalists) was expected to play an important part in putting OCTS into practice (128). This united-front strategy was successfully carried out by assuring the capitalists the protection of their property rights, actively engaging them by offering them important roles in drafting the Basic Law (Fong 2015, 103–17; Goodstadt 2000), and providing them with investment opportunities in the mainland.

The middle class (professionals, managers, and administrators) reacted strongly to the unanticipated changes in Hong Kong's political status. Most of them had enjoyed upward social mobility under colonial rule in the postwar decades. Any change in the existing socioeconomic system would jeopardize their interests. They were skeptical of the promise of keeping "two systems" within "one country." Faced with an uncertain future, they were anxious and restless.

Though some middle-class professionals and former university student activists formed political groups and took part in various newly established channels of political participation, the dominant coping strategy adopted by the middle class was emigration (Lui 1999b). It was a strategy of obtaining some kind of "political insurance" by acquiring a foreign passport (Salaff and Wong 1994, 220). By doing so, they could dissociate the personal from the social: no matter what happened to post-1997 Hong Kong, they would have the option of exit. In practice, many sent their family members abroad to process their foreign-citizenship papers while they themselves stayed in Hong Kong to take advantage of the booming economy. Also, many went back to the colony as returnees once they had obtained their new passports.

The rest of the population had few options. Life experiences and personal attitudes under colonialism and laissez-faire capitalism varied, but few saw themselves as victims of oppression and/or injustice. Given the rapid pace of economic growth and development in the postwar decades, many families had been able to improve their standard of living and find opportunities for intergenerational mobility. Their preference was to keep things as they were. As long as the status quo was preserved, they remained acquiescent.

It was out of a balance of such diverse interests and concerns that OCTS was taken as a promise that could partially satisfy the concerned parties. For China, Hong Kong would be returned to its motherland in 1997, upholding China's national unity and territorial integrity. Yet China's actual power over the SAR would be compromised in selected areas. It had to accept the existence of a capitalist economy within the national framework. Article 8 of the Basic Law states, "The laws previously in force in Hong Kong, that is, the common law, rules of equity, ordinances, subordinate legislation and customary law shall be maintained, except for any that contravene this Law, and subject to any amendment by the legislature of the Hong Kong SAR" (One Country Two Systems Economic Research Institute 1992, 6). Such compromises imposed certain restrictions on the exercise of power by the socialist state. For Britain, the deal allowed it to step down from its previous role as the sovereign state over colonial Hong Kong in a dignified manner. At least, there would be sufficient measures (e.g., the drafting of the Basic Law) to ensure that Hong Kong would continue to be a capitalist free port with the rule of law and protection of personal freedom. For Hong Kong, the threat of an immediate or premature takeover was ruled out, and the status quo would be kept in 1997 and thereafter for at least another fifty years. True, in the eyes of many, this promise was still not reassuring enough. Thus, there were waves of emigration to countries like Canada, Australia, and the United States in the 1980s and early 1990s (especially after the Tiananmen Incident in 1989). Yet, despite people's doubts and reservations, the future of Hong Kong was largely settled then.

Institutional Continuity and the Minimization of Change
in Political Transition

Being, however, the outcome of a historical compromise, OCTS also left some expectations unmet. China, though eager to fully utilize Hong Kong's contributions to push its modernization and market reform, had to stay alert to negative influences, like "spiritual pollution," emanating from the future SAR. As for Britain, how OCTS would be worked out remained uncertain, and this could be a source of tension in future Sino-British relations. For Hong Kong, the return to an authoritarian regime inevitably created worry and anxiety. And the sense of anxiety lingered throughout the process of political transition (Lui 1999a). In this connection, tensions, disagreements, and conflicts emerging from the implementation of OCTS were almost inevitable. Each of the concerned parties found that OCTS in practice fell short of their expectations. In particular, China faced constraints in the exercise of its sovereign rights over Hong Kong. Meanwhile, Hong Kong looked forward to the realization of a higher degree of autonomy. Questions concerning the pace and scope of democratization captured more attention from 2003 onward.

Beijing's resistance to such political demands was seen, at least by the political opposition, as a sign of the curtailing of the SAR's autonomy. Such frustrations continued to build up and subsequently led to major confrontations between Beijing and Hong Kong.

Yet, at one point in time, the promise of institutional continuity had formed the basis of the historical compromise. Indeed, the main theme underlying OCTS was the maintenance of the status quo—changes in the existing institutional arrangements should be minimized. Any change other than a change of Hong Kong's political status should be as small as possible. It was on the basis of such a tacit understanding that China's representatives described the process as not much more than a change of flag at 00:00 on July 1, 1997.

In a broad stroke, the Hong Kong SAR was prescribed to remain a capitalist economy with a partially democratized political system. The so-called executive-led administrative system, largely modeled on the previous colonial bureaucratic administration, was expected to continue to function smoothly. Institutional features found to be conducive to Hong Kong's success in attaining economic prosperity and political stability in the postwar decades were written into the Basic Law. Free-market capitalism was upheld to curb potential threats from the mainland and to contain growing demands for welfare provision from local social activists. The political system was only partially democratized so that politics would be downplayed (with the Hong Kong SAR government's bureaucratic administration managing daily public affairs). The judicial system was basically kept unchanged, and this, together with the guarantees of civil liberty and personal freedom, formed a shield to protect Hong Kong from interference by the authoritarian socialist state. These key ingredients of the recipe for Hong Kong's success in the 1980s were "deep-frozen" in the Basic Law, to be "defrosted" in 1997 so that the success story would continue. Meanwhile, Beijing was quite happy to inherit the colonial institutional structure so that the future SAR would still be a "business city." It was a farewell to colonial rule without doing much about the preexisting socioeconomic and political system.

The design of OCTS intentionally included the preservation of certain colonial legacies. The use of the English language was one (Article 9 of the Basic Law). The continuation of the common-law legal system was another (Basic Law, Chapter IV, Section 4). Such conscious attempts at preserving some of the key elements of the colonial superstructure had to do with the belief that such institutional arrangements had assisted Hong Kong in becoming a global city and assuming an important role in the international business world. So, from the very beginning, the resumption of sovereignty over Hong Kong was not intended to liberate the former British colony. It was not intended to turn the world upside down. Institutional continuity was underlined for the practical reason of maintaining economic prosperity and political stability after 1997. In this connection Li Ruihuan 李瑞環, then the head of the Political Consultative Conference, drew an analogy comparing Hong Kong to an old teapot—in order to recognize the subtlety and value of Hong Kong's preexisting practices, instead of performing a thorough cleanup, one had to appreciate the sedimentation and accumulation of its historical past (Yahuda 1997, 204). Li's statement in March 1995 during a meeting with the Hong Kong and Macau representatives to the Chinese People's Political Consultative Conference served to comfort the people of Hong Kong at a time when the relationship between Britain and China soured. But it was also a reinstatement of the pragmatic considerations built into the OCTS framework. If certain ingredients of its superstructure could promote capitalist development and thus economic prosperity, then they would be allowed to stay.

Yet, in retrospect, the assumption that Hong Kong would continue to excel after 1997 without making any changes to its recipe for success in the colonial eras seems untenable, as the macro-, meso-, and microenvironments underwent rapid changes from the time the Basic Law was drafted to the establishment of the SAR. Also, to guide Hong Kong's navigation of the transition into an unknown political future, OCTS should have looked into the future. Yet, paradoxically, the main theme of the political compromise then was a minimization of economic, social, and political changes. Instead of looking ahead and anticipating emergent problems in the process of political transition, the prevailing view heavily emphasized preservation, preserving what was already there in Hong Kong's economic, social, and political system and ensuring that it would continue to function in the way it did under colonial rule.

As a passive measure, the promise of maintaining the status quo and minimizing changes meant that things would remain the same after 1997. But in the deeper structure of this status quo discourse, there was a belief, or, say, a projection, that Hong Kong's system would prevail despite its embeddedness in China's one-country framework. In different forms, the modes of thinking of all the concerned parties shared such a belief. As shown in an earlier section, Governor MacLehose saw the importance of retaining British management, the preexisting legal system, and a separate currency to maintain investors' confidence in a Hong Kong under Chinese rule. He seemed skeptical of the socialist sociopolitical system. Yet doing business according to capitalist norms would allow for a loosening of the socialist grip. It would take years for China to catch up, but this was possible. On the Chinese side, the notion of "two systems" was developed at a time when it had just launched its special economic zones. It was China's intention to fully capitalize on Hong Kong's advantageous position and competitiveness to further its market-reform project. Though the need to guard against bourgeois liberalization repeatedly came up in official statements on OCTS, Deng Xiaoping saw OCTS in a wider context of national strategic development. The promise of upholding OCTS for at least fifty years after 1997 rested on longer-term changes in the Chinese economy:

> Why 50 years? . . . We need not only to reassure the people of Hong Kong but also to take into consideration the close relation between prosperity and stability of Hong Kong and the strategy for the development of China. The time needed for development includes the last 12 years of this century and the first 50 years of the next. So, how can we change our policy during those 50 years? Now there is only one Hong Kong, but we plan to build several more Hong Kongs in the interior. In other words, to achieve the strategic objective of development, we need to open wider to the outside world. Such being the case, how can we change our policy towards Hong Kong? (Deng 1993, 61)

Underlying Deng's comment on the promise of maintaining OCTS for at least fifty years was a vision of gradual liberalization of China's socialist economy. The deepening of economic reform in the mainland would smooth the process of integrating Hong Kong into the master framework of "one country." Economic liberalization would ease the tension between capitalist Hong Kong and the socialist mainland.

On the side of Hong Kong, China's commitment to economic reform allowed its people to develop a new sense of optimism. Maoist politics belonged to the past, and modernization as well as marketization would soften the CCP's authoritarian rule. The proliferation of private business, growing affluence, and a new environment with emphasis on economic drives reshaped the role of the socialist state and ordinary people's mentality and everyday life. Deng Xiaoping's visit to southern China in 1992 confirmed the commitment to a deepening of economic reform. The pace of marketization galloped. Anxieties arising from the crash of the student movement in 1989 lingered but were gradually diluted by the imagination of a marketized and liberalized China. Outside the political domain, everyday-life China was becoming less intimidating. With such a positive outlook for a marketized

China, many Hong Kong people saw progress in China's socioeconomic development and evaluated the post-1997 future from a new perspective.

The shared premises of the projected future of Hong Kong as a relatively autonomous sociopolitical entity rested on a discourse of economism. Hong Kong's future hung on the promise of remaining a capitalist economy—China would continue to "fully utilize" the benefits of a capitalist Hong Kong SAR. A very important assumption in OCTS and the contents of the Basic Law is to ensure that Hong Kong will remain a capitalist economy. The stipulations in the Basic Law have done more than just keep capitalism intact in the SAR. The intention was to preserve "a special kind of capitalism" (Ghai 1999, 139)—according to the prescriptions in Chapter V of the Basic Law, "no foreign exchange control policies shall be applied," the status of a free port and the policy of free trade would be upheld, a low-tax policy would be pursued, and "the principle of keeping expenditure within the limits of revenues in drawing up its budget" would be followed (One Country Two Systems Economic Research Institute 1992, 38).

It is also important to recognize that the "two systems" in the framework of OCTS referred to capitalism and socialism. The separation of the two systems was emphasized (Ghai 1999, 140–41). At one point, many saw the separation of capitalism from socialism as a means to ensure the future SAR's autonomy (i.e., autonomy from socialist intervention). But, ironically, it was exactly during the drafting of the Basic Law in the late 1980s that there witnessed the relocation of Hong Kong's manufacturing industries to the Pearl River Delta (S. Chiu and Lui 2009). While many Hong Kong people, including the factory owners who had relocated their plants across the border, were worried about the potential threat of the imposition of socialist practice on Hong Kong, the capitalist imperative drove the colony's economy toward regional integration. Hong Kong became the main source of "foreign" investment in China, and its capital played an important role in the marketization of the Chinese economy. Such a trend of development gradually reshaped the interface between Hong Kong and China.

Changing the Hong Kong–China Interface

Given the focus on maintaining the status quo, little effort had been made to project the progress of socioeconomic reforms in China and anticipate issues and problems that might arise when 1997 approached. In fact, before 1997, social development in China was largely conceived as static. At best, in the eyes of many people in Hong Kong, given the constraints of an authoritarian socialist regime, social and economic reforms there would progress only slowly. So, few policy makers bothered to consider whether a socioeconomic and political system designed in the 1980s would assist Hong Kong in coping with a China that by 1997 had been undergoing economic reform for almost twenty years. Even up to 1997, there was limited awareness of how further socioeconomic changes across the border might pose new challenges to the assumptions embedded in OCTS. But very soon Hong Kong found itself overwhelmed by the flows of money and people from China. Marketization had brought Hong Kong and China closer to each other. The boundary between the two systems was blurred. More important, the one-way flows of capital and economic activity from Hong Kong to the mainland in the earlier stage of development began to change. In fact, Tung Chee-hwa 董建華, then Hong Kong's chief executive, was aware of the growing strength of the Chinese economy, stating in his 2001 Policy Address that "Hong Kong's unique position, with the Mainland as our hinterland and extensive links to all corners of the globe, is a major and enviable advantage" (Hong Kong SAR Government 2001, 5). He called for a repositioning of Hong Kong: as a major city in China and Asia's world city, its future rested on the strength of China's growing economy. It was a repositioning because it implied a change from making use of Hong Kong's global connections to provide services to China to relying on "the backing from the Mainland and openness to the world" (*beikao neidi mianxiang quanqiu* 背靠內地, 面向全球) (6) for building existing and new economic strengths. The uniqueness of Hong Kong's position was summarized as follows: "Compared with other places, Hong Kong is indeed fortunate. At a time when foreign investors are vying to enter the China market, we are already well positioned to seize the opportunities they seek" (5).

While this repositioning did not immediately bring about major policy change, this line of thinking subsequently came to shape the basic orientation of the Closer Economic Partnership Arrangement, a measure launched by Beijing to help Hong Kong recover from its depressed economy as a result of the severe acute respiratory syndrome (SARS) in 2003 and to respond to growing political discontent in Hong Kong, as shown in the mass rally held on July 1 of the same year (Ma 2015, 44–45). Whereas in the past Hong Kong was always seen as a platform through which China could reach out to the world, with the former playing an active role in leading the latter onto the stage of the world economy, there was an increasing realization that a globalizing China was now shaping Hong Kong's future development. Hong Kong would have to adjust its own position and role to the new requirements of

China as an emerging economic power. With China's booming economy with high rates of economic growth, it was suggested that perhaps Hong Kong should try to make the best use of the wealth and consumption power in the mainland by bringing the money into the SAR's economy.

In these talks about letting flows of money, people, and activities into the Hong Kong SAR, the perspective was characterized by abstraction and disembeddedness. Money and people moving in and out of Hong Kong were barely abstract statistical figures for the gross domestic product, retail sales, and tourism. The economistic perspective simply assumed that such new inflows of money, people, and activities had limited connections to and effects on the community. Few, if any, attempts were made to evaluate the impacts of such flows on the local economy and community. Of course, by 2009–10 the impacts of mainland mothers giving birth in Hong Kong, the rapid increase in mainland tourists, and the shortage of milk powder owing to food-security issues across the border were strongly felt by the locals. By then, *regional integration* was no longer seen as a neutral term to describe the intensified flows of activity as well as more frequent interactions between Hong Kong and the mainland. Increasingly, it was seen as a problem, one that fueled rising hostility toward China, both the Beijing government and the mainlanders (Kwong and Yu 2013; also see K. Wong, Zheng, and Wan 2016).

Paradoxically, OCTS was undermined by the newly discovered two-way flows of money and people between the mainland and the SAR. That some fifty-one million Chinese tourists visited Hong Kong in 2018 gives the gist of the intensity of the traffic between the SAR and the mainland. This flow of people created other business opportunities as well. Between 2013 and 2016, "the office premium share in respect of new long term [insurance] policies issued to Mainland visitors had grown markedly from 16.1% to 39.3%" (Research Office, Legislative Council Secretariat 2019, 2). The growing trend was reversed after a tightening of control over capital outflow. In terms of capitalization in the Hong Kong stock market, China-related shares (i.e., H shares, Red Chips, and mainland private enterprises) constituted almost three-quarters (73.4 percent) of the Main Board's total in 2019 (Hong Kong Exchanges and Clearing Ltd. 2020). It was the marketized Chinese economy that posed the most serious challenge to OCTS. Market capitalism was once assumed to be a protective shield for Hong Kong. Not only would socialist China be softened as it went along the paths of economic liberalization, rejoining the world economy and thus conforming to standards prescribed by global business. It would also become more dependent on the SAR, which had the necessary experience and professional business support for conducting transnational business and reaching out to business partners in different parts of the world. Also, the market mechanism would help Hong Kong guard against interference by the socialist visible hand. Increasingly, however, China encroached on Hong Kong via the market. The size and scale of the purchasing power from China, ranging from tourist consumption to the acquisition of real estate, was simply daunting.

Missing Pieces in OCTS

There are two major missing pieces in the design of OCTS. First, the commitment to further democratization was ambivalent. While China took on board the idea of rule of law with some reluctance, its appropriation of the rather anachronistic colonial political structure of Hong Kong was a happy inheritance. That colonial Hong Kong was able to attain rapid economic development with a partially democratized administrative state gave China a good reason to hold back changes in political development that had been initiated by the colonial government. Its resistance to democratization was supported by the local business community. The worry, at the beginning, was about growing demands for social welfare and other state provisions that would undermine the smooth operation of market capitalism (Cheng 2004). After the crackdown on the Beijing student movement in 1989 and the reconstitution of the pro-democracy camp in the local political arena, the business community as well as the pro-Beijing groups found the voice for democratization a challenge to their political power. China simply did not believe it was necessary to make further concessions to the pro-democracy camp. Some form of election, as promised in the Joint Declaration, was introduced in the selection of the chief executive. And the legislature had already been partially democratized. Questions about legitimacy and political mandate were taken as something of minor importance. On the basis of such an understanding, the SAR's political structure could largely follow what had been practiced in the colonial days. In the eyes of Beijing, a controllable and predictable political structure was of paramount importance. Such a mode of political reasoning continued despite growing discontent and rising challenges to the SAR government from 2003 onward.

As pointed out by most observers of Hong Kong politics after 1997 (e.g., Fong 2015), the termination of colonial rule reshaped state-society relations. The SAR government was repeatedly challenged for not being able to secure popular support and a political mandate from the people. Its political authority was badly eroded, and both its political capacity and effectiveness of governance were undermined. If the political institutions were part of Hong Kong's colonial legacy that China consciously and eagerly inherited, this colonial inheritance was no longer functional after the change in the colony's political status.

Second, there had never been a clear statement on the relations between the central government and the SAR. Hong Kong is a "local administrative region of the People's Republic of China," "enjoying a high degree of autonomy" (One Country Two Systems Economic Research Institute 1992, 9). But as noted earlier, the definition of *autonomy* was not clearly stated (Ghai 1999; Gittings 2013). The statement that the SAR had "a high degree of autonomy, except in foreign and defence affairs which are the responsibilities of the Central People's Government," gave many people the wrong impression that all domestic matters, seen as internal affairs, would be completely under the control of the SAR government (One Country Two Systems Economic Research Institute 1992, 90). But when the SAR was no longer a political and socioeconomic entity segregated from the mainland, the central government would inevitably assume a role in its governance.

In the drafting of the Basic Law, there were conscious efforts to contain the power of the central government. For instance, Article 106 states that the Hong Kong SAR "shall have independent finances." It "shall use its financial revenues exclusively for its own purposes, and they shall not be handed over to the Central People's Government." Also, "the Central People's Government shall not levy taxes in the Hong Kong SAR" (One Country Two Systems Economic Research Institute 1992, 38). The hidden agenda of the above stipulations was to prevent the central government from taking money out of Hong Kong. Furthermore, Article 105 states that "the Hong Kong SAR shall . . . protect the right of individuals and legal persons to the acquisition, use, disposal and inheritance of property and their right to compensation for lawful deprivation of their property. Such compensation shall correspond to the real value of the property concerned at the time and shall be freely convertible and paid without undue delay" (38). The hidden message was a fear of socialist interference in the SAR's domestic finances and of the socialist government's confiscation of personal property. All the above stipulations pointed to a certain perception of China in the 1980s—Beijing was heavily guarded against the possibility of appropriating money, property, and other assets from Hong Kong.

In Chapter II of the Basic Law, again there are stipulations that would curb the central government's interference and prevent non–Hong Kong government bodies from managing the domestic affairs of the SAR (see, for example, Article 22). But all these measures failed to equip Hong Kong to live with China when the two parties became counterparts within the same market. Nor did they prepare Hong Kong to face the challenge of being a "local administrative region" under the central government. The 1997 question was about China's resumption of sovereignty over Hong Kong. But it turned out that the question of sovereignty had not been adequately addressed. It was deliberately downplayed, largely for the sake of pacifying Hong Kong's people at a time when they found the prospect of the colony's return to China worrying. Stationing the People's Liberation Army in the SAR was taken as a symbol of Chinese sovereignty. But even then restrictions were imposed on the garrison: "Military forces stationed by the Central People's Government in the Hong Kong SAR for defence shall not interfere in the local affairs of the Region" (One Country Two Systems Economic Research Institute 1992, 9). However, when Hong Kong returned to China, the central government would not be just a backdrop. Beijing's fear of subversive activities and issues of national security, according to its definition, would pop up in a matter of time. As China's economy continued to be vibrant and to expand, again it was a matter of time before its economic planning, as shown in its Five-Year Plan, touched on the SAR. Hong Kong, an open and largely liberal social environment, had to deal with coexisting with an authoritarian regime. Tensions, always there, gradually came to form cleavages. The Basic Law did not offer a clear statement on the relations between the central government and the SAR at the operational level. And this sowed the seeds for future conflicts.

From Tensions to Open Conflicts

The framework based on economism was not able to contain the spread of conflict along political cleavages after 1997. The compromise reached in the 1980s to maintain the status quo set out to deal with the major differences between a capitalist and a socialist economy. Protection of private property, safeguards against socialist interference, and a guarantee of personal freedom addressed most, if not all, of the main worries at that time. Moreover, China's rapid economic growth along the path of marketization gave many people the hope of further liberalization with the rise of the middle class and the formation of civil society. China's economic growth and development would help reduce uneasiness and anxiety about living under the one-country framework. But this mode of thinking could not handle confrontations over political matters.

The appeal of economism was significantly weakened when regional and national integration did not necessarily bring opportunities and tangible material rewards to people from different walks of life (Lui 2015). Also, as noted earlier, the intensification of flows of money and people created tensions between the locals and the mainlanders. More important, when it came to matters concerning Hong Kong's future political development, especially the pace and extent of democratization, the conventional discourse of economism simply failed to address the growing discontent arising from stagnation in democratization. Different chief executives and their administrative teams repeatedly failed to win the support of the public. The decay of political legitimacy was seen more as a structural issue than an issue of flawed individual politicians. Tung Chee-hwa's premature resignation from the office of the chief executive in 2004 barely eased the political tensions, and only for a short time. The loss of confidence and trust happened again when Donald Tsang and C. Y. Leung led the Hong Kong SAR government in 2004–12 and 2012–17, respectively. Debates on political reform resumed. In an attempt to preempt the political opposition from pushing their agendas, Beijing propagated its positional document entitled *The Practice of the "One Country, Two Systems" Policy in the Hong Kong Special Administrative Region* (Information Office of the State Council 2014). It was emphasized that Beijing had *quanmian guanzhiquan* (全面管治權) over the Hong Kong SAR. In the English version of the paper, the term was translated as "overall jurisdiction"; in fact, it was intended to mean an encompassing power of domination. Accordingly, "the system of the SAR . . . is a special administrative system developed by the state for certain regions" (Information Office of the State Council 2014, 9), and the high degree of autonomy enjoyed by the SAR was under the supervision of the central government. This was not able to stop those planning "Occupy Central" from pursuing political mobilization. Later, the Standing Committee of the National People's Congress simply announced its decision to retain strict control of the nomination procedure for candidacy for election as chief executive. This subsequently led to the eruption of the Umbrella Movement, a massive political mobilization and extended protest that lasted from September 26 to December 15, 2014.

Concluding Remarks

To a large extent, Hong Kong's political crisis persisted after the end of the Umbrella Movement. Divisions and cleavages stayed on and would sooner or later come back into the public arena. That said, few observers anticipated an even bigger-scale, and more confrontational, political contention in 2019. The Anti-Extradition Bill Movement, an extended confrontational campaign triggered by an attempt to amend the Fugitive Offenders Ordinance—perceived as a move to undermine legal protection and to allow for Beijing's intrusion into the SAR—erupted in a context of "movement abeyance" (Lee et al. 2019, 7), expressing deep-seated distrust of the SAR government and China. On one side, there were peaceful demonstrations, road blockades, rail sabotage, attacks with petrol bombs, and the destruction of allegedly pro-Beijing cafes and restaurants; on the other, there were dispersals of crowds, firing of tear gas and pepper spray, shooting of rubber bullets, and disproportionate application of violence. As the confrontation escalated, violence, from both sides, also spiraled. While the Hong Kong SAR government failed to respond to the protesters and restore social and political order, the activists were also unable to rearticulate their demands and go beyond street confrontation. The latter tried to rally international support by appealing to foreign governments. But this ended up becoming swirled into the vortex of the growing Sino-American rivalry. The deadlock opened a window for Beijing to crudely step in, sidestepping the SAR's legislature through the passage of the Hong Kong National Security Law by the National People's Congress Standing Committee in June 2020. The whole matter was handled in a most un–Hong Kong manner; the new national security law is the first law in Hong Kong to be gazetted without an English version.

Is this the end of OCTS? Probably not in the sense of the coexistence of capitalism and socialism in the SAR. Hong Kong's stock market has continued to be vibrant in the midst of political contention and the COVID-19 pandemic. No more autonomous Hong Kong? That depends on the judgment of what constitutes relative autonomy. Hong Kong's autonomy is always conditional and rests on a delicate balance of different forces. Now the balance has been upset, and the one-country and two-system balance will be redefined. In the past the emphasis of OCTS was on institutional continuity. But this simply failed to equip Hong Kong society to deal with the underlying contradictions. Once it was also believed that economism would help bypass questions arising from decolonization. Now the writing is on the wall.

Notes

Archival research for this chapter was supported by a Start-Up Research Grant from the Education University of Hong Kong.

1 Objections came from Venezuela, Fiji, and Sweden. Britain only expressed the view that the resolution would not affect the current status of Hong Kong. Nihal Jayawickrama (1991, 165) connects Britain's acquiescence with the deci-

sion to exchange ambassadors with the PRC and the withdrawal of its official representation in Taiwan in the same month.

2 David Owen to prime minister, "UK/China Relations: Hong Kong," February 9, 1979, the National Archives Commonwealth Office and Foreign and Commonwealth Office (TNA FCO) 40/1047.
3 MacLehose to McLaren, "Visit to China and the Leases," April 10, 1979, TNA FCO 40/1047.
4 MacLehose to Owen, April 11, 1979, TNA FCO 40/1047.
5 MacLehose to McLaren, "Visit to China and the Leases," April 10, 1979, TNA FCO 40/1047.
6 W.E. Quantrill on "Governor of Hong Kong's Visit to China," April 20, 1979, TNA FCO 40/1047.
7 MacLehose to Donald, "Leases and the Future of Hong Kong," July 7, 1980, TNA FCO 40/1162.
8 Meeting between the Secretary of State and the Governor of Hong Kong, November 5, 1980, TNA FCO 40/1156.

Elaine Yee Lin Ho

Locating Anglophone Writing in Sinophone Hong Kong

The narrative of colonial loss, anticolonial resistance, cultural retrieval, and national renewal offers one of the most globally recognizable discursive frameworks in which the Hong Kong decolonizing story might be told. Until recently, this story was largely regarded as having reached its conclusion as the sovereignty of the People's Republic of China (PRC) over Hong Kong appeared undisputed. When Occupy Hong Kong erupted in 2014, what had long been labeled a capitalist consumerist enclave where peaceable natives prioritized economic well-being above sociopolitical concerns appeared to transform overnight into a site of fervent political dissent. As usual, international attention focused on daily events as they happened, and the Occupy movement provided a partial framework in which the Hong Kong protests could be globally legible. But as both local and global Occupy movements receded, Hong Kong was co-opted back into predictable narratives of financial enterprise aligned to the PRC's economic ascendancy.[1] When protests erupted again in 2019, their vigor and persistence despite escalating government suppression again captured world headlines. Beyond the feverish daily updates, the protests called out for attention to a particular "Hong Kong story" that had yet to become globally legible.[2] In 2020 the crushing response of the central Chinese government to these events showed that they had in mind an entirely different story for Hong Kong.

While the sociohistorical conditions of Hong Kong's postcoloniality have been the subject of a number of illuminating studies, what has been lacking are longer-term studies, from the perspective of literature and literary culture, that could offer an explanatory framework for the more recent social movements.³ This chapter aims to contribute to ongoing critical inquiry, in this volume and others, into the "Hong Kong story." Whether the passage of the new national security law n(NSL) in July 2020 will bring an end to the protest movements or hasten their transformations in civil society, and what this will mean for anglophone, as for other, writing, is part of Hong Kong's unfolding story. Historically, the space of anglophone writing had long been restricted, its prospects often no more than the hope of committed individuals and small collectives. How this experience may be brought to bear on expressiveness and publication under the NSL's draconian and global proscriptions will open up another chapter of trial and struggle.⁴

In many former British colonies that achieved independence, the history of decolonization flowed into the timescale of the fragmenting nation and failing state. Writing about postcolonial Nigeria, Simon Gikandi speaks of "a past of promise" betrayed in "a present of failure" (1991, 136) that captured the imagination of postcolonial writers. From this perspective Hong Kong, not an independent nation but promised a high degree of autonomy under One Country, Two Systems, as a special administrative region (SAR) of the PRC after 1997, has become the latest site of this betrayal. The crucial question for this chapter is how anglophone Hong Kong writing can be read, not as literature per se, nor as allegories of postcolonial failure, but as profoundly engaged with telling the story of the place. From the past century to the present, in its habitats, practices, reception, thematics, and poetics, anglophone writing is marked by Hong Kong's colonial-capitalist self-identity. Struggling against this identity, it also resonates in and of a more remarkable story.

In probing the Hong Kong story instantiated in anglophone writing, this chapter acknowledges from the outset that the use of English in fictional and literary writing has long been the practice of a minority in Hong Kong, while the language itself enjoyed privileged colonial status and continued as an official language post-1997. Access to English was long perceived as the route to success, the ability to use English proficiently in everyday work a mark of this success achieved, in a neocolonial perversion of the critical import of Frantz Fanon's remark that "a man who has a language consequently possesses the world expressed and implied by that language" ([1967] 1986, 18). Because English as the colonial language was often regarded as the oppressive other, many Hong Kong writers, especially those who could write in Chinese, felt politically and ethically compelled to define themselves against it. The late Ping-kwan Leung (Yarsi), poet and public intellectual, has spoken eloquently of a resistant formation: "I think growing up in Hong Kong has put a particular psychological block on us in the use of English. It has become in this society a means of evaluation, a measure of one's social or economic status, a source of snobbery or mockery and so on, rather than a means of communication" (1992, 180–81). Leung's comments highlight the paradox of anglophone literary writing: its very minoritization is a function of the hegemonic elaboration of the English language, which enjoys high social status as symbolic capital in modern, capitalist Hong Kong before and after 1997.

Undistinguished by the kind of names and titles that constitute the postcolonial English literary pantheon of former British possessions like, for example, India and unlike Hong Kong film or the airport page-turners that exoticize Hong Kong, anglophone writing is largely invisible to international view. While in Singapore a state-sponsored literary culture flourished, English-language fictional writing was never officially promoted in Hong Kong.

Receiving little support from private and commercial sponsors, amid an English-language publishing industry invested in textbooks and self-help manuals, anglophone writing was largely pursued in private, paid for by authors working in a capitalist economy but detached from the economy itself. Its readership was largely drawn from writers' circles and others in the education and cultural sectors for whom English usage was not simply instrumental, as it was for society at large. Under the colonial hegemony of English but in its own latitude outside official approval and commercial or mass appeal, anglophone writing appears as a condition of negative freedom that Isaiah Berlin, extrapolating from intellectual history, understands as "freedom from," or the absence of, external interference in what "the subject . . . a person or group of persons" does or is capable of doing (2002, 178, 169). Berlin makes the important point that negative freedom is "not incompatible with some kinds of autocracy, or . . . with the absence of self-government" (176). Surviving in obscurity, anglophone writing is subject to many of the conditions that maintain a stranglehold on Hong Kong's long-term aspirations to self-actualization, social well-being, and participatory politics, as this chapter will discuss in a moment.

Before doing so, I need to expand on the context and constraints in which this writing takes place.[5] *Anglophone writing* in this chapter denotes fictional and literary writing as a discourse and space of engagement between English and Cantonese-Chinese, or Sinophone, indigenous culture and language use in Hong Kong. To say this is not to insinuate exclusionary practices against other intra-Chinese linguistic intermixings in Hong Kong, or literature in non-English and non-Chinese languages. To locate anglophone writing in sinophone Hong Kong is to argue that a substantive study of Hong Kong history is unimaginable without reference to the majority Chinese population in Hong Kong and to the Cantonese-Chinese language in which most of this population lives its everyday life, communicates, and engages in acts of meaning making.[6] While this may sound uncontentious, scholars in different disciplines have identified two sources of pressure against which the Hong Kong story needs to struggle to be heard. According to translation studies scholar Martha Cheung, "A plethora of images has been imposed and superimposed on Hong Kong—by Western writers as well as those from the Mainland" (1998b, x). Describing Hong Kong as "a story that is hard to tell," Ping-kwan Leung, speaking in the context of Chinese-language writing, explained the difficulty as follows: "Over the years, there has been a steady stream of people from the outside seeking to tell the story of Hong Kong" (1998, 3, 4). These include "mainland artists" disparaging Hong Kong's lack of culture and "stories of Hong Kong as a colony" produced by "the state apparatus in China." "Such an angle," Leung adds, is "not so different from that of Western tourists in their search for novelty and the exotic" (5). Leung's comments draw attention to a mimetic tradition in which Western writing, largely encoded in English, works with writing in Chinese from mainland China to exercise a binaristic grip on the Hong Kong story.

As a belated colony in the global decolonizing process, Hong Kong's experience of modernity took shape under a colonial aegis. From a Western historiographical perspective on Hong Kong, the historian Steve Tsang (2004) has identified freedom of expression and the rule of law as the two achievements of the late colonial decades, a period more generally considered by scholars as the time when Hong Kong became a modern city. Other scholars who study this period through the lens of culture are much more ambivalent about the modern progress that has typically been associated with Hong Kong's development into a financial center and urban metropolis where people enjoyed different kinds of freedoms not available in mainland China during the same period, or in many other former British colonies on the eve of decolonization. From the late 1970s, Hong Kong was remodeled as a financial hub where free flows of money, goods, and capital came to be regarded as the exclusive denomination of its self-worth and global value. Such are the capitalist "social and economic systems" and "lifestyle" enshrined in the 1984 Joint Declaration between the PRC and Britain (quoted in Brooke-Holland 2019, 8, 9). that shall remain unchanged for fifty years after 1997. Far from the fundamental change that is the inaugural promise of many postcolonial polities, the fifty-year guarantee of no change posits a Hong Kong future in the shape of a quasi-colonial social imaginary. From this perspective the recent suppressions of political dissent can be seen as the logical outcome or cynical fulfillment of the promise of the guarantee. When change did come, it took the form of the NSL, which reprocesses Hong Kong's colonial control into subservience to Beijing. The sinophone writer and cultural critic Koonchung Chan offers a historical narrative that shows how the attempts at reform of the late-colonial decades have been gradually effaced by the adoption of neoliberal economic policies. The subjects and culture enjoying the euphemistic "life-style" in the Joint Declaration are foregrounded in their dubious monopoly of the Hong Kong story and then spellbound by the guarantee of fifty years of no change, no further narrative. Chan has attacked as the product of a "colonized mind" (2007, 384) an elitist self-identification premised on complacent assumptions about Hong Kong as an economic miracle and cultural meeting place between East and West. In the decades following 1984, Chan argues, Hong Kong people have yet to articulate a wider cultural narrative of their own emergence that seriously contests their economistic definition.

There has long been a general concern in Hong Kong, especially prominent in studies of literary history and culture before and after 1997, about the absence of narratives that are, on one hand, better coordinated with global scholarly frameworks of cognition and recognition about colonialism and its aftermath and, on the other, adequate to Hong Kong's historical realities. The narrative of colonial progress elaborated into a teleology of national reunion, familiar in British and other Western imperial historiography, is seen by many writers and scholars as inadequate to Hong Kong as cultural inhabitation. At the same time, the model of an integrative nation and politically unified state did not succeed in incentivizing popular anticolonial resistance in the last colonial decades. The blandishments of a return to Chinese origins, central to the anticolonial rhetoric of nativist historiography, may be attractive to mainland loyalists but cannot articulate Hong Kong's cultural self-consciousness or inspire a credible postcolonial imaginary. Rey Chow has argued that Hong Kong's supposed transition in 1997 from loss to retrieval, absence to presence, speaks not of change but of continuity, in a process that defies wider global understanding. To Chow, the actual terms of the Joint Declaration that decided on Hong Kong's "retrocession" to China in 1997 violated "the *telos* of the conventional thinking about coloniality, in which coloniality is followed by emancipation" (1998, 174).[7] Chow elaborates on Hong Kong as "anomaly": "Hong Kong confronts us with a question that is yet unheard of in colonial history: how do we talk about a postcoloniality that is a forced return (without the consent of the colony's residents) to a 'mother country,' itself as imperialistic as the previous colonizer? Is Hong Kong then simply an anomaly in the history of colonialism? Or does it not, in its obligatory 'restoration' to China, in fact crystallize and highlight the problem of 'origins' that has often been suppressed in other postcolonial cultures because of ethnic pride?" (151).

Long before the recent protests in Hong Kong, Chow's prescient comments, first made in 1992, queried the integrative nation-state model that dominated an earlier postcolonial temporality and is now being imposed on supposedly autonomous Hong Kong.[8] It is questionable, however, whether Hong Kong is an anomaly: its tortuous passage between British and Chinese sovereignties may be usefully studied as a late twentieth-century coordinate of the serial colonialisms experienced by Asian countries like Taiwan and the Philippines that are discussed in different chapters in this volume. Importantly, Chow's question about "origins" draws attention in another direction to what has long been sidelined by the Chinese-British struggle that dominates Hong Kong's postcolonial narrative: the *longue durée* of the Hong Kong story in which the recent popular dissent visibly enacts the emergence of the "local." To tell this story, Ping-kwan Leung urged, "We need a fresh angle, / nothing added, nothing taken away, / always at the edge of things and between places" (1992, 34).

No less engaged with acts of narrating Hong Kong, anglophone writing needs to confront the same forces as Sinophone narratives: the symbolic order of English in the colonial past and globalized present and the power of a centristic Chinese discourse claiming cultural authenticity and legitimacy exclusively for itself. From the historical privilege of its negative freedom, throughout the British colonial period and beyond, select texts of anglophone writing have attempted to present Hong Kong as locality. A very early instance came in the form of W. H. Auden's sonnet "Hongkong," written when the poet visited the colony on his way to mainland China in 1938. Before turning to the poem, a few caveats need to be entered. To begin with Auden's sonnet would appear to raise several problematic questions familiar—perhaps too familiar—to contemporary readers. First, it seems to postulate an outdated notion of origins, that is to say, an attempt to locate and fix in a particular historical moment the sources and resources of subsequent literary endeavor. Then there is the specific choice of Auden himself—metropolitan, canonical. It is with these two caveats in mind that my discussion of the sonnet eschews situating the poem in Auden's oeuvre. The fact of the matter is, in almost all the compendious scholarship on Auden, the poem passes unnoticed. "Hongkong" has no place in Auden's oeuvre, while Auden, English and transient, could claim no "place" in Hong Kong. For this reason, to use the poem to claim an association with Auden as a strong precursor of anglophone Hong Kong writing is of dubious benefit and can only serve to emphasize the invisibility of the writing, as observed earlier. For this chapter the poem points to another story, another map.

Commissioned by Random House to write a travel book, Auden and his friend Christopher Isherwood decided to report on the Chinese war of resistance against Japanese invasion. This war was, for Auden, the opening of a new front in the global conflict between socialism and fascism over the future of world history. In traveling to China, Auden was expressing, as a left-wing intellectual, "solidarity with China's resistance to invasion" in an "obligation similar to support for the Republican cause in the Spanish civil war" (Kerr 2008, 160–61). Hong Kong was his first port of call. Auden's journey and the sonnet inscribe the colonial-capitalist privilege of anglophone writing; both were enabled by the circuits of free trade in imperial globalization. More important for this chapter, it brings into question how a representation of Hong Kong in English can possibly develop traction as "local."

"Hongkong" is one of the sonnets that Auden contributed to the published book, *Journey to a War* (Mendelson 1997, 235).[9] Satirically, in the octave, the sonnet stages the colonial bankers and civil servants—"wise and witty," "substantial men of birth and education"—as "leading characters" in a drawing-room comedy. Knowing "the manners of the modern city," they "have erected / A worthy temple to the Comic Muse." In the background are the Chinese servants, unseen and unheard by the main actors and audience but not the poet, distanced as participant-observer, who alone registers their entrance as "unexpected" and who perceives that their "silence has a fresh dramatic use."[10] As the sestet reveals, a crucial distinction is drawn between histrionics and history: the critique of a colonial histrionics self-assured of its importance in the "Late Victorian" drama of empire, oblivious to what Auden sees as world history unfolding "off-stage," in a "war [that] / Thuds like the slamming of a distant door"—the Chinese resistance against fascism in the Asian sphere that Auden would go on to narrate in *Journey to a War*.

Looking askance at Britain as colonial-capitalist master, the poem, in its own time and place, has no quarrel with China as Hong Kong's ethnocultural overlord. It does raise several questions very germane to my argument about the necessary elaboration of anglophone writing in Hong Kong with Chinese and "sinophone" in telling the Hong Kong story: Where are the native subjects in the narrative of colonial-capitalist Hong Kong? And in piercing the "silence" that marks their presence, how are they to be heard speaking and writing themselves in and into world history? Despite its title the poem does not address these questions as particular Hong Kong issues. Instead, it is already pivoting away from Hong Kong, drawn by "the slamming of a distant door" that is the war in China.[11] In this turn, the poem's anticolonial imperative is ineluctably bonded to its assumption, principled in its own time, that the nation and the struggle between nations are what locate world history. Its trenchant colonial critique gives sanction to a perspectivalism that collapses Hong Kong into China even as it calls out, in all conscience, for native subjects to be represented and for native voices to become audible.

In select anglophone texts after Auden, to critique the colony is to critique the self as colonial; reaching out to the Chinese subject, the self-in-writing pushes against colonial complacency and enacts its struggle for self-authentication. Edmund Blunden's contemplative poem "The Sleeping Amah," for example, begins with the premise of opposition between East and West, familiar in the British Empire since Rudyard Kipling. Line 1 of the poem, "'The East has all the time, the West has none,'" rehearses an imperial cliché but immediately questions what it means to the individual subject— "But I know not what I say" ([1961] 2001, 9).[12] The loss of verbal and self-coherence is the speaker's colonial predicament, from which he begins to extricate himself when he lights on the titular amah, someone "unknown" to him and now seen, for the first time, it seems, in the poem. Momentarily, she appears as coherent form, located in place and time, "in her chair / After the long day's labor," with an assured history: "A child, a mother, the wise face now begun." In apprehending her, the speaker enacts his own transition out of colonial loss; the poem ends with their identity in silence: "Like me she falls asleep / Quietly moored upon the warm time-deep" (9). "Time-deep," the third term beyond time and place, is accessible to the speaker only in this singular moment of illumination. Blunden's romantic utopianist visualization of his identity with the native amah is clearly premised on unseeing her—and himself—in history.

Other poems, like Joyce Booth's "The Old Boat Woman" and "The Letter Writer" (in Hsia and Lai 1977, 56, 60), struggle to reintroduce this history by microdetailing the native milieu of their working-class subjects. Voluble descriptions of Hong Kong sights and sounds are meant to emphasize by contrast the ineffable dignity of the boat woman who "sits in silence with a placid face," or the letter writer who "sits quite unperturbed." From a related perspective, the Orientalized silent native in Blunden and others can be seen as the unexceptional outcome of a colonial language divide that confronts the Hong Kong writer, expatriate or otherwise, who dwells exclusively in Standard English. Even as the poem breaks out of English's dominant instrumentalization into literary self-expressiveness, it is thrown back by its own monolingualism into a quasi-colonialist discursive iteration of the native as silent.

This conundrum develops an ironic, if unsurprising, global turn early in this century in the retitling of Martin Booth's (2004) memoir of his Hong Kong childhood. Arguably the finest of the end-of-colonial-era narratives (see E. Ho 2019b, 306), the book was first published with the short title *Gweilo*, which is glossed in the paratext: "*Gweilo*—Chinese slang for a European male—translates literally as *ghost (or pale) fellow*. . . . Once a derogatory or vulgar term, referring to a European's pale skin, it is now a generic expression devoid of denigration." Appropriated as the title of an emotive personal narrative, the generic term, transliterated from Cantonese, gestures toward Booth's self-branding as native to Hong Kong. This is frustrated, internally, by native characters who speak in "deplorable phonetic pidgin" (Harrison 2006, 34) and, externally, in the Standard English retitling of the book as *Golden Boy*, which was deemed more marketable to American readers.[13]

The texts discussed above seek to perform their author-speakers' movement from colonial to postcolonial agent; simultaneously, they reinscribe linguistic segregation as the inimical condition of their coloniality. In other texts, the self-authenticating moves against coloniality develop a Chinese nationalist tenor also illuminated by transactions between English and Chinese. To Man Wong, Blunden's left-wing contemporary, the systemic divide between Modern Standard English and Modern Standard Chinese (Mandarin/Putonghua) is, for the writer who uses both languages, a historical condition of his being "between" East and West. Wong's quasi-autobiographical poetic collection, *Between Two Worlds*, is published in parallel texts. In this arrangement the two languages are spatially distinct, but the presumption is that they are translatable and mutually intelligible, and their colonial hierarchization is erased. In the book the colony is thematized as "an easy place, created for / The delights of a selected few" (1956, 153). True egalitarian mutuality when "East meets West / Where no line is" (71) is possible only away from Hong Kong, in the colonial prodigal's welcome "home return" (72) to early socialist China.

Wong Man was active in the early years of the PRC, around the time of the Bandung Conference (1955) of nonaligned nations, and was inspired, like

Auden, by socialism as both a nationalist and internationalist cause (see E. Ho 2009b). As Hong Kong approached 1997, the nationalist impulse developed an irredentist turn sustained by a doubled erasure: of Hong Kong's modern history politically separate from the PRC and of the calamitous decades of political turmoil on the Chinese mainland since 1949. Some of these issues are thematized in a realist short story, "Red Amber Green," by David T. K. Wong (1990). The story is set in 1960s Hong Kong but was published after the Joint Declaration of 1984. The 1960s, a period of political instability and social deprivation in the PRC, are commonly regarded by scholars as the first decade of Hong Kong's recent capitalist modernity. The text conflates capitalist modernity with both colonial rule and severance from a Chinese homeland. A refugee from famine in China, the protagonist, Old Mak, becomes a rickshaw puller in Hong Kong. As a subject of labor, he has no locus in the colonial developmental narrative. Debilitated by his daily drudgery on the busy streets, he succumbs to opium addiction. Arrested by the police, he is taken to court and, in the extract from the trial that follows, is given the opportunity to tell his own version of events, his "Hong Kong" story:

> The magistrate told the police sergeant to step down from the witness box and then addressed the interpreter: "Tell the defendant that he may now speak in his own defence. Explain to him that he may give evidence under oath in the witness box or he may make a statement from the dock. If he testifies under oath, his words will carry more weight with the court, but he will also have to submit to cross-examination by the prosecution. If he elects to make a statement from the dock, his words will carry less weight, but he will not be subjected to cross-examination. Of course, he may also remain silent."
>
> "You can speak now," the interpreter said. "You can speak from where you are or you can speak from the witness box. If you speak from the witness box, the inspector can ask you questions. If you speak from where you are, no one will ask you questions. If you speak from the witness box, your words will be more believable. If you speak from where you are, your words will be less believable. You can also say nothing, if you like. What do you wish to do?" . . .
>
> "Speak up," the interpreter said. ". . . It is now your turn to speak. Do you not wish to tell your side of the story?"
>
> Old Mak shook his head. "I want to go home," he repeated.
>
> "The defendant does not wish to make any statement, your Worship," the interpreter said, "He states that he wishes to go home." (117–18)

The extract shows the pathetic subject of labor becoming a captive of colonial-capitalist law through an act of linguistic and mimetic violence. For the text this act of violence marks the inauguration of Hong Kong's colonial-capitalist modernity in the 1960s and makes a mockery of its vaunted "rule of law." The text shows how the gruesome mutilation of English and Chinese vis-à-vis each other, in capturing the court and trial process, develops biopower; Old Mak's "Hong Kong" story is, in other words, already scripted. But if this is the case, then his desire for return—"to go home"—cannot be voluntaristic but is, at best, symptomatic of a reaction formation against the breaking up of the linguistic and social world he knows. Subjected to capitalist exploitation and colonial violence, Old Mak becomes the object of nationalist fascination.

The subject as abject is amplified in the realist narrative's causal connection of anticolonial critique and national return. While the story begins with Old Mak's escape to Hong Kong from famine and persecution on the mainland, it ends with him in jail desperate to return to rural China, now transformed, in his prison reverie, into "life-giving land" (118). This realist causality transcribes, in part, the nationalist narrative from separation to return. And yet in the realist closure, the "life-giving" motherland imaginary also emerges as an *effect* of colonial violence and, as such, cannot but be disavowed by a "motherland" claiming authenticity for itself, in itself. If, from a nationalist-irredentist perspective, the Sino-British Joint Declaration of 1984 has scripted the Hong Kong story as one of colonial rejection and national return, "Red, Amber, Green" discloses that such a script hardly offers genuine political and ethical choices but instead inscribes colonial capitalism and nationalism as historical forces enmeshed with each other that foreclose on individual and social agency.

In the above texts and others from the 1950s and after, anticolonialist and nationalist-irredentist impulses subtend an inquiry into linguistic transactions between English and Chinese. But in a narrative of Hong Kong as locality, such an inquiry is necessarily complicated by two historico-linguistic exigencies: first, that of Cantonese as a majority language resistant to incorporation into Modern Standard Chinese and, second, a continuous linguistic hybridization that mixes Chinese, Cantonese, English, and, to a lesser extent, other languages. In the years before and after 1997, these linguistic practices become postulates of a particular Hong Kong identity, entrenched in the cultural and sociopolitical resistance against both mainland Chinese incorporation and the colonial-capitalist capture of modern Hong Kong. The rest of the chapter explores anglophone texts that probe this identity and its struggles in their linguistic and representational practices.

In Hong Kong's linguistic and social history, Cantonese-Chinese sinophonism, oral and written, inscribes what the anthropologist Michael Herzfeld calls "cultural intimacy," or "those aspects of a cultural identity that are considered a source of external embarrassment but that . . . provide insiders with their assurance of common sociality" (2005, 3). For many Hong Kong writers, what is at stake is how to introduce Cantonese features into Modern Standard Chinese and Modern Standard English so as to generate effects of the local that are also legible to global readers of the two languages. If there is embarrassment, it is a function of the perception that sinophone hybridization is a sign of colonial Hong Kong's deculturation from Chinese language and ethnicity—a perception that often accompanies the centristic Sinological dismissal of Hong Kong as an inauthentic "cultural desert" (Ping-kwan Leung 1992, 177). This embarrassment is no less the lived experience of Cantonese users of English. In an iteration of the silent, silenced native, the poet Tammy Lai-ming Ho writes, "We dare not open our mouths, lest our strong HK / Accent betrays our humble origin. The terrible / Flatness of our tone, the inflexibility of our tongue" (2015, 84). Louise Ho's poem "Well-Spoken Cantonese" (1994) takes up the challenge of the "silent" native but also deftly sidesteps it:

> How praise the beauties of a gracious man
> Except that they are the graces of a beautiful man?
> Tone, stress, diction, timing, all combine
> To make the texture of his voice:
> So rare anywhere
> But rarest of all, *here*.
> His modulated resonance
> Creates a civilized space
> Or a proper silence,
> Which was not there
> Before he spoke. (L. Ho 2009, 60, my italics)

Rather than speech itself, the poem characterizes a speech act in Cantonese. The link enabled by Cantonese between the aesthetic—"beauties . . . beautiful"—and the "civilized" is clearly thematized. Much more opaque is the word "here"—a resonant pause, at the midpoint of the poem, that disrupts the flow of its fluid praise. Does "here" denote the poem itself, the textual location where English negotiates its representation of Cantonese?[14] Or is it metatextual, pointing to the poem's Hong Kong location, where Cantonese has been derided as "harsh, guttural and cacophonous" (L. Tam 2017, n.p.)?

In another, longer poem, "Jamming," also by Louise Ho, each of the stanzas presents a variant viewpoint on exchanges between English and Chinese. Interspersing the stanzas is a refrain, "geeleegulu," that is glossed by the poet as "a Cantonese colloquial onomatopoeic reference to English as 'Double Dutch.'" An example:

> He wants "to be married"
> China Bride wants out of the country
> She has minimal English
> He has minimal Chinese
> Between them it can only be
> > geeleegulu
> Have you ever tried merging
> The time-stressed with the syllable-stressed
> Within one discourse
> > geeleegulu . . .
> Bacon didn't trust it much
> But Churchill thought it rather grand
> On these our very own shores
> Let us make our very own
> > geeleegulu (L. Ho 2009, 42–43)

The extract moves from mutual incomprehension in the first stanza to isochronous differences that appear to prevent Chinese and English from merging, through to the third stanza, which issues a clarion call to language making as self- and place-making—"our very own shores . . . / our very own." The poem sites this creative activity firmly in the familiar Cantonese Chinese phrase *geeleegulu*; the transliteration of the phrase actualizes the poem as anglophonic. In form and thematics, Ho's poem embeds anglophone writing in the already existing everyday practice of linguistic intermixing that has, for long, simultaneously pushed English toward the anglophonic and Chinese into the sinophonic.

To experiment with an anglophonic usage translated from Cantonese is, from another perspective, to turn Cantonese and the Hong Kong self-identity it encodes toward the world, to steer the cultural and social intimacy of Cantonese away from an exclusionary, nativist linguistic politics. This has developed a special urgency in the past decade; amid rising protests against the PRC's erosion of Hong Kong's autonomy, a nativist localism that targets mainland Chinese immigrants and visitors became increasingly vocal and visible.[15]

Both enigmatic and direct, Tammy Ho's "Cantonese Idioms" traces the line between inclusion and exclusion in a poem that is quirkily self-expressive. Each of the poem's five stanzas takes off from a common Chinese idiom easily comprehensible to a Cantonese user. For example:

> Four horses, all whipped,
> fail to chase after an uttered word.
> Who knows if the mammals
> have not been drugged
> or who they really serve?
>
> A dragon is bullied
> by baby shrimps in shallow water.
> It should inhale deeply and
> breathe those lowly creatures in.
> That said, who put the dragon there? (2015, 80)

The first two lines of each stanza translate a commonly used Chinese idiom that carries cautionary import. The first warns against hasty or indiscreet speech, and the second about the fall and humiliation of even the greatest. The idioms are the inherited source of the poem's inventiveness, which goes on to exceed them; their conventional social force is repeatedly displaced, overturned by a whimsical and transformative curiosity. The poem's title can be seen as a misnomer, in the sense that the idioms are also legible to Mandarin Chinese users. In appropriating the idioms and then playing with them, the poem becomes both a closed and open space: the idioms cocoon Cantonese Chinese users as knowing insiders while proffering a series of puzzles to non-Cantonese Chinese or non-Chinese users. It is a beguiling invitation to all readers to enter into its unique image making, to share its curiosity as it crosses from convention into the unknown, from the local-national to the international.

In the *longue durée* that is the Hong Kong story, an English-language inquisitiveness about Chinese subjects and Cantonese Chinese goes hand in hand with the hybridizing of English with Cantonese to form new descriptive, often highly colorful, verbal compounds and idioms.[16] In this linguistic hybridization, agency is located in everyday users of the languages, often in acts of spontaneous creativity that go on to develop social currency. Before social media as a platform for linguistic invention and dissemination, anglophonic inventions often emerged from institutional clusters like university campuses, where English is often commingled with Cantonese in everyday communication. As early as 1931, eight years before Auden's arrival in Hong

Kong, a group of students at the University of Hong Kong conversed about language and in particular about their own acts of language violence. The university was set up in 1911 to educate ethnic Chinese students from Hong Kong, mainland China, and the Chinese diaspora, as well as students of Eurasian and other ethnicities, in Western learning through the imperial lingua franca of English (see E. Ho 2006). With characteristic youthful vigor, the culturally diverse group of editors and readers of a student magazine invented their own idioms to talk about their everyday lives:

> All animals, the human among them, give voice to their feelings in one way or another, and thus groups here and there have combined to form words and sentences that are not only original but also intelligible only to the few or many who have evolved them. . . . Not being adept at either Greek or Latin and being very near to China and Malaya, what is more natural than this, that the undergrads should mutilate the languages of these two countries and after slaughtering a few English verbs should evolve, what is popularly known as "farmerism."
>
> To expound "farmerism" would take a greater genius that [sic] the writer claims to be, but a few sentences and one or two anecdotes would aptly illustrate it.
>
> To an ordinary person this would perhaps sound senseless: "Witness hey! chow fishings grub time." But one in the know would interpret it thus: "Very witty to-day eh! Had plenty of fish for tiffin, I suppose." Or "Everything's wrong chilakar even battins' chows ducks" would mean: "Dam [sic] it all! Nothing seems to go right, even in batting I made a duck." . . .
>
> Or after a hockey or football match: "First half cheap, but after halftime, siap, and we no chance" would be interpreted as "We were leading in the first half, but in the second half they scored in rapid succession and we had no chance to win." (A. Grico La. 1931, 94–95)[17]

The article goes on to describe more of what it calls "greater homicidal tendencies" (95) that issue in further language crimes, as the daily need to communicate in different situations seems to demand, and concludes with the following:

> I think the cream of "farmerism" is this:—A freshman totally ignorant of the existence of "farmerism" happened to inquire of one, who was a great supporter of the tongue, his nationality and place of residence. This was the reply he received:
>
> "What do you think? I is Chinese and I come from local." (96)

The students' invented code is, like Tammy Ho's poem, both insular and cosmopolitan. As the extracts show, in stripping English of its normative power as an imperial lingua franca, it is also open to being translated back into everyday Standard English communication. For the "local" student, as the text suggests, it is an act of self-identity that both establishes her location on campus and bonds her to an undergraduate community. Auden lived at the university during his visit, but it is difficult to imagine what form of attention he might have turned to these loquacious young subjects of empire who appeared so radically different from those, colonial or native, he made visible in his compact fourteen-line sonnet.[18] The young students and their "impure" utterances speak of a life elsewhere *within* Hong Kong, a diasporizing momentum framed but not consumed by systemic regimes of English and Chinese predicated on colonial, nationalist, or capitalist segregations.

These utterances, more than eighty years ago, are acts of identity that appear to contain the embryonic potential for a twenty-first-century performance in languaging such as Arthur Sai-cheong Leung's 2008 poem "What the Pig Mama Says." Throughout Leung's poem, not only do English and Chinese disrupt each other, but their entanglements are also, in turn, augmented and disrupted by other languages. Here is the poem:

> The pupoh stopped to cheer. Leklek
> was took away. He was mine biggest boy.
> A good heart. Saved the best for Yenyen
> and Hokhok. His self eating leftovers.
> I cried I cried. Not knew the bastang
> took him where. Gokgou told me was hell.
>
> We ate much as we liked. The white fence
> put us safe. Always we talked, cheered.
> The pupoh liked to play with Hokhok.
> Mine little boy talked to them sweet.
> He knew how make community.
> But Hokhok too was took away by same
>
> same bastang they took Leklek before.
> Mine only girl Yenyen too sad to see
> her little brother went. She kept quiet
> everydays think think. I begged the bastang
> not took mine boy. They not understood.
> Heard only something like "pok is good."

> The pupoh talked little little. Yenyen
> stopped to eat. She said, "No Hokhok play
> wis me!" I sorry sorry for her. The bastang
> came to take Yenyen. I saw her away.
> I not cried. Maybe it better for Yenyen.
> She will stop to think. No more think.
>
> No more think think. Maybe I say
> too much. Who is listening to my story?[19]

Who, indeed, is listening to the story? The poem tells a story of separation between parent (mother?) and child supposedly drawn from a local news item about the price of pork imported from the mainland. But the story is almost completely displaced by the poem's languaging—its singular syntactic and lexical intermix of English, Cantonese, Malay, and possibly Thai and Tagalog.[20] The poem displays the formal structure of English but also delivers an act of formal disobedience. Grammatically intersectional, its interest goes far beyond the thematic to locate the everyday as language mixing in action. The utterance, one can say, is the story.

Arthur Leung once declared, "We are writers of the twenty-first century and what is written should reveal *our times*; hence, no archaisms of expression or thought" (2012, my italics). In 1938 Auden's gaze as traveler was, in many ways, fixated on the monumentalist struggle between fascism and socialism as world historical forces. Affirming the epic magnitude of the cartographic project that is his "journey to a war" in China has the collateral effect of deriding colonial Hong Kong as minuscule—no bigger than a theater stage—and trivial: his anticolonial text is also necessarily a colonial one. To place the 1931 "farmerism" speech acts together with Auden's sonnet has the curious effect of making Auden's questions about the silent native already seem premodern. A narrative of anglophone Hong Kong writing as the Hong Kong story of "our times" needs to construe and explain the historical movements between Auden and Leung, *and* between "farmerism" and the "pig mama." There is violence in all these moments, for this is a story of contested unions and ruptures, and one in which, after all, there is no end yet in sight. Folding "farmerism" and "What the Pig Mama Says" into each other, we see language acts that are also socially imaginative acts: hybridized speech that constructs and identifies community in a linguistic activism that diasporizes English and Cantonese Chinese Hong Kong.

Notes

1. Articles from Anglo-American and Hong Kong presses (see, for example, Bowring 2014; Branigan and Kuo 2020; Lide 2019; Sala 2019) have begun to capture the Hong Kong protests through a longer historical lens, but whether such analyses are sustainable remains to be seen.
2. See Martin Purbrick's (2019) useful chronological overview of the protesters' and government's actions in 2019.
3. Wing Sang Law's (2009) important work on how Hong Kong Chinese elites collaborated with British colonial power in education and culture is complemented by Leo Goodstadt's (2013) studies of government mismanagement that is responsible for and exacerbates the inequities between rich and poor. See also Lui Tai-lok's chapter in this volume.
4. For the international consequences of the NSL, see Peterson (2020).
5. In using the word *anglophone* instead of English, this chapter references the scholarly-critical tradition of separating the two, one that has not been uncontroversial (see Madsen 1999). That a "phonic" literature presumes a center of literature and culture has also made some readers wary about using the term *anglophone*, because of English's imperial history and current international dominance (Prendergast 2008). If this chapter has the effect of making anglophone Hong Kong writing more visible globally, such visibility is not primarily intended to be that of a subcategory in an expanded metropolitan canon or in world anglophone literatures; despite its long colonial lineage, Hong Kong never developed into a fully fledged "anglophone ecumene" (Boehmer and Tickell 2015, 11). In an earlier study (E. Ho 2019a), I have presented arguments, justified in historical usages, for how *anglophonic* may be considered a keyword in theorizing Hong Kong culture. The term *sinophone*, rather like *anglophone* when it first emerged, is the subject of dispute, especially over whether it includes or excludes mainland China (see D. Wang and Tsu 2010). Shu-mei Shih, who earlier theorized the use of the term (2004), was thinking about literature written in Sinitic languages outside mainland China that loses recognition and visibility because it becomes incorporated into a nation-based concept of "Chinese literature." Sinophone studies, she reiterates, is the "study of Sinitic-language cultures, communities, and histories on the margin of China and Chineseness" (2008, 13). This maps onto two phases of the anglophone controversy: first, when critics and scholars dispute the incorporation of writing and writers of, for example, European origins into English literature; and, second, when the dispute extends to writing from the former colonial world. In the second phase, what is at stake is not incorporation but marginalization by canonical English literature. My use of the word *sinophone* does not, in the first instance, connote the center-periphery relations that define these two phases of the anglophone debate. It refers specifically to linguistic practices of intermixing Modern Standard Chinese and Cantonese.

6 In talking about the proximity of the two languages, the sociolinguist David C. S. Li (2018, 8) observes, "Linguistically, Hong Kong English is enriched by extensive borrowing from the local language(s), notably words for naming local places and various aspects of local culture from flora and fauna to dining and social taboos."

7 *Retrocession* is the actual English term used in the Joint Declaration. Other words, such as *handover* or *return*, are popularly used. The Chinese term, *huigui* (回歸), suggests return, reaffiliation, and belonging.

8 Stephen Vines (1998) has explicitly described Hong Kong as "China's New Colony." For Candice Delmas (2020), the 2019 protest "bears resemblance to decolonization struggles."

9 Auden revised the poem at least twice (Mendelson 1996, 825). The revisions do not alter the colonial critique or the issue of the inaudible Chinese subject, only the reflection on what the visit meant to the poet.

10 The issue of verisimilitude has been debated in relation to labor subjects in Auden's earlier poems: "Auden's workers are mostly . . . a rather shadowy, physically vague ideal according to which the capitalists and their cohorts are judged and found wanting" (Firchow 2002, 122).

11 A line clearly resonant of the revolutionary offstage slam of Henrik Ibsen's Nora in *A Doll's House*.

12 *Amah* refers to a Chinese woman domestic helper. Rudyard Kipling, "The Ballad of East and West" (1889), Kipling Society, https://www.kiplingsociety.co.uk/poem/poems_eastwest.htm. For discussions of Blunden's poems in a Hong Kong context, see E. Ho (2009a).

13 Booth died in January 2004, shortly after the publication of *Gweilo*. Whether he could have been involved in the decision to change the title a year later is uncertain.

14 Douglas Kerr avers that the poem is "where the medium of written English and the subject of Cantonese speech collaborate . . . to make 'a civilized space'" (Kerr 2009, 160).

15 This was captured during the protest movement of 2019–20) and, most recently, during the pandemic, by Hong Kongers calling mainland Chinese "virus spreaders" (JN 2020).

16 This hybridization has fascinated sociolinguists of "code-mixing" in Hong Kong since the 1980s, who tend, however, to focus mostly on formal descriptions of linguistic features. For studies analyzing their sociocultural import, see D. Li (2018) and A. Lin (2015).

17 The author, who signed himself as "A. Grico La.," clearly expected his identity to be known to his readers.

18 Auden and Isherwood stayed with the vice-chancellor of the university during their visit (Colletta 2005, 107).

19 "What the Pig Mama Says" was awarded third prize in the Edwin Morgan International Poetry Competition at the Edinburgh Book Festival in Scotland

(August 2008), in the summer when the Hong Kong media were totally focused on coverage of the Olympic Games in mainland China. Hong Kong did not pick up on Leung's award until the Home Affairs Bureau issued a press release on September 4 that contained the following self-congratulatory comment: "The award not only represents success for a Hong Kong Chinese poet writing in English in international literary circles, but also showcases to the world the cluster of top talent in the cosmopolitan world city of Hong Kong" (China.org.cn 2005).

20 On the formal qualities and reception of the poem in another context in an earlier article, see E. Ho (2010, 431–34).

Part IV

Taiwan Postcoloniality between Japanese and Chinese Colonialisms

The Slippage between Empires

As a place with a multilayered colonial past, including colonial encounters with both European and Asian powers, Taiwan makes a great case for postcolonial studies.[1] Postcolonial theories as an academic discipline tend to, by and large, focus on the third world locales formerly colonized by the West.[2] Consequently, Taiwan is often "already written out of mainstream Western discourse" (Shih 2003, 144). Despite its relative marginality in postcolonial studies, there have been some theoretically informed debates in Taiwan since the 1990s surrounding Taiwan's postcoloniality. Vehemently debated issues include when exactly Taiwan entered its postcolonial phase, whether Taiwanese nationalism existed during the Japanese colonial period, and, if so, what constituted this collective awareness. Regarding the start of Taiwan's postcoloniality, scholars often opt for either 1945 (the end of Japanese colonialism) or 1987 (the end of Taiwan's martial law period). The former sits particularly well with the mainlanders' ideology, whereas the latter is widely adopted by Hoklo-Taiwanese scholars. However, from the perspective of Taiwan's aborigines, the Han people's "colonial" power remains prevalent even nowadays. Kuan-hsing Chen claims that "colonialism would continue to exist for the aborigines, workers, gays, lesbians and women, until the removal and decolonization of ethnocentrism, class, heterosexuality and patriarchal structure" (1996b, 54), calling attention to the remaining subaltern groups and ongoing neocolonialism raised in Dai Jinhua's chapter in this book.

As for the genesis and ingredients of Taiwanese nationalism, the scholarly discussion is frequently entangled with the politics of ethnicity and polemics about unification versus independence. Viewed from another angle, it is the divide in ethnicity and political ideologies among critics that continues to prompt debate on Taiwan's subjectivity.

Postcolonial is not only a diversely defined term but also a disciplinary umbrella consisting of various methods and approaches.[3] It can also be manifested in different ways and to varied degrees, including an outright resistance against, a moderate negotiation with, or a passive acceptance of colonialism. If we take postcolonial as a general global condition or a universalizing framework, then when did it start? How are different postcolonial societies related? Is *postcolonial* applicable to former colonizer societies too, or is it merely a trendier name to refer to the third world? If the term in a temporal sense refers to the end of official colonization, and postcolonial literature is understood as an anticolonial writing in which the colonized register their subjectivity, how do we account for the search for and construction of subjectivity that existed before the end of colonization? In this chapter I take *postcolonial* not so much as a temporal term to refer to the end of a colonization but more broadly as a term covering "all the culture affected by the imperial process from the moment of colonization to the present day" (Ashcroft, Griffiths, and Tiffin 2002, 2).

Although the years 1945 and 1987 are handy to explain Taiwan's political decolonization, they fail to capture the more discursive cultural aspect of Taiwan's decolonization. For example, despite the general recognition of Taiwan's political decolonization, the recent controversies over a history-book revision are seen as evidence that Taiwan remains colonized by the China-centric mentality of the Nationalist Party (Kuomintang [KMT]).[4] In what follows, I start my discussion from Taiwan's Japanese era, the island's first encounter with a relatively comprehensive and strategic colonial system, since the Qing frontier governance was loose.

The Problematic of Taiwan's Postcoloniality

Owing to the unsettled political situation of Taiwan, Taiwanese scholars have offered varied views on Taiwan's postcoloniality. Regarding the emergence of Taiwanese consciousness, Wu Rwei-ren 吳叡人 (2006) and Chen Cuilian 陳翠蓮 (2008) both argued that a Taiwanese identity existed around the 1920s and 1930s, although Chen posited it was at best a "protonationalism" instead of Taiwanese nationalism, because it overlapped with Chinese nationalism.

Li Xiaofeng 李筱峰 (1996) and Fang Xiaoqian 方孝謙 (2001) considered the Taiwanese consciousness during the colonial era ambiguous because it was tangled up with the yearnings for Japan's modernity and the imagination of China as a motherland. More specifically, Chen Zhaoying 陳昭瑛 (1995) and Leo Ching (2001) tried to tease out the implications of China and Japan respectively in the making of Taiwanese consciousness. The former's claim that Taiwanese people are "innately Chinese" was almost antithetical to Ching, who viewed "becoming 'Japanese'" as a collective political unconsciousness, particularly for colonial Taiwan's educated class.

Debates on Taiwan's colonial and postcolonial identity, as illustrated, were a highly contested ground that spotlights the critics' ideological divide between unification and independence. The various perspectives highlight one central aspect of Taiwan's postcoloniality—how can the intricate triangular Taiwan-Japan-China relationship be understood when facing the Fanonian question "Who am I in reality?" (Fanon [1963] 2004, 182). Existing postcolonial theories, formulated largely on a single colonial experience, tend to suggest a neat Manichean divide in which the subjectivity of the colonized is constructed on the basis of resistance against the colonizer. Although this anticolonial resistance discourse is useful and has been employed by both Taiwan-centric critics and China-leaning writers, it does not address the dynamics Taiwan had with Japan's and the Nationalists' rules historically.

To better grasp and explain Taiwan's conundrum of identity, it is necessary to contextualize the trilateral (or even quadrilateral if adding America as a neocolonial power in postwar Taiwan) entanglements within which Taiwan's postcoloniality is situated. I focus on three historical periods (the Japanese colonial era, the early postwar era, and the post-1987 years) in which the literary manifestations of Taiwan's subjectivity and postcoloniality were clearly visible, and issues surrounding Taiwan's identity were fruitfully debated. I start with a reappraisal of some articulations of Taiwanese consciousness under Japanese rule before examining the nativist discourse in the 1970s to illustrate how it hinges on the criticism of America's neocolonial presence in Taiwan at that time. Finally, I discuss the debates and challenges of Taiwan's postcolonial discourse in the 1990s. In view of the KMT's top-down "re-Sinicizing" cultural policy and high-handed martial law control in post-1945 Taiwan, I consider its rule Taiwan's "recolonized" period under the larger Cold War cultural logic, although strictly speaking the KMT was a one-party authoritarian regime instead of a typical colonizer with its own empire, and the year around 1987 the beginning of Taiwan's postcolonial phase, at least politically.[5]

Tangled Beginnings: A Triangular Tie among Taiwan, Japan, and China

The expressions of Taiwanese consciousness under Japanese rule unsurprisingly germinated among Taiwan's gentry-class people and intellectuals. This elite-centric collective awareness of being Taiwanese during the colonial period from the outset was not a radical decolonization but a moderate demand for Taiwan's local self-governance. This was largely due to Japan's suppression of armed uprisings during the first two decades of their rule. Therefore, Taiwan's gentry-class intellectuals by the mid-1910s accepted Taiwan's colonial reality and turned to seek more rights *within* the colonial system. For instance, the Taiwan Assimilation Society, established by Itagaki Taisuke 板垣退助 and some Taiwanese gentry intellectuals in 1914, aimed to eliminate the unequal treatment of Taiwanese people and promote Taiwan's role in facilitating inter-Asian peace.

Another prominent example of this "curbed" nationalist practice is exemplified by the founding of the Taiwanese Cultural Association in 1921. Jiang Weishui 蔣渭水, its founder, made it clear that he had to promise the chief of police that the association was for promoting local culture, not political movements, in order to get the required approval. Nevertheless, members of the association supported home rule, submitting annual petitions from 1921 to 1934 to demand the establishment of a local parliament in Taiwan. Regrettably, the request was dismissed. During the assimilation phase (1919–September 1936), Taiwanese had a chance to serve as advisers to the colonial government and receive (Japanese-language) education, but the assimilation policy also revealed the gap between the ideal of impartiality and equal treatment and the reality of discrimination. However, although Cai Peihuo 蔡培火 referred to assimilation as "an alias for exploitation" and a "people-fooling policy" (1928, 86) because it failed to deliver what it had initially promised, he did not oppose assimilation completely. Cai (1920) supported what he termed "natural assimilation," such as abandoning the bad practices of foot-binding and opium smoking, and quibbled only about "artificial assimilation," such as wearing Japanese costumes.

Cai's view on assimilation signals the ambivalence among Taiwanese elites toward the Janus-faced colonial modernity brought into Taiwan by the Japanese colonizers.[6] As it coincided with Japan's political oppression and economic exploitation, colonial modernity in Taiwan was embedded with multiple paradoxical features such as progress and oppression, enlightenment and discipline. Cai's stance largely represented that of the gentry intellectuals who advocated cultural enlightenment and sought a milder local self-rule. Others, such as the self-determination devotees Jiang Weishui and Wang Minchuan 王敏川 and the anarchist Lian Wenqing 連溫卿, opted for a more radical route of national liberation. The disparity between these two groups can be understood in Frantz Fanon's ([1963] 2004, 97–144) terms as the distinction between elite (or bourgeois) nationalism and the national-popular that is more genuinely emancipatory. Those intellectuals' broad spectrum of positions under Japanese rule was shaped by a number of factors, including their generation, linguistic and educational background, and social class, in addition to external colonial policies such as assimilation and imperialization. To accentuate the co-relationship between the colonial context and the intellectuals' varied ways of enunciating a Taiwanese voice, I choose the Taiwanese Cultural Association and some of its members as examples for the assimilation period and select a few authors to illustrate how Taiwan's subjectivity was articulated through creative writing during the imperialization period.

The difference between Cai's wish to establish a Taiwan Assembly and Jiang Weishui's more proletariat-aware political agenda is worth noting. In his essay "Clinical Diagnosis," Jiang ([1921] 1950) personifies Taiwan as a patient who is living in Taiwan's Government-General Office and is diagnosed as culturally backward owing to prolonged and severe intellectual malnutrition. This highly allegorical diagnosis encapsulated the Taiwanese Cultural Association's members' profound sociopolitical concerns and their fervent ambitions for cultural enlightenment. Despite its goal of cultural enlightenment, its objective was closely intertwined with its members' extensive sociopolitical engagements. As early as 1912, Jiang joined the Taiwan branch of the Chinese Revolutionary Alliance to support Sun Yat-sen's revolutionary movement. In 1913 he even planned to assassinate Yuan Shikai 袁世凱, then the first president of the Republic of China. In 1914 he joined the aforementioned Taiwan Assimilation Society, hoping to eliminate Japanese discrimination against the Taiwanese people.

Beginning in the 1920s, Jiang was supportive of the farmers' and peasants' movements. The Taiwanese People's Party, founded in 1927 by him together with Cai Peihuo and others, later became the center for labor movements after the Japanese colonizers began to more closely monitor the new, more radical left-leaning association.[7] Jiang's devotion to labor movements, though enhancing the public support of the Taiwanese People's Party, deepened his conflict with the "right-wing" members of the party (such as Cai Peihuo and Lin Xiantang 林獻堂), so they left the party and established the League for Local Self-Rule in Taiwan in 1930. The right-wing gentry-class members' withdrawal from the Taiwanese People's Party revealed the different routes of cultural enlightenment taken by Taiwanese writers. Those disparate choices are well illustrated in the works of Lai He 賴和 and Yang Kui 楊逵.

Studying Chinese at an early age but later attending the prestigious Medical School of the Taiwan Government-General, Lai He is a good representative of the "second-generation" intellectuals caught between old and new in terms of social change and the literary transformation from traditional Chinese poetry to vernacular writing.[8] In a classical Chinese poem written to commemorate the short-lived Republic of Formosa, Lai lamented its failure and mulled over Taiwan's status. The earlier version of the poem says, "Heavens constrained Taiwan, making Taiwan's independence difficult" (Lai 2000, 322). But Lai (2000, 322) later changed the sentence to "Heavens and Taiwan are originally independent." Whether the "independence" in the poem referred to an anti-Japanese decolonization, an interpretation preferred by Chinese or pro-China scholars, or a potentially de-Sinified independent political entity, as suggested by some Taiwanese scholars, remains debatable. If one takes Lai's other poems into consideration, both views are partially true. Lai was concerned about China's social chaos (such as the warlords, people's addiction to opium, and officials' corruption) in the early twentieth century, but he also cared about Taiwan's future. The disillusionment he encountered during his sojourn in Amoy made him realize that Taiwan must be self-reliant because China was "an unrelated sinking continent" (385) and that life under Japanese rule was "without justice, like cows and horses that are being whipped" (402).

After settling back in Taiwan, Lai exhibited similar criticisms of Taiwan's social malaise in his works. "Raising Hell" and "Scale of Injustice" both condemn corrupt social practices and Japanese oppression. The former caricatures the unnecessary excessiveness of a traditional Taiwanese deity-worshipping fair. The latter is an account of a vegetable vendor who tries to please a Japanese patrolman but ends up being arrested for violating the rules of weights and measures and eventually killing the policeman and himself. The scale is supposed to signify fairness and justice, but it serves exclusively the economic interests of the Japanese and ratifies their control under colonialism. Despite Lai's humanitarian concerns for the proletariat, his political tendency stayed mild. After the split of the Taiwanese Cultural Association, Lai was involved in both the new left-wing Taiwanese Cultural Association and the pro-reform Taiwanese People's Party. When the reformist League for Local Self-Rule in Taiwan was formed, Lai did not articulate his ideological preference, although in his writing he mocked the elite class and their enlightenment goal and gradually adopted a leftist stance. Lai's socialism, however, remained fairly idealistic.

In Yang Kui, literary writing and social movements became one. Yang reiterated his socialist ideas in several of his works, but his semi-autobiographical "The Newspaper Boy" ([1932] 1979; published in Chinese under the title 送報伕) is probably the most renowned. Set during the economic recession, it tells of the narrator (a Taiwanese newspaper boy) being exploited by his newsagent boss. While he nearly gives up, a Japanese student worker helps the narrator out of his financial difficulty. The newspaper boy eventually joins the Japanese workers' organization, realizing that the enemy is not the Japanese but capitalists all over the world. If we take this story as an enunciation of Taiwan's subjectivity under Japanese rule, then this expression places class struggle prior to national consciousness. Unlike the dichotomy between Japanese policemen and Taiwanese farmers in Lai's writing, Yang minimized the Japan-Taiwan difference, highlighting instead the opposition between the capitalists and the proletariat. In other words, the class-focused socialist ideal provides Taiwanese writers a dimension for constructing a voice for Taiwan that eschews national boundaries.

In addition to the difference in their sociopolitical inclinations, Lai's and Yang's cases also evoke the question of form and language in formulating a Taiwanese consciousness. This question was especially acute for members of the Taiwanese Cultural Association because the target audience for their enlightenment goals was largely illiterate and the majority spoke only Taiwanese. Classical Chinese and Japanese were obviously unsuitable for reaching the common people in colonial Taiwan, but whether Taiwanese writers should adopt vernacular Chinese, as advocated by the May Fourth–inspired Zhang Wojun 張我軍, or strive to transliterate the Taiwanese language remained unsettled. While using vernacular Chinese gradually gained momentum from the mid-1920s, some Taiwanese writers attempted to write in Taiwanese.

To deal with the accelerating assimilation policy of Japanese imperialists, Lai He employed at least three strategies to authenticate Taiwanese culture and evoke a national narrative. His restoring of local folklore indicates a call to return to Taiwan's precolonial local cultural tradition, whereas his linguistic characteristics—a mixture of colloquial Taiwanese and Japanese (and Chinese) expressions—ratify syncretized elements of the heterogeneity created during Taiwan's Japanese period. His third tactic was to experiment with writing in Taiwanese. This was intimately associated with Lai's concern for underprivileged people. With an aspiration to reach out to the wider community, Lai began to experiment with Taiwanese writing—composing in classical Chinese before converting it into vernacular Chinese and then finally into Taiwanese (Wang S. 1979). His "transcription" of Taiwanese using

Chinese characters can be seen as an effort to search for a local identity so as to respond to Japan's assimilation, but the "Taiwaneseness" in Lai's works is *already* hybridized (with noticeable influence of Japanese and Chinese expressions). Unfortunately, his 1935 work "A Letter from a Comrade," written entirely in Taiwanese, was not as easily understandable as he had hoped.

With the outbreak of the Second Sino-Japanese War in 1937, the Japanese intensified their assimilation policy. The use of Chinese in newspapers and journals was banned, although some Chinese publications survived. To incorporate the colonies into Japan's imperial expansionism, the colonizers encouraged the writing of the local customs of the colonies on the basis that a vivacious regional or local (*chihō* 地方) culture would lead to a powerful Japanese Empire and maintain the latter's hierarchy. Yet savvy Taiwanese writers took advantage of this turn in policy to register their own versions of local culture, with distinct concern for Taiwanese folkways. While works by Lü Heruo 呂赫若 were criticized for being too gloomy, numerous Taiwanese authors managed to continue publishing despite the intensified wartime censorship. This indicates that Taiwan's rejuvenated literary subjectivity in the 1940s was precisely carved on the verge of colonial control.

Another example highly illustrative of Taiwan's literary subjectivity in the late years of Japan's colonial rule can be found in the debate surrounding realism. In the debate Japanese critic Shimada Kinji 島田謹二, a scholar of comparative literature who taught at the Taipei Imperial University during the colonial period, defined literature from Taiwan as "colonial literature." The scope covered works written by Japanese writers residing in the colonies only. But unlike Nishikawa Mitsuru 西川滿, an active Taiwan-residing writer known for his literary exoticism, Shimada advocated realism—not the class-sensitive proletariat realism but a literary mode in which authors described the "uniqueness of the [colony's] modes of thinking, feelings, and ways of life in a lively fashion according to the way they are" ([1941] 1995, 476).

Shimada's emphasis on Taiwan's indigenous color is in this regard not incompatible with Taiwanese critic Huang Deshi's 黃得時 notion. Yet Huang was more Taiwan-centric and inclusive than Shimada. In Huang's (1943) historiography, Taiwan's literature could be dated back to the Ming dynasty's Koxinga era, and all works could be considered part of Taiwan's literature as long as they are about Taiwan. Huang was so inspired by the French critic Hippolyte Taine's work on the history of English literature that he conceptualized Taiwanese literature from the factors of race, milieu, and the historical moment. His effort can be seen as an attempt at a quasi-national literature made possible during the colonizer's call for revitalizing local cultures in the colonies to assist in the war effort. Although one may argue that the uniqueness emphasized in Shimada's notion could eventually lead to Taiwan's literary subjectivity, Shimada did not address this. Quite the opposite, Huang's literary historiography seemed to pick up where Shimada left off and therefore constituted a salient example of Taiwanese writers' practice of cultural resistance under imperialization.

Stories dealing with the process of becoming Japanese, generally referred to as imperial-subject literature, offer another great case in point for the representation of Taiwan's subjectivity. In Wang Changxiong's 王昶雄 "Torrent," the cultural difference between the two competing identities (Japanese and Taiwanese) is represented by the difference between dream and reality. Obsessed with his student life in Tokyo yet asked to return to Taiwan, the protagonist, Doctor Hong, is placed in a dilemma in which the colonial space is divided: vulgar Taiwan versus cultivated Japan. It starts with Hong's reminiscence of his student life in Tokyo three years earlier, before he departed for Taiwan, an experience in which his youthful sentiment and love for Japan yielded to reality (Wang C. 1991, 325).

After returning home and becoming a doctor in the countryside, Hong projected his nostalgia for Japan onto one of his Taiwanese patients, who adopts the Japanese name Itō Haruo. While Hong is impressed by the degree to which Itō has Japanized himself, he feels uneasy when he discovers that Itō has abandoned his parents and lives only with his Japanese wife and mother-in-law to cover up his Taiwanese background. Hong later learns that Itō financially supports Itō's student Bonian, who is studying in Tokyo. Bonian sends Hong a letter, encouraging Hong to be a "dignified Taiwanese" without feeling inferior. Unlike Itō, who drastically severs his connection with Taiwan, and unlike Bonian, who finds a balance between Japanese modernity and his love for Taiwan, Hong is stuck in indeterminacy, yearning for Japan but simultaneously seeing the falsity of this pursuit. Although a hybrid Taiwanese identity is suggested through Bonian, the cultural hierarchy within it remains unsolved.

Hong's indeterminacy is further compounded by the "orphan complex," coined by Wu Zhuoliu's 吳濁流 *Orphan of Asia* ([1956] 1973), in which Wu situated his protagonist Hu Taiming's Taiwanese identity in a double negation—neither Japanese (the hierarchy with the Japanese cannot be resolved) nor Chinese (the gap between Taiming's imagined China and the China he experiences in reality is unbridgeable). Taiming chooses, and is warned, not to reveal his Taiwanese background no matter whether he is in Japan or China. The negation is threefold, as the political and economic oppressions accompanying colonialism make Taiwan, the "local," unlivable and cause Taiming's insanity. While Taiming is often seen as a victim trapped in a specific historicity without a reliable identity, his "no identity" can also be interpreted as a possibility for a fresh Taiwanese identity no longer hinged on a sense of inferiority or repression with reference to Japan and China.

Critiques of Western Modernity and Cultural Contentions

With the founding of the People's Republic of China in 1949 and the KMT's retreat to Taiwan, the two sides of the Taiwan Strait remained confrontational ideologically within the larger global Cold War context in the second half of the twentieth century. In the midst of the KMT's call for an anticommunist literature, both the émigré writers and those Taiwanese writers living through the Japanese rule sought alternatives. The former quickly found resonance with (Western) modernism, a literary mode sponsored indirectly by America. For instance, Ji Xian 紀弦, a leading figure of Taiwan's postwar modernist poetry, in his controversial manifesto (1956), claimed stylistic inheritance from Charles Baudelaire and declared that new poetry in Taiwan is the result of "horizontal transplantation," not "vertical inheritance." While there was a three-century-long history of modernism developing in Europe, modernity in Taiwan was compressed (if understood as sociohistorical progress) and premature (if understood as a translated aesthetic movement). Its emergence around the mid-1950s and culmination in the 1960s and 1970s coincided with Taiwan's transformation from an agricultural society to a labor-intensive, export-oriented industrial society, different from the social conditions of high capitalism, materialism, and urbanization in the case of Western modernization.

Nevertheless, this time lag and the KMT's martial law control helped generate an "indigenized" version of cultural and literary modernism in Taiwan. A distinct feature of Taiwan's modernism was its relatively apolitical take. Several promoters of modernism clustered in the Department of Foreign Languages and Literatures of National Taiwan University, particularly the flagship modernist journals *Literary Review* and *Modern Literature*, supported by America through the US Information Agency. While reservations about the KMT's politicized literary policy were discernible in *Literary Review*, its protest was relatively latent. A by-product of modernism in Taiwan was the introduction of new criticism and close reading as a paradigm in Taiwanese academia. Although some modernist works can be read as a critique or reflection of Taiwanese society at that time, and new criticism practitioners' attenuation of sociohistorical reference may be understood as a political act, modernist literature eventually became an elitist experiment insufficient to address Taiwan's external and internal sociopolitical turmoil in the 1970s.

Internationally, the Baodiao movement stirred up the anti-imperialist and anticolonialist spirit of the decade. In 1971 Taiwan was forced to withdraw from the United Nations as the Beijing government was recognized as the sole legitimate government of China. Shortly afterward, Japan and the United States cut diplomatic ties with Taiwan in 1972 and late 1978 respectively. These setbacks smashed the KMT's myth of "counterattacking the mainland" and urged writers to face Taiwan's reality and think about their moral imperative. Domestically, the KMT's arrest of liberalism-embracing émigré academics from late 1972 to mid-1975 heated up people's discontent over the KMT regime. Chiang Kai-shek's death in 1975 further prompted Taiwanese to mull over the future of Taiwan. While Chiang's death may have been considered an ill omen among the unification-leaning population, it made room for *dangwai* (黨外: literally, outside the party) efforts to further wrest power from the ruling KMT. All those factors converged on the urgency of engaging with society among Taiwanese people and brought about the 1977–78 nativist literary debate.

On the surface, it was a dispute between nativists and modernists, who were disparaged for being overly Western leaning and escapist. In fact, it was politically embedded because critics in the oppositional camps had diverse views on "native soil." Among the advocates of nativist writing, both Wang Tuo 王拓 and Ye Shitao 葉石濤 were Taiwan-centric, calling on writers to reflect Taiwan's here and now and its cultural-historical particularities. Chen Yingzhen 陳映真 shared their preference for a socially engaged literature but considered Taiwan's nativist literature an integral part of Chinese national literature. The "oppositional" camp included writers such as Zhu Xining 朱西甯 and Yu Guangzhong 余光中. Zhu criticized the provincialism of Taiwan literature, questioning Taiwan's cultural loyalty to China. Yu (1977) went so far as to label those promoting nativist literature as advocates of class struggle and of "literature for workers, farmers, and soldiers." The ambiguity of the term *native soil* was the cause of all the contention. But the frustration with the KMT's rule and ardor for social reform enabled critics of nearly incompatible political inclinations (such as Ye Shitao and Chen Yingzhen) to align together vis-à-vis those (such as Zhu Xining and Yu Guangzhong) who were pro-KMT ideologically. In this regard, the vagueness of *native soil* made the alliance between Taiwan-centric and pro-China critics possible.

The term was, principally, a safety shield for articulating Taiwan-centric views, as directly using the word *Taiwan* would alert the KMT. It was not until the 1983–84 debates on Taiwanese consciousness that *Taiwan* was placed in the foreground of a public debate as a national identity. But the social transformation and cultural debates that occurred throughout the 1970s, dubbed the Karl Jaspers–esque "Axial Age" for the development of Taiwanese identification (Hsiau 2013, 176), provided a solid foundation for the greater momentum in Taiwan's subjectivity formation in the 1980s. The historical conditions pushing the KMT to initiate democratic reform and transition itself from Giovanni Sartori's "party-state system" to a "one party dominant regime," in T. J. Pempel's terms (Zhu 2001, 4), included its need to win support from native Taiwanese people to sustain its legitimacy, and the high cost of political suppression as dissatisfaction with the KMT continued to grow among Taiwan's younger generation (i.e., those born after 1945) and middle-class people. The KMT's constitution-based ideology, which allows the possibility of a multiparty system, helped too. With China-Taiwan relations becoming more relaxed in the 1980s, the martial law implemented as an emergency measure appeared increasingly unjustifiable. The KMT around the late 1970s and early 1980s also gradually lost its senior legislators and assembly delegates, who had been elected as early as 1947, leaving it with little choice except to hold supplementary elections and open up political space for native Taiwanese candidates.

Although nativist literature and modernist writing in Taiwan are not irreconcilable as a literary practice, the pro-nativist critics polarized them and somewhat scapegoated the modernist practitioners for Taiwan's rising social problems. Huang Chunming's 黃春明 "The Taste of the Apples" (2000a) illustrates the literary tendency of returning to Taiwan's daily reality and exposes Taiwan's predicament with American imperialism. The protagonist, Afa, is a hardworking laborer. Owing to his being hit by an American colonel's car, he and his family become "better-off" as a result of the colonel's generous compensation. When admitted to the hospital, jokingly called "the White House" because of its white decor, Afa for the first time in his life gets to taste apples, the symbol of America's economic hegemony over Taiwan, only to realize they are "not quite real." The American colonel at the end informs Afa of his wish to send Afa's deaf-mute daughter to the United States for education. This further symbolizes the Taiwanese people's inability to voice their oppression, as the unequal power is ironed out through the colonel's "benevolence." In "Xiaoqi's Cap" (Huang 2000b), a story about two Taiwanese salesmen peddling Japanese pressure cookers, Huang extends his concerns over foreign supremacy in Taiwan to Japanese technology. While one is fatally injured in an unexpected explosion, the other discovers the ugly skull underneath the cap of Xiaoqi, a little schoolgirl with whom he becomes friendly. Both the explosion and the removal of Xiaoqi's cap hint at the latent crisis of the seemingly beautiful future (foreign) materialistic modernity has promised.

While Huang portrays the humble lives of Taiwan's working class, Wang Zhenhe 王禎和 straddles nativist themes and modernist techniques with his hilarious satire of the uncritical admiration of American culture among Taiwanese (mostly the white-collar class) to register his social concerns. In *The Beauty Trap* (Wang Z. 1982), the manager insists that the employees sing the American national anthem daily. While the high-ranked people in the company send their children to the United States to study, mocked as "assisting America" in the novel, the low-ranked workers are busy running around for a tiny salary. The contrast between these two classes generates a profound irony embedded in the title: Is the "beauty" those who embrace America or those who are industrious and unpretentious low-ranked workers? His *Rose Rose I Love You* (Wang Z. 1984) represents Taiwan's postcolonial experience in his trademark profane satiric mode. It depicts how a few business-savvy people make plans to set up a bar (ironically at a church) and offer sex services to the American soldiers in the Vietnam War, who are anticipated to visit Taiwan. Here Wang pushes the limit of patriotism to an extreme: Is the export of Taiwanese and aboriginal female bodies an accomplice of American hegemony or a potential "resistance" by making profits from the Americans? Simultaneously, he paints a dark picture of the expected loss of an ideal native soil, as the town anticipating the arrival of the GIs cannot be exempt from degeneration. Another aspect distinguishing Wang from other nativist writers is the linguistic heteroglossia in his works. In *Rose Rose I Love You*, one can find the usage of Chinese, Taiwanese, Japanese, and English. This linguistic hybridity, an important and common attribute of postcoloniality, emerges in the debate surrounding whether Mandarin in Taiwan is a colonizer's tongue imposed on Taiwan's population in the 1990s, which is discussed later.

The Interplay between Postcolonial and Postmodern in Post–Martial Law Taiwan

The trend of rethinking Taiwan's subjectivity continued to advance throughout the 1980s. The lifting of martial law generated a wave of reflecting Taiwanese identity and previously repressed historical memory (such as the February 28th narrative). It also overlapped with the introduction of postmodern theories and, slightly later, postcolonial theories into Taiwan's academia. In 1992 Chiu Kuei-fen 邱貴芬 employed the "decentering" characteristic commonly shared by postmodern and postcolonial theories to explain Taiwan's subjectivity. She claimed that Taiwanese is a subject position, not an essentialized identity, proposing to understand the Taiwan-styled Mandarin through Homi Bhabha's concept of hybridity. However, Liao Chaoyang 廖朝陽 (1992) argued that hybridity works for the stronger culture, whereas the weaker culture would only be assimilated. He questions where Taiwan's selfhood stands if Taiwaneseness is by default an intercultural entity. Given Taiwan's influence from the Han culture, Japanese rule, and the West, and its status as a migrant society, the Taiwaneseness raised by Liao can be articulated only in the process of becoming.

In 1994 Liao Chaoyang introduced the idea of "emptiness" as a possibility to conceptualize one's subject position. Liao's radicalism elicited virulent debates, with Chen Zhaoying (1995) uttering her China-leaning sentiments to redress this nearly absolute constructivist notion of the "empty subject" and Liao Xianhao 廖咸浩 (1995) questioning Liao Chaoyang about the foundation for identity construction. Both Liaos quoted Slavoj Žižek to further their arguments. Liao Chaoyang stressed that in the order of being, the gap (from leaving the matrix) could be the empty subject itself. Liao Xianhao highlighted Žižek's notion of "constitutive antagonism"—the tension between the empty subject and the pursuit of the subject—and indicated that this tension in Taiwan is usually expressed through hostility toward the mainlanders. While the two Liaos' debate touched on crucial issues surrounding Taiwan's postcoloniality, it later turned into an emotionally charged argument about the difference in political tendencies. This ideological divergence was replicated in the debate between the pro-China Chen Yingzhen and the Taiwan-centric Chen Fangming 陳芳明 concerning Taiwan's literary historiography from 1997 to late 2000 in the magazine *Unitas*. Interestingly, while Chen Fangming (1999) regards the era of KMT rule as Taiwan's "recolonial" period, he considers émigré writers "Taiwanese" writers instead of colonizers. This demonstrates that cultural syncretism is inevitable when practicing postcolonial studies in Taiwan's multicultural society. While excluding émigré authors from Taiwan's literary historiography can lend weight to a Hoklo-centered nationalism, it leaves the Han people's suppression of indigenous culture unanswered.

With the ongoing debates on Taiwan's palimpsestic colonial past, *postcolonial* has become an almost inevitable term to carry out any Taiwan-centric discourse. But in terms of literary practice, works produced after the lifting of martial law are tinted with both postcolonial and postmodern hues. A striking example is found in the fictional representation of the formerly suppressed February 28 incident (henceforth 2.28). A nearly opposite take on 2.28 is exhibited through the 1990s works of Li Qiao 李喬 (the history-loaded *Buried Grievance of 1947* [1995]) and Lin Yaode 林燿德 (the playful and subversive *1947 Lilium Formosanum* [1990]). Lin eschews the Han Taiwanese perspective, retelling 2.28 from the aborigines' viewpoint. The novel focuses on the period from noon to 11:59 p.m. on February 27, 1947, challenging immediately the authority of the very date of the tragedy and all the signifiers that may attach to it. It is no longer remembered as the bloody conflict between Taiwanese and the mainlanders. Rather, it is remembered as an Atayal youth's search for his tribal tradition. Squashing Taiwan's four-hundred-year history into half a day and juxtaposing the four ethnocultural constituents (the Atayal myth, Western imperialism, Japanese colonialism, and Han society), Lin successfully decenters Han hegemony as well as the lineal trajectory and monophonic record of history. But the possibility of Atayal subjectivity seems to be deconstructed too. However, the ending of the novel—interpreted as a postmodern work—reminds us of the danger of assuming that the aboriginal culture is more authentic than the Han culture and that the aborigines have an unchanged tradition ready for them to return to. Quite the reverse, the heir of the Atayal heritage has interacted with other cultures and has yet to renegotiate his identity and reengage with his tribal tradition upon his return to the community.

Written after a decade of archival research and interviews, Li Qiao's *Buried Grievance of 1947* makes a stark contrast to Lin's representation of 2.28. For him, 2.28 is not merely a historical event but *the* event determining Taiwanese people's fate. This compels him to explain its meanings and offer his understanding of it to his readers. Li's wish to represent the complete scenes of 2.28 yields a tension between historical narration and fictional writing. To make allowance for both the factuality and fictionality of 2.28, he divided the work into two volumes, with the first one "tightly drawn to the historical facts" and the second one "purely dedicated to literature" (1995, 644). Through the characterization, Li detailed how Taiwanese people, after coming to terms with their "impure" Japanese past and the KMT-engineered Chinese imagination, finally become self-assured Taiwanese. Li once commented that 2.28 had damaged Taiwanese's collective mentality. Hence, he called for a positive attitude to walk through the trauma to develop an "autonomous cultural system" and a "new independent and autonomous state" (1998, 406–7).

While Li's "vulnerary" postcolonial take is commendable, we must stay vigilant about the reheard voices in his considerably Han-Taiwanese-focused redemptive narrative. This explains why the *Isle Margin* published a special issue on "alter-Native Taiwanese" (*jia Taiwanren* 假台灣人) in 1993, proposing this as Taiwan's fifth ethnic group. Written by "Taiwanren" (Taiwanese), the article states that alter-Native Taiwanese do not possess any subjectivity or essence. Nor can they form any center, nor are they represented. They are "a group without ethnic history or tradition, a (post)modern group constituted by broken, fragmented, and chaotic signs and experiences" (Taiwanren 1993, 45). Its website touts itself as a "marginal and left wing" website that "leads the (new) Taiwanese astray" and "creates historically informed and theoretically profound new discourses in the midst of the blue and green opposition" (*Isle Margin* 1993). This notion of alter-Native Taiwanese not only parodies the politicized ethnicity-centric identity but also challenges mainstream slogans such as "four major ethnic groups," "community of shared destiny," and "New Taiwanese" (Taiwanren 1993). It is partially compatible with the critical model of postloyalism discussed in David Der-wei Wang's chapter, mainly because of both terms' implication of proactive destabilizing and reenvisioning of extant, or foreseeable, dominant forms of identity discourse. Yet the alter-Native Taiwanese notion appears more radical. Unlike the (Chinese) loyalists who construct their identity as survivors of political upheaval and continue to be haunted by it, the alter-Native Taiwanese identity purposely refuses to claim any tradition, let alone the rather orthodox Chinese political lineage drawn by Wang. It is also more extreme than the postloyalist concept in a way: while the Chinese-centric postloyalism does not concern Taiwan's aborigines, alter-Native Taiwanese rejects the normalizing official discourse of "four major ethnic groups" (including the aborigines) outright.

Indeed, the calls for "major" ethnic groups and "shared" destiny risk ignoring the "minor" voices during the process of homogenization. A similar effort at ensuring multiple options for Taiwanese identity was made by David Chou 周威霖 in 1994 with his proposal for "Club 51"—turning Taiwan into the fifty-first state of America (Club 51, 1994). Chou's proposal of "state" building marks an interesting postnational move and an alternative mapping of Taiwan against the less discussed US cultural imperialism rather than the ambivalence toward China or nostalgia for Japan. In the era of speedy globalization, Chou's proposal becomes curiously pragmatic about Taiwan's survival. However, it still pivots on the traditional national identity and perhaps makes sense only to those with English proficiency, like Chou, who holds a law degree from America. Unsurprisingly, Kuan-hsing Chen (1996a) calls for a postnational critical syncretism, an "ethical" project to internalize one's subjectivity as the minoritarian others such as women, homosexuals, aborigines, the poor, and the Black. Chen's proposition endeavors to empower the weaker in various categories of identification. Yet, before this well-meaning internalization can take place, the determination of which group is to be internalized still requires the subject's agency, which is likely to be tendentious one way or the other.⁹

Conclusion

This chapter has analyzed some distinct characteristics of Taiwan's postcoloniality throughout the twentieth century with a focus on cultural discourses, scholarly debates, and literary expressions. It takes the postcolonial as a general search for and forging of subjectivity by Taiwanese intellectuals and writers in different sociohistorical contexts, including the Japanese colonization, the KMT-ruled era, and the post-1987 period. It examines how Taiwanese elites strove to maneuver a compromised voice within the colonial reality and how a Taiwan-focused discourse was carried out in the modernist-nativist polemics under the vague term *native soil*. Finally, it explores the convergence of the postcolonial and the postmodern in contemporary Taiwan. The diverse manifestations of postcoloniality remind us of Taiwan's divided political ideologies and ongoing imbalanced power configurations in aspects such as class, gender, and ethnicity.

Despite its theoretical limits, the postcolonial has been useful for expounding the conflicted yet kinetic Taiwan-Japan-China triangulation before and after 1945 and for reviewing America's impact on Taiwan. In the colonial era, Taiwan's subjectivity was situated largely between a Chinese loyalist mentality and not quite Japanese self-worth. In postwar politics, the KMT government engaged in military diplomacy with the Japanese on the one hand while disseminating anti-Japanese sentiments on the other hand, seeking the United States' aid for its dream of recovering the mainland. This background engendered a modified Taiwan-specific modernist practice. It, too, brought about the alliance of ideologically diverse critics in releasing their discontent together toward the KMT, whose policy left Taiwan at the mercy of (mainly American and Japanese) capitalist modernity. If British rule made Hong Kong more prepared to demand democracy, as Lo Kwai-Cheung's chapter observes, then Taiwan's Japanese past could lend strength to the construction of a Taiwan-centric historiography in literary practices. Wu Zhuoliu's switching "back" to write in Japanese for the "politically incorrect" details about the KMT's involvement in 2.28 in his *Taiwanese Forsythia* (1995) demonstrates how the ex-colonizer's language can be appropriated to document the repressed Taiwan-centric historical memory under the KMT's authoritarianism.

Taiwan's lingering nostalgia for Japan, more distinctively among the older generation of the native Taiwanese population who lived through the colonial and the KMT-ruled eras, further points to a peculiar response to the moral self-flagellations of Japan about its imperialist past. In parallel to the Japanese nostalgia among Taiwan's older population is the Japanophilia (*hari*) of the youngsters who grew up under the influence of Japanese youth culture and are not necessarily interested in their (grand)parents' firsthand colonized experience. Although the Japanophilia among Taiwan's younger generation is a 1990s phenomenon referring specifically to the influence of popular culture (such as Japanese TV dramas and popular writings about Japan in newspaper columns or books) and commercial products (Taiwanese youngsters' general fondness for Japanese goods, either for their better quality or for the cuteness with which the products are associated), the behavior of those fans is hardly related to the heavy colonial memory. Actually, Japan is not their only object of desire. Korea also has its share in Taiwanese young people's pattern of consumption. With more Japan-informed bloggers involved in the role of cultural translators, it would be unjust to rebuke all those youngsters as passive admirers of Japan.

The generational gap, however, remains palpable in the reception of Japanese colonialism. Wei Desheng's 魏德聖 blockbuster *Cape No. 7* (2008), criticized for being Japan pampering by Xu Jielin 許介鱗 (2008) and for "portraying (Taiwan's) despondency over not winning Japan's love" by Chen Yizhong 陳宜中 (2008) but celebrated among the younger audience for its fresh expression of a bottom-up "Taiwanese subjectivity," exemplifies this. As Wei aimed to make a popular film to raise money for his *Seediq Bale* (2011), an epic film about the Atayal's anti-Japanese Musha Incident, one can argue that Wei's deft co-opting of the style of Japanese idol drama (including the casting of Japanese pop star Atari Kōsuke 中孝介) in his fairly localized southern Taiwan–based narrative has contributed to the film's box office success. In other words, Taiwan's Japanese past has been appropriated as an audience-appealing tactic in popular culture despite the controversies.

In post-1987 Taiwan, the postmodern theory accentuating antitotalization, plurality, and heterogeneity operated in tandem with the postcolonial call for constructing a non-KMT-imposed Taiwanese subjectivity. Yet the deconstruction celebrated by postmodernists is more ideologically ambiguous than that of those employing postcolonial theory. Writers utilized the deconstruction aesthetics for different purposes, and postmodernists' rejection of a coherent subject continued to challenge the potential homogenization of newly constructed mainstream discourses. The postcolonial is anticipated to entail novel deployments because the negotiations of Taiwan's subjectivity are subject to new power slippages and cultural legacies generated by the island's forever-changing internal sociopolitical reality and neocolonial conditions. The unexpected outbreak of the COVID-19 pandemic, for instance, seems to have pushed Taiwan into escalating tensions between the two superpowers—China and the United States—over the latter's vaccine donations to Taiwan.

Despite Taiwan's relative marginality in global academic discourse, this fringe position can be considered "a space of power," enabling this "weak power" to "speak for themselves for the first time" (Hall 1997, 183). Taiwan's historical trajectory, as a fragment of multiple empires, has paradoxically served as a continuous driving force for the construction of its postcolonial subjectivities. A more fruitful way of applying postcolonial theory in Taiwan, however, is not just about subjectivity construction per se but ensuring that this imagination and production of an opposing force or alternative perspective remains open and emancipatory, making allowance for difference and diversity and taking heed of the election-driven political manipulations and homogenizing neoliberal cultural and economic globalization. While ethnic tension might have waned (as it cannot be simplified as the mainlanders favoring the People's Republic versus the independence-leaning Taiwanese) and the difference between the major political parties has decreased, Taiwan's limited global recognition is likely to make the national identity of Taiwanese people a thornier issue in the years to come.

Notes

1 Southern Taiwan was under Dutch rule from 1624 to 1662, whereas northern Taiwan was under Spanish rule from 1626 to 1641. Zheng Chenggong (Koxinga) conquered the Dutch colony of Formosa and established the Ming-Zheng Kingdom (1661–83) before Taiwan fell to Qing rule (1683–1895) and Japanese colonial rule (1895–1945). Some consider the Nationalist Party's rule under martial law (1945–87) Taiwan's "recolonial" period.
2 This view of colonialism as the Western powers' domination over the third world is limiting even within Europe. The Soviets' imperialist expansion within Europe, for instance, is not fully addressed.
3 Despite the diverse perspectives that postcolonial studies invite, Ella Shohat (1992) argues that postcolonial theory remains "ahistorical," "universalizing," and potentially "depoliticizing" in its deployments.
4 In the 2014 revision of the book, a noticeable change was referring to the Japanese rule as *riju* (Japanese occupation) instead of *rizhi* (Japanese rule). Some high school students protested against the then ruling Nationalist government's "brainwash" (Lin 2015).

5 Some may prefer to use 2000, the year Taiwan for the first time had a president from an opposition party, as the starting point of Taiwan's postcoloniality, but this view privileges political change and risks downplaying the perspective of Taiwanese aborigines.
6 The modernity introduced by Japan into Taiwan was already a mediated/translated one, Japan's Meiji Restoration being itself a transplantation of Western modernity.
7 The Taiwanese People's Party was allowed to be established partly because its political appeal for setting up a Taiwan Assembly was comparatively mild and partly because it could check and balance the radicalism of the postsplit Taiwanese Cultural Association.
8 *First generation* refers to writers born around the mid-nineteenth century who experienced China's cession of Taiwan to Japan as adults. They often wrote classical Chinese poems full of loyalist sentiments. The second-generation Chinese-language writers were born roughly between 1895 and the 1910s. Although Lai He did not compose in Japanese, Wu Zhuoliu and Yang Kui of this cohort did.
9 The former Chiang Kai-shek Memorial Hall, renamed Liberty Square, and the Taipei New Park 2.28 Memorial Park are two cases in which political values are privileged. In the latter the rights of homosexual people become underrepresented because the venue used to be a major cruising site for gays in Taipei. Compared to the Taiwanese indigenous peoples, who have been demanding more rights since the 1980s, Taiwan's Southeast Asian migrant workers are more marginalized.

Questions of Postcolonial Agency

Thought of the Other is occasionally presupposed by dominant populations, but with an utterly sovereign power, or proposed until it hurts by those under them, who set themselves free. The other of Thought is always set in motion by its confluences as a whole, in which each is changed by and changes the other.
—ÉDOUARD GLISSANT, *Poetics of Relation*

Democracy in Retreat

For many third world countries, the postcolonial phase may well mean continuing struggles with contradictory colonial legacies and mixed blessings, with a large proportion of them falling into autocracies and oligarchies. The postcolonial elites tend to reinvent new forms of colonialism and to introduce ethnonationalism to discriminate and to expunge. As a result, since the 1940s, despots all over have held on to almost permanent positions and manipulated electoral polls to consolidate their powers. According to a recent special report in the *Economist* (2020), ten years after the Arab Spring, the Middle Eastern and African world is in disarray, with millions displaced, tens of thousands dead. Increasingly, the catchword is *development* rather than *democracy*, as the postcolonial political leaders take advantage of "opportunity zones" or infrastructure construction projects, while putting their opponents in prison and declaring themselves to be presidents or prime ministers for life. From China to Peru, the postcolonial picture doesn't look bright indeed, with mainstream citizens turned populist and right-wing supporters of dictatorship, or, in the words of Achille Mbembe (2019), of necropolitics, rendering their societies torn by worsening inequality, militarization, racism, and banal brutality.

Part of the reason for such a dismal postcolonial situation may have to do with the shortcomings in local constituencies and the psychosocial structure of provincial inadequacies. However, a major contributing factor is the decline of democracy in the West and, with it, the impending questions of postcolonial agency in many parts of the world—with the exception of probably East Asia—in forging national identity and doing cultural translation to bring home such concept metaphors of colonial modernity as democracy, freedom, minority rights, social progress, and so on, in any hybridized or catachrestic styles imaginable. Scholars have examined postcolonial European nations' "imperial exceptionalism," which often evokes nostalgic (albeit regressive) memory of colonial endeavor as a benevolent strategy of "denial and simultaneous legitimation of continued racial exclusion at the national and international level," especially in relation to mediatized, backward, and reactionary images of postcolonial migration (Jensen et al. 2017, 3). To undercut such a claim of exceptionalism, postcolonial Europe has, however, been enmeshed in a series of financial crises that threatens to tear Europe apart from the inside and from the outside—illegal migrants from former colonies, on top of China's Belt and Road Initiative challenge and US tariffs or high-tech monopoly, among others.

On the rise of antidemocratic (and apocalyptic) politics in America, Wendy Brown has teased out the intensification of "nihilism, fatalism, and ressentiment"—against fact-checking, science, or even mask wearing, for example—among white male supremacists. "Perhaps there is a form of nihilism shaped," she writes, "by the waning of a type of social dominance or the waning social dominance of a historical type" (2019, 180). "As this type finds itself in a world emptied not only of meaning," she suggests, "but of its own place, far from going gently into the night, it turns toward apocalypse. If white men cannot own democracy, there will be no democracy. If white men cannot rule the planet, there will be no planet" (180). This is also what Steven Levitsky and Daniel Ziblatt observe regarding the guardrails of American democracy today: "The erosion of our democratic norms began in the 1980s and 1990s and accelerated in the 2000s" (2018, 9). They attribute such weakening to "extreme partisan polarization—one that extends beyond policy differences into an existential conflict over race and culture" (9). With the empires going amok, it is small wonder that the world jeers in postcolonial cynical reason. Donald Trump's incitement of insurrection on January 6, 2021, for instance, appears to be déjà vu, just another staged coup all too familiar to peoples in Belarus, Egypt, Kazakhstan, Nigeria, Syria, Venezuela, and indeed many other places. To find alternatives, Levitsky and Ziblatt urge us to look elsewhere for inspiration. Along such a line of argument, I propose here to discuss two recent films from Taiwan on the questions of postcolonial agency, not only to raise issues regarding the ways in which resistance and social change may be implemented, but also to address this topic as the new religion in the time of democracy in ruins and the apocalypse.

The rise of new Buddhist sects in 1980s Taiwan, as this chapter demonstrates, has much to do with the island's postcolonial conditions, with the local Taiwanese new class beginning to dominate in the economic and industrial manufacturing sectors. They demanded fairer political representation, retribution or social justice, and, in particular, an end to a long period of double or internal colonization: Dutch conquest (1622–61), Chinese settlement (1636–1895), Japanese occupation (1895–1945), and Nationalist "recovery." Between 1945 and 1985, Taiwan was under the rule of the Nationalist (Kuomintang) government, which introduced re-Sinification policies by reversing the national identity construction process and by undermining the local languages and cultures. By 1985 a new and vibrant opposition, the Democratic Progressive Party (DPP), began to transform the public sphere by mobilizing the critical mass to launch large-scale social movements in raising ecological consciousness, upholding minority rights, consolidating popular sovereignty through general elections, and seeking opportunities to rejoin the United Nations as an independent country: no longer the first world's dumping ground, or even just a renegade province of China, as claimed by the Republic of China or the People's Republic of China. Taking over as president in 1989, Lee Teng-hui tried to cut ties with China by proposing localization and steering away from China by going south—that is, promoting offshore investment in Vietnam, Indonesia, the Philippines, and so on—rather than depending on Chinese cheap labor. In response to Lee's "South Advance" projects, mainlander Chinese in the administration turned against the local power bloc, faulting Lee for betraying the national interests, causing partisan strife, and generating distrust and fear among the people. Seeing the internal split as an opportunity, the mainland Chinese government made it a habit, if not an everyday practice, from then on to send fighter jets and missiles across the Taiwan Strait to warn the "secessionists" in Taiwan.

It is within these contexts that movies like *The Terrorizers* (directed by Edward Yang 楊德昌, 1986) and *City of Sadness* (directed by Hou Hsiao-hsien

侯孝賢, 1989) zoom in on political polarization, ethnic tensions, implosive anxieties, suicidal impulses, and the apocalypse. In such times of political upheaval and turmoil, resuscitation of Japanese Zen Buddhism became a fashionable spiritual trend of attaining inner peace and "second harmony," as the local elites were mostly businesspeople or manufacturers who came of age in the Japanese period and then survived the White Terror imposed on them by the Nationalist regime. Heqi Tao (Hochi, life forces brought into harmony) was a product of such a volatile era, evolving as a way to get rid of the "negative" messages, to battle ecopolitical stagnation, and to boost energy, especially when Taiwan not only had become increasingly isolated but also was constantly harassed by China through all sorts of economic coercion and military threats. New Buddhist cults boomed as a result, and the practitioners would often embrace and even disseminate problematic apocalyptic narratives that Taiwan's economic miracle had come to an end and its political future was doomed.

It is interesting that both Wendy Brown and Achille Mbembe relate new religious practices or dark messianism to the age of posttruth, postcolonialism, and postdemocracy, particularly with regard to the ways in which apocalyptic narratives grow out of fear and anxiety to exclude or purge ethnic others. Evidently, postcolonial spiritual agency has worked side by side with those economic (Brown sums these up as "neoliberal") and political institutions that function to discriminate, deport, or destroy. Brown asks, "What if supremacy is the rosary held tight as white civilization itself appears finished and takes with it all futurity?" (2019, 180). This is probably why lots of Christian evangelicals are behind Donald Trump and his plea to overthrow the government in violence, in total rejection of the changing social reality, of civil movements (like Black Lives Matter), and of choice.

However, unlike the American version of evangelical prosperity theology that unites white supremacists with the Republican regime, new Buddhist cults in Taiwan and in the Sinophone communities actually cultivate the arts of survival through mediated healing and a collective therapeutic process of self-maintenance. They agonize over the ambivalent consequences of Taiwan's localization and democratization. To many mainlander Chinese and Taiwanese on the island, the new postcolonial situations not only disrupt social stability but also put Taiwan at risk by provoking China, which has become an aggressive superpower. In the past the ruling class, made up of a large body of bureaucrats, educators, members of the military, and technocrats, used to enjoy sociopolitical privileges and to benefit from favor networks that provided lifetime security—for example, once they retired, they had good pension plans with a return of 18 percent interest. As Taiwan enters a postcolonial phase by going local and democratic, the residual ruling class clashes with the emerging middle class, finding themselves increasingly left out and lost, with no certain future in sight. Tormented by profound fears and anxieties, the disciples of these Taiwanese Buddhist cults desperately look toward their masters for lessons on how to overcome domestic and international negative components in hard times. As Mbembe puts it more succinctly, "Contrary to biblical messianism, contemporary avatars of messianism are not concerned about the fate of the slave" (2019, 106). "Negative messianism is a kind of messianism that has either forfeited the idea of redemption as such or has been reduced to a crude belief in the expiatory power of bloodshed. It is not about salvation. In its minor version, it is about survival and the willingness to sacrifice or to be sacrificed. Its aim is to turn a forgiving God into an ethnic and angry god. In its major version, it is about collective suicide before the Apocalypse" (106). That is, if we update such a phantasmagoric narrative, the end of the world might assume the image of a panicking Batman ensnared in the webs of coronavirus variants, flying in cycles over a hot, trounced landscape that is charred by forest fires. Or, as Mbembe observes, "The clock is ticking down and nothing is sustainable. The seas are boiling, filthy with plastic bags and drowning polar bears; the smoggy air will soon be swarming with (more) U.S. military drones, rogue-states nuclear drones, homemade bioweaponry, and Amazon's fleet of robotic delivery services" (106).

Two 2017 Films from Taiwan

The two recent films from Taiwan discussed in this chapter zoom in on such an apocalyptic vision and dark messianism. *Great Buddha Plus (+)* 大佛普拉斯 (directed by Huang Hsin-yao 黃信堯) and *The Bold, the Corrupt, and the Beautiful* 血觀音 (directed by Yang Ya-che 楊雅喆) came out in 2017, the year in which lots of the Taiwanese middle class vented their frustration and anger against President Tsai Ing-wen 蔡英文, the "empress and dictator" who had drastically revised established nationalist policies by reducing the rate of return on elites' pensions from 18 percent to just 2 percent in the name of political justice and economic equity. The year saw the unprecedented rise of fake news on the island, as local educators and social media workers teamed up to promote antigovernment sentiments, on top of disseminating pseudopublic discourses to call for collective action in response to the perceived betrayal of people's trust and, above all, President Tsai's pro-independence stance. Tsai urges people not only to "put down local roots" but also, under the guise of "moving south," to invest in Southeast Asian countries and welcome more immigrants from the region. According to the right-wing voters, who helped establish a pro-unification cult under the leadership of Han Guoyu 韓國瑜, the incoming Kaohsiung mayor, the Tsai administration's actions would inevitably push Taiwan toward a crash course with China and thereby bring about the apocalypse. As fears and anxieties accumulated, large- and small-group communications across Line, WeChat, and other mobile internet channels promulgated survival strategies by emphasizing, on the one hand, "saving oneself" (*zijiu* 自救) but also by demanding, on the other hand, the reinstatement of the pro-China Nationalist regime in the coming elections, so as to cherish the hope of coexistence in peace and prosperity.

No Asian religion fits better in the intellectual and spiritual contexts of caring for oneself than a new Buddhist conviction inspired by Catholicism, a way to do good and revitalize energy in the everyday as advocated by the Reverend Tzu-chi and then promoted by several Zen monks across the local and overseas Chinese communities. This sort of new Buddhist sect and club membership is highlighted in the two films in question here, with the contrasting image of doing good on a superficial level in *Great Buddha Plus* and of doing something evil to one's own daughter, an intimate enemy, in *The Bold, the Corrupt, and the Beautiful*. In diverse ways these two films raise the issue of the possibility of resisting or speaking back to power; both address local disparities in terms of the moral ironies that the most corrupt and materialistic elites are key members of electro-spiritual Buddhist societies. On the surface, these "true believers" aim to regain innocence and redemption through practicing Zen Buddhism; however, they actually commit horrendous murders and betray their loved ones.

As the title suggests, *Great Buddha Plus* draws on the Buddhist doctrines that consider kindness to all living beings and benevolent deeds as moral imperatives. But nothing can be further removed from the truth, as the film begins with a group of social outcasts who struggle to eke out a living by recycling boxes and bottles, undertaking multiple dangerous jobs to pay off family medical bills, enduring hunger or unemployment, and, at best, serving as a security guard. Unlike these poor subalterns, who show goodwill to each other in spite of their financial difficulties, the superrich and the most powerful members of the Buddhist club are abusive, lustful, selfish, and indifferent to human suffering and even death. The elitist class, represented in the film by the boss of the factory and his congregants, uses Buddhist gatherings to build their business network, to revive their energy, and to overcome obstacles, that is, to sublimate and achieve a greater harmony by practicing meditation and reciting scriptures. To these elites, the most remarkable way to get elevated is by donating to the club and by contributing to the construction of a temple or a great Buddha statue. At the launch ceremony of the great Buddha, with which the film concludes, however, all the candles get blown out, and suddenly in the eerie silence somebody is playing a drum inside the great Buddha's belly. A person must have been murdered or buried alive there. Can it be that the deceased has returned in the form of a female ghost to haunt? A typhoon is coming, and the clouds darken, as if the apocalypse prevails over the island. It seems the Messiah never arrives and in his stead just a hauntological specter demanding musical attention: not even political justice, as there is only darkness, and people just freeze.

Throughout the film everything seems to gain added (hence "plus") values or meanings as unexpected situations start to unfold new dimensions or inside perspectives. The ragpicker, for one, thinks of his recycling job as essential to environmental protection. He demands that his friend pay him more handsomely, only to realize that the boxes and bottles collected are dumped as added-on garbage: the small sum of money he has been getting is in fact just charity from a sympathetic but by no means forgiving friend. The security guard has the additional responsibility of taking care of his boss's expensive SUV, but he learns a way to retrieve the digital data recorded in the car during traffic. The CD-ROMs turn out to contain pornographic tapes of what has been illicitly going on between the boss and his mistresses. The sex tapes are not only entertaining but also enabling, as the security guard, supposedly a powerless little man, by now has acquired enough inside knowledge to cultivate his agency over the boss and his "affective affiliates." Together with the ragpicker, he witnesses his boss's quarrels with a mistress and later on learns that the extramarital affair might have ended badly—a female body inserted and cemented into the great Buddha's belly. In the film no protagonist dominates; it is the small and distracting narratives around the lives of all these minor characters that reveal. Director Huang adds a traditional narrative formula to the film—a singer of tales, accompanied on the three-string lute, a local musical instrument—on top of providing from time to time his voice-over, to illuminate the background, to offer commentaries, and to moralize (if a bit sarcastically) about local and global disparities. In the face of poverty and misery, death and loss, the elitist Buddhist club appears only to add more corruption and hypocrisy. The state is superfluous or simply evaporates.

The picture in *The Bold, the Corrupt, and the Beautiful* is even grimmer and more apocalyptic. The film can be interpreted as a gender-bending Taiwanese version of *The Godfather* (directed by Francis Coppola, 1972) or as a thriller and political film that foregrounds the femme fatale and social anxiety (Chen 2020, 247). However, the Buddhist club is depicted, along with its symbolic capital, exclusive political networking, and ensuing corruption, in such a way that it is at the core of the film, which ends with Madame Tang (the godmother) sending her men to take out her daughter so that the latter won't be able to escape or to confess to the authorities all kinds of evil deals done by the family. It is interesting that the film is titled *Guanyin in Bloodshed* in Chinese, while director Yang opts for *The Bold, the Corrupt, and the Beautiful* in the English subtitles, perhaps indicating the film's indebtedness to the famous western movie *The Good, the Bad, and the Ugly* (directed by Sergio Leone, 1967). As a matter of fact, Guanyin is a male (albeit minor) bodhisattva in India, but in the process of cultural translation and transport, he switches gender to symbolize feminine grace and "mercy," gaining more prominence in Chinese Buddhism, almost an equivalent to the Christian Madonna. The film begins with an elaborate close-up shot of a historical Guanyin relic imported from Thailand, having one of her arms slightly twisted but glowing nevertheless with a rare jade body as if burning or stained with blood. Madame Tang, our hardly merciful protagonist, immediately is drawn to the religious icon and precious commodity. In many ways, she gives an appearance of embracing the graceful motherly image, but she actually embodies something completely opposite to Guanyin: she is ruthless, bloodthirsty, and, above all, brutal in hunting down her rivals—including her most intimate friends and family members. In the film Madame Tang corrupts practically everybody else, the only exception being her granddaughter, who manages to grow like a lotus out of the muddy water. Madame Tang utilizes her daughter to seduce leading politicians and businesspeople to secure her shares in many grand construction projects, while at the same time trying to keep her grandchild close to her as a figure of innocent beauty. But of course the granddaughter sees all the obscenities and knows better. She just pretends to be childlike, constantly awaiting her chance to do good or save her mother—though always already too late. The three women form an evil trinity in such complex ways that there is no exit from the godmother's predetermined plans. Even when the daughter attempts a daring escape, she ends up having no other option but to be sacrificed, with no redemption in sight.

As the daughter plans to free herself and starts a new career in South Asia, Madame Tang bids her farewell but immediately sets off the timed bomb to blow up the boat. Such a horrendous and totally unexpected implosion plot from a supposedly loving mother who is deep down a femme fatale and a domestic terrorist sums up the apocalypse in a most dreadful manner. It seems that in an increasingly dangerous and uncertain world, intimacy and affection feed only greed and a thirst for bloody revenge. However, something scary and subtly political may be embedded here in terminating the no-longer-obedient daughter, who has decided to start anew in the south. Can we read this incident as an implied critique of the Tsai administration's renewed and more vigorous "South Advance" investment project? Or as a blunt rejection of Taiwan's "self-determination" (hence postcolonial) path to move away from China? Is Taiwan's political and economic future doomed?

Madame Tang is originally from Hong Kong but is married to a powerful Chinese officer in Taiwan. Her given name alludes to a particular type of begonia flower that actually resembles the shape of China on the map. Her late husband is a prominent Nationalist general from mainland China. His picture hangs in the living room to ensure that all local business transactions with China will be successful. Madame Tang is ambitious and skillful in using numerous tricks to entice, enslave, and expunge. (A literal intertextual allusion here could be the Yu political family in Kaohsiung, at least three generations of whom became county mayor or served in the state legislature, after Grandpa Yu Dengfa was murdered at home on September 13, 1989, as a frontrunner of the DPP and also a martyr.) In the early years, Madame Tang draws on her husband's prestigious networks, but she goes on to expand them and gains even more power through sex, lobbying, misinformation, intimidation, and especially organized Buddhist club activities—spiritual but often materialistic sessions, by sacred and secular means, often combined. Madame Tang practices what the new Buddhist schools would call "giving a new life to the dharma on the profane earth" (Sheng Yan 2003, 10), to make the best of the hardest times before the apocalypse hits, before a wrathful Buddha appears to mete out justice and end the world in violence.

That Yu Dengfa was murdered on the eve of Taiwan's forty-year-old martial law being lifted in 1987 (hence the start of the postcolonial phase) is part of the island's slow and traumatic democratization processes. Martial law was introduced by Chiang Kai-shek in 1949 when he fled to Taiwan, thinking that he would use the island as a bastion to reclaim China from the hands of the communists. The law banned unauthorized political activities—including illegal social gatherings and organizations, as the Generalissimo had learned his bitter lessons only too well in losing his war to Chairman Mao Zedong. Under martial law, tens of thousands of Taiwanese and mainlander Chinese were arrested or put to death. In 1979 a major crackdown on the "insurrection" and its aftermath as generated by the Formosa Incident took place at Kaohsiung, Yu's hometown. Yu was therefore singled out as a main organizer of the subversive plot and "riot," but he went free as international amnesty organizations, American congresspeople, and world news agencies expressed their concerns over the incident. Because of Yu and many of his allies, Taiwan's DDP moved forward to urge President Lee Teng-hui to lift the outdated martial law. As a reactionary gesture to vent their frustrations, the nationalist secret police targeted and assassinated Yu, staging it as a suicide.

In the film, even though Yu's name is not mentioned, the progenitor is implied as a likely model for the important political family that produces corrupt governors and legislatures in the south. (The DDP leader, President Tsai, is from Pingdong, a neighboring prefecture farther south.) While partially based on a true story, the film zooms in on the pseudoreligious bonds that Madame Tang forges to suggest something even more politically and ethically disturbing. Madame Tang exploits Buddhism and its icons (including the Guanyin relic) as state commodity fetishes to reinforce moral blackmail and economic control over others. She assumes the role of the Guanyin bodhisattva to strengthen favor networks and to provide friends with many opportunities to take advantage of governmental projects, just like a savior or, more accurately, a dark Messiah. When her daughter is tortured by an inner sense of guilt and tries to seek redemption, Madame Tang urges her men to wipe her out in a massive act of destruction and in sheer violence to justify it as intercepting or even "purifying" the potentially ugly and disastrous scenario of an undesirable failure, the "mess" or unnecessary hindrance. In Madame Tang's postcolonial crypto-cynical reasoning, human emancipation is unequivocally not an option. This is how she absorbs and thereby becomes transfigured by the qi (vital life force) from the jade body of a stained Guanyin relic, so that she may survive treason and unwanted situations. Achille Mbembe has argued that "neoliberalism has created the conditions for a renewed convergence, and at times fusion, between the living human being and objects, artifacts, or the technologies that supplement or augment us and are in the process transfigured and transformed by us" (2019, 108). On top of such neoliberalism (that brings ruin to our democracy, as Wendy Brown advocates), commodity fetishism and Buddhist electro-spiritualism operate in such a way that they bring precious religious relics into perfect (albeit destructive and apocalyptic to others) fusion with the new aura and cult of purity, feng shui, organic vitality, and therapeutic healing or cleansing.

Money, Meditation, Music, Magic, and Medicine

Several cultural and medical anthropologists have delved into perhaps a number of the more prominent and globally successful Buddhist organizations, like Tzu Chi (Mercy Charity) and Fagu (Dharma Drum), in terms of their founders' "charisma and compassion" and their institutional structures, rather than their impact on the believers' mind and body in the constitution of a sense of well-being (Pazderic 2004; C. J. Huang 2009). These Buddhist organizations have attracted millions of disciples to "build a better world through their collective good work" (Huang 2009, 217). To accomplish their good work, the disciples are constantly engaging in very orchestrated forms of qi circulation and transformation, involving, as Huang witnesses, collective "weeping and musical corporeality" (124–52). And no Buddhist sect is more popular among the superclass—engineers, medical professionals, scientists, and intellectuals—on the island than the Dharma Drum, which fuses Zen Buddhism and meditation or physical-mental therapy. Just like Indian yoga, which brings physical, mental, and spiritual exercises together to discipline and to heal, Dharma Drum urges practitioners to spend three to seven days in isolation to do meditation lessons, boost their vital energy, and rid themselves of negative elements in their mind and body.

But in the films the references may be to more hybrid Buddhist societies that are indebted not only to Tzu Chi and Fagu but to some other sects that promote communal well-being through large gatherings, as initiated by Michael Chou and a number of masters from Vietnam or overseas Chinese communities. As a founder of Heqi Tao (the practice to bring vital forces or energies into harmony, a popular trend in the electro-spiritual communities), Chou (1997) explains it this way in terms of electromagnetic audio technologies of transmission, reception, and recording: "The entire environment is an ill condition. . . . What causes it? Each of us is like a small radio station continuously transmitting messages. These messages are accumulated in the cosmos and in our bodies . . . because these many different small radio stations continuously transmit various negative messages (complaints, hatred, resentment, and feelings of suppression and fear). These messages, accumulating in the outside world and within our own bodies, result in a very forceful negative effect."

How does one rid oneself of these negative messages? Disciples can learn from the master to open their hearts by going through the process of overcoming, practicing an energy-revival exercise (qigong), or repeating key popular songs to generate an emotional atmosphere conducive to universal love, so as to recover their true selves. Heqi Tao promises to take people back to their childhood and create a situation to let practitioners find something they have lost. However, the concept of qi derives more from a creolized version of traditional Chinese Taoist doctrines as illuminated by modern physics and electromagnetics. Drawing on Taoist and Chinese kung fu notions of the body, Chou suggests that the magnetic field is the essence of both life and social power, generated in the paradoxical process of overcoming and transcending old formats. As the magnetic field pervades a society, the smart one knows that he or she must smash traditional institutional or ideological structures such as small, family-centered businesses, so that these can be replaced and revitalized by large-scale, value-added, and computerized biotechnical production. This technological imagination and its promises of success are at the core of the discourse to transform one's capacity to be able to compete in, and outwit, the world network of trade.

Chou's life experience indicates such promises of success. A motorcycle accident in Taiwan left him partially paralyzed from a spinal injury in 1980. He learned from his mother, a martial arts teacher, but managed to cure himself through alternative means. Following his miraculous recovery, he went to the United States to study Chinese medicine. In the mid-1980s, he began to teach a hybrid form of martial arts and spiritual arts that he had learned from his mother and grandmother. In 1994 he called his practice Heqi and thereby gave traditional martial and spiritual arts new meanings in light of physics and psychotherapy. The term Heqi in fact derives from Japanese karate, which has a long tradition of blending Chinese kung fu with a holistic view (Tao) of energy building for a sudden breakthrough. In many ways, Heqi Tao has always already been a creolized form of sustaining spiritual biopower, of cultural retranslation. Whereas in the Japanese version the philosophy is to synthesize bodily energy for self-defense, the doctrines advocated by Chou emphasize a "harmonious atmosphere" and "primordial *qigong*" (Pazderic 2004, 195). Heqi is said to have performed miracles and to have generated enormous interest in alternative healing, such that by 1999 not only Heqi Tao but several Buddhist organizations had set up TV networks, CD circulation channels, websites, and email editions of magazines and became globalized. Electro-spiritual communities are electrified not simply by illuminating lasers, fiber-optic transmitters, radio waves, and microwaves but also by asserting universal love to extend, as part of a Greater China discourse, the revolutionizing of the world in the image of their middle-class enlightened selves. It is only natural that more and more engineers, managers, and makers of cell phones (especially the iPhone, which outsources the assembly to Foxconn) find themselves attuned to such electro-spiritual practices in fending off all sorts of malaises and disorders, not to mention emotional vulnerability, unconscious tensions, and other negative messages from everyday life.

Heqi Tao practitioners often begin their workout rituals by reciting scriptures and popular songs (such as "Hardworking, the Only Way to Win") that are hybrid products. The matters and methods used indicate a long history of the evolution of Chinese kung fu in response to Western concepts of colonialism and modernity, of magic and medicine. Nikola Pazderic associates the rise of Heqi Tao with the structural transformation of the contemporary Taiwanese political economy. To him, Heqi Tao practitioners appear to have "had intimate institutional experience" with the shift in Taiwan's economic success in the 1980s as a sign to "fill in the gap of recognition caused by the exclusion of the Republic of China from the status of nationhood" (196). In his view, Heqi Tao serves to compensate for or to renegotiate the benefits of "nationalist ideologies, policies, and power" (196). That is partly why Pazderic opens his essay with these succinct but general remarks: "Promises of success and specters of failure permeate public life in contemporary Taiwan" (196).

Heqi practice began in the United States in the early 1990s, but by 2002 its centers and training programs numbered in the dozens, operating successfully in many major cities, following the seed practice institutes in Los Angeles, San Jose, and Taichung. The membership fee as of spring 1997 was NT 18,000 (over US$600 per year), but the cost to join has been reduced quite drastically as more and more disciples started to donate money and even contribute substantially to help build or sustain Heqi centers (Pazderic 2004, 199). Pazderic points out quite correctly that the story of Heqi's success "testifies to the personal charisma of the founder and to the dedication, organization, and wealth of his followers" (199). He highlights the relevancy of media discourse, psychotherapy, love, and electronics to the subject in question. A lot of what Chou preaches in fact conforms to Buddhist doctrines; however, Chou (1996) not only adds a new psychophysical dimension but also associates bodily movement with magic, music, and memory retrieval: "While we do the bows, a stream of thoughts will come to mind. Do not attempt to suppress them, for they have greater importance than mere random thoughts. They are records from our deepest subconscious memory, i.e., our worries, our fears, issues that we don't want to face, or events that we have forgotten. These may be matters whose accumulation have caused damage to the various corresponding systems of the body." Pazderic reports that during one training session a theme song from *Oshin*, a Japanese soap opera that took Taiwan by storm in 1994 and since then has enjoyed constant reruns, was used for its highly powerful message regarding a young lower-middle-class girl from the countryside who endures and overcomes hardships. The affective as well as acoustic ambience of the song helps generate an emotional atmosphere conducive to spiritual love and psychomagnetic dynamics. On other occasions, Pakistani Sufi hymns and African drumbeats are said to be popular among the followers.

Music and magic thus work together to evoke the communal sense of a second harmony, moving through a self-emptying and overcoming process to reach a fulfilling mental as well as physical state of positivity, endowed with love and tranquility. During the session "expressive gestures to accompany the song were taught to the group by senior disciples. . . . The songs, gestures, and stories created an appropriate atmosphere . . . for further transmission and reception of Heqi," so as to move the body more expansively to eliminate negative messages and diseases (Pazderic 2004, 206–8). Those who experience the recovery of their true selves are asked to speak out and share with other group members what they have gone through. An informant told Pazderic this: "All the practitioners said Heqi really opened their hearts. . . . By the fifth day all practitioners became innocent like children; they showed themselves entirely; that means they all opened their hearts before the class ended. I talked about how Heqi takes people back to childhood or infancy with some practitioners, and they all agreed. Actually, Heqi creates a situation to let practitioners go and find something they lost before" (210).

It is precisely against the backdrop of the 1980s economic miracle (and, with it, stressful political-economic situations) that Heqi Tao gained popularity as a form of recovering one's true self, of overcoming the sense of loss. As numerous Heqi Tao practitioners are at the same time disciples of Buddhist organizations such as Tzu Chi and Fagu, they help promote new hybrid forms of meditation and therapy, particularly in turning to Buddhist masters for magical healing. The late 1980s saw Taiwan in its interregnum with the lifting of martial law in 1987 and with more tensions arising across the strait as the island launched its localization processes under the leadership of President Lee Teng-hui. It is small wonder that intellectuals, engineers, cell phone makers, and the superrich are attracted to the vital energy-retrieval activities orchestrated by many Buddhist societies, so that they can stay strong and healthy—but in a rather repressive, narcotic, and selfish manner, as portrayed in the two films.

The Questions of Postcolonial Agency

The Bold, the Corrupt, and the Beautiful depicts Buddhist cults in 1980s Taiwan, not only considering their healing power in keeping superrich people like Madame Tang from aging and her family members from earthly worries—so as to be able to maintain childlike innocence and heavenly beauty—but also singling out the miraculous functions of the jade Buddha relics and the master's spells over the disciples. The contemporary reference is to quite a few morally depraved yet commercially highly successful sects led by such ingenious masters as Song Qili 宋乾琳, Miao Tian 妙天, and Miao Chan 妙禪. Song is so powerful that his disciples include major politicians and CEOs of transnational corporations like James Soong 宋楚瑜 (president of the People First Party, better known as the former governor of Taiwan Province and twice a presidential candidate) and the late Zhang Ronfa 張榮發 (of EVA Airways and Evergreen). However, instead of demonstrating their sophisticated interpretations of foundational Buddhism doctrines such as selflessness and spiritual emptiness, these masters often show off their materialistic accumulations. Miao Tian ("Heavenly Miracle"), for example, prides himself on putting his predecessor Song to shame, as he counts several of the most expensive Lamborghinis and Rolls-Royces as gifts from disciples, whose standard uniforms are golden robes. But Miao Tian's wealth and power are eclipsed by those of Miao Chan (the name means "Marvels of Zen"), whose congregation is far larger and all dressed in purple. Accordingly, Miao Chan is hailed as the Purple Buddha in the Chinese kingdom on earth, at least across the Taiwan Strait.

Evidently, it is no longer inner harmony or redemption that concerns important members of these Buddhist clubs or organizations. Director Yang uses Madame Tang to tease out the contradictory practice of dedication and manipulation, of boom and doom: the matriarch single-handedly renders the family highly powerful (albeit corrupt) but at the same time destroys it by taking out her daughter. As a power broker and intimidator, Madame Tang does not fully control or even prevail. The granddaughter in fact cultivates her postcolonial agency in resistance. She is the child growing up in 1980s Taiwan at a truncated historical juncture, experiencing the shift from totalitarianism to democracy. She lives in a grand Japanese-style house, which calls her attention to the colonial and postcolonial trajectories in terms of place and identity. The house must have been designed and inhabited by a Japanese colonial officer and his family. Then, after the Nationalist Party took over Taiwan in 1947, the house was given to Madame Tang's husband, a high-ranking general. As a widow, Madame Tang inherited the house, but she uses it as a social space for conducting business transactions and showing off her wealth, artifacts, and privileges. In the film the granddaughter is the only person who lives and stays in the house. Unlike her grandma, who is originally from Hong Kong and defines herself as a mainlander's wife, the little girl picks up localized hybrid languages and cultures—Chinese, Japanese, Taiwanese, and Southeast Asian—more than any other family member. In many ways, she is a character who might well be featured in director Yang's other films on such themes as coming of age, in the light of place, ethnicity, gender, and politics. Through her lens, slowly and darkly, we see how things have gone wrong. But she also points toward alterity and heterogeneity in unfolding secrecies and betrayals, though often reticently. The film brings forth an ambivalent sense of Taiwan's postcolonial volatility and vulnerability, underscoring that the opportunity to set the island free from China's control (symbolized by what the grandma does to the girl's mother) has not yet arrived, or might arrive only belatedly.

Great Buddha Plus, in contrast, addresses the issue of moral and political agency head-on. The Buddhist gathering at the end of the movie is portrayed in such a way that it indicates the bad faith of the electro-spiritual club members in covering up a murder and then being forced to listen to the repressed (but certainly not silenced) voice of the subaltern. Finally, against the background of the apocalyptic shimmering flames that quickly blow out, the "marvels of Zen" or grand masters of meditation and magical cures are thrown into question, exposing their hypocrisies and indifference to the sufferings of the common people. As the scripture recitation and the enlightenment ritual come to a halt, the sky turns black, and then we hear the drum from the belly of the great Buddha. We can certainly interpret this scene and the political economy of "noise" here as the subaltern raising its voice in the figure of a female phantom or a monster in response to the historical momentum that has been repressed, as Judith Zeitlin (2016) or David Wang (2004) might advocate, or, even better, as an echo in the Marabar caves to generate a series of postcolonial panics, as Homi Bhabha (1994, 126–27). Even though the mysterious drum music seems to present an apocalyptic moment in which the subaltern speaks, the environment turns pitch dark, and the audience is dead silent, afraid and unwilling to confront the truth. Thus, the question of agency raised here is around truth: Who lies buried in the great Buddha's belly? What is the drum music about? What actually happened? Which institution is going to launch the investigation? Will a member of the congregation be persecuted to restore justice? May the music lead to the discovery of truth in terms of epiphany, enlightenment, and even, as Édouard Glissant (1997, 137) suggests, "a following through [of] whatever is dynamic, the relational, and the chaotic" to cultivate the "Thought of the Other"? Could it function as a fluid, uncertain, and surreal instance to disrupt or simply to distract?

In interviews posted online, director Huang appears to go for the version with the subaltern speaking: "All of us may well be the one who is making her voice heard in the great Buddha" (Huang 2017b). However, in the film the ragpicker and the security guard deliberate as to whether they should report the case to the police after finding out that the boss might have murdered his mistress and inserted the corpse into the great Buddha's belly. The ragpicker's nickname in fact is a pun in Taiwanese on the "belly button," not only alluding to the great Buddha's lower body part but also associated with food and by extension poverty and income disparity. He ponders the issue of truth versus power, that is, whether the authorities will believe the story the poor people tell or more likely side with the rich and powerful. On top of the credibility and legal-evidence problems, the ragpicker and security guard are troubled by the possible consequences if they reveal the truth. They can easily lose their employment and even be hunted down. So can the subaltern speak to power without putting themselves in jeopardy? Both of the defenseless decide to stay quiet and wait for the right moment or for better opportunities, entertained with the idea of a willing suspension of belief.

Great Buddha Plus, the first feature film by director Huang (2017a), won ten nominations in the 2017 Golden Horse Film Awards. Over the years Huang has been known mainly as a documentary filmmaker, detailing Taiwan's ecological degradation and the struggles of poor folk (in spite of their goodwill and planetary consciousness) against human-caused catastrophes caused by global warming, the rising sea level along the west coast, the continuing flooding of the submerged areas, the contamination of the seashore by industrial wastes and plastic bags, and the island's increasingly minoritized status in the world, in addition to its own worsening internal economic disparities and political polarization. In spite of all these dismal images, director Huang appears to be hopeful: he often singles out numerous small groups of bird-watchers and amateur environmentalists who try to save wetlands or swamps for tens of thousands of avian migrants from elsewhere, to clean up dumps, and to recycle. And this may be why the ragpicker in the film *Great Buddha Plus* is a significant deployment in calling attention to the problematic of postcolonial agency—local, regional, and global. The ragpicker recycles but survives only because of the kindness or companionship of his friends—few indeed and also struggling. A major problem in local disparities, as the ragpicker and security guard see it, derives from outsourcing; that is, more and more Taiwanese companies and industries invest in China. The superrich, who spend most of their time away from home, are indifferent to local economic pains. Not only that, but they are mobilized by the Chinese government to disrupt the island's democratization procedures, often by endorsing pro-China candidates. As a result, the incoming Kaohsiung mayor, Han Guoyu, won a landslide election in 2018, one year after both films came out. Han's very next move—to take over the island in the presidential campaign—suffered a dramatic defeat, however, as the Taiwanese people were in horror when they watched the news regarding the ways China had tightened its grip on Hong Kong in the name of national security, in blunt rejection of the promised One Country, Two Systems policy to sustain the port city's semi-autonomy (see Lui Tai-lok's chapter in this volume).

To director Huang, being small and going local are beautiful. The Tzu Chi Buddhist Association was initially launched by founder Zheng Yan 證嚴, who famously urged poor countryside housewives to save just two pennies per day to help others, but as the revenue grew, the association became an industry constantly targeting the superrich for fundraising through orchestrated means of empathetic compassion around a charismatic "bodhisattva" turned CEO. It evolved gradually into a colossal transnational corporation that bought lands and stocks and ran TV channels, hospitals, schools, and the like. One of the documentaries that director Huang helped team-produce for local public TV is about the Buddhist association's controversial land transactions, which flourished by building facilities over environmentally fragile waters. He develops the cinematic agency to record and reveal, so as to bring about change. Very much like the granddaughter in Yang's film *The Bold, the Corrupt, and the Beautiful*, the little men in *Great Buddha Plus* develop their agencies in cultivating a discerning, intense (albeit voyeuristic) gaze to disclose while withholding the partial truth. In our world today, filled with many "apocalyptically minded, violent far-right extremist[s]" (quoted in Bennhold and Schwirtz 2021, on the Capitol riot in the United States), we see different narratives from the 2017 Taiwan film examples.

Conclusion

This chapter highlights Taiwan's postcolonial experiences so that we may move beyond the old paradigms that tend to be built on cultural nationalism (in spite of its fragments and intimate enemies) and challenge the "white mythologies," provincialize Europe (and, along the same line, take issue with America's and, increasingly, China's claims to exceptionalism), and criticize neoliberal capitalism and systemic racism, on top of singling out materiality and local everyday practices. During the COVID-19 pandemic, several former British, French, and Japanese colonies such as Singapore, New Zealand, Vietnam, South Korea, and particularly Taiwan have stood out as models for keeping their information and media transparent, making their data and sources accountable, and ascertaining that their contact tracing and messaging are democratic (rather than invasive), on top of making the best use of medical and technological facilities. As reported in Natifix Asia Research (2021), Taiwan actually experienced "stellar growth" in sustaining a very limited impact from COVID and in manufacturing world-class chips for Tesla and many others: "If 2020 was a test, Taiwan has passed with flying colors. As the world is trapped in the endless cycle of lockdowns, Taiwan is out of the woods with stellar growth. The early containment measures have paid off with a less bumpy ride in domestic demand. Export growth has also held up well with demand in high-tech products. Together with the rollout of vaccines and the recovery in global economy, these factors will continue to bring momentum to Taiwan in 2021."

In many ways, countries like Taiwan reveal that we may be better off learning from alternative postcolonial narratives. The two 2017 films from Taiwan are in this regard integral to the critical responses to the questions of postcolonial agency. Together, they point us to the many intellectual organizations, global networks, political institutions, and artworks that connect the world with "Underground Asia" (as Tim Harper [2020] has just mapped out for us), on top of what is on the ground and on the screen.

Part V

Diasporas in East and Southeast Asian Postcoloniality

Sinophone Geopoetics

Sinophone has arguably been the most provocative keyword of Chinese literary studies since the turn of the new millennium. Although the term has been used since the 1990s in various contexts, it was not made popular until 2007 when Shu-mei Shih published *Visuality and Identity: Sinophone Articulations across the Pacific*.[1] In her book Shih invokes the Sinophone as a language-based critical perspective from which to engage the linguistic, cultural, ethnic, and political dynamics in China, as well as Chinese-speaking communities worldwide (Shih 2004, 2010, 2011). In opposition to the convention of referring to China as a homogenized entity, she argues that the dispersal of the Chinese people across the world needs to be reconceptualized in terms of vibrant or vanishing communities of Sinitic-language cultures rather than of ethnicity and nationality. With the Sinophone paradigm, Shih seeks to intervene in both Sinology and Chinese area studies, in the hope of unleashing (or dispelling) the contested forces in the discourse about China.

In the wake of Shih's groundbreaking work there have been waves of attempts to rethink the conditions of Sinophone literature, its spatiotemporal boundaries, its methodological feasibility, and, above all, its geopolitical and geopoetic implications. For instance, Jing Tsu (2010) tackles "linguistic nativity" as both an innate competence and an acquired aptitude in the sound and script systems of the Chinese language. Tee Kim Tong (2010, 77–93) calls attention to the plural trajectories always already embedded in the Chinese linguistic and semiotic system. E. K. Tan (2013), Alison Groppe (2014), and Brian Bernards (2015) all focus on the Chinese imaginaries in Southeast Asia. Andrea Bachner (2013) studies the media proliferation of the Chinese language, taking issue with the "signology" through which Sinology is constructed and deconstructed.

Meanwhile, questions have been raised as to the relationship between Sinophone literature and the extant paradigm of Chinese literary studies: Is *Sinophone* merely a nomenclature in place of the familiar term *overseas Chinese literature*? If not, what new theoretical ground and critical goal are at stake? Is it a Sinitic brand of popular theories in North America, such as postcolonialism, multiculturalism, diaspora studies, and empire studies? How can it be brought to bear on the literary productions in Chinese-speaking communities? Most important, what is its relevance to Chinese national literature produced in China?

In this chapter I engage with Sinophone Chinese literary studies in three directions. First, I review the strengths and limitations of the extant model proffered by Shih, which is largely predicated on postcolonialism. Second, instead of the postcolonial model, which stresses the politics of spatiality, I introduce postloyalism as a way to tease out the historical bearings of Sinophone discourse, thereby calling forth its inherent politics of temporalities. Third, with fictional examples drawn from Taiwan, Hong Kong, and Malaysia, I highlight the textual and spatial loci where postcolonial and postloyalist inscriptions are intertwined with each other and contend that these loci generate some of the most perplexing Sinophone conditions for further deliberation.

Interrogating the Sinophone

To begin with, Sinophone literature represents a recent intervention with the mapping of Chinese literary modernity based on national boundaries. For decades, the writing and reading of modern Chinese literary history has been couched in the national discourse, as part of the world circulation of nationalism and literary representation. By way of contrast, Chinese-language literature produced outside the territory of sovereignty (of either the Republic of China or the People's Republic of China) has been treated as subordinate to, or derivative of, the corpus of Chinese national literature. Sinophone literature seeks to reconsider such a dichotomized view of Chinese literature by projecting a sphere where multiple Chinese-language literatures are being produced, circulated, and contested. Shu-mei Shih derives her definition of *Sinophone* from the Sinitic language family, an immense network comprising more than four hundred topolects, dialects, and ethnic languages (Shih 2011; see also Mair 1991). While recognizing the dominant position of the Han Chinese, Shih stresses that the "Chinese" language is a multitude of Han and non-Han regional and ethnic utterances of the Sinitic language family. To this we should also add the multitude of utterances in various social, gender, and class communities (McConaghy 2013). Thus, when studied from the Sinophone perspective, Chinese literature appears to be a kaleidoscopic constellation of soundings, spaces, and identities, as opposed to the enclosed, homogenized corpus upheld by the national apparatus.

A coinage in the vein of terms such as *Anglophone, Francophone,* and *Hispanophone, Sinophone* was first used in the late twentieth century to refer to the state of "Chinese speaking" or to a "Chinese-speaking person." Shih brought to the fore the term's colonial undertone, thus igniting its critical power. For Shih, "Sinophone studies takes as its objects of study the Sinitic-language communities and cultures outside China as well as ethnic minority communities and cultures within China where Mandarin is adopted or imposed" (Shih, Tsai, and Bernards 2013, 11). She contends that, just as is the case for anglophone, francophone, or hispanophone articulations, *Sinophone* brings to mind the colonizing and colonized conditions in Great China in military, economic, and cultural terms. She criticizes the Han-centered Chinese language policy and the canonical structure of Chinese literature, and assigns *Sinophone* to those texts that have been given the "torturous and confusing nomenclature 'literature in Chinese' (*huayu wenxue* 華語文學) as opposed to 'Chinese literature' (*Zhongguo wenxue* 中國文學 written inside China)" (Shih 2011, 710).

One discerns in Shih's endeavor a complex of theoretical attempts, from postcolonial criticism to minority studies, from humanist Marxism to multiculturalism. Of these theories, postcolonialism stands out as her main stake. Shih tackles the common wisdom that colonialism is a modern political and economic maneuver undertaken only by Western imperialist powers. She calls attention to three types of Chinese colonialism. First, instead of maritime expeditions, the Qing engaged in multiple military and political actions at the borders and in adjacent areas of inland China, and as a result commanded an immense territory on the Asian continent. Accordingly, the Qing empire thrived on "continental colonialism" (Shih 2011, 711) and its legacy was inherited by the Republic of China and the People's Republic of China. Second, although the Qing did not develop overseas colonies, the way it ruled minorities *within* the territory of China, making them cower to the hegemonic culture, amounted to internal colonialism. This phenomenon finds a modern counterpart in contemporary China's rule in areas such as Tibet and Xinjiang. Third, the large influx of Chinese into a target place of immigration may form an emergent force over time, such that it affects local institutional, political, economic, and even demographic structure. Hence, it gives rise to settler colonialism (713). Shih's research concludes with the claim that the Sinophone subjectivity is predicated on the disavowal of diaspora. If diaspora studies focuses on issues such as the loss of roots and the yearning for homecoming, Sinophone studies, according to Shih, seeks to pin down the "expiration date"(717) of diaspora. That is, insofar as (im)migration points to immigrants' eventual assimilation into the culture of the area to which they relocate, Sinophone subjectivity may very well be gradually minoritized as time passes and even become de-Sinicized in the end (Shih, Tsai, and Bernards 2013, 11).[2]

Shih has made an enormous contribution to Sinophone studies, in particular her observations of the manifold individual voices, regional soundings, dialectical accents, and local expressions—alternative "mother tongues"—that are in constant negotiation with the standardized, official national language. Meanwhile, her approaches also point to areas where additional critical efforts are desired. Whereas Shih's distinction between (socialist) China and the Sinophone world unwittingly duplicates the polarized agenda of the Cold War era, her support of the politically and ethnically underprivileged embraces a classic humanism in both leftist and liberal veins. *Colonialism* has been used as a blanket term to describe variegated forms of conquest, oppression, and hegemony in such a way as to lose its historical specificity and critical rigor. For one thing, in view of the fact that the Qing was an empire established by the Manchus, who by Shih's definition should have been labeled a minority, how do we deal with the paradox that the Han-ethnicity-centered China under Qing rule is already a colonized polity while exerting its colonial power over other ethnicities? Shih's critique of settler colonialism brings into view the predatory side of the narrative of Chinese diaspora, but it may at the same time downplay the existential circumstances, for good or ill, that underlie overseas Chinese's need of linguistic and ethnic solidarity. Finally, although her concept of "anti-diaspora" projects a desired horizon of multicultural assimilation, global immigration history, as illustrated by the Hakka and the Jewish people, belies any sanguine belief in the immigrant subjectivity's unilateral "plasticity" in joining a new society.

I suggest that, despite her interventional efforts, Shih does not go far enough to confront the most polemical dimension of Sinophone studies. In my view, for a Sinophone project to exert its critical potential, one must not engage merely with the domain of conventional overseas Chinese literature plus ethnic literature on the mainland. Rather, one should test its power *within* the nation-state of China. In light of the translingual dynamics on the global scale, one needs to reimagine the cartography of the Chinese center versus the periphery so as to enact a new linguistic and literary arena of contestations. As a matter of fact, to truly subvert the foundation of Chinese national literature, we should no longer consider it apart from the Sinophone literary system. My argument actually derives from Shih's logic. If "Chinese" is not a homogenized entity but a constellation of Sinitic utterances amid the flux of historical changes, a Sinophone scholar can conclude that even the official Han language, however standardized by the state, comprises complex soundings and transformations and is therefore subject to the rhizomatic tapestry of Sinoglossia.

Moreover, Shih's discourse treats the Sinophone as a modern phenomenon, resulting from the fragmentation of China when challenged by modern forces. While acknowledging her observations on issues from immigration to diaspora, colonialism, and nationalism, I call for a more serious inquiry into the historical implication of Sinophone discourse, and instead of postcolonialism, I propose the model of postloyalism (D. Wang 2007, 23–70).

Postloyalism

Postloyalism is a coinage derived from a critical reflection on loyalism, or *yimin* 遺民, a unique political and cultural discourse in Chinese history. The term *yimin* originally meant "one who remains loyal to a former dynasty and is ashamed to serve a new dynasty when a change in state power occurs" (Struve 1979, 327; Jay 1991, 6). In Chinese it is a compound of *yi* 遺 ("to leave behind" or "the leftover") and *min* 民 ("people" or "subjects"). Loyalism is a discourse premised on the politics of anachrony and displacement. When a political subject in ancient times insists on retaining their bereavement of a fallen dynasty or a lost culture against all odds, loyalist sentiment abounds. There is an underlying paradox in loyalism, however, as it derives its claim to legitimacy, be it political, cultural, emotional, or ethical, from a reluctant awareness of the loss of that legitimacy. In other words, loyalism gestures toward the belatedness of time and yet gains an unlikely agency in the hope of restoring that which is forever lost. Caught between the desire for the past to be realized in the future and the desire for the future to be restored to the past, the loyalist plays out a unique politics of time "in fold."

The etymological root of *yi* already contains a semantic ambiguity. *Yi* suggests losing something (*yishi* 遺失); at the same time, it means the leaving of something (*canyi* 殘遺). The former points to a total loss, the latter to a leftover or a remnant. But *yi* also means giving or bequeathing (*yiliu* 遺留), implying leaving someone a thing or a gift. The three meanings of *yi* speak to the complex historical and affective syndrome that is loyalism: thrown into the abysmal condition of dynastic cataclysm, a political subject feels entrenched in an irrecoverable loss of their affiliations while cherishing all the more their identity as a survivor, a remnant of the loss; more engagingly, they are compelled to preserve the loss as a legacy, a gift, from the past into the future, despite the historical fact that suggests otherwise.

When one comes to *post*loyalism, something more complex arises. The prefix *post* as I am using it here partakes of a postmodernist undertone. Literally, *postloyalism* refers to that which happens, in conceptual, affective, and political terms, *after* loyalism. But insofar as *loyalism* already implies temporal posteriority, and a resultant sense of mourning and nostalgia, the *post* of *postloyalism* doubles the temporal and psychological complexity inherent in loyalism. It could mean either that which is over with loyalism or that which is subsequent to loyalism. More intriguingly, in line with the postmodern subversion of the causal sequence of time, postloyalism could point to an anticipatory revisioning of the past on behalf of the future, therefore implying a reopening of the pastness of the past. As such, the *post* of *postloyalism* refers to a desire for a timeline that comes prior, rather than posterior, to the extant historical closure: it implies the (renewed) beginning rather than the ending of a desired history.

As a political identity, the loyalist tradition goes back to ancient times. When King Wu (r. 1046–1043 BC) of Zhou (1046–256 BC) conquered the Shang (1760?–1122 BC), he moved all of its peoples to the various states of Song, Wei, and Lu to consolidate Zhou control of the Central Plains. This created the first mass migration of people in China's recorded history. Pining for the former dynasty, the Shang people were unable to control themselves and strove to retain the attire and rituals of the bygone era. Throughout medieval China, loyalist discourse was observed mainly in a descriptive rather than a self-descriptive manner. *Yimin* was invoked in association primarily with the remnants left behind by the fallen dynasty and made only sporadic appearances in records. It was the Song dynasty that witnessed the subtle transformation of loyalist discourse, primarily for two reasons. On the one hand, the rise of neo-Confucianism fostered a totalistic view that linked self-cultivation to moral and political integrity vis-à-vis historical contingencies. On the other hand, the existence of a multipolar China in which the Song dynasty confronted the threat of the rival contemporaneous Liao (Khitan), Western Xia (Tangut), and Jin (Jurchen) dynasties to its north gave rise to the ethnic and territorial awareness suggestive of an incipient mode of nationhood.

Loyalism since the Song took on a decisively political dimension, reaching its climax at the fall of the Ming. In 1644, when the Manchus stormed the capital, Emperor Chongzhen (1611–44) hung himself, and the empire changed hands. In an era of dynastic change, the righteous few who refused to surrender to the Qing formed a loyalist solidarity. Only decades later did their cause finally dissolve. The routes taken by these loyalists can be categorized according to a few distinct trends. In some cases they aspired to recover their former positions of rule (such as Koxinga or Zheng Chenggong 鄭成功, 1624–64, and Zhang Huangyan 張煌言, 1620–64). In other cases, they retreated hermit-like into the mountains and forests, where they pined for the past (such as Zhang Dai 張岱, 1597–1684); found refuge from the times in religion and the arts (such as Shi Tao 石濤, 1642–1707, and Zhu Da 朱耷 [aka Bada shanren 八大山人], 1626–1705); or abandoned themselves to hopelessness or indulged in a decadent life (such as Mao Xiang, 1611–93). Most noticeably, some others, such as Gu Yanwu 顧炎武 (1613–82) and Huang Zongxi 黃宗羲 (1610–95), engaged with political and philosophical treatises on the prospects of a civilization's survival, thus opening up a new epistemological dimension of Chinese humanistic studies (Idema, Li, and Widmer 2006; W. Li 2014).

The loyalist consciousness is further complicated when discussed in the light of modernity. By logic, as an ideology closely tied up with dynastic transition and feudal loyalty (and its disavowal), loyalism should have gone extinct after the fall of the Qing, the last Chinese dynasty. When the Republic of China was founded, the seeds of democracy are said to have been planted, and the blossoming of equal citizenship projected; to talk about one's unconditional dedication to a royal house was deemed obsolete. Nevertheless, specters of loyalism haunted the republican era, as attested by a lineup of renowned Qing loyalists.

But such a loyalist consciousness need not be aligned merely with conservatism. Insofar as the modern is only such because of the term's indication of a violent temporal rupture between past and present, tradition and reform, one can even explore the loyalist dimension embedded in the conceptual makeup of Chinese modernity. Critics have long pointed out that the irony of modernity is both its emphasis on a temporal rupture that creates a distinct "experience of the past" and its exposure of a sense of nostalgia for the irrecoverable past. In one respect, modernity exaggerates the necessity of meanings and values that have no precedent, while in another it cannot hide the hauntings looming behind radical reforms or ulterior motives. Faced with omens of civilizational rupture, intellectuals of the late Qing expressed shock at the magnitude of an unprecedented crisis. They were aware that the shock of the modern was even more assaulting than the aftermath of another dynastic transition. This indirectly explains the sense of tremendous loss following the founding of the republic.[3]

Politically, loyalism engages itself with the polemics of (dynastic and cultural) legitimacy; it generates the force of its platform from that which has already been overthrown. That is to say, if loyalism is a thought or act predicated on anachronistic desire, to turn back the clock so as to return to the primal state of nationhood and selfhood, postloyalism is an exercise that anachronizes anachronism. It is aimed at altering or displacing a timeline that is already irrecoverably altered or displaced. As such, postloyalism intensifies the precarious nature of loyalism as it seeks to upset—delegitimize—what has already been delegitimized. The result is the opening of Pandora's box, unleashing multiple demons with regard to the politics of recognition and loyalty.

Here Jacques Derrida's notion of hauntology finds its complex Eastern parallel (Kamuf 1997; Mapp 1999). With hauntology, Derrida intended to draw attention to the haunting influence of the "specters of Marx" after the decline of Marxist thought in the West. He criticizes the ontological style of dialectics perpetuated by theorists and philosophers who evade discussion of the shadowy origins of these theories. He writes that "haunting is historical, to be sure, but it is not dated, it is never docilely given a date in the chain of presents, day after day, according to the instituted order of a calendar" (1994, 4). In other words, the specter not only comes from the past but also foretells its continuous, lingering presence in the future. Based on Derrida's argument, we can speak of the postloyalist's refusal to comprehend the mandate. On the one hand, this act ultimately dislodges the loyalist memory from the neat order of time, while on the other hand it extends and exaggerates the postloyalist ego's a priori attachments to the loyalist consciousness. Time's continuum becomes disjointed, and forms of remembering become unrestricted. The postloyalist's sense of loss and their inability to let go of their love and resentment are no longer bound by systematic thinking. These feelings rather become endlessly evolving burdens and quagmires—or ghostly seductions.

Now we turn to the Sinosphere and ask how postloyalism can help us better understand the polemics of Sinophone literature. As already argued, despite incessant foreign encroachments since the early nineteenth century, which amounted to a colonial threat, China was not totally colonized except in the cases of Taiwan, Hong Kong, and partially Manchukuo. Nor can one describe China as a colonial power unless one expands the definition of colonialism to cover all hegemonic systems, from the empire to the totalitarian regime. One should also look into the fact that, during the colonial periods of Taiwan and Hong Kong, where Japanese and English were mandated as the official languages, respectively, Chinese, especially in dialectal forms, appeared to have a firm grip on the society at large. That the Chinese people under colonial rule were still capable of preserving their linguistic and cultural habitus, however hybrid in practice, may have to do with either the colonizer's language policy or merely the short duration of the colonial rule. Still, these cases compel one to think beyond the model of (post)colonialism.

One also should pay attention to the Sinophone diaspora, particularly in Southeast Asia, where more than thirty million people are of Chinese heritage. Ever since the late eighteenth century, hundreds and thousands of Chinese have immigrated to Southeast Asia, forming extensive social, economic, and cultural networks. As the region went through drastic transformations in political systems, especially from colonialism to nationalism, throughout the twentieth century, the Chinese settlers were forced to cope with various challenges with regard to their ethnic and cultural identities. While the Chinese in countries such as Indonesia and Thailand were assimilated into the indigenous culture as a result of either coercion or gentle naturalization, those in countries such as Malaysia and Singapore were able to preserve their heritages, at different degrees of cost.

Shih has used *settler colonialism* to describe the Han Chinese immigrants' predatory inclinations in their new space of settlement. For her, *settler colonialism* refers to both overseas Chinese's relocated provincialism and their newly acquired colonial mentality. We need to stress equally, however, that these overseas Chinese settlers were in turn victims when confronted by ferocious colonial powers (the Japanese, Dutch, French, Americans, English, etc.) and subsequent indigenous nationalist campaigns. By the conventional logic, the Chinese should have succumbed to the colonial oppression or the nationalist hegemony at the cost of giving up their cultural heritage. Or they should have recognized that they had reached the "destination" of diaspora, for good or ill, and acted out a new identity and linguistic affiliation. The reality, however, is more complicated. Their interaction with colonial and indigenous cultures has led to varied consequences that cannot be described merely as postcolonial.

This is where the Sinophone becomes an arena between postcolonialism and postloyalism. One sees a wide range of responses to the use of the Chinese language—and its denial—on the levels of both sound and script, both cognitive recognition and affective negotiation. At the height of the anti-Chinese days in Indonesia, the Chinese language was repressed in the public sphere for fear of affecting national unity. In contemporary Singapore the Mandarin Chinese language was acknowledged as the "mother tongue," only to be ironically "learned" by Chinese-heritage citizens. But the most striking case happens in Malaysia, where the Chinese constitute almost one-fourth of the population but occupy an unstable social and political position. The Malaysian government has systematically added pressures to the Chinese-language education system since the late 1960s so as to solidify Malay-centrism. For the Chinese-descendant residents, preserving the Chinese language has become a voluntary cause of sustaining cultural identity and political solidarity.

All these facts remind one that the Sinophone conjuration of Chineseness is a matter of hauntology; it involves considerations ranging from sentimental fabulation to political engagement, such that it cannot be streamlined into either resistance or governance. I have therefore used postloyalism as a way to engage with these facts. Let me stress again that postloyalism is invoked in the first place as a critique of loyalism. But by adding the prefix *post* to *loyalism*, I mean to highlight the temporal anomaly inherent in the concept of loyalism and the doubly anachronistic implication of loyalism in the modern Sinophone context. Psychologically, we may consider postloyalism a deferred effect of the trauma syndrome, even its ghostly double. But in the Sinophone cases to be examined in the next section, postloyalism casts something more perplexing—in either a conservative or a radical vein. Instead of looking merely backward, a Sinophone postloyalist may anticipate a futuristic loss of something they hold valuable now. Or they may preempt such an "anticipatory nostalgia" by projecting—inventing—a memorable object or moment that may have yet to come into existence. Even more paradoxically, where connections with or memories of China have long been suspended or never existed, a Sinophone postloyalist's newborn desire may call for a "prosthetic memory" through the conduit of new media forms (Landsberg 2003).[4] When the future is being mortgaged as if it were the legacy of the past, when the mechanism of memory turns out to be run by a desiring machine, the specter of loyalism reveals its postloyalist thrust.

Three Sinophone Spaces

In the following I introduce three Sinophone spaces that are rich in both postcolonial and postloyalist traditions: Taiwan, Hong Kong, and (the Sinophone community of) Malaysia. Whereas Taiwan was under Japanese rule from 1895 to 1945, Malaysia and Hong Kong were colonized by Britain, respectively, from 1786 to 1957 and from 1842 to 1997. While the Chinese people of the three areas each underwent a distinct process of assimilation, they strove to develop their own Sinophone legacies. Decolonization nevertheless did not bring these areas a streamlined itinerary of political authenticity or determination. Since 1949 the Nationalist regime has made Taiwan become a substitute China, and the island country has experienced a contentious struggle to define its ties with mainland China to date. After the 1997 handover, Hong Kong purportedly entered a new era free from colonial rule, only to fall into an increasingly tense relations with her mother country, the implementation of the National Security Law in 2020 being only a recent example. Finally, in Malaysia, since 1957 the Chinese-speaking community has never ceased their confrontation with the government in their struggle to safeguard their civilian rights and ethnic heritage. In all three postcolonial cases, the coexistence of Sinophone and Chinese factors leads to a highly volatile political environment that is consequently rife with eruptions of postloyalist impulses and the demands of alternative histories.

TAIWAN.   In light of the dynamics of modern Taiwanese history, one can describe multiple strains of (post)loyalist writing on the island. In the aftermath of 1895, Taiwanese writers exhibited great ambiguity regarding their political allegiances. They directed their loyalist longing toward either the Qing or Ming regimes, the legacy of the mainland, or the local culture of the island. The founding of the republican regime further complicated their loyalist discourse. Taiwanese literature during the colonial period registers the conflict and compromise between colonial discourse and indigenous consciousness; between modern viewpoints achieved via Japanese mediation and revolutionary thoughts brought back from China; and, most relevant to our purposes here, between nipponophone and Sinophone discourses. Taiwan was both the "Island of Beauty," or Formosa, as early foreign explorers saw it, and the "Orphan of Asia," as viewed by Wu Zhuoliu 吳濁流 (1900–1976), the pioneer of post-1945 Taiwan literature. Wu sought to engage all these issues in *Orphan in Asia* (*Ajia no koji* アジアの孤児, first published in Japanese in 1946), the first novel published after Taiwan's retrocession to China. Despite its strong yearning for the truncated Han cultural heritage, the novel was written in Japanese and could be read as a Sinophone project implicated in nipponophone writing.

In 1949 the Nationalist regime lost the mainland and retreated to Taiwan. By conservative estimates, 1.5 million people made the journey. The majority came to Taiwan as commoners, military personnel from both the lower and middle classes, or government employees and teachers. Their mainland backgrounds differed, as did their reasons for coming to Taiwan, but as soon as they arrived on the island, they were lumped into the category of mainlanders. During times of hardship linking both sides of the strait (both past and present), many found solace in writing. The People's Republic scholar Li Xiangping describes the narrative and ideological imaginary of Taiwanese writing of this period as a "new loyalist complex" (2003, 292–93).

Li's observation risks oversimplification. It is worth noting that "new loyalist" literature began to undergo a qualitative change after the 1970s. As time relegated the mainlanders' migration to Taiwan further into the past and the numbers of those who migrated steadily declined, writings about the past became unable to recover the heart-wrenching pain of the early years following their arrival. Yet the literature changed also because the island's political structure changed, calling a new territorial consciousness into being. The previous "new loyalist" writings no longer bore the stamp of political orthodoxy. Nativist literature's transplantation of attachments from the opposite side of the strait to the Taiwanese side gave rise to a different object of loyalist desire.

For the activists seeking Taiwan's self-determination, the island has always been under colonial rule since the seventeenth century, a condition that could be altered only by declaring independence. Paradoxically, in an effort to create a polity free of any Chinese political and cultural influence, they find in (post)loyalism a source of rationale. As the nativists call all preceding ruling forces colonial (whether Chinese, Japanese, Qing, or those of the Republic of China), they couch their national consciousness in a (Chinese) loyalist discourse they should have disinherited at the outset. Before the idealized Taiwanese Republic can even be founded, they have already imagined it as a long-lost utopia. They cast an anticipatory nostalgia for the prehistory of the futuristic nation. As they are striving to create a national history predating the founding of their nation, they turn their postloyalism into an uncanny preloyalism.

Meanwhile, a counterexample can be found in the case of Chu Tien-hsin 朱天心 (b. 1958). As an author among the second generation of mainlanders in Taiwan, Chu witnessed the rise of passionate nativism and felt compelled to voice her sense of despondence and estrangement. In *Gudu* 古都 (The old capital, 1996), the middle-aged female narrator, who seems to be Chu's alter ego, returns from Japan and discovers that if she reexamines Taipei from the perspective of a Japanese tourist, the city where she grew up suddenly seems extremely unfamiliar and even terrifying. Relying on a map from the era of the Japanese occupation, she wanders the main streets and narrow alleys of fin-de-siècle Taipei, where the sights appear wretched and dilapidated like ruins. She seeks a moment of repose in Taipei but is actually a wandering spirit, migrating along the margins of amnesia and vain hopes in search of the dregs of history.

Lo Yi-chin 駱以軍 (b. 1967) is arguably one of the most important writers of contemporary Taiwan. Lo's early writing shows the indirect influence of Chu Tien-hsin. In terms of postloyalist discourse, however, the two are quite different. Chu is forlorn and resentful toward the inevitability of the changing times and the dissolution of values that accompanies it. Lo's works do not put the sequence of time's advance or retreat in such a simple chronological order. He is certainly aware of the ruthlessness of the tricks that time plays, which causes him anxiety, but he does not devote much energy to voicing this anxiety, and he does not assume that he is on the side of justice. Lo's postloyalist complex culminates in *Xixia lüguan* 西夏旅館 (Western Xia Hotel, 2008). The novel parades endless bizarre encounters that occur within the insular space of the Western Xia Hotel, from a necrophilic romance to a phantasmal manhunt, from burlesque intrigues to senseless carnivals. Behind the absurd-turned-quotidian, Lo describes the diasporic experience of a generation of Chinese exiled to Taiwan. The hotel with no exit thus becomes a topos haunted by nostalgia and hysteria. More intriguingly, the name of Lo's hotel is a reference to the Western Xia dynasty (1038–1227) of the eleventh century, a dynasty that once thrived on a hybrid civilization of Han and non-Han origins. Western Xia was ruined by the Mongols and as a result thrown into oblivion, its short-lived cultural splendor becoming an enigma.

Lo's novel thus invokes an unlikely parallel between a postmodern haunted hotel and a premodern "barbarian" regime. One leitmotif of the novel is the mingling and unmingling between the Han and the Hu (barbarian) cultures throughout history. In regard to our concerns, such a fact speaks to the Sinophone geopolitics of exception through assimilation or vice versa. The game of exclusion and inclusion was as precarious in the Western Xia era as it is in contemporary Taiwan. The result is a bizarre national allegory of Taiwan trapped in multiple temporalities and multiple states of exceptions. At a time when radical Taiwan nativists are seeking a state free from Chinese experience, Lo contemplates not only the position of second-generation mainlanders as adherents to a lost cause—postloyalists—but also the fate of Taiwan at large. Once a self-appointed overseas stronghold of Chinese civilization, in the face of the double challenge of self-de-Sinicization on one hand and mainland-Chinese political encroachment on the other, will Taiwan become another disappearing Western Xia?

HONG KONG.   Despite its colonial status, Hong Kong has served as an unlikely base for Chinese literary production since the 1930s. Although the British colonial government imposed an anglophone political and pedagogical system, Hong Kong developed a unique Sinophone discourse by not only preserving local Cantonese literary and popular traditions but also hosting waves of modern Chinese intellectuals and writers bound for the south (*nanlai* 南來). The colonial government played an intriguing role. It is well known that during his service as governor of Hong Kong, Cecil Clementi (1875–1947) promoted classical Chinese-language literature, which led to the founding of the first Chinese Department at Hong Kong University. Granting the political motivation underneath his pro-Chinese antiquity campaign, Clementi, a Sinologist by training, must have harbored his own vocation of Orientalism. Lu Xun nevertheless found in the campaign a loyalist overtone, one that was fostered by the colonial ruler: "The foreigners are smarter than us. At this point, not only can we not assimilate them, but they are using our culture that is already corrupted to govern us, a corrupted nation" (1981b, 324).

Thanks to, and in spite of, the colonial conditions over the past century, the literary configuration of Hong Kong is closely related to its amorphous status as a *city* short of national identity. Hong Kong has become a unique urban space where the forces of politics and commerce, colonialism and nationalism, have been brought into play. Amid ever-changing political, economic, and cultural factors, what has remained unchanged in Hong Kong is, paradoxically, its changeability. As the "deadline" of 1997 loomed over the fin-de-siècle moment, Hong Kong writers were compelled to contemplate their colonial and national identities and to reimage the political past and future of their city. Dung Kai-cheung 董啓章 (b. 1967) is one such a case. Since the mid-1990s, Dung has created a series of works about the mysterious V (for Victoria) City. Instead of expressing nationalist longing, his narrator observes the rise and the fall of the metropolis from the perspective of a postapocalyptic future. He recollects its grandeur in the vein of ancient Chinese cities such as Chang'an (Xi'an), Bianliang (Kaifeng), and Hangzhou, pondering the illusory and ephemeral nature of *all* cities in world history. Fiction becomes the final locus where the city can sustain its mesmerizing power.

In particular, in novels such as *Menghualu* 夢華錄 (Dream of splendor) and *Fanshenglu* 繁勝錄 (Account of prosperity), Dung relates in the future perfect tense the splendor and prosperity of V City, which will have been ruined by a certain point in time. The titles of the two novels are of special historical significance. *Dream of Splendor* brings to mind Meng Yuanlao's 孟元老 *Dongjing menghualu* 東京夢華錄 (East Capital: Dream of splendor) (first published in 1187), arguably the most famous loyalist account of everyday life in classical Chinese literature. Meng became a refugee from Kaifeng when the thriving capital of the Northern Song fell into the hands of Jurchen barbarians in 1126. In a quasi-encyclopedic manner, his book catalogs the old capital's commercial life, seasonal products, and festivals, as well as foods, customs, and traditions, all of which had evaporated like a dream. Likewise, *Account of Prosperity* is derived from *Xihu laoren fanshenglu* 西湖老人繁勝錄 (Account of prosperity by a senior gentleman on the West Lake)(Xihu laoren [pseud.], dates unknown), a book recollecting the bygone urban life of Hangzhou, where the Song royal house built its southern capital after the fall of Kaifeng. By copying the style and structure of the two Song accounts, Dung's novels about life in Hong Kong generate the sensation of a ghostly déjà vu, while the sense of pastness of Hong Kong is projected to the time after 2046, fifty years after her return to China (Wang D. 2013).

By the nationalist logic, the people of Hong Kong should have welcomed the restoration of the Chinese regime to the island, following 156 years of colonial rule. Dung's fiction reverses such an assumption. On the eve of the handover, according to Dung, Hong Kong is experiencing not so much a wish fulfillment as a deeper sense of loss. Instead of the jubilant postcolonial fervor, Dung entertains a postloyalist nostalgia—most ambiguously for the lost time of British colonial rule. By "anticipating" that Hong Kong will become a ruined city like Kaifeng and Hangzhou, he enacts a historical melancholia, one that speaks to the "eternal return" of a fallen city. Moreover, insofar as both Kaifeng and Hangzhou were Song capitals, Dung's analogy between Hong Kong and the two ancient cities insinuates the political taboo that Hong Kong might as well enjoy the status of independent sovereignty in its own fantastic moment.

In his study of Hong Kong and 1997, Ackbar Abbas (1997) describes the city as thriving on "the politics of disappearance." Hong Kong's peculiar lack of identity is due to its status as "not so much a place as a space of transit" (1) whose residents think of themselves as transients and migrants on their way from China to somewhere else. Abbas invokes "déjà disparu" to describe the structure of feeling of Hong Kong, "the feeling that what is new and unique about the situation is always already gone, and we are left holding a handful of clichés, or a cluster of memories of what has never been" (25). As such, Abbas contemplates the fate of a colonial city in the postcolonial time. Dung's novels seem to fit Abbas's theory at first glance, but in effect he strives to picture a Hong Kong that is not necessarily as transient as Abbas would have his reader think. By understanding the fate of Hong Kong along the lines of the great cities in premodern China, Dung means to share with us something more tangible: he is relating a history constituted by numerous variations of the city in disappearance and reappearance. The cultural politics of Hong

Kong need not be trapped in postcolonial vacuity; rather, it gives rise to the surfeit of postloyalist yearnings.

MALAYSIA.   Finally, we come to Sinophone literature in Malaysia. As already mentioned, more than thirty million people of Chinese descent live in Southeast Asia, demonstrating a variety and vitality of Sinophone cultures that can hardly be homogenized by the conventional paradigm of "overseas Chinese heritage." Particularly in Malaysia, Sinophone language and writing have long served as tokens of Chinese ethnic solidarity. However, ever since the 1940s, Malay(si)an Chinese-language authors have had to negotiate between a Chinese identification—fostered by language and the inevitably powerful influence of the Chinese literary tradition—and a sense of belonging to their local environment of Malay(si)a.

Take a look at the case of Li Yung-ping 李永平 (b. 1947). Born and raised in Malaysian Borneo, Li has always harbored a dream of "Mother China," and he went to Taiwan to study in 1967. For him, the island is a miniature projection of the mainland, to which he feels destined to return in the long run. Li's passion is such that he creates a textual phantasmagoria, as if only the Chinese script can actualize his loyalist desire. In 1992 he published *Haidong qing* 海東青 (Haidong blues), a work of more than 500,000 characters. The novel has no plot to speak of but is rather a detailed account of the nocturnal wandering of a middle-aged scholar and a seven-year-old girl on the streets of Haidong (Taipei) city (Li 2006). Mixing a sensuous exposé of the nightlife of the metropolis and an ambiguous narrative of the two characters that brings to mind *Lolita*, the novel impresses nevertheless for its fetishistic indulgence in Chinese vocabulary of the most obscure and archaic kind. For Li, this kind of language is the only way to call back the diminishing "essence" of China. Above all, Li frames his novel as an unabashed celebration of the Nationalist regime and its erstwhile leader Chiang Kai-shek.

The Chinese Malaysian postloyalist tradition takes another turn in the works of Ng Kim Chew 黃錦樹. Born in the year that Li Yung-ping embarked on his voyage to Taiwan, Ng grew up witnessing the ever-tightening control of the Malaysian government over the Chinese community. Following in Li's steps, Ng went to study in Taiwan in 1986 and ended up settling down on the island. Nevertheless, Ng has engaged in a literary career as if he had never left Malaysia. He remains to date a vehement critic of Chinese Malaysians' ethnic culture. On the one hand, he wants to heighten Chinese Malaysians' vigilance regarding their diasporic position vis-à-vis governmental hegemony; on the other, he lashes out at their longing to transplant anything Chinese to a new land, likening their effort to a necrophilic ritual. Oscillating between the "wandering Chinese" complex and its disavowal, Ng demonstrates a Sinophone "obsession with China" of the most perplexing kind.

Ng has sought to turn such an obsession with China into an interventional move in recent years. One such move can be illustrated by "Yuhai" 魚骸 (Fish bones, 1996), a story about the discovery of the "oracle bones" in relation to Sinophone literary modernity. In 1899 a late-Qing official purchased pieces of medicinal "dragon bones," only to realize that they were animal bones inscribed with the earliest Chinese characters identifiable to date (Ng 2016). But the fact that the bones—as well as the history they represent—were not discovered until the turn of the modern century works to synchronize, so to speak, the temporalities of past and present. In Ng's story, a Chinese-Malaysian scholar performs a nocturnal ritual of killing tortoises and producing "oracle bones," so as to communicate with the dead and the missing who were lost as a result of colonial rule. Thus, through the medium of the oracle-bone inscriptions, his story brings together premodern augural technology and postmodern media haunting, late-Qing archaeological discovery, and fin-de-siècle diasporic nostalgia.

Ng intensifies his Sinophone politics with a series of novels under the title *Nanyang renmin gongheguo* 南洋人民共和國 (The People's Republic of the South China Sea, 2011–13). The Republic of the South China Sea is said to be a socialist state that could have been founded by Chinese communists on the Malay Peninsula in the 1950s. It is a phantom polity that vanished no sooner than it was conceived by leftist activists. In a way, Ng takes up where Jin Zhimang left off in the 1960s, when the nation-building project of the Malayan People's Republic fell through. Nevertheless, as history has proven to be other than Jin's socialist dream, all Ng can do is to describe either the prehistory of the republic, when the leftists underwent severe trials to realize their nation-building dream, or the posthistory, when the leftists were either co-opted by the Malaysian government or simply died off as time passed. What was supposed to take place in history—the founding of the People's Republic of the South China Sea—remains an abysmal lacuna, something that can be captured only by fiction.

Ng's fictional project brings home the aporia of the postloyalist discourse we have discussed so far. It speaks to both the wildest dream and the deepest melancholy of overseas Chinese in regard to their expatriate circumstances. More than sixty years after the establishment of the Malayan Federation (1957), Ng's characters are seen as wandering ghosts in the "homeland," the Malay Peninsula, which they refuse to call home. They are citizens of the phantom

People's Republic of the South China Sea or the aborted Malayan People's Republic—either of which is merely an imagined diasporic mimicry of the People's Republic of China. Nevertheless, at a time when the People's Republic regime is trying to shed its image as the instigator of leftist insurgencies in Southeast Asia, these characters are destined to be denied by their "spiritual" mother country too. They are postloyalists of the most abject kind.

Conclusion

This chapter represents an attempt to broaden the scope and methodology for studying modern Chinese-language literature. It does not seek to overwrite the extant imaginary of China but rather seeks to tease out its complexity. Is it not a paradox that critics can subscribe to a "politics of marginality" and pontificate about a "clash of empires" and "global contextualization," all the while rigidly marginalizing forms of Chinese/Sinophone modernity and historicity that do not emerge within some preconceived mainstream? If one of the most important lessons one can learn from modern Chinese literature and history is the tortuous nature of Chinese writers' attempt to grapple with a polymorphous reality, then this knowledge can be appreciated in full only through a criticism and literary history equally exempt from formulaic dogma and geopolitical blindness. By examining two critical models of postcolonialism and postloyalism, I argue that one must genuinely believe that Chinese and Sinophone writers have been, and still are, capable of complex and creative thought, constructing and deconstructing the nation and the world in the literary domain and beyond. Any critical endeavor in the name of Chinese literature must be unafraid to look squarely at this historical reality—a reality of contested Sinophone modernities.

Notes

1 *Sinophone* had been used in various contexts before the publication of Shih's book. Ruth Keen defines *Sinophone communities* in Chinese literature as "the Mainland, Taiwan, Hong Kong, Singapore, Indonesia and the U.S." (1988, 231). Chong Fah Hing 莊華興 (2012, 101) suggests that the term was used by Chen Peng-hsiang 陳鵬翔 as early as the 1990s to refer to Chinese-language literature at large. Geremie Barmé (2005) describes the "Sinophone world" as "one consisting of the individuals and communities who use one or another—or, indeed, a number—of China-originated languages and dialects to make meaning of and for the world, be it through speaking, reading, writing or via an engagement with various electronic media."

2 Shih's reflection leads one to Jing Tsu's theory of governance (2010, 1–17). At the core of Sinophone governance is the polemics of "linguistic nativity"—which Tsu (2010, 3) believes encompasses hereditary competence, institutional cultivation, and, more polemically, "acquired" passion. Tsu finds in the Sinophone a complicitous participation in the antagonistic relations between standard and nonstandard language use of Chinese (46).

3 For instance, the drowning in 1927 of Wang Guowei 王國維 (1873–1927), one of the most important modern Chinese intellectuals, caused a big controversy as to the cause of his suicide.

4 With American mass culture as her case in point, Alison Landsberg (2003) argues that the technologies of mass media make it possible for anyone, regardless of race, ethnicity, or gender, to share collective memories—to assimilate as personal experience historical events through which they themselves did not live. The result is a new form of public cultural memory—"prosthetic" memory—that transcends the essentialism and ethnic particularism of contemporary identity politics.

Multiple Colonialisms and Their Philippine Legacies

The Philippine experience of multiple colonialisms is often pithily rendered as "350 years in a Spanish convent, 50 years in Hollywood" (Tatad 2015), and four years in a "Japanese concentration camp" (Maslog 2000, 373).

Benedict Anderson (1998, 227) notes the power of sequential colonization by spatially, temporally, and epistemically differentiated colonizers to induce a deep feeling of "historical vertigo" among observers of the Philippines. The shifting "grounds of comparison" (P. Cheah and Culler 2003) make it impossible to view and understand the Philippines from a single, fixed perspective: "Seen from Asia, the armed uprising against Spanish rule of 1896, which triumphed temporarily with the establishment of an independent republic in 1898, makes it the visionary forerunner of all the other anticolonial movements in the region. Seen from Latin America, it is, with Cuba, the last of the Spanish imperial possessions to have thrown off the yoke, seventy-five years after the rest" (Anderson 1998, 227). The "spectre of comparisons" (Anderson 1998, drawing on Filipino national hero José Rizal's phrase "el demonio de las comparaciones" [1887]) haunts not only the classic colonial relationship between the so-called metropole and its periphery but also relationships among multiple metropoles and peripheries.

Indeed, scholars trying to make sense of the "anomalous, economic experience" of a laggard, crisis-prone postcolonial Philippines in an East Asian region of high-performing late-industrializing or newly industrialized countries have sought an explanation in the Philippines' shared experience of Spanish colonialism with Latin America and the enduring "historical and cultural traits" that are supposedly its legacies (Elson 2013, 54–55; Krugman et al. 1992, 1–78). The Philippine trajectory follows the arc of Latin American history, shaped by anglophone Black Legend (*leyenda negra*) narratives of reactionary Catholicism; predatory, rent-seeking elites with strong agrarian-export interests and little interest in producing manufactured goods for export; deep-seated inequality and periodic political and economic instability; patron-clientelistic and nepotistic ties in politics and business; and administrative states bereft of bureaucratic autonomy (Elson 2013, 54–55). Out-of-place Philippines is simultaneously Philippine time-out-of-joint, for to speak of the Philippines as an "outlier" (54) whose history belongs more properly in Latin America than in East Asia is also to speak of historical timing, of simultaneously being ahead of one's time while also lagging behind the times.

In these assessments of multiple colonialisms, the figure of the Filipino elite stands out. Neither reducible to colonial object nor identifiable with/as a national subject, *elite* signifies both potentiality and botched reality and for this reason attracts both praise and opprobrium in Philippine nationalist historiography. *Ilustrados* (the educated, enlightened) were members of the Propaganda Movement that advocated colonial reform through the incorporation of the Philippines into Mother Spain. Their writings, however, also inspired the separatist 1896 revolution. From their ranks are drawn many of the country's "national heroes." But the Filipino elite have also been taken to task for "betraying" the revolution; for putting their selfish, factional interests above those of the nation and the masses; for collaborating with the Americans; and for being the principal coarchitects and beneficiaries of the "colonial democracy" (Paredes 1989) installed by the Americans in the early twentieth century (Constantino 1975; Constantino and Constantino 1978).

In elite hands, the postcolonial Philippines would be bogged down in a series of failures: the failure of a procedural democracy to achieve redistributive social justice and the failure of developmentalism under both democratic and authoritarian governments to jump-start industrialization and raise the income of the majority of the Filipino people. Instead, the Philippines would contribute two keywords to contemporary political discourse: *crony capitalism*, to describe the systematic favoritism and plunder exercised by the Ferdinand Marcos dictatorship of the 1970s, and *People Power*, to describe the relatively peaceful revolution that toppled that dictatorship in 1986 and restored democracy (albeit elite dominated). *Crony capitalism* would serve as a buzzword for Lawrence Summers's and Alan Greenspan's attempts to pin the blame for the Asian financial crisis in 1997–98 on the close ties between business and state (supposedly typical of the "developmental state" [Johnson 1982], of which Japan provided the paradigmatic example) that led to financial regulation based on relations rather than rules, while People Power would have a "demonstration effect" on neighboring Taiwan and South Korea, among many other countries, and help reorient American policy toward democracy promotion among its noncommunist allies (Hau 2017, ch. 5).

Over decades the Filipino nationalist grand narrative of *ilustrado* betrayal, co-optation, and predation has ossified into intellectual and popular orthodoxy. But recent scholarship has complicated this grand narrative by questioning its assumption of a great divide between elite and masses and by reexamining the differential impact of the policies and practices of Spanish and American colonialism on the Philippine state, economy, and society. Building on such research, this chapter seeks a more nuanced understanding of the long nineteenth and twentieth centuries and the vicissitudes of Filipino cosmopolitan nation making (and otherwise).

This chapter focuses on national artist Nick Joaquin's (1917–2004) first novel, *The Woman Who Had Two Navels* ([1961] 1991, hereinafter *Woman*) and the portrait it paints of the elite as Filipinos. One of the most influential Filipino writers in English, Joaquin had long been attentive to the transformative roles of Spanish and American colonialisms and their postcolonial legacies. *Woman* deals with two decisive moments of transition—from Spanish to American colonial rule in the late nineteenth to early twentieth centuries, and from the American Commonwealth era (1935) to the Japanese occupation (1942–45) to the postindependence period (1946)—and the political possibilities that were opened up, and foreclosed, within these historical junctures.

Joaquin's vision of "culture and history" ([1988] 2004) meditates on the possibilities and dead ends of the *ilustrado*-mediated anticolonial revolution that emerged out of the Spanish-era birth and reorganization of the modern world-system, and the subsequent American valorization of the *ilustrados* as "representative men" in the fraught process of collaborative state building and decolonization (Kramer 2006, 196). The artistic recovery of a forgotten history and of the roads not taken that might have led to a different political outcome and future for the Philippines is exemplified by Joaquin's decision to set his novel in Hong Kong rather than the familiar transregional cultural circuit linking the Philippines, Europe, and the Americas. Joaquin memorializes Hong Kong's role, as colony and free port, in the world-spanning, world-making ecumene that enabled—and was also enabled by—Filipino anticolonial, pan-Asianist, anti-imperialist, and socialist projects, activities, and networks, proof that multiple sites of (post)coloniality were critical in nurturing what Vicente Rafael (2005, 13) calls the "originary cosmopolitanism" out of which the Filipino national community was made, unmade, and remade.

Moreover, Joaquin's novel is remarkable for its literary prolepsis. In the six decades since its publication, the novel's evocation of a world populated by diasporic Filipinos, a world of "Filipino-foreign" children, Filipino musicians working in Asia, and seafaring Manilamen, has anticipated a Philippine future (now present) in which the deterritorialized Filipino not only is crucial to the continued economic survival of the Filipino nation but also performs the work of shoring up—of guaranteeing the viability of—the project of national community making. Deterritorialized Filipinos are now routinely hailed as "new heroes" (*bagong bayani*) and "new *ilustrados*," vectors of the modernity that the elite had once embodied but failed to actualize. While they are invested with *ilustrado* potentiality (to use Miguel Syjuco's term; quoted in W. Tam 2010), their multifarious engagements (including the lack thereof) with, and beyond, the multisited Filipino "imagined community" (Anderson 1991), like those of the nineteenth-century *ilustrados* themselves, have proven to be recalcitrant, not easily assimilable to narratives of home, belonging, loyalty, and patriotic contribution to the nation.

Hong Kong as a Site of Philippine Post-Coloniality

Nick Joaquin was particularly well equipped to dissect the adversities (*mésaventures*) (translated as "trials and tribulations" in Fanon [1963] 2004) of national consciousness. Fluent in Spanish, Tagalog, and English, Joaquin was a prolific translator, poet, playwright, journalist, biographer, and fictionist. Joaquin's trademark "baroque, Spanish-flavored English" of lush, long sentences has been much imitated by other Filipino writers (Lanot 1999, 10).

While Joaquin's writings valorize the worldliness of the city of Manila, the conditions of production of *Woman* are transregional: "I finished the first part [of the novel], chapter one, very fast in Hong Kong. Then I got the Rockefeller grant and I went to Spain. After my year in Spain I spent a year in New York. Part of the last part of the novel was written in New York. And then I got a Harper's grant to go to Mexico, where I stayed almost a year and the novel was finished" (in Joaquin 1990, 64). The significance of Spain and America is obvious enough. Mexico, too, was decisive in the changing fortunes of the Spanish Empire and its Philippine colony: from the late sixteenth to the late eighteenth century, the Philippines had been administered and subsidized by the Viceroyalty of New Spain, the capital of which had been Mexico City. Mexico had been a major hub of the galleon trade that brought silver from the Americas to China and Europe and Chinese silk and other goods to Mexico and Europe via Manila (through which passed some one-third of the silver produced in the Americas over 250 years; Legarda 1999, 44). Economic historians (Flynn and Giráldez 1995, 201; Nakajima 2018, 26) date the birth of world trade, the reorganization of the East Asian tribute-and-trade system, and China's commercial revolution to the establishment of the entrepôt city of Manila in 1571. The galleon trade was the linchpin of the silver-based world economy spanning centuries and oceans, linking continents and cities (such as Quanzhou, Nagasaki, Lima, and Seville).

"And why *here*?" wonders Pépé Monson in *Woman* when Connie Vidal comes to see him in Hong Kong for the first time (Joaquin [1961] 1991, 6).

In the late 1940s, Joaquin spent a formative year on scholarship at St. Albert's College, a seminary in Hong Kong. Moreover, Hong Kong had a significant role in Philippine and Asian history in the closing years of the nineteenth century, as Filipinos waged the first anticolonial revolution in Asia and Americans broke the eighty-year "white peace" of European collective imperialism in the region by waging war against Spain. That period between the French and British occupations of the Dutch Indies in the Napoleonic era (1806–15) and the Spanish-American War (1898) was marked by repression (often violent) of the non-European populations within the colonies.

Hong Kong emerged as a major hub of the British-led intra-Asian and world-trade system (Hamashita 1996) into which the late-colonial Philippine economy would be integrated after Latin American independence from Spanish rule ended the galleon trade. Between 1880 and 1938, intra-Asian trade grew faster than world trade and faster than Asia's trade with the West (Sugihara 2019, 74). The growth and expansion of this regional system were comparable to those of intra-European trade, creating different pathways for labor-intensive (as distinct from capital-intensive) economic development in Asia (78).

Not only was the bulk of the funding for foreign trade in the Philippines in the late nineteenth century sourced from Hong Kong (Nagano 2015, 61) and instrumental in promoting cash-crop production in the Philippines. Hong Kong also served as the base of Filipino political activism, providing a safe haven and launching pad for various forms of anticolonial nationalist resistance against Spain and America (Schumacher 1981; Owen 2005, 155; Joaquin [1997] 2005, 218).

Hong Kong was the Asian hub of the Philippine Propaganda Movement, which was active in Spain and other parts of Europe in the 1880s and 1890s. Printed works such as the periodical *La Solidaridad* were smuggled into the Philippines from Barcelona via Hong Kong, and the Hong Kong colony of Filipino exiles and expatriates served as the principal source of news from the Philippines, which they relayed by letter and telegraph to compatriots in Madrid, Barcelona, Paris, London, Berlin, and Ghent (Kramer 2006, 28; R. Reyes 2008, 192–93n15).

Hong Kong was the official base of exile chosen by the revolutionary government of Emilio Aguinaldo following the Pact of Biak-na-Bato (the truce between Spain and the Philippine Republic) in 1897. Hong Kong was also the site of the naval base (off Mirs Bay) that supported American commodore George Dewey's squadron of seven cruisers during the Spanish-American War in 1898. From Hong Kong, Aguinaldo and, after him, other Filipinos such as Marcelo H. Del Pilar launched repeated attempts to continue the war against the Americans, even after the Americans had declared an end to the "Philippine Insurrection."

Until the Filipino revolutionaries were kicked out of Hong Kong by the British authorities (owing to American pressure), the port city had also served as a hub (along with Tokyo/Yokohama) of the pan-Asianist network that connected Filipino revolutionaries to Miyazaki Tōten, Inukai Tsuyoshi, Pak Yong-hyo, Yu Kil-chun, An Kyong-su, and others in the common cause of fomenting national revolution across China, the Philippines, Japan, Korea, and other parts of Asia (Joaquin [1997] 2005, 218–23; Hau and Shiraishi 2009).

Even as Hong Kong functioned in the Cold War era as an American military bastion and base for anticommunist intelligence-gathering activities (Share 2007, 120–23), it had historically served as a hub of the early communist network in Southeast Asia. In the 1920s Hong Kong had been the Comintern's base for organizing meetings, publishing revolutionary pamphlets, collecting funds, and planning activities against the governments of Malaya, Indonesia, Indochina, and Thailand (91). The Vietnamese Communist Party held its founding National Congress there in 1930, and Ho Chi Minh used the port city as a base from which to network with fellow communists in Shanghai, Bangkok, and other cities (92).

Scions of the late nineteenth-century Philippine elite were sent to Hong Kong for English-language schooling years before the American occupation. Hong Kong was a major travel destination in the colonial and postcolonial eras, the place where the Marcoses stashed their ill-gotten money (Chaikin and Sharman 2009, 170). It would also be a major workplace of overseas Filipino workers in the late twentieth and early twenty-first centuries.

The main characters of Joaquin's novel cross paths in Hong Kong in the early postwar period. There are the Monson brothers, Tony and Pépé, one a priest, the other a veterinarian. Both men are born in Hong Kong to a veteran of the Philippine Revolution who had chosen a lifetime of exile in Hong Kong over surrender to and accommodation with the occupying American forces back home and the Filipino daughter of a Manilaman ship captain. Both have never been to the Philippines.

Their father, the Monson patriarch, had sworn "not to go home, neither himself nor his sons, until it [the Philippines] was a free country again" (Joaquin [1961] 1991, 15). Not long after the Philippines was "granted" independence by the Americans in 1946, the Monson father had gone back to the Philippines, only to return in haste to Hong Kong a month later, a broken man "quietly going to pieces" (26) and resorting to drugs for solace and forgetfulness.

A similar traumatic experience befalls the Filipino-Portuguese Paco Texeira, a childhood friend of the Monsons and someone who nowadays would have been called a *Fil-foreigner* (a term designating children born abroad to at least one Filipino parent), a Hong Kong–born musician contracted with his band to play music in Manila, in clubs with names like "Manila–Hong Kong" and "Shanghai Boulevard." Married to fellow Filipino-Portuguese Mary, Paco embarks on an affair with the socialite Concha Vidal (44). Paco had been "deeply interested in Manila" (40), but his actual experience of that "evil city where rich and poor alike huddled in terror behind their beasts and guns" (60) sends him fleeing back to Hong Kong.

At the heart of the novel is the mother-daughter pair of Concha and Connie, mirror images of each other. Concha Vidal had previously been married to a poet who had risen to prominence at the end of the Spanish regime but whose career as a writer had been nipped by the precipitous decline of the Spanish language and literature in the American-speaking twentieth century. After the death of her first husband, Concha, faced with the upbringing of four sons (two of whom would die in the Pacific War), has an affair with another writer but after his suicide decides to abort the baby she is carrying and ends up marrying her abortionist, the ironically named Manolo Vidal.

On the eve of World War II, Concha falls in love with a younger man, Telemaco "Macho" Escobar, scion of a prominent family that owns a vast sugar plantation in the Visayas region, but then takes it on herself to marry off her daughter Connie to her ex-lover. Married for just over a year, Connie runs away from her husband to Hong Kong and encounters the Monson brothers, to whom she turns for counsel both practical and spiritual, as well as yet another of her mother's former lovers, Paco the musician. The mother and daughter's soul-searching in Hong Kong leads to a shocking scandal that, by implication, ends the career of the politician who is Concha's husband and Connie's father: Connie elopes with Paco, and a despairing Macho Escobar shoots Concha before turning the gun on himself.

The Vidal (the surname in Spanish means "life-giving") women find themselves chafing against the life that is expected of privileged women of their class. Daughter Connie's first act of rebellion as a teenager is sparked by her discovery, via the newspapers, that her father had put her name on the government payroll even though she was only a schoolgirl and had never been inside a government office. Cursed with a "conscience" (20), Connie runs away. Her mother finds her daughter "working as a dishwasher in a chop suey joint in the Chinese quarter. . . . She kept denying her name and actually seemed to have forgotten who she was" (22). Connie had told her mother that she "absolutely refused to be educated on 'stolen money,'" and when her mother objected to Connie's phrase "stolen money," Connie "said no, it wasn't stolen money, it was money sucked from the people" (21).

Connie's second flight is to another "Chinese" quarter farther afield, Hong Kong. The journey is coded as a search for a true father, for traces of the man her own father had been before his transformation from idealistic patriot into cynical, opportunistic politician. Connie's father (Concha's second husband) had been educated in Spain and had fought in the revolution. "But he had been quick to see that . . . the coming culture, unlike that of the Revolution, would have a political, not a literary accent" (178), and opted for a lucrative career in politics.

In Hong Kong, Connie finally comes face to face with the living proof of patriotic integrity, recognizing in the dying, elderly Monson "the hero they had all betrayed" (303), who had maintained his allegiance to the lost cause of revolution, as her biological father had failed to do.

Mother Concha suffers a harsh fate. She witnesses firsthand the rapid eclipse of the *ilustrado* patriotism of the revolutionary period in favor of the "ilustrado politics" (Cullinane 2003) of the American period. She tells Pépé Monson, "When I was a little girl people like your father were my conscience walking around in elegant clothes" (19). Concha remembers the days of the revolution as an age of insurgent activity, an "age of heroes" (167). The waning of that age is encapsulated by the linguistic shift from Spanish to English. "In two swift decades they would find themselves obsolete. . . . The future of which they had so happily babbled had turned into a dead end.... A people that had got as far as Baudelaire in one language was being returned to the ABC's of another language, and the young men writing in the 1900s would find that their sons could not read them. The fathers spoke European, the sons would speak American" (167).

The Misadventures of *Ilustrado* Nationalism

The transformation of the Philippines from entrepôt to agricultural-export economy (Legarda 1999, 119) was crucial in engendering the social forces that nurtured the ascendancy and militancy of the *ilustrado* class. The most distinctive feature of this transformation is that it did not follow the classic colonial pattern of tying a colony to the metropole in a relation of one-sided dependency. The Philippines was not economically complementary to Spain and in this sense was not a typical colonial economy (Legarda 1999, 4). In the export trade, its main trading partners in 1818 had been Mexico, India, America, China, and France, but by 1846 they would be Great Britain, China, America, Spain, and Australia, with Spain coming in only in fourth place (131–32).

The imperial crisis wrought by the Seven Years' War (1756–63) and the Bourbon reforms were instrumental in centralizing the colonial administrative apparatus while extending control over the colony proper through local and provincial reforms that promoted a "politics of collaboration" with the native elite and transformed the fiscal base of the bankrupt colony (Fradera 1999). By the nineteenth century, the key players in the Philippine colonial economy were private British agency houses and American firms that formed working relationships with Filipino and Chinese intermediaries in local operations. The Philippines was part of the intra-Asian and global trade system, underpinned by "forced free trade" (Martin 1832) and mediated by Anglo-American (the British controlled 70 percent of the Philippines's foreign trade; Kramer 2002, 1330) and Chinese players, leading one Spanish critic to characterize the Philippines as an "Anglo-Chinese colony with a Spanish flag" (Carlos Recur, quoted in Wickberg 1965, 280). A substantial portion of the Philippine trade with other countries was conducted through Hong Kong and Singapore (Legarda 1999, 126).

Ilustrados were scions of natives and mestizos (people of mixed ancestry, mainly Chinese-indigenous and to a lesser extent Spanish-indigenous and Spanish-Chinese-indigenous) who accrued enough money to send their sons to municipalities, to Manila, and to Europe or Hong Kong for education, secure their social status within their own society, and clamor for greater participation in the colonial government (Cullinane 1982, 279). Native entrepreneurship, modern technology, and rural wage labor gave these cosmopolitan colonials (some of whom now took to calling themselves Filipinos, a term that originally denoted only Philippine-born creole Spaniards) in Manila and other municipalities an independent socioeconomic base outside the state, as well as the necessary clout to challenge the increasingly repressive Spanish colonial authorities.

The colonial economy also expanded the urban middle sector. Not as rich or as highly educated as the "principales" who held office and the *ilustrados* who obtained their professional degrees abroad or from the University of Santo Tomas in Manila, they were nonetheless literate and had connections with the *principales*, the colonial bureaucracy, and the economy through their work (Cullinane 2014, 87). This urban middle sector, along with leading men from the municipalities, constituted the "emerging elites" (89) who, along with blue-collar workers (Escalante 2017, 462), joined the cross-class movement Katipunan (Richardson 2013, 400). While the *ilustrado*-led Propaganda Movement agitated for political representation in the Spanish Cortes, the socially heterogeneous Katipunan called for independence.

Apart from material power, these emergent Filipino elites differed from other colonial elites by virtue of their polyglot epistemic power. With their working knowledge of European (Spanish, German, French, English), Asian (Sanskrit, Malay, Japanese), and Philippine/Austronesian languages, *ilustrados* were active participants in the production of knowledge in the Philippines (Thomas 2012, 3; see also Mojares 2006). They were themselves contributors to European Orientalism, even as they essayed concepts of history and society through knowledge that had hitherto been deployed for colonial projects. Their discourses constructed a notion of Filipino that breached ethnolinguistic boundaries while simultaneously excluding (or else selectively including) specific segments of the population: mestizo, Muslim, Chinese, and highland "infidel" (Thomas 2012, 54; see also Aguilar 2005).

The key feature of this Filipino knowledge production lies in the fact that the "European" knowledge created by an Orientalist tradition and dominated by English, French, and German authors was *not* part of the Spanish colonial repertoire (Thomas 2012, 4), since, other than folklore, Spain was not a significant contributor to Orientalist knowledge production. For this reason Filipinos had far more leeway (linguistically, materially, and intellectually) to participate in the global creation of knowledge and to use that knowledge for anticolonial purposes, rather than receiving and having to grapple with the terms set by a preestablished and—in the case of India, for example—extensive, deeply learned body of work. Filipino intellectuals were often among the first to publish scholarly works on the Philippines in Spanish (40) and other languages and acted as the Spanish-language representatives in the various academic meetings in Europe in which they actively took part. Megan Thomas argues that the "young [Filipino] colonial subjects positioned themselves as modern scholars and intellectuals in a broader [European] field in which their colonizers, the Spanish, often lagged behind" (2012, 10).

The material and epistemic bases of *ilustrado* ascendancy in the late nineteenth century complicate Frantz Fanon's ([1963] 2004) idea of a national bourgeoisie bereft of sufficient material or intellectual resources. Fanon's national bourgeoisie is economically and intellectually "underdeveloped" (98), lacking economic power and incapable of accumulating capital other than as intermediaries (98), but, just as important, incapable of achieving epistemic mastery (Sekyi-Otu 2006, 143) that allows them to participate in knowledge production. While there is plenty of evidence showing that Filipino *ilustrados* often acted in their own interests, there are also examples of *ilustrado* patriotism that bear out Fanon's other observation concerning an "authentic middle class" that "betray[ed] the calling fate has marked out for it, and . . . put itself to school with the people, . . . put at the people's disposal the intellectual and technical capital that it has snatched when going through the colonial universities" (150).

Fanon's excoriating critique of the "misadventures of national consciousness" (Sekyi-Otu 2006, 143) is accompanied by an acknowledgment that there exist "honest intellectuals": "There are intellectuals, civil servants, and senior officials who sincerely feel the need for a planned economy, for outlawing profiteers and doing away with any form of mystification. Moreover, such men, to a certain degree, are in favor of the maximum participation by the people in the management of public affairs" (Fanon [1963] 2004, 121; on postcolonial theory's disavowal of the role of intellectuals in revolution, see Lazarus 1999; Hau 2000).

Joaquin's concern to recover the abortive history of a youthful, heroic *ilustrado* patriotism rests on the contention that the revolution had been "untimely" and had already "flopped before [US admiral George] Dewey steamed into Manila" ([1997] 2005, 87). Joaquin identifies two geographically and sociologically distinct revolutions that broke out in 1896: the Manila-based revolt (led by Andres Bonifacio) that "ended less than a week in failure" in the last days of August 1896, and the Cavite-based one (led by Emilio Aguinaldo) that lasted five years, from late August 1896 until Aguinaldo's capture in

1901 (88). The revolution, he argues, was "bourgeois" from the start (104). But this "bourgeois" revolution would quickly be mired in murderous factional conflict and result in the execution of the founder of the Katipunan, Andres Bonifacio. Under Aguinaldo, the revolutionary government's heavy taxation, military conscription, and failure to curb military abuses were resented and resisted by peasants and urban workers alike.

The failure of the revolution did not, however, spell the end of the revolution. Joaquin stresses that after 1901 the insurgency was continued by "outlaws, outcasts, peasants, laborers, the poor, the ignorant, the have-not classes in general" (225), who had been part of the 1896 revolution but who took up the cause the "mass of intelligent men"(226) had abandoned. Joaquin contends that "the Revolution was indeed 'captured,' not *from* the masses, in the 1890s, but by them in the 1900s" (226).

Far more crucially, American colonialism would drastically vitiate the critical stance of *ilustrado* nationalism. In institutionalizing municipal and national elections, the Americans cemented the power of *ilustrados* as "representative men" at a time when the revolution itself had been downgraded by the Americans as a "movement of 'the more ignorant people of the laboring masses'" (227). Brutal as the torture, massacre, and concentration camps had been, Joaquin sees the rise of the native elected official (whom he calls *politico*) and the public school system, both of which operated on a model of education-based tutelage to "prepare" the country for eventual independence (Kramer 2006, 201), as the true betrayal of the revolution.

Just as crucial as the political co-optation of the *ilustrado* was the narrowing of the Philippines' economic horizon and the attenuation of its linkages with different national markets. The "price of twentieth-century progress," as the historian Benito Legarda (1999, 340) puts it, "would be economic dependence" on the United States, the reduction of the multisited global trade to bilateral US-Philippines trade. In 1930, 63 percent of imports came from the United States, and 79 percent of exports went to the United States (Hawes 1987, 25–26); by 1933, 87 percent of Philippine exports went to the United States, two-thirds of which income came from sugar alone (Doronila 1992, 32). This state of affairs in which the Philippines was tied by an umbilical cord to the United States would persist into the next few decades of the postindependence era.

More, American knowledge production (McCoy 2009) differed from other varieties of Orientalism. It was "inherently superficial" in character and did not entail the erudition that was rooted in long-term service, language acquisition, and deep cultural knowledge (42–43). Stressing "quick, cost-effective solutions" (43), it exercised global domination through the "surface reconnaissance" of cadastral surveys, census taking, geography, photography, and police surveillance (44). Superficial knowledge by no means suggests frivolous knowledge: what the Americans did in the Philippines already signaled a transitional moment in the evolution of governmentality away from the older, European "territorial colonialism of plantations, police and bolt-action repression" to a "postcolonial, supranational regime of military bases, electronic surveillance and psychological warfare" (45).

Neither the Philippines' "special relationship" with America during the Cold War era (as part of an American-led hub-and-spokes system of bilateral security alliances and economic ties that helped jump-start some of the Cold War developmental projects in anticommunist "Free Asia," notably Japan, South Korea, and Taiwan) nor the Filipino elite's capture of the commanding heights of the economy and polity has served the Philippines well. Instead, the Filipino elite would bear the brunt of the blame for the fiscal instability and political impasse of an electoral system—touted as a showcase of America's Asia-style democracy (Friedman and Selden 1973)—that spawned a "political economy of permanent crisis" (Bello 2004). The failed attempt at creating a "developmental state" (Johnson 1982) during the Marcos era ended in yet another economic crisis in the early 1980s: the global debt crisis triggered by the US Federal Reserve Board decision to raise interest rates (for a critique of the developmental state as concept and model, see Hau 2017, 217–23).

The Philippines did not simply provide the archetype of the "antidevelopmental state" (Bello 2004), the messy-democratic Other that Singapore's Lee Kuan Yew and Thai politicians invoked to justify their authoritarian rule. The two keywords it popularized, *People Power* and *crony capitalism*, provided intellectual ballast for American attempts to restructure the East Asian region by criticizing if not dismantling the East Asian (authoritarian) developmental state in the 1980s and 1990s. National and global mass media and scholarship alike blamed the Filipino elite's failure to develop their country on the recalcitrance and persistence of the "traditional" Filipino political culture of patron-clientelism, nepotism, and personalistic exchange (Ileto 1999). Filipinos would be no better than "raw men" (Spivak 1999, 26, drawing on Immanuel Kant), not yet and not fully subjects spatially, temporally, and epistemically differentiated from their American colonizers (despite the American colonial provenance and postcolonial buttressing of Filipino elite dominance and the corruption, cronyism, nepotism, and personalism of leaders like Donald Trump) and impervious to the civilizing imperative of education and governance along Weberian legal-rational state lines.

Joaquin's siting of the lost promise of an abortive *ilustrado* revolution outside the Philippines, in a nearby Hong Kong that had served as a political haven and enabling ground for Filipino revolutionaries, underscores that the American-era and postindependence Philippines that his main characters are in constant flight from has itself become a "foreign" country, a *terra aliena*. In recent years, however, Hong Kong itself has become a *terra aliena* to Hong Kongers who support democracy (see chapter 6 in this volume).

Diasporic Filipinos: The "New *Ilustrados*"?

If the Philippines itself is a *terra aliena*, an alien nation inhospitable to the Philippine Revolution and a source of alienation, the Monson patriarch pins his hope on his surviving sons to carry on the unfinished project of "the Revolution and the Republic": "There it was now in their faces—the Revolution and the Republic, and that small private past for which he had come so far away to die" (Joaquin [1961] 1991, 331).

In the decades since the publication of *Woman* in 1961, overseas Filipino workers (OFWs) have come to embody the critical potentiality that had been lost by the *ilustrados*. In *Woman*, the Filipinos in Hong Kong number not only the "expatriate" Monson and his Hong Kong–born sons but also the Filforeigner (Filipino-Portuguese) musician Paco Texeira and the dead Monson matriarch (the daughter of a Manilaman seafarer).

Indeed, travel abroad and education had never been the exclusive privilege of the *ilustrados*. Propagandists like Graciano López Jaena (1889, 7) hailed the more than twelve thousand to twenty thousand Filipino seafarers (*marineros*) scattered all over the ports of England, France, America, and Spain as fellow countrymen and potential *ilustrados*.

López Jaena projects the Propaganda Movement's concern with patriotic intent and political exile onto the far more diverse, complex motives and decisions of these sailors to work abroad (see Aguilar 2014). *Ilustrado* investment in diasporic potentiality is no guarantee that diasporic activities can be channeled for national, let alone even anticolonial, purposes. Manilamen (not all of whom were Filipinos) manned the galleon ships and Captain Ahab's harpoon boat in Herman Melville's novel *Moby-Dick* (1851). Some would be involved in collecting money to support Aguinaldo's revolutionary junta in Hong Kong (Aguilar 2014, 49). Others hired themselves out as mercenaries under Frenchman Hyppolite Bouchard as he attempted to "liberate" California in 1818 (37), and under Frederick Townsend Ward as he contracted with the Qing government to defend Shanghai and quell the Taiping Rebellion in China (37–40). Currently, over one-quarter of the 1.2 million seafarers who make it possible for nine-tenths of global trade to be conducted by sea are Filipinos (*Economist* 2019).

Filipino musicians of the Paco Texeira sort have also been active in the Asian music scene since the late nineteenth century (S. Ng 2006). They formed part of state bands such as Malaya's Selangor state band and played in Norodom I's royal orchestra in Cambodia, the nightclubs of French Indochina, the dance halls of Shanghai, and the high-class hotels and clubs of Tokyo, Hong Kong, Taipei, Bangkok, Singapore, and Guam (46–47). These Filipino musicians were purveyors of American jazz and other forms of Western music, mediating the Asian consumption of American and "Western" culture (59). Joaquin calls them "agents between the East and West, building the Harlem gods a bamboo habitation on this side of the Pacific" ([1961] 1991, 35). Superstar Bruce Lee learned the intricacies of the cha-cha from a Filipina (Polly 2018, 67).

In the past three decades, a new term has emerged to encompass the earlier waves of international travel by Manilamen and musicians but with a far wider geographic and occupational scope. *Overseas Filipino workers* replaced an earlier term dating back to the Marcos-era 1970s, *overseas contract workers*. The official policy of sending workers abroad had begun as a stopgap measure to deal with the country's current-account deficit in the Marcos period. By the 1980s the trend of international labor migration would be irreversible, with a significant impact on Philippine society. The combined remittances of these workers, based mainly in Asia and the Middle East, have effectively transformed the Philippine economy. Their growing significance has been confirmed by President Corazón Aquino's characterization of these workers as "bagong bayani" (new heroes), saviors of the Philippine economy (Republic of the Philippines Presidential Management Staff 2002). Their remittances, representing more than 9 percent of the gross domestic product in 2019 (Rivas 2020), have boosted the country's current account, domestic consumption, and domestic investment.

The Connie who washed dishes in Manila's Chinatown would find her present-day, less privileged compatriots washing dishes in Hong Kong, where large numbers of them work as domestic helpers (see Rafael 2000, 231–32n16). Drawn mainly from the middle sector (Albert, Gaspar, and Raymundo 2015), these OFWs would be hailed as the "new ilustrados," "influential agents of change," and the "most demanding constituency of the Philippine nation" and compared to "Filipino travelers of Rizal's generation" in terms of loyalty to, and concern over, the nation (David 2010). "Their mobility, their broad international experience, and their rich encounters with various cultures have made OFWs truly modern" (David 2010). They would be the "critical fulcrum of our society's transition to modernity" (David 2010).

International labor migration and market forces have created a situation in which a large number of Filipinos, in the course of pursuing their own interests and those of their families, have become middle class by Philippine standards because of their greater earning power abroad but, because of their occupations, are not necessarily considered middle class either in their home country (at least in the eyes of the elite) or in their host countries. As with the emerging elites of the late nineteenth century, their shifting subject positions endow OFWs with political potentiality, affording them access to more than one world view, site of experiences, and arena of contestation. Filipino domestic-worker activists have been at the forefront of foreign workers' struggle for legal rights in Hong Kong and other places and have established a political party in the Philippines to push for Philippine government protection of OFWs (Constable 2007, 215).

While the Philippine state has been actively incorporating the OFWs into the Philippine national imaginary as new heroes, acts of migration are neither easily nor safely subsumed into a narrative of loyalty to, and heroic sacrifice on behalf of, the Filipino nation, let alone progressive politics. The idea of the OFWs' flight to other countries does not necessarily carry with it the historical association of travel with (political) exile and resistance but is instead coded as economic "necessity" and "opportunity." The mobilities and subject positions of OFWs may promote or discourage attachment to place(s), underscoring the existential and intellectual motility and political potentiality, but also the limits, of place making. Place making without guarantees may exceed both governance and resistance, translating into neither loyal contribution to one's country (which one?) nor political action to transform it (see David Der-wei Wang's "postloyalism" and Lin Pei-Yin's ambiguous "native soil" in this volume). In other words, diasporic Filipinos' complex, variegated motivations and decisions to live and work abroad do not lend themselves to being simplistically coded as political critique and social transformation of the nation. The Monson brothers' and Paco Texeira's attitude toward the Philippines is rife with ambivalence.

Paco "never felt any curiosity about nor the least affection for the country of his musician father; and when he went to Manila, was stirred by no sentiments of filial piety. Unlike the Monson boys, who were always conscious of being Filipinos, exiles, and the sons of a patriot, Paco was a guileless cosmopolitan and would have felt at home—or rather, would have failed to notice that he was at the North Pole as long as he had his piano, his drums, a good radio, some people to play football with, and Mary" (Joaquin [1961] 1991, 35). For Paco, there is always the option to leave the Philippines when things become unbearable there.

The Monson brothers—both presumably carrying Philippine passports—have an even more ambivalent relationship with both the Philippines and Hong Kong, for both countries have in common the fact that they represent a "home" that is not home. Tony Monson, watching from the window in St. Andrew's Convent in Hong Kong (which is tellingly bounded by the racetrack, the red-light district of Wang Chai, and manure-fed vegetable gardens) and hearing the distant cannon that meant war in the Chinese mainland, "felt a sudden bitter tenderness for the city spread out and humming joyously beneath him, this doomed heathen town that was home and not home, that was birthplace but not native land, that he had loved and feared and finally rejected, but whose beauty—soggy in springtime, steamy in summer, perfect in autumn, perverse in winter—his foreign bones knew like a wife and regarded like a stranger" (130–31).

Mary tells Pépé Monson, "We all of us more or less belong over there [the Philippines], but only Paco here—and your father, Pépé—have gone back, and see what it did to them" (27). The Monson ancestral house burned down in the Japanese war, and the Monson patriarch's exhortation that "*the house of our fathers is waiting for us to come home!*" (12) now rings hollow. Moreover, the quick, disappointed return of the Monson father and Paco to Hong Kong means that from here on, all these Filipinos must sing the Lord's song in a foreign land (a reference to the Latin Old Testament verse the elder Monson is fond of quoting: "Quomodo cantabo canticum Domini in terra aliena?" (14, based on Psalm 137:4), *foreign* here meaning the Philippines and Hong Kong.

There remains the risk that the song may not even be sung at all, as Pépé Monson realizes, for "they had apostasized, leaving the old man to carry on his cult alone. Now the cult had abruptly come to an end; the candles had all been extinguished and removed. There was only vacant darkness, a vacant *silence*" (69, emphasis added).

The Monson patriarch may see in his sons' faces "the Revolution and the Republic," but nothing in the actions of the Fil-foreign sons, save for the succor they give to Connie to find herself through their father, serves as a final guarantee that they will take up their father's cause, let alone return to the mother country. The potentiality may remain only a potentiality, rather than translate into purposive action, even as the decisions, actions, and forced return of many OFWs are already reshaping the Philippine state and economy in ways that go beyond the capacity of the present-day state and *ilustrado* leaders to direct, let alone command.

For all of Joaquin's efforts to memorialize a heroic *ilustrado* patriotism that was quenched but not fully lost in the transition from Spanish to American colonialism, and from colonialism to postcolonialism, Joaquin knows full well that investing faith and hope in the overseas Filipinos carries its own risk of nonreturn, of nonsacrifice, of outright indifference even.

Joaquin's writings indicate that the promise of the "unfinished revolution," as it is called in Philippine historiography (Ileto 1993), survives not a priori in any group or class as a whole but in the actions and languages of people in the course of their struggle against oppression and for liberation, wherever they may find themselves, whoever they are.

One final legacy of multiple colonialisms: Spanish and American colonialism failed to extinguish the languages of the colonized. The Philippine Revolution had a salutary effect on Philippine languages: it ushered in the first golden age of Tagalog and vernacular literature in the early to mid-twentieth century (S. Reyes 1982; Mojares 1983). While English remains a language of privilege and power, neither the use of Spanish nor the imposition of English during the two colonial eras succeeded in obliterating the Philippine languages, which are spoken in everyday life today (Guillermo 2010). Speakers of these languages have demonstrated their capacity for decolonial thinking (Mignolo and Walsh 2018), appropriating and resignifying, and above all generating, enlightened ideas, while retaining the semantic richness and political efficacy of their languages, far in excess of any transmitted ideas. Far from being mere captives of the ideological discourses emanating from the colonial state or from the cosmopolitan-colonial elite, people whose labor enabled the transformations of the past centuries have time and again used their many mother tongues to adopt positions of "reflexive detachment" and produce "standpoints" from which "colonial rule could be criticized" (Guillermo 2010, 203, 209). This is but a way of reminding readers that world-making revolutionary discourses and practices of the nineteenth, twentieth, and twenty-first centuries have never been limited to the so-called *ilustrados*.

Note

An earlier version of chapter 11 appeared in Caroline S. Hau, *Elites and Ilustrados in Philippine Culture* (Quezon City: Ateneo de Manila University Press, 2017), 83–122.

Pheng Cheah

Diasporic Worldliness in Postcolonial Globalization

With regard to its provenance, the concept of diaspora in contemporary academic discourse originates from the social sciences, especially sociology and anthropology. Consequently, its relation to topics in the humanities such as cosmopolitanism has not been explicitly theorized. Because diasporic subjects circulate globally and can have multiple affiliations and affective ties, it is inferred that they are cosmopolitan. More important, diaspora theorists sought to connect diasporic cosmopolitanism to a distinctive form of time. Taking as a point of departure Benedict Anderson's (1991) argument that the nation is produced and governed by homogeneous empty time and the progressive linear time of modernity, they argued that the discontinuities and displacements of diasporic experiences and memories generate disruptive temporalities and broken histories that subversively interrupt dominant forms of time.

In this chapter I argue that diaspora became conflated with cosmopolitanism because the initial theorization of diasporic consciousness focused on its destabilization of national identity and belonging in the British imperial metropolitan center and its main settler colony, the United States. Migration is the fundamental material condition of diasporic subjectivity. Its vectors and significance have drastically changed in the contemporary conjuncture of postcolonial globalization, which is structured around the new empire of the Pax Americana, its conflict with the Islamic world, and its competition with postsocialist Chinese global capitalism. New forms of diaspora have emerged that problematize the axiomatic affiliation of diaspora with cosmopolitanism. Their condition is characterized by an experience of time quite different from disruptive temporality. In postcolonial globalization the vectors of migration are governed by the temporal regime of global capitalist modernity, which appropriates disruptive temporalities within the North Atlantic for multiculturalism and makes them untenable outside the North Atlantic. I suggest that a return to an original worldliness offers some respite.

The bildungsroman is an apposite literary genre for understanding the worldly and temporal dimension of diasporic consciousness. Like the concept of *Bildung* that it dramatizes, its narration of a protagonist's progressive development from restless naive youth into worldly maturity symbolically personifies modernity's representation of time as linear progress, while its portrayal of this development's global itinerary dramatizes the geographical schema of capitalist modernity's temporal regime. By contrasting Hanif Kureishi's *The Buddha of Suburbia* (1990) and K. S. Maniam's *The Return* ([1981] 1993), two bildungsromans about the older kind of South Asian diaspora set on different sides of the international division of labor (IDL), I argue that the impossibility of cosmopolitan *Bildung* for a diasporic subject on the subordinate side of the IDL shows the limits of the North Atlantic diasporic model. Mohsin Hamid's *The Reluctant Fundamentalist* (2007), a novel about a new South Asian diasporic subject who embraces fundamentalist nationalism after his failed cosmopolitan *Bildung* in the post-9/11 United States, suggests that the North Atlantic diasporic model belongs to a superseded conjuncture of global capitalism. Finally, I examine Tash Aw's *Five Star Billionaire* (2013), a bildungsroman about the new Chinese diaspora, to elucidate why a return to a more fundamental worldliness is necessary for such subjects in the postsocialist Chinese empire: not to the nation fetishized as the natural place of natality but to the uncanny moment where we first come into the world and can envision making it anew.

Diasporic Subjectivity: Cosmopolitan *Bildung* and Diasporic Temporality

The key features of the sociological and anthropological conceptualization of diaspora are, first, coerced or involuntary departure from a putative homeland metaphorized as a scattering of seed from a parent tree; second, the continued identification with that homeland and maintenance of a cultural identity through collective memory and cultural practices; and, third, the preservation of connections with the homeland, often expressed as a desire to return physically or symbolically, for example, through travel, gift relations, or memory and nostalgia. It is only with the theorization of diaspora as a form of group consciousness—subjectivity in the loose sense—that the term began to have a strong traction in literary studies, where it became associated with worldliness.[1]

Paul Gilroy's work is exemplary in this regard. Although a sociologist by training, his account of Black diaspora consciousness in the North Atlantic was largely based on a study of literary works. Gilroy links diasporic consciousness to cosmopolitanism by arguing that because the diasporic experience foregrounds the transnational processes of identity formation, it challenges fixed and essentialist conceptions of identity. Identities, he suggests, are "the outcomes of worldly cultural processes" (1997, 310). In contrast, the territorial regime of the nation-state seeks to close off identity formation from worldly processes by determining identity according to a "sedentary politics of either soil or blood" (317). The fixed primordiality of national identity thus needs to be destabilized by an alternative notion of identity based on movement. Because it personifies mobility, diasporic consciousness is a worldly process of *Bildung* that leads to a more expansive sense of social belonging and political solidarity that welcomes difference and otherness. "Diaspora," Gilroy suggests, "is a valuable idea because it points towards *a more refined and more worldly sense of culture* than the characteristic notions of soil, landscape and rootedness" (328). "Diasporas are the result of the 'scattering' of peoples ... with the inevitable opening of their culture to new influences and pressures. Diaspora as a concept, therefore, offers new possibilities for understanding identity, not as something inevitably determined by place or nationality, and for visualizing a future where new bases for social solidarity are offered and joined, perhaps via the new technologies" (303–4). An engagement with time and temporality is fundamental to the theorization of diasporic consciousness in the 1980s and 1990s, although, as with literary and cultural studies, the use of these terms is metaphorical.[2] The concern with time arises from a polemic against two related conceptions of time: the linear time of the modern state's drive for progress and the homogeneous empty time of the nation as an imagined community (Anderson 1991). I focus on Gilroy's and Homi Bhabha's reflections on diasporic temporality.[3]

Gilroy's account of diasporic time in *The Black Atlantic* is part of his critique of the inadequacy of the conceptual opposition of tradition/modernity for understanding the experiences of the Middle Passage and its legacies for the political cultures of the Black Atlantic diaspora. Afrocentrism, which celebrates an atemporal African civilization that has been preserved despite slavery and colonialism, is commonly opposed to the modernity of Western civilization. Gilroy, however, argues that they share the same linear conception of time. The Afrocentric celebration of African tradition claims the linear time of Western modernity for a pure African civilization. In contrast, Black Atlantic diasporic intellectuals, writers, and musicians question this conception of time because they experience time as simultaneously modern and fragmented by the memory of a lost time that slavery has made inaccessible. Consequently, Black Atlantic political culture is neither simply traditional nor modern. It "grew inside modernity in a distinctive relationship of antagonistic indebtedness" because it has "diaspora temporality, historicity, memory and narrativity . . . [as its] articulating principles" (Gilroy 1993, 191). The history of slavery engendered complex encounters between the respective temporalities of (African) tradition and (Western) modernity such that "diaspora time is not . . . African time" (196). However, because race bars the diasporic subject from attaining full citizenship in the North Atlantic nation-state, black intellectuals experienced "the tension between temporalities that leads [them] to try to press original African time into the service of their attempts to come to terms with diaspora space and its dynamics of differentiation" (196–97). Diasporic temporality is the disruption of the modern nation-state's linear time of progress: diasporic intellectuals "shared a sense that the modern world was fragmented along axes constituted by racial conflict and could accommodate non-synchronous, hetero-cultural modes of life in close proximity" (197).

What does Gilroy mean by *time*? One looks in vain for a definition. Instead, Gilroy alludes to the meaning of temporality by using *historicity*, *memory*, and *narrativity* as equivalent terms. In his most precise attempt at a definition, he suggests that diasporic temporality is the interruption of linear temporality by space: "The idea of diaspora might itself be understood as . . . a utopian eruption of space into the linear temporal order of modern black politics which enforces the obligation that space and time must be considered relationally in their interarticulation with racialised being" (198). Gilroy's primary concern is clearly not with time but with how black diasporic subjects mark its passage, especially through aesthetic processes. Indeed, he invariably explains diasporic temporality by noting its affinity with aesthetic modernism's sense of time and illustrates it with musical examples. Rhythm and blues introduces "a syncopated temporality—a different rhythm of living and being in which 'the night time is the right time' and . . . 'everything is on The One.' Ralph Ellison describes the effects of this temporal disjunction thus: 'Invisibility, let me explain, gives one a slightly different sense of time, you're never quite on the beat. Sometimes you're ahead and sometimes behind. Instead of the swift and imperceptible flowing of time, you are aware of its nodes, those points where time stands still or from which it leaps ahead. And you slip into the breaks and look around'" (Gilroy and Ellison quoted in Gilroy 2003, 202). Gilroy's reliance on musical terms such as *accents* and *breaks* indicates that what he means by *time* is the meaningful patterns black diasporic subjects use to express and order their experiences of time, which are marked by the violence and suffering of slavery and ongoing racism. Gilroy cites a comment from James Baldwin to propose that black music expresses "distinct conceptions of time that have a special political and philosophical significance" (203): "Music is our witness, and our ally. The beat is the confession which recognizes, changes and conquers time. Then, history becomes a garment we can wear and share, and not a cloak in which to hide; and time becomes a friend" (quoted in Gilroy 1993, 203).[4] Read in context, Baldwin's comment, the last two paragraphs of a review on jazz history, is not about conceptions of time but the conversion of time into history. Baldwin suggests that black music offers an expressive narration of black American history that emphasizes slavery's destruction of human civilization's ideals. Black music conquers time insofar as it appropriates time's passage and gives ethical significance to what was experienced as meaningless violence. It makes time into a friend: it expresses a meaningful history forged from slave experiences, gives consolation, and builds community.

In Bhabha's work, diasporic temporality is metaphorical. Bhabha yokes Anderson's argument that national community is imagined in homogeneous empty time to a linear conceptualization of history. Because migrant and diasporic subjects carry the memory of other places and are subject to discrimination in Western host nations, they are uneasily interpellated by the linear historical narratives that constitute a national community's culture. When these narratives are examined as a textual performance, a mode of address that disciplines their recipients and makes them into members of the nation, they undergo slippage and become ambivalent, thereby subverting national cohesion. Such is the nation's "temporal dimension," which is coextensive with "the iterative temporality" of the enunciative split, the lag between the subject of enunciation and the enounced subject (1990, 293, 305). A nation's culturally constructed character means that it is a metaphorical entity that requires interpretation. Hence, the nation is governed by "a temporality of representation," which requires a mode of writing different from the linear narratives of national history, one that is attuned to "the ambivalent temporalities of the nation-space" (293, 294). "Such cultural movements disperse the homogeneous, visual time of the horizontal society.... We need another time of writing that will be able to inscribe the ambivalent and chiasmatic intersections of time and place that constitute the problematic 'modern' experience of the western nation" (293). What does Bhabha mean by *time* and *temporality*? While the complexity of diasporic experiences may need to be represented by different modes of writing, the latter's connection to time is unclear. Anderson's argument was not about time itself but the manner of its apprehension in modernity. More precisely, he contrasted the modern apprehension of simultaneity as the meaningless temporal coincidence of clock and calendar with that of religious communities and, more broadly, an enchanted cosmological worldview, where the past and future are always part of the present as its prefiguration and fulfillment (Anderson 1991, 22–24). These are fundamentally different historical modes of experiencing and ordering time's passage so that we can make sense of it. When Bhabha suggests that diasporic experience problematizes the nation's time, he is similarly unconcerned with time itself. Diasporic temporality is metaphorical in two senses: first, it refers to the metaphorical forms we use to organize and render meaningful time's passage. Second, insofar as the modern nation's temporal simultaneity is generated by metaphorical processes, attending to their "time" foregrounds the disruptive tensions covered over by the nation's "time."

The Temporal Regime of Global Capitalist Modernity

Theories of diasporic temporality use *time* and *temporality* without precision and fail to distinguish between the two terms. *Temporality* refers to that which constitutes time, the "essence" that makes time what it is. For example, in Western philosophy, time has been understood as the succession of "nows" (Aristotle), the interiority of the subject (Immanuel Kant), or the protention and retention of traces (Edmund Husserl), or as constituted by temporalization, which reveals the present on the basis of anticipating the future as having-been (Martin Heidegger), and so on. Moreover, they do not distinguish between time and our apprehension and experience of it. Our experience of time is shaped by representations and interpretations that we, as individual and social subjects, prescribe to give it meaning. When we describe time as linear or cyclical, we use geometrical figures to represent its passage and attribute a value to these figures through concepts of progress or cosmic fulfillment. In contrast, temporality in an ontological sense concerns questions such as, Why does time come and persist? How and why do we exist and continue to be by receiving the gift of time? Theorists of diasporic temporality are uninterested in these questions. They are concerned with how sociopolitically hegemonic interpretations of homogeneous time that structure national belonging and global modernity are contested by the "disjunctive temporalities" and "broken histories" of diasporic experiences.

Although diasporic temporality has its basis in the slave trade and colonialism, the horizon for its ethico-political stakes is constitutional democracy in the North. Gilroy's emphasis on Black *Atlantic* political culture and Bhabha's focus on the problematic modern experience of the *Western* nation clearly indicate that diasporic subversion and the desire for redress and transformation occur through the channels of the civil societies of North Atlantic constitutional democratic nation-states. Such theories have some purchase for analyzing racial and cultural relations in North Atlantic societies constituted by the forcible displacement and migration dictated by chattel slavery and Western colonialism. The cultural politics of Black Britain, Arab France, hyphenated America, and the Indisch Netherlands, and, more broadly, cosmopolitan multiculturalism, belong to this formation. Their relevance to postcolonial sites, however, is questionable. Despite the global dimension of Black Atlantic diasporic politics, for example, the third worldist/Afro-Asian solidarity of Richard Wright's Bandung-influenced humanism and W. E. B. Du Bois's reflections on the global color line (see Wright 1956; Du Bois 2005), its primary focus is civil rights and social, political, and economic equality in North Atlantic nations. Diasporic temporality's subversiveness derives from the fact that the dominant representation of time is a necessary component of sociosymbolic cohesion and political legitimation in nations in the North. This avenue of redress is unavailable in the postcolonial South because the fundamental inequality of the global system obstructs the establishment of functioning institutions of constitutional democracy in the South required for the legitimation process.

Indeed, global capitalist modernity is sustained by a temporal regime that is not merely metaphorical and that reaches far deeper into social life than the legitimation of nation-states through symbolic-cultural representation. "The measurement of labour by its duration" and this measurement's expression in the magnitude of the product's value, Marx (1990, 174) notes, is axiomatic to capitalist accumulation.[5] Accordingly, capitalism functions through rational calculations and technologies for the macrological and micrological management of time at the levels of material production, social life, and group and individual consciousness. They generate an abstract form of time, quantifiable labor time, and a correspondingly abstract form of human labor, to maximize value extraction.[6] The homogeneous empty time of clock and calendar—time as an independent framework and measure for all events and action—is one of these technologies. The global dissemination and evolution of homogeneous empty time into the cartographical cage of world time zones centered on Greenwich Mean Time enabled capitalist accumulation on a global scale through the transnational coordination of production, exchange, consumption, and financialization.[7] Temporal technologies are also at work at the micrological level of power. Michel Foucault (2000, 86) points out that a set of political techniques were elaborated in the nineteenth century to convert the bodies of peoples and their time into labor power and labor time so that they could be efficiently transformed into hyperprofit. At the level of the biological species and subjectification, global capitalism is sustained by biopolitical technologies for the production of populations and corresponding types of human subjects. These calculations and technologies constitute a temporal regime of which space-time compression is the highest achievement.

The teleological time of historical progress, the dominant representation of time in modernity, is an expression of abstract time that invests it with the meaningful end of universal human progress. From the Latin *modernus*, *modernity* is by definition a time-consciousness, one obsessed with the time of the *now* (*modo*). The always-disappearing present is a precious resource we must maximize in its fleeting duration. G. W. F. Hegel offers a poignant figuration of time's corrosiveness. As the category for understanding change and transience, time is our relation to nonexistence. Time's central principle, personified by Chronos's devouring of his children, is the destruction of all that exists (Hegel 1955, 153; 1980, 127). It is an "unhistorical power" that annihilates all human efforts to leave a permanent mark in the world (Hegel 1998, 459). However, because humanity is endowed with reason, we can harness the dynamism of temporal change for our ends. This ability is expressed in quotidian exhortations about the prudent use of time in education, work, or leisure: Do not waste time! Make the most of it! Rational humanity calculatively reckons with time by measuring how much we can accomplish in a given duration. This magnitude confirms humanity's capabilities. As Jürgen Habermas puts it, a modern consciousness experiences "time as a scarce resource for mastering the problems that the future hurls at the present. This headlong rush of challenges is perceived as 'the pressure of time'" (2001, 132). The rational appropriation of time is the fundamental axiom of modernity. Its calculations are the ontological structure of global capitalism's temporal regime. At each conjuncture of capitalism, this regime produces corresponding subjects that perform the appropriate calculations, for example, the managers and workers of the industrial factory, the global executives of transnational corporations, and the creative workers of the new economy.

The globalization of this temporal order by European colonialism introduced a fundamental modulation that makes subversive diasporic temporality impossible outside the North Atlantic. Colonialism organized the world according to an international division of labor that involved the extraction of natural resources and agricultural commodities from the peripheries as raw materials for industrial value-adding in core countries. This division, which continues in neocolonialism, was justified by a geographical transposition of universal linear progress, which became understood through the cognate terms *modernization* and *development*. This transposition naturalized the structural hierarchy of the narrative of progress. As world-systems sociologists and political economists have pointed out, the telos of universal development cannot be fulfilled because global capitalist accumulation thrives on uneven development, even the active development of underdevelopment. Consequently, "backward" regions lag behind the developed West and emulate Western modernization as an ideal model in their frustrated development. It has been argued that postcolonial nation-states in the South are Europeanized institutions imposed by Western colonialism and that statist development subscribes to the same exclusionary pedagogical project of cultivating national community as European states (Chakrabarty 2005). Postcolonial nations are eo ipso also vulnerable to the subversion of alternative temporalities similar to diasporic temporality. My point, however, is that the geographical hierarchy of the IDL obstructs the formation in the South of a public democratic culture where disjunctive temporalities can lead to fundamental social transformation.

Journeys and Returns: The Limits of
the North Atlantic Diasporic Model

Theories of diasporic temporality hit their limits in the IDL, which makes the global actualization of public democratic political culture impossible. The bildungsroman is an apposite literary genre for illuminating the constraining force of capitalist modernity's temporal regime for two reasons. First, the plot of a protagonist's development from restless youth into maturity is a symbolic expression of the dialectic between dynamism and regulation that characterizes modernity's time-consciousness and its representation of time as linear progress (Moretti 2000). Second, the bildungsroman offers a realistic portrayal of the cultivation of different types of diasporic subjects as elements of capitalist modernity's temporal regime.

The three novels about South Asian diasporas discussed in this section have a conventional narrative structure: a first-person protagonist-narrator recounts his experiences and justifies his successful *Bildung* or explains its obstruction. A journey abroad and a return across different regions of the world-system is fundamental to the plotting of this *Bildung*. When the worlds evoked by these novels are brought into relation to each other as different sites of the postcolonial global capitalist system, they offer a geopolitical cartography of how the temporal calculations of global capitalist modernity shape the protagonist's itineraries and determine his *Bildung*'s success or failure. In *The Buddha of Suburbia*, Karim's *Bildung* begins in the Greenwich Mean Time of London, moves to New York's Eastern Standard Time, and returns to Greenwich Mean Time. The *Bildung* of Ravi, the protagonist of the Malaysian Indian writer K. S. Maniam's semi-autobiographical novel *The Return*, begins on the other side of the IDL, in British Malaya, and involves a two-year sojourn in England and a return to postindependence Malaysia. Changez, the protagonist of Mohsin Hamid's *The Reluctant Fundamentalist*, travels to the United States for an education at Princeton a few years before the September 11 attacks and returns to Lahore in their aftermath. Kureishi projects a vision of multicultural Britain as a future for British Indian diasporic citizens. The despairing outcome of Ravi's *Bildung* in postcolonial Malaysia, where multicultural democratic citizenship cannot be realized, indicates that we cannot transplant a theory of diasporic temporality formulated from North Atlantic experiences to the peripheries. The obstruction of Changez's cosmopolitan *Bildung* in post–September 11 Manhattan confirms the implausibility of a general theory of diasporic temporality. His transformation into a fundamentalist suggests that cosmopolitan *Bildung* symbolically reflects a conjuncture of global capitalism that has passed.

The Buddha of Suburbia explores the cultural politics of the old diaspora subject in the racist xenophobic climate of 1970s England. Karim, the novel's narrator, the offspring of a migrant from Bombay and a working-class Englishwoman, describes himself in the opening page as "an Englishman born and bred, almost. I am often considered to be a funny kind of Englishman, a new breed as it were, having emerged from two old histories" (Kureishi 1990, 3). His comical account of his *Bildung* sketches a series of fabricated South Asian diasporic subjectivities: Haroon, his father, the eponymous Buddha, who reinvents himself as a new age Orientalist spiritual guru by syncretizing a mishmash of Eastern philosophies and religions; and Jamila, his childhood friend, who is forced by her father, Anwar, into an arranged marriage and becomes politicized from reading Angela Davis.

For Haroon's generation, diasporic consciousness is a reaction-formation to English racism and the failure to assimilate into English society. Sent to

England to be schooled in the culture of imperialism, he begins his English life as a "mimic man," only to rediscover his Eastern roots late in life. In Karim's words, "Perhaps it was the immigrant condition living itself out through them. For years they were both happy to live like Englishmen. . . . Now as they aged and seemed settled here, Anwar and Dad appeared to be returning internally to India, or at least to be resisting the English here. It was puzzling: neither of them expressed any desire actually to see their origins again" (64). Haroon's homeland is a psychic reaction to his disaffection with England: "We old Indians come to like this England less and less and we return to an imagined India" (74).

The diaspora of the older generation at least had access to cultural traditions that they initially rejected in their desire to become English but can use to construct an imaginary homeland as a refuge when their assimilation is obstructed. The England-born younger generation can only identify as English. Karim's skin color belies his utter disconnection from India. His mother remarks, "You're not Indian. You've never *been* to India. You'd get diarrhea the minute you stepped off that plane" (232). Karim begins his acting career by being cast as Mowgli. The director berates him for his inauthenticity. To play the part, he smears his body with brown makeup and assumes a fake Indian accent. Karim develops a diasporic subjectivity when he strategically identifies with a fabricated India to cope with racism. His imagined India supplements a psychic lack: "But I did feel, looking at these strange creatures now—the Indians—that in some way these were my people, and that I'd spent my life denying or avoiding that fact. I felt ashamed and incomplete at the same time, as if half of me were missing, and as if I'd been colluding with my enemies, those whites who wanted Indians to be like them. . . . So if I wanted the additional personality bonus of an Indian past, I would have to create it" (212–13).

However, instead of fetishizing Eastern authenticity, Karim's diasporic consciousness resignifies Englishness by projecting a political future of being an Indian English citizen. The novel reimagines England as a cosmopolitan multicultural nation open to the minority cultures engendered by immigration from its former colonies by overlaying two returns: Karim's return to his imagined India and his return to England after a sojourn in the United States. Kureishi's novel marks a new conjuncture where the United States has displaced Britain as the center of global capitalism. When Karim accompanies his play to its New York run, his feelings of provincialism suggest that America is now the metropolis of the world and England has become its province, just as colonial India was London's province. Karim completes his

Bildung by spurning the center. He rejects America as the land of the endless pursuit of self-interest, where ethnic and class authenticity are commodified fetishes. The novel's affirmative ending opens a future horizon by echoing William Shakespeare's image of England as a "scepter'd isle" (*Richard II*, II.i.40). Karim is spiritually recentered, at home in London as a black British diasporic subject: "And so I sat in the centre of the old city that I loved, which itself sat at the bottom of a tiny island. I was surrounded by people I loved, and I felt happy and miserable at the same time. I thought of what a mess everything had been, but that it wouldn't always be that way" (284). Earlier, he had described Jamila's path even more hopefully: "She went forward, an Indian woman, to live a useful life in white England" (216). Kureishi sees constitutional patriotism as a solution to Britain's racial problems. The plight of the South Asian diaspora will not be solved by an illusory fantasy of home but by "a fresh way of seeing Britain and the choices it faces: . . . a new way of being British" that involves "the continual struggle against racism; . . . the continual adjustment to life in Britain" (1992, 36, 35). The novel's telos of cosmopolitan multicultural citizenship achieved through a new public culture open to diasporic differences is the optimal outcome of diasporic temporality's problematization of British homogeneous empty time.

But this telos's fruition depends on the unequal generation of socioeconomic growth by global capitalism's temporal regime. It is unrealizable on the other side of the IDL. The sheer heterogeneity of migrations resulting from the British Indian colonial legacy makes any general theory of diasporic subjectivity implausible. Migration from South Asia to England in the 1940s was for educational reasons, with no initial intention of settlement. Kureishi's novel portrays this type of diaspora: the privileged upper-caste colonial who makes a pilgrimage to the metropolis "to be educated by the old colonial power" (Kureishi 1992, 3). This is Haroon's and Kureishi's fathers' itinerary: unlike the second wave of lower-caste economic migrants in the two decades after decolonization, "like Gandhi and Jinnah before him, Dad would return to India a qualified and polished English gentleman lawyer and an accomplished ballroom dancer" (Kureishi 1990, 24). Driven by economic distress and labor demand in other parts of the British Empire, the migration of Indian peasants and untouchables to Southeast Asia from the nineteenth century onward is a drastically different trajectory (Latham 1986). *The Return* portrays the despairing consciousness that arises from the vitiation of the *Bildung* of this type of Malaysian Indian diaspora by the IDL.

Maniam's novel is a semi-autobiographical bildungsroman set in British Malaya/Malaysia from 1940 to 1962, the last seventeen years of colonial rule and the first five years of postcoloniality. Ravi, its protagonist-narrator, is of Tamil descent. His grandmother, Periathai, migrated with her sons, and he grows up on a colonial rubber plantation, a geographical creation of the IDL. Because of his low caste status and rural background, Ravi has no childhood access to the culture of British imperialism. Hence, his imaginary India is shaped by transplanted religious traditions absent from the India of Kureishi's novel. The Indian community in rural Malaya maintained a strong connection to rural India. Its members imported an Indian carver to re-create "the typical rustic look of an Indian village" by building a communal cooking place resembling those in India (Maniam [1981] 1993, 4). For Periathai, the Indian past is embodied by objects of worship contained in two tin trunks—a deity statue, trays, bangles, and ceremonial brass lamps. "Perhaps Nataraja [the deity] spoke to her of the original spirit, and her personal articles of the home she had left behind. It was a re-immersion, a recreating of the thick spiritual and domestic air she must have breathed there, back in some remote district in India" (5–6). Her stories evoke an imaginary homeland that the glowing lamps illuminate: "Her voice transformed the kolams into contours of reality and fantasy, excitingly balanced. I felt I stood on the edge of a world I may have known" (6). The community's Hindu festivals confirm this homeland's reality, and supernatural forces suffuse Ravi's childhood. This enchanted world provides spiritual freedom from the humiliating drudgery of plantation life. "These festivals, together with Thaipusam and Ponggal, created a special country for us. We were inhabitants of an invisible landscape tenuously brought into prominence by the lights . . . and the many taboos that covered our daily lives" (13).

But Ravi's connection to the Hindu rituals from an Indian past is not analogous to the Black Atlantic diaspora's inventive appropriation of African rituals or the disjunctive temporality of diasporic hybridization. A diasporic subject from a working-class plantation family in the periphery cannot project a cosmopolitan multicultural future from his past. Ravi undergoes two journeys in his cultivation as a modern educated colonial subject and member of the comprador middle class: he renounces his childhood rituals as shameful irrational superstitions and travels to the metropolitan center. His education in a local English school is an internal journey through the cultural landscape of colonial textbooks, which destroys and supplants the invisible landscape of his childhood: "We were issued glossy books, each page containing a picture, a letter and a word. . . . They transported us into a pleasant, unreachable land. . . . We were already bewildered and fascinated. Dobbin and Ernie absorbed our tiny souls" (24). Ravi's internal journey leads to a two-year sojourn in London on a scholarship. He becomes an English teacher on his return to postcolonial Malaysia.

But Ravi's *Bildung* is a painful process of self-alienation, deculturation, and deformation (*Verbildung*).[8] Maniam presents two existential paths for the Malaysian Indian diaspora. The first path, taken by Periathai and by Ravi's father, Naina, the attempt to belong to Malaysia by investing the local soil with transplanted cultural traditions or invented hybrid ones, ends in dispossession and madness. In Ravi's words, "I began to understand the simple mechanism . . . of the Malaysian Indian. I recognised the spirit that had touched Periathai and now possessed Naina. He continued the battle Periathai had begun: *to drive some stake into the country*. The restlessness that had motivated Periathai into building her houses and keeping the kolam courtyard decorated, meaningful, and intact, took another form in my father" (140). But the colonial state and its postcolonial successor, with their racial and class hierarchies, do not recognize their claims of belonging. The town council evicts Periathai, and she dies of cancer, her spirit broken by her failure to root her dreams of India in Malaysian soil. Ravi's father undergoes a similar tragic fate. When the postcolonial government expropriates the land on which he has built his new house, he burns his house and immolates himself, leaving behind Periathai's charred lamps and statue of Nataraja.

The alternative path of becoming a modern bourgeois subject is equally bleak. Ravi's successful return from his English journey is a failed homecoming. He rejects his family because his education and social progress have made him ashamed of it. After Naina's death he undergoes a catharsis and seeks to spiritually "return" to his origins, expressing his desire in a poem dedicated to his father. But the poem does not open a future horizon and is instead a sobering recognition of the modern Malaysian Indian diaspora's irreparable cultural alienation:

> Have you been lost?
>
> Then words will not serve.
> They will be like the culture
> you refused at adolescence,
> drinking from the tap
> instead of the well.
>
> The dregs at the bottom
> of well water is the ash
> of family prayers you rejected.

> The clay taste
> the deep rootedness
> you turned aside from—
> for the cleanliness of chlorine.
>
> Words will not serve.
>
> You will be twisted by them
> into nameless impulses
> that roam dark city roads, raging.
> They will be vague knots
> of feelings, lusterless, cultureless,
>   buried in a heart that will not serve. (Maniam [1981] 1993, 173)

The poem draws on the poetic imagery of William Blake, William Wordsworth, and Samuel Taylor Coleridge to juxtapose a modern subject shorn of cultural attachments to the child organically rooted in a rural community. But instead of enabling Ravi to overcome his alienation and return to his roots, the poem performatively underscores his subject deformation. He is capable of expressing his alienation only in English blank verse using romantic imagery. The lyric objectifies him and separates him from himself by addressing him in the second person.

The romantic opposition between the alienated modern individual and his childhood self in harmony with his rural community is irrelevant in postcolonial Malaysia because no revitalizing return to the rural past is possible. Periathai's and Naina's fates indicate that hybridized Hindu traditions cannot flourish in Malaysian public culture. In his madness Naina envisioned an ideal postcolonial community by inventing a private ritual language composed of Malay, Indian, and Chinese, a synecdoche of the ideal public language of a multiracial nation where the Indian diaspora can belong. But the geographical hierarchy of the global capitalist temporal regime makes this polity unrealizable. Malaya's position as a supplier of raw materials (tin, rubber, etc.) led to the establishment of an export economy that required the importation of Chinese and Indian immigrant labor. The late nineteenth-century colonial state shaped social relations between indigenous Malays and other ethnic groups through racial ideology and policies of divide-and-rule that prevented social solidarity across ethnicities. Although Chinese and Indians could benefit economically from the colonial system, their political marginalization meant that entry into anglophone society was the best means for social mobility (Hirschman 1986, 355). This dictates Ravi's repudiation of his childhood Hindu traditions. The deep entrenchment of colonial racial ideologies of innate differences among the ethnic communities continues to shape postcolonial Malaysian ethnic relations, resulting in the racialization of political representation. From its inception the postcolonial state institutionalized a form of unequal multiculturalism that gives Malays more rights and privileges than other communities to compensate for their "economic backwardness" (B. Cheah 2005, 103). Because ethnic relations are a primary issue in Malaysian politics, the overwhelming concern with the minority status of Indians has hampered their effective democratic participation in political life (Ramasamy 2001). Malaysia's focus on economic development as it seeks to ascend the IDL has pushed the establishment of a multicultural democracy based on the equality of all groups further into the background.

Reading *The Return* alongside *The Buddha of Suburbia* illustrates the diverse range of diasporic subjects engendered by global capitalism's temporal regime: a colonial elite that fulfilled a bureaucratic function and migrated to the metropolitan center for education (Haroon), lower-class migrants to other peripheries who perform the menial labor of agriculture and resource extraction (Periathai and her sons), the new cosmopolitan diasporic Indian citizen of multicultural England (Karim, Jamila), and the alienated bourgeois Indian subject of postcolonial Malaysia (Ravi). Discussions about cosmopolitan multiculturalism in the North and multiracial national belonging in the South feel dated today because these migrations are driven by the old IDL of the colonial era and its neocolonial aftermath. The new IDL, established by the outsourcing of production to developing countries through foreign direct investment and international subcontracting (Fröbel, Heinrichs, and Kreye 1980) within the political framework of the American informal empire that emphasized the economic development of the peripheries through export-oriented industrialization (Maier 1978), marks a new conjuncture of global capitalism. Here an important development is the culturalization of global politics in a world after September 11 and the rise of Asian growth economies followed by postsocialist China. I call this conjuncture *postcolonial globalization* because the major players are no longer just North America or Europe but also formerly colonized or semicolonized places like China, Hong Kong, and Singapore.

This conjuncture produces a new type of diaspora: economic migrants seeking work in the finance, high-tech, and business-management industries in the global cities of North America and Europe and the rapidly industrializing and postindustrial East and Southeast Asia. Changez, the protagonist-narrator of Mohsin Hamid's *The Reluctant Fundamentalist*, is a South Asian diasporic subject who embarks on a *Bildung* to become a cosmopolitan citizen of the transnational corporate world. In his global path of upward mobility, he migrates to the United States for higher education at Princeton and professional success on Wall Street. The novel portrays the new subjectifying processes of the capitalist temporal regime: the internalization of temporal calculations for the maximization of accumulation. Unlike Karim and Ravi, Changez's *Bildung* is not about reevaluating the ethical values of the diasporic subject's host nation but about becoming a member of a cosmopolitan professional class. Cosmopolitan consciousness is no longer linked to Western nations but to the spirit of global capitalism. Changez notes the American empire's cosmopolitan openness: its prodigious capacity to integrate the best global talent to augment its human capital. "We international students were sourced from around the globe, sifted not only by well-honed standardized tests but by painstakingly customized evaluations . . . until the best and the brightest of us had been identified. . . . Students like me were given visas and scholarships, complete financial aid, mind you, and invited into the ranks of the meritocracy. In return, we were expected to contribute our talents to your society, the society we were joining. And for the most part, we were happy to do so. I certainly was, at least at first" (Hamid 2007, 4). He resolves his ambivalence toward the United States by identifying with cosmopolitan New York, which he regards as having transcended its American borders: "I was, in four and a half years, never an American; I was *immediately* a New Yorker" (33). As "a testament to the open-mindedness and—that overused word—*cosmopolitan* nature of New York in those days," Changez feels "completely comfortable" riding the subway in a starched white kurta (48). He disidentifies with his country and becomes interpellated as a homogeneous citizen of the global corporate world: "On that day, I did not think of myself as a Pakistani, but as an Underwood Samson trainee, and my firm's impressive offices made me proud" (14). The values he internalizes are not the ethical norms of a society but the values of the corporate world, such as "systematic pragmatism." He is trained to make temporal calculations about competitive advantage such as valuations of corporate assets and future profitability aimed at maximizing accumulation and repeatedly undergoes ranking exercises that compare him to his peers.

But despite his enthusiastic embrace of this temporal regime, the caesura of his qualification—"at least, at first"—suggests that cosmopolitan diasporic subjectification has become problematic. The confluence of several events obstructs his *Bildung*: public racism in the wake of the September 11 attacks, his growing disaffection with his work, and his failed romance with an American woman. Changez links these frustrations to alterations in the temporal order. America is no longer the site of universal progress. The appearance of American flags all over New York City is the recidivist nationalization of global space: "America, too, was increasingly giving itself over to a dangerous nostalgia at that time. There was something undeniably retro about the flags and uniforms, about generals addressing cameras in war rooms and newspaper headlines featuring such words as duty and honor. I had always thought of America as a nation that looked forward; for the first time I was struck by its determination to look back" (115). Gradually, Underwood Samson no longer functions as a cosmopolitan space of refuge from American tribalism, and he finds his work meaningless. Changez becomes aware of his ideological victimage. Likening himself to a janissary, an abducted Christian boy deprived of memories of the past in order to be trained as a dedicated soldier for his adopted Muslim empire, he recognizes that his cosmopolitan *Bildung*, which decultures him of his homeland traditions, is a function of American empire.

Changez's reevaluation of the openness of global mobility celebrated by theories of diasporic temporality is especially striking. The loss of regulative boundaries leads to aimless flux instead of the liberating destabilization of national identity and cosmopolitan progress: "Such journeys have convinced me that it is not always possible to restore one's boundaries after they have been blurred and made permeable by a relationship: try as we might, we cannot reconstitute ourselves as the autonomous beings we previously imagined ourselves to be. Something of us is now outside, and something of the outside is now within us" (173–74). His *Bildung* ends with his return to Lahore and his assumption of a bordered identity. He becomes a university lecturer and participates in demonstrations for Pakistani independence from the United States in its foreign affairs. After one of his students is arrested for planning to assassinate a US development aid officer, the global media brand him a fundamentalist.

Despite its cognitive mapping of the limits of cosmopolitan *Bildung*, the novel does not offer a feasible alternative to global capitalism's temporal order. There is nothing affirmative about Changez's *Bildung*. His transformation into a religious nationalist is the unwitting result of contingent circumstances beyond his rational control. Indeed, we are unsure of the sincerity or rationality of his justifications. Because the narrative is a conversation with an American visitor whose response is not portrayed, it is suffused with the irony of an extended dramatic monologue whose speaker contradicts what he professes, not least because Changez repeatedly reassures his addressee that he is not insane.

The difficulty of portraying a plausible alternative to the global capitalist temporal order may be germane to the bildungsroman because of the centrality of the idea of progress. Hence, the novels I have discussed portray the impossibility of developing a cosmopolitan consciousness, its frustration as the return to a premodern ancestral tradition outside public life (*The Return*), or the espousal of a fundamentalist national future (*The Reluctant Fundamentalist*). Indeed, theories of diasporic temporality leave this pervasive temporal regime intact. They presuppose the same understanding of time as an independent framework for all events and actions. A modern time-consciousness gives value to time's passage. We measure it by clock and calendar, appropriate it, and make good use of it. The normative standard for measuring our use of time in global capitalism is the economic value accumulated over quantified units of time. Theories of diasporic temporality challenge this standard by suggesting other ways of giving meaning to human existence. But diasporic temporality and the broader idea of alternative temporalities are also human appropriations of time. Instead of questioning modernity's ontological basis, these theories merely contest the Eurocentric, secularizing, and progressivist tendencies of homogeneous empty time by invoking other "temporalities." They ironically subscribe to a form of teleological time because they envision a sociopolitical order that is open to the disruptiveness of difference as the telos of universal human progress. They are thus easily integrated into global capitalist modernity as a multicultural or postcolonial supplement that remedies a deficit in North Atlantic nation-states by creating more value through the injection of cultural difference.

Moreover, the onset of postcolonial globalization has cast doubt on the feasibility of an alternative world-system based on the spirit of Bandung. The People's Republic of China (PRC), once a key champion of solidarity among Asian and African nations in the struggle against colonialism, is now the emergent global economic hegemon with its own African and Latin American peripheries for resource extraction. In the globalization of the Beijing Consensus through the adoption of the Sanya Declaration by the five major emerging economies of Brazil, Russia, India, China, and South Africa (BRICS), the ideology of intra-South cooperation is used to hide China's asymmetrical relations with these peripheries. The PRC's Belt and Road Initiative is a modulation in global capitalism's temporal order that aims to recenter the world-system in hyperdeveloping China (Ziegler 2020; Bradsher 2020).

Tash Aw's *Five Star Billionaire* is instructive for two reasons. First, it situates the new Chinese diaspora within the capitalist temporal regime by focusing on their *Bildung* as entrepreneurial subjects of human capital. Second, it suggests that when these subjects fail to achieve belonging in the postsocialist ancestral homeland, they find respite by embracing an uncanny localism. Instead of invoking an alternative temporality, they "return" to the world in the original sense: the "site" that precedes any temporal order because it is where we first come into the world with the gift of time.

Aw's novel is set in contemporary Shanghai, the cosmopolitan financial center of postsocialist China, to which four Malaysian Chinese diasporic subjects of different social backgrounds, Yinghui, Justin, Phoebe, and Gary, have journeyed as economic migrants to pursue the Chinese dream of economic success and self-betterment. Their Malaysian pasts link them although they are largely unaware of these connections. They are Chinese diaspora to a second degree: their ancestors migrated to Southeast Asia to escape economic hardship, and they have lost all ties with the communist mainland. Their cultural relation to their ancestral homeland is limited to the traditions they brought to Southeast Asia and flows of global Chinese popular culture. Malaysia is their homeland and the destination of return from their return to the ancestral homeland. Their relation to Chinese culture is not postcolonial: they do not invoke it via recuperative memory as a source of resistance to or amelioration of British colonial or postcolonial Malaysian culture, and they do not have the sense of deferential inferiority that Creoles feel toward an ancestral culture. More precisely, these English- and Chinese-educated characters are not the postloyalist subjectivities portrayed by Sinophone writers such as Li Yung-ping or Ng Kim Chew (Wang, this volume) or the older Chinese diaspora with militant loyalties to the Chinese communist cause (Hau 2014). They do not harbor cultural nostalgia for their ancestral homeland or revolutionary nostalgia for the PRC. They are contemporary Anglo-Chinese (Hau 2013) who have a purely instrumentalist attachment to mainland China as an emerging economic center. Aw's novel is written for an anglophone reader, but the chapters about the primary characters mark the center's linguistic milieu with titles in simplified Chinese followed by their English translation.

Unlike the bildungsromans discussed earlier, which have first-person protagonist-narrators, Aw uses an omniscient narrator in the main chapters to foreground the pervasiveness of Chinese globalization's temporal regime. These chapters recount how the main characters' paths become entwined because of the machinations of Walter Chao, the titular five star billionaire.

Walter, a Malaysian-Chinese billionaire who writes self-help books under a pseudonym, narrates the story of his own success in short interludes presented as how-to lessons. An interlude called "How to Manage Time" thematizes the affinity between the temporal order of global capitalism and the new Chinese diasporic temporality. Walter recounts how he learned to appropriate time when he was sent to live with his great-aunt. "Like all children, I had never before appreciated what *time* meant—the years stretched infinitely beyond me, waiting impossibly to be filled. But all of a sudden I began to feel the urgency of each day. I counted down, saddened by how much I could have been doing with every sunrise and sunset, if only I had been at home" (70). "You must appreciate that time is always against you. It is never kind or encouraging. It gnaws invisibly at all good things. Therefore, if you have any desire to accomplish anything, even the simplest task, do it swiftly and with great purpose, or time will drag it away from you" (70). This calculative management of time is the spirit of postsocialist accumulation. The book's first chapter, "Foreword: How to Be a Billionaire," portrays the new Chinese diaspora's time-consciousness. Walter recalls being impressed as a child by the vision of American capitalism in the opening sequence of a US television legal drama. It opened a prospect of *Bildung*: "One day, I will own a building like that, a whole tower block filled with industrious, clever people working to make their fantasies come true" (Aw 2013, 2). But he notes that he has outstripped these inadequate ambitions.

This time-consciousness drives the main characters' *Bildung*. It provides the quantitative standard for their progress and for positioning their home country vis-à-vis the emerging center. Phoebe, an unscrupulous girl from a small Malaysian town who has assumed a stolen identity and progressed from being a karaoke hostess, to a garment-factory clerk in Shenzhen, to a spa receptionist in Shanghai, views her hometown as a place of stagnation: "She thought of her mother, living alone in that small town in the north of Malaysia, a town that was shrinking, becoming less and less alive as each year passed. It was the opposite of the Chinese villages that these girls spoke of, that grew and grew with the money they earned in the big cities on the coast, the fields of rice and wheat shrinking and eventually turning into industrial parks and high-tech factories, the villages becoming towns, the towns cities.... Phoebe had left, but she could not go back" (205).

Walter is not merely a frame narrator but is arguably also the omniscient narrator. The maxims driving the characters' desires and actions are similar to those of his books. Such temporal calculations are ingrained in their subjectification. Consequently, Walter attains omniscience over them. He knows their

Malaysian pasts, and his complete understanding of their motivations allows him to anticipate and manipulate their desires and actions in his pursuit of vengeance. His uncanny ability to observe events from above also applies to himself. In a striking passage, he regards himself as another person and judges himself as an omniscient narrator judges a character: "Sometimes when I read an article about myself even I recoil at the seeming callousness of my financial manouvering. . . . What a dreadful life this Walter Chao must have, I think. Imagine being *him*. Often I forget that *he* is in fact *me*" (98). This totalizing view makes him a personification of the global capitalist temporal regime. His narrative envelops himself and other characters, and we encounter them as though they were cases in his self-help book. The Chinese titles of the main chapters are four-character idioms (*chengyu* 成语), but their English renditions are pseudostrategies that mimic Sun Tzu's *The Art of War* adapted for anglophone business types. This is the extent of the new diaspora's Chineseness.

The novel, however, points to something that exceeds the teleological time of Chinese diasporic circulation. The main characters' Chinese dreams fail, and their *Bildung* eludes Walter's totalizing calculations. The ethical awakenings of Phoebe and Gary, characters from a poor social background, are of particular significance. Phoebe has fallen in love with Walter and cannot continue her charade as an entrepreneur from Guangzhou. She realizes that belonging to the global city of Shanghai is impossible. Its inhabitants are migrants in the service of accumulation and are replaceable by newer migrants. The Chinese empire's metropolis cannot be the location of meaningful memories because it is not a place where one can leave traces. "People say [Shanghai] is the size of a small country, but it is not, it is bigger, like a whole continent, with a heart as deep and unknown as the forests of the Amazon and as vast and wild as the deserts of Africa. People come here like explorers, but soon they disappear; no one even hears them as they fade away, and no one remembers them" (381).

Aw transposes the moral hell of the European colonial adventure portrayed by Joseph Conrad's *Heart of Darkness* ([1902] 2007) as the glittering misery of postsocialist Shanghai. Phoebe renounces the new diaspora's axiom of forsaking the past in the relentless march toward a global future. She rejects her earlier identification with Guangzhou and decides to return to the place of her childhood. "I didn't grow up in that huge ugly polluted city. I grew up in a place surrounded by forests and lakes and warm winds, not far from the sea, where you could walk in the heavy rain and not fall sick with cold, where the tallest building was four storeys high—a place many thousands of miles from here" (387). But what appears like a commonplace return to restorative rural origins is more complicated. Phoebe does not invoke the cultural traditions of her ancestral land to alleviate the alienating deculturation of the postsocialist Chinese temporal regime. Just as her journey to Shanghai was not a quest for ancestral culture, her return is not an embrace of Chinese traditions eradicated by communist and postsocialist temporal orders. Nor is it an identification with her birth nation's culture. Instead, she affirms local elemental forces.

Gary experiences a similar return. A singer from a provincial town who became a teen idol pop star in Taipei after winning a talent contest, Gary attempted to penetrate the mainland market. But he descends into alcoholism and internet porn addiction when his dreams of superstardom fail. He finds redemption by reinventing himself as a grassroots singer who performs in Hokkien, a language spoken by the diaspora from southern Fujian that is incomprehensible to a putonghua- or Mandarin-speaking mainland public. When he sings a Hokkien song at a charity concert in aid of Sichuan earthquake victims, he is transported to the peaceful solitude of his childhood. "He sings in *Minnan hua*, the dialect of his mother, of his youth—an earthy rustic language that some would call coarse. Maybe that is why it suits the song so well; maybe that is why it suits him so well. . . . Singing in his mother tongue reminds him of the quiet loneliness of his childhood—of the long hours sitting on the porch of his village house watching the rain falling, hoping it would end" (435).

How are we to understand these returns? Reappropriative place making is central to postcoloniality, which is primarily concerned with the self-determination of national, regional, or continental territorial sites against colonizing forces. The identification with homeland is generally represented by an equation of the nation with nature, exemplified by the etymological link between the words for nation (*naissance*, *natio*) and natural origin/birthplace in European languages and the widespread figure of the nation as mother. Hence, postcolonial writers often contrast the denaturing character of colonial cultivation with the attunement to nature in precolonial traditions and their alternative temporalities. In particular, anglophone writers represent the nation in high-romantic fashion as the place of the subject's original harmony with nature. Theorists of diasporic temporality sought to denaturalize the Western nation by arguing that the complex diasporic identifications resulting from slavery and colonialism are forms of cosmopolitanism from below. But global capitalism makes cosmopolitan *Bildung* unrealizable in the postcolonial South.

Aw's novel suggests that the Chinese diaspora in postcolonial globalization cannot achieve reappropriative place making by returning either to their ancestral homeland or to their birth nation. The former is not the source of an alternative temporality because the new diaspora's relation to postsocialist

China is purely instrumental and marked by cultural and emotional alienation. Although they physically or imaginatively return to their birthplaces, the novel is silent on reclaiming political membership in their birth nation qua semiperiphery of the PRC. Postcolonial national belonging is problematic because of political discrimination against non-Malay ethnic groups. They cannot be in harmony with the nation qua nature (*tanah air*) because they are not *bumiputera*, sons of the soil. Hence, Phoebe and Gary do not return to a geographically bounded territory but simply to lakes, forests, winds, the sea, and the sound of rain. The final chapter is entitled "跋山涉水 The Journey Is Long" (*bashansheshui*). "Traversing mountains, crossing waters," a more literal translation, would be an apt description of the worldly trials of a bildungsroman's protagonist. But Gary's most difficult journey is not his cosmopolitan circulation but his cathartic inner return home. This is figured as a rebirth, the coming-again into worldly phenomenality, just as an infant's cry expresses its original coming into the world: "He feels . . . that he is completely alone, but it is a solitude that feels calm, as it did many years before, when he was small. Only he can appreciate the quality of the voice filling his lungs, filling the vast space above him" (Aw 2013, 435).

The conventional theme of homecoming and its ordinary prose become uncanny. We see a stripping of the external accoutrements of cosmopolitan cultivation and an affirmation of a place that is prior to the nation as natural origin. The elemental imagery suggests an original worldliness that precedes the appearance of nature in the conventional sense of our biological origin and the milieu of our growth, progressively metaphorized as family, community, nation, and, finally, humanity. This worldliness is not the place of biological birth but its ontological ground. We obscure birth's ontological significance when we understand it in biological terms, just as we obscure original worldliness when we view it as a state of unity with nature. Heidegger elucidates worldliness by recalling the Greek φύσις: "In early [Greek] thought, the essence of life is not represented biologically [*biologisch vorgestellt*] but rather as φύσις, the emergent, that which arises [*das Aufgehende*]" (2002, 208; 1977, 279). Beginning with its Roman translation as *natura*, Western thought has obscured the meaning of φύσις by likening it to the generation and course of natural phenomena such as the genesis and growth of plants or the rising of the sun, when coming-into-presence, such that there is something instead of nothing, is the condition of anything like nature (Heidegger 1979, 90; 2018, 68).

The Roman translation of φύσις as *natura* and, moreover, the ensuing domination of the notion of nature [*Natur*] in Occidental-European thought, completely cover over the original meaning of φύσις: that is to say, that which arises from out of itself into its respective limit and here comes to dwell.

Even today, we can experience the mystery of φύσις in Greece—and only here, where in an equally astounding and restrained manner there appear to us a mountain, an island, a coast, an olive tree. (Heidegger 2013, 121)

If we set aside Heidegger's Greco-centrism, we can say that the rain, forests, lake, and winds that Phoebe and Gary find comforting are simply what is there. Their import lies in their thereness. Being there affords repose not because it is an objective natural home in which we recognize our unity with nature but because it is our propulsion into existence. Aw's portrayal of the returns of the Chinese diaspora in postcolonial globalization thus addresses the temporal order of global capitalism by broaching the question of time in a fundamental manner. Global capitalism is a limitless field of instrumentality that can integrate all nonhegemonic interpretations of time such as diasporic temporality. Returning to an original worldliness is a tacit acknowledgment of the coming of time. We cannot take this coming for granted. Nor can we reckon with time and humanize it by appropriating it and making it harmonize with our ends because it is the inhuman ontological condition for our rational processes. Hence, time is the limit to human appropriation. There cannot be any experience of time—linear, cyclical, disjunctive, or iterative—if it does not continue to come. As the limit to the global capitalist temporal order, its coming gives respite from the vicissitudes of diasporic circulation.

Returning to world means going back to the first giving of place before the world becomes geometrically and quantitatively reduced to a spatio-geographical object to be divided into regions and countries. This original placing gives us a stake in the world and, hence, is the ground of any political claim to self-determination and sovereign place making. But contrary to Heidegger's equation of authentic temporality with an elect people's authenticity, the Chinese diaspora of Aw's novel are thrown back to the giving of time and place by the historical contingency of their scattering in postcolonial globalization. They are ethnoculturally impure because they cannot identify with their ancestral homeland or the public culture of their birth nation. The solitude of original worldliness is not a solipsistic withdrawal. As Gary's singing in Hokkien in a putonghua public world illustrates, this is where we are *in statu nascendi* and always already with others before we are for or against them. This is the basis for envisioning new alignments and establishing new solidarities for acting in concert.

We hear an echo of this placing in an Occupy Hong Kong slogan appropriated from Lu Xun's story "Hometown" ("Guxiang" 故鄉, 1981a, 485): "Originally, there is no path on the ground, but when many walk on it, a path comes into being" (*dishang ben meiyou lu, zou de ren duole, ye bian chengle lu* 地上本沒有路，走的人多了，也便成了路). The narrator of this homecoming story is depressed when his cherished memories of childhood freedom are crushed by traditional social barriers that separate him as an adult from his former playmate. When he despondently reflects on hope's illusoriness, a vision of a moonlit seascape suddenly comes upon him. This leads him to formulate the story's humanist lesson: hope is like a path created on the ground by repeated steps. But pathmarks can only be formed if there is already a ground to tread. The seascape's unexpected propulsion into phenomenality intimates the emergence of the ground for hope.

Notes

1 This turn extends the meaning of *diaspora* beyond the classical Jewish, Greek, and Armenian examples in an inflationary and sometimes purely metaphorical manner (Tölölyan 1991, 1996; Safran 1991).
2 For an overview of the role of time in theories of diasporic consciousness, see Clifford (1994, 317–18).
3 Gilroy's and Bhabha's reflections on diasporic and migrant time are consonant. Gilroy acknowledges his indebtedness to Julia Kristeva's essay "Women's Time" and cites Bhabha's adaptation of her work "to the post-colonial predicament" (1993, 247n8).
4 Baldwin places "beat" in quote marks.
5 The computation of value in terms of quantified labor time reflects "a social formation in which the process of production has mastery over man." Bourgeois political economists fail to question this because it appears as a natural necessity to their "bourgeois consciousness" (Marx 1990, 174–75).
6 Moishe Postone notes that socially necessary labor time is "a general temporal norm resulting from the action of the producers, to which they must conform" such that their labor time must be the same as that of the norm. The domination of abstract time over human life as a normative measure of human activity is fundamental to alienated social relations in capitalism (1993, 191). Historical time is a form of concrete time that expresses abstract time (291–98). See also Thompson 1967.
7 For a study of the technologies and politics of the transnational unification of time, see Galison 2003.
8 For a similar diagnosis of alienation in Africa, see Ngũgĩ wa Thiong'o 1986.

References

Abbas, Ackbar. 1997. *Hong Kong: Culture and the Politics of Disappearance.* Minneapolis: University of Minnesota Press.

Agnew, Junko. 2013. "Constructing Cultural Difference in Manchukuo: Stories of Gu Ding and Ushijima Haruko." *International Journal of Asian Studies* 10 (2): 171–88.

A. Grico La. 1931. "Farmerism." *Hong Kong University Union Magazine*, November 1931, 94–96.

Aguilar, Filomeno V. 2005. "Tracing Origins: *Ilustrado* Nationalism and the Racial Science of Migration Waves." *Journal of Asian Studies* 64 (3): 605–37.

Aguilar, Filomeno V. 2014. "Manilamen and Seafaring: Engaging the Maritime World beyond the Spanish Realm." In *Migration Revolution: Philippine Nationhood and Class Relations in a Globalized Age*, 24–52. Kyoto: Kyoto University Press.

Ahmad, Aijaz. (1992) 2008. *In Theory: Nations, Classes, Literatures.* London: Verso.

Albert, Jose Ramon, Raymond Gaspar, and M. J. Raymundo. 2015. "Who Are the Middle Class?" *Rappler*, July 8, 2015. http://www.rappler.com/thought-leaders/98624-who-are-middle-class?cp_rap_source=yml#cxrecs_s.

Amin, Samir. 1974. *Accumulation on a World Scale: A Critique of the Theory of Underdevelopment.* Translated by Brian Pearce. New York: Monthly Review Press.

Amin, Samir. 2014. *Capitalism in the Age of Globalization: The Management of Contemporary Society.* London: Zed Books.

Amin, Samir. 2019. *The Long Revolution of the Global South: Toward a New Anti-Imperialist International.* New York: Monthly Review Press.

Anderson, Benedict R. 1991. *Imagined Communities: Reflections on the Origins and Spread of Nationalism.* Rev. ed. London: Verso.

Anderson, Benedict R. 1998. *The Spectre of Comparisons: Nationalism, Southeast Asia, and the World.* London: Verso.

Anghie, Anthony. 2005. *Imperialism, Sovereignty, and the Making of International Law.* Cambridge: Cambridge University Press.

Aravamudan, Srinivas. 2005. "Carl Schmitt's *The Nomos of the Earth*: Four Corollaries." *South Atlantic Quarterly* 104 (2): 227–36.

Arendt, Hannah. 1951. *The Origins of Totalitarianism.* New York: Harcourt Brace.

Arrighi, Giovanni. 2009. *Adam Smith in Beijing: Lineages of the Twenty-First Century*. London: Verso.

Ashcroft, Bill, Gareth Griffiths, and Helen Tiffin. 2002. *The Empire Writes Back: Theory and Practice in Post-colonial Literatures*. London: Routledge.

Auerbach, Erich. 1946. *Mimesis: Dargestellte Wirklichkeit in der abendländischen Literatur*. Bern: Francke.

Auerbach, Erich. 1957. *Mimesis: The Representation of Reality in Western Literature*. Translated by Willard R. Trask. New York: Doubleday Anchor.

Auden, W. H. 1939. *Journey to a War*. New York: Random House.

Aw, Tash. 2013. *Five Star Billionaire*. London: Fourth Estate.

Bacevich, Andrew J. 2002. *American Empire: The Realities and Consequences of U.S. Diplomacy*. Cambridge, MA: Harvard University Press.

Bachner, Andrea. 2013. *Beyond Sinology: Chinese Writing and the Scripts of Cultures*. New York: Columbia University Press.

Baker, Hugh D. R. 1983. "Life in the Cities: The Emergence of Hong Kong Man." *China Quarterly* 95:469–79.

Baldwin, James. 1984–85. "Of the Sorrow Songs: The Cross of Redemption." *Views on Black American Music*, no. 2: 7–12.

Banner, Stuart. 2005. *How the Indians Lost Their Land: Law and Power on the Frontier*. Cambridge, MA: Harvard University Press.

Barlow, Tani. 1993. "Colonialism's Career in Postwar China Studies." *Positions: East Asia Cultures Critique* 1 (1): 224–67.

Barmé, Geremie. 2005. "Towards a New Sinology." *Chinese Studies Association of Australia Newsletter*, no. 31 (May 2005): 4–9.

Barnes, Trevor J., and Claudio Minca. 2013. "Nazi Spatial Theory: The Dark Geographies of Carl Schmitt and Walter Christaller." *Annals of the Association of American Geographers* 103 (3): 669–87.

Bary, William Theodore de. 1988. *East Asian Civilizations: A Dialogue in Five Stages*. Cambridge, MA: Harvard University Press.

Baudelaire, Charles. 1964. *The Painter of Modern Life and Other Essays*. Translated by Jonathan Mayne. London: Phaidon.

Baudrillard, Jean. 1975. *The Mirror of Production*. Translated by Mark Poster. Saint Louis: Telos.

Bauman, Zygmunt. 1976. *Socialism: The Active Utopia*. New York: Holmes and Meier.

Bello, Walden. 2004. "The Political Economy of Permanent Crisis." In *The Anti-developmental State: The Political Economy of Permanent Crisis in the Philippines*, by Walden Bello, Herbert Docena, Marissa de Guzman, and Marylou Malig, 9–31. Quezon City: Department of Sociology, University of the Philippines, and Focus on the Global South.

Bendersky, Joseph W. 1983. *Carl Schmitt: Theorist for the Reich*. Princeton, NJ: Princeton University Press.

Benedict, Ruth. 1946. *The Chrysanthemum and the Sword: Patterns of Japanese Culture*. Boston: Houghton Mifflin.

Bennhold, Katrin, and Michael Schwirtz. 2021. "Capitol Riot Puts Spotlight on 'Apocalyptically Minded' Global Far Right." *New York Times*, January 24,

2021. https://www.nytimes.com/2021/01/24/world/europe/capitol-far-right-global.html.

Benton, Gregor. 2007. *Chinese Migrants and Internationalism: Forgotten Histories, 1917–1945*. London: Routledge.

Berlin, Isaiah. 2002. *Liberty*. Edited by Henry Hardy. Oxford: Oxford University Press.

Bernards, Brian. 2015. *Writing the South Seas: Imagining the Nanyang in Chinese and Southeast Asian Postcolonial Literature*. Seattle: University of Washington Press.

Bernstein, Thomas P., and Hua-yu Li, eds. 2010. *China Learns from the Soviet Union, 1949–Present*. Lanham, MD: Lexington.

Bhabha, Homi K. 1990. "DissemiNation: Time, Narrative, and the Margins of the Modern Nation." In *Nation and Narration*, 291–322. London: Routledge.

Bhabha, Homi K. 1994. *The Location of Culture*. New York: Routledge.

Blanco, John D., and Ivonne del Valle. 2014. "Reorienting Schmitt's *Nomos*: Political Theology, and Colonial (and Other) Exceptions in the Creation of Modern and Global Worlds." *Política común* 5:1–20.

Blunden, Edmund. (1961) 2001. *A Hong Kong House: Poems, 1951–1961*. Hong Kong: Hong Kong University Press.

Boehmer, Elleke, and Alex Tickell. 2015. "The 1990s: An Increasingly Postcolonial Decade." *Journal of Commonwealth Literature* 50 (3): 315–52.

Booth, Martin. 2004. *Gweilo: Memories of a Hong Kong Childhood*. London: Doubleday.

Borras, F. M. 1967. *Maxim Gorky the Writer: An Interpretation*. Oxford: Clarendon.

Bosteels, Bruno. 2005. "The Obscure Subject: Sovereignty and Geopolitics in Carl Schmitt's *The Nomos of the Earth*." *South Atlantic Quarterly* 104 (2): 295–305.

Bowring, Philip. 2014. "How Hong Kong's Business Elite Have Thwarted Democracy for 150 Years." *South China Morning Post*, October 19, 2014.

Bradsher, Keith. 2020. "China Renews Its 'Belt and Road' Push for Global Sway." *New York Times*, January 16, 2020.

Branigan, Tania, and Lily Kuo. 2020. "How Hong Kong Caught Fire: The Story of a Radical Uprising." *Guardian*, June 9, 2020.

Bray, Mark. 2013. *Translating Anarchy: The Anarchism of Occupy Wall Street*. Winchester, UK: Zero Books.

Brooke-Holland, Louisa. 2019. *Hong Kong: The Joint Declaration*. Briefing Paper no. 08616, July 5. London: House of Commons Library.

Brown, Chris. 2007. "From Humanized War to Humanitarian Intervention: Carl Schmitt's Critique of the Just War Tradition." In *The International Political Thought of Carl Schmitt: Terror, Liberal War and the Crisis of Global Order*, edited by Louiza Odysseos and Fabio Petito, 56–69. Abingdon, UK: Taylor and Francis.

Brown, Wendy. 2019. *In the Ruins of Neoliberalism: The Rise of Antidemocratic Politics in the West*. New York: Columbia University Press.

Button, Peter. 2009. *Configurations of the Real in Chinese Literary and Aesthetic Modernity*. Leiden: Brill.

Cai Peihuo 蔡培火. 1920. "Wuren zhi tonghuaguan" 吾人之同化觀 [My view on assimilation]. *Taiwan seinen* 臺灣青年 [Taiwan youth] 1 (3): 16–28.

Cai Peihuo 蔡培火. 1928. *Nihon honkokumin ni atafu* 日本々国民に与ふ [For the Japanese population in Japan]. Tokyo: Taiwan mondai kenkyūkai.

Cai Yi 蔡仪, ed. (1963) 1979. *Wenxue gailun* 文学概论 [Introduction to literature]. Beijing: Beijing renmin chubanshe.

Cams, Mario. 2016. "Recent Additions to the New Qing History Debate." *Contemporary Chinese Thought* 47 (1): 1–4.

Cervinkova, Hana. 2012. "Postcolonialism, Postsocialism and the Anthropology of East-Central Europe." *Journal of Postcolonial Writing* 48 (2): 155–63.

Césaire, Aimé. 1939. "Cahier d'un retour au pays natal" [Notebook of a return to my native land]. *Volontés* 20:23–51.

Césaire, Aimé. 1942. "En guise de manifeste littéraire" [By way of a literary manifesto]. *Tropiques* 5: 7–12.

Césaire, Aimé. 1947. *Cahier d'un retour au pays natal/ Memorandum on My Martinique* [Notebook of a return to my native land]. With translation by Lionel Abel and Yvan Goll. New York: Brentano's.

Césaire, Aimé 1948. "L'impossible contact." *Chemins du monde*, nos. 5–6:105–11.

Césaire, Aimé. 1950. *Discours sur le colonialism* [Discourse on colonialism]. Paris: Réclame.

Césaire, Aimé. 1955. *Discours sur le colonialisme* [Discourse on colonialism]. Paris: Éditions Présence Africaine.

Césaire, Aimé. 1990. *Lyrical and Dramatic Poetry, 1946–82*. Translated by Clayton Eshleman and Annette Smith. Introduction by A. James Arnold. Charlottesville: University Press of Virginia.

Césaire, Aimé. 1995. *Notebook of a Return to My Native Land/Cahier d'un retour au pays natal*. Translated by Mireille Rosello with Annie Pritchard. Tarset, UK: Bloodaxe Books.

Césaire, Aimé. 2000. *Discourse on Colonialism*. Translated by Joan Pinkham. New York: Monthly Review Press.

Césaire, Aimé. 2013a. *Aimé Césaire: Poèsie, théâtre, essais et discours*. Edited by Albert James Arnold. Paris: CNRS Éditions.

Césaire, Aimé. 2013b. *The Original 1939 Notebook of a Return to the Native Land*. Translated by A. James Arnold and Clayton Eshleman. Middletown, CT: Wesleyan University Press.

Chadwick, Justin, dir. 2013. *Mandela: Long Walk to Freedom*. Paris: Pathé, Videovision Entertainment, Distant Horizon, Origin Pictures.

Chaikin, David, and J. C. Sharman. 2009. *Corruption and Money Laundering: A Symbiotic Relationship*. New York: Palgrave Macmillan.

Chakrabarty, Dipesh. 1989. *Rethinking Working-Class History: Bengal, 1890–1940*. Princeton, NJ: Princeton University Press.

Chakrabarty, Dipesh. 2000. *Provincializing Europe: Postcolonial Thought and Historical Difference*. Princeton, NJ: Princeton University Press.

Chakrabarty, Dipesh. 2005. "Legacies of Bandung: Decolonisation and the Politics of Culture." *Economic and Political Weekly* 40 (46): 4812–18.

Chan, Koonchung. 2007. "Hong Kong Viscera." *Postcolonial Studies* 10 (4): 379–89.

Chan, Ming K. 1994. "Introduction: Hong Kong's Precarious Balance." In *Precarious Balance: Hong Kong between China and Britain, 1842–1992*, edited by Ming K. Chan, 3–8. Hong Kong: Hong Kong University Press.

Chang, Chi-Hsien. 1936. "Japan Stops Chinese Migration to Manchuria." *Information Bulletin* 1 (4): 1–23.

Chari, Sharad, and Katherine Verdery. 2009. "Thinking between the Posts: Postcolonialism, Postsocialism, and Ethnography after the Cold War." *Comparative Studies in Society and History* 51 (1): 6–34.

Chatterjee, Partha. 1984. *Bengal, 1920–1947: The Land Question*. Calcutta: K. P. Bagchi.

Cheah, Boon Kheng. 2005. "Ethnicity in the Making of Malaysia." In *Nation Building: Five Southeast Asian Histories*, edited by Wang Gungwu, 91–115. Singapore: Institute of Southeast Asian Studies.

Cheah, Pheng, and Jonathan Culler, eds. 2003. *Grounds of Comparison: Around the Work of Benedict Anderson*. New York: Routledge.

Chen Cuilian 陳翠蓮. 2008. *Taiwanren de dikang yu rentong 1920–1950* 台灣人的抵抗與認同 [The resistance and identity of Taiwanese people, 1920–1950]. Taipei: Yuanliu.

Chen, Fangming 陳芳明. 1999. "Taiwan xin wenxueshi de jiangou yu fenqi" 台灣新文學史的建構與分期 [The construction and periodization of modern Taiwanese literary history]. *Unitas* 178 (August): 162–73.

Chen, Kuan-hsing. 1996a. "Decolonization and Cultural Studies." *Taiwan: A Radical Quarterly in Social Sciences* 21:73–139.

Chen, Kuan-hsing. 1996b. "Not Yet the Post-colonial Era: The (Super) Nation-State and Transnationalism of Cultural Studies: Response to Ang and Stratton." *Cultural Studies* 10 (1): 37–70.

Chen, Shu-ching. 2020. "The Secret Beauty of History." In *Locating Taiwan Cinema in the Twenty-First Century*, edited by Paul G. Pickowicz and Yingjin Zhang, 245–63. Amherst, NY: Cambria.

Chen, Tina Mai. 2009. "Socialist Geographies, Internationalist Temporalities, and Traveling Film Technologies: Sino-Soviet Film Exchange in the 1950s and 1960s." In *Futures of Chinese Cinemas: Technologies and Temporalities in Chinese Screen Cultures*, edited by Olivia Khoo and Sean Metzger, 73–93. Bristol, UK: Intellect Books.

Chen, Tina Mai. 2012. "The Human-Machine Continuum in Maoism: The Intersection of Soviet Socialist Realism, Japanese Theoretical Physics, and Chinese Revolutionary Theory." *Cultural Critique*, no. 80, 151–81.

Chen, Yizhong 陳宜中. 2008. "Haijiao qihao de Tairi kulian" 台日苦戀 [The Taiwan-Japan bitter love in *Cape No. 7*]. *Zhongguo shibao* 中國時報 [China times], October 9, 2008.

Chen Yong 陈涌. 1979. "Wo de daonian" 我的悼念 [My mourning]. *Renmin wenxue* 人民文学 [People's literature], no. 11, 43–47.

Chen Zhaoying 陳昭瑛. 1995. "Lun Taiwan de bentuhua yundong: Yige wenhuashi de kaocha" 論台灣的本土化運動：一個文化史的考察 [On Taiwan's nativization: An investigation of its cultural history]. *Zhongwai wenxue* 中外文學 [Chung-wai literary monthly] 23 (9): 6–43.

Chen, Zhimin. 2005. "Nationalism, Internationalism and Chinese Foreign Policy." *Journal of Contemporary China* 14 (42): 35–53.

Cheng Y. S. 鄭宇碩. 2004. "Cong 'yishangweizheng' kan Beijing dui Xianggang de tongzhan zhengce" 從「以商圍政」看北京對香港的統戰政策 [Beijing's united-front strategy policy toward Hong Kong—securing political power through the support of the business community]. *Yuanjing Foundation Quarterly* 遠景基金會季刊 5:197–217.

Cheung, Martha P. Y., ed. 1998a. *Hong Kong Collage: Contemporary Stories and Writing*. Hong Kong: Oxford University Press.

Cheung, Martha P. Y. 1998b. Preface to Cheung 1998a: i–xiii.

Chibber, Vivek. 2006. "On the Decline of Class Analysis in South Asian Studies." *Critical Asian Studies* 38 (4): 357–87.

Chibber, Vivek. 2013a. "How Does the Subaltern Speak?" Interview by Jonah Birch. *Jacobin*, April 10, 2013. https://www.jacobinmag.com/2013/04/how-does-the-subaltern-speak/.

Chibber, Vivek. 2013b. *Postcolonial Theory and the Specter of Capital*. London: Verso.

Chibber, Vivek. 2014. "Marxist Theory, Universalism and the Left: Postcolonial Thought's Blind Alley." *Middle East Online*, October 5, 2014.

China.org.cn. 2005. "Hong Kong Poet Wins 3rd in Global Competition." China.org.cn, September 5, 2005. http://www.china.org.cn/living_in_china/news/2008-09/05/content_16392647.htm.

China Review. 2001. "The 1950s: China and the Soviet Union." Editorial. Fall 2001.

Ching, Leo T. S. 2001. *Becoming "Japanese": Colonial Taiwan and the Politics of Identity Formation*. Berkeley: University of California Press.

Chiu Kuei-fen 邱貴芬. 1992. "'Faxian Taiwan': Jiangou Taiwan houzhimin lunshu" 發現台灣：建構台灣後殖民論述 ["Discovering Taiwan": Constructing Taiwan's postcolonial discourse]. *Zhongwai wenxue* 中外文學 [Chung-wai literary monthly] 21 (2): 151–68.

Chiu, Stephen W. K., and Tai-lok Lui. 2009. *Hong Kong: Becoming a Chinese Global City*. London: Routledge.

Chong Fah Hing 莊華興. 2012. "Mahua wenxe de jiangjiehua yu qujiangjie hua: Yige lishi demiaoshu" 馬華文學的疆界化與去疆界化：一個歷史的描述 [The territorialization and deterritorialization of Chinese Malaysian literature: A historical sketch]. *Zhongguo xiandai wenxue* 中國現代文學 [Modern Chinese literature] 22: 93–106.

Chou, Michael. 1996. "The Process of Hochi Practice: Summary of a Lecture by Master Michael Chou." *Hochi Universal Love*. Accessed January 1, 2006. http://www.hochi.org/pubs/vol3/practice.htm.

Chou, Michael. 1997. "Breaking Our Formats." *Hochi Universal Love*. Accessed January 1, 2006. http://www.hochi.org/msgs/breakformat.htm.

Chow, Rey. 1998. "Between Colonizers: Hong Kong's Postcolonial Self-Writing in the 1990s." In *Ethics after Idealism: Theory, Culture, Ethnicity, Reading*, 149–67. Bloomington: Indiana University Press.
Chu Tien-hsin. 1996. *Gudu* 古都 [The old capital]. Taipei: Ryefield.
Chua, Beng Huat. 2008. "Southeast Asia in Postcolonial Studies: An Introduction." *Postcolonial Studies* 11 (3): 231–40.
Chun, Allen. 2012. "Toward a Postcolonial Critique of the State in Singapore." *Cultural Studies* 26 (5): 670–87.
Chung, Sze-yuan. 2001. *Hong Kong's Journey to Reunification*. Hong Kong: Chinese University Press.
Clausen, Soren. 1998. "Party Policy and 'National Culture': Towards a State-Directed Cultural Nationalism in China?" In *Reconstructing Twentieth-Century China: State Control, Civil Society, and National Identity*, edited by Kjeld Erik Brødsgaard and David Strand, 253–79. Oxford: Clarendon; New York: Oxford University Press.
Clifford, James. 1994. "Diasporas." *Cultural Anthropology* 9 (3): 302–38.
Club 51 五一俱樂部. 1994. 讓台灣參加美利堅合眾國：終極之解決 [Let Taiwan join the United States of America: The ultimate solution]. *Haixia pinglun* 海峽評論 [Straits review monthly] 48:28–36.
Colletta, Lisa. 2005. *Kathleen and Christopher: Christopher Isherwood's Letters to His Mother*. Minneapolis: University of Minnesota Press.
Conrad, Joseph. (1902) 2007. *Heart of Darkness*. Edited by Owen Knowles. Harmondsworth, UK: Penguin.
Constable, Nicole. 2007. *Maid to Order in Hong Kong: Stories of Migrant Workers*. Ithaca, NY: Cornell University Press.
Constantino, Renato. 1975. *The Philippines: A Past Revisited: Pre-Spanish–1941*. Quezon City: Tala.
Constantino, Renato, and Letizia Constantino. 1978. *The Philippines: The Continuing Past*. Quezon City: Foundation for Nationalist Studies.
Cook, Alexander C., ed. 2014. *Mao's Little Red Book: A Global History*. Cambridge: Cambridge University Press.
Coppola, Francis, dir. 1972. *The Godfather*. Los Angeles: Paramount Pictures.
Cornut-Gentille D'Arcy, Chantal, and Lawrence Grossberg. 2010. "An Interview with Lawrence Grossberg: Personal Reflections on the Politics and Practice of Cultural Studies." *Atlantis* 32 (2): 107–20.
Cullinane, Michael. 1982. "The Changing Nature of the Cebu Urban Elite in the 19th Century." In *Philippine Social History: Global Trade and Local Transformation*, edited by Alfred W. McCoy and Edilberto C. De Jesus, 251–96. Quezon City: Ateneo de Manila University Press.
Cullinane, Michael. 2003. *Ilustrado Politics: Filipino Elite Responses to American Rule, 1898–1908*. Quezon City: Ateneo de Manila University Press.
Cullinane, Michael. 2014. *Arenas of Conspiracy and Rebellion in the Late Nineteenth-Century Philippines: The Case of the April 1898 Uprising in Cebu*. Quezon City: Ateneo de Manila University Press.

CuUnjieng Aboitiz, Nicole. 2020. *Asian Place, Filipino Nation: A Global Intellectual History of the Philippine Revolution, 1887–1912*. New York: Columbia University Press.

Dabashi, Hamid. 2012. *The Arab Spring: The End of Postcolonialism*. London: Zed.

Dai, Jinhua. 2018. "History, Memory, and the Politics of Representation." Translated by Rebecca Karl. In *After the Post–Cold War: The Future of Chinese History*, edited by Lisa Rofel, 141–59. Durham, NC: Duke University Press.

David, Randolf S. 2010. "What Should Truly Matter to Filipinos?" Lecture delivered at the University of the Philippines Academic Congress, "Beyond 2010: Leadership, Public Administration and Governance," University of the Philippines, Diliman, Quezon City, February 1–5, 2010. Accessed September 21, 2012. http://dilc.upd.edu.ph/index.php/events/421-what-should-truly-matter-to-filipinos.

Davidshofer, William J. 2014. *Marxism and the Leninist Revolutionary Model*. New York: Palgrave Macmillan.

Day, Richard B., and Daniel Gaido, eds. 2009. *Witnesses to Permanent Revolution: The Documentary Record*. Leiden: Brill.

Delmas, Candice. 2020. "Uncivil Disobedience in Hong Kong." *Boston Review*, January 13, 2020.

Deng, Xiaoping. 1993. "We Should Draw on the Experience of Other Countries: June 3, 1988." In *Deng Xiaoping on the Question of Hong Kong*, 59–62. Hong Kong: New Horizon.

Denton, Kirk A., ed. 1996. *Modern Chinese Literary Thought: Writings on Literature, 1893–1945*. Stanford, CA: Stanford University Press.

Denton, Kirk A. 1998. *The Problematic of Self in Modern Chinese Literature: Hu Feng and Lu Ling*. Stanford, CA: Stanford University Press.

Derman, Joshua. 2011. "Carl Schmitt on Land and Sea." *History of European Ideas* 37 (2): 181–89.

Derrida, Jacques. 1994. *Specters of Marx: The State of the Debt, the Work of Mourning, and the New International*. Translated by Peggy Kamuf. New York: Routledge.

Dikötter, Frank. 2015. *The Discourse of Race in Modern China*. 2nd ed. Oxford: Oxford University Press.

Dirlik, Arif. 1998. *The Postcolonial Aura: Third World Criticism in the Age of Global Capitalism*. Boulder, CO: Westview.

Dittmer, Lowell. 1987. *China's Continuous Revolution: The Post-liberation Epoch, 1949–1979*. Berkeley: University of California Press.

Dittmer, Lowell. 1998. *Liu Shaoqi and the Chinese Cultural Revolution*. Armonk, NY: M. E. Sharpe.

Doronila, Amando. 1992. *The State, Economic Transformation, and Political Change in the Philippines, 1946–1972*. Singapore: Oxford University Press.

Dreyer, Edward L. 2007. *Zheng He: China and the Oceans in the Early Ming Dynasty, 1405–1433*. New York: Pearson Longman.

Du Zhidong 杜志东. 2016. "Ershi shiji liushi niandai 'Yafeila geming zhuti' Zhongguo diansu yanjiu" 二十世纪六十年代「亚非拉革命主题」中国雕塑研究 [Chinese statues made in the 1960s with themes related to Asia–Africa–Latin America revolutions]. *Rongbao zhai* 荣宝斋 [Rongbao studio], no. 6, 146–55.

Duara, Prasenjit. 1997. *Rescuing History from the Nation: Questioning Narratives of Modern China*. Chicago: University of Chicago Press.

Duara, Prasenjit. 2001. "The Discourse of Civilization and Pan-Asianism." *Journal of World History* 12 (1): 99–130.

Duara, Prasenjit. 2003. *Sovereignty and Authenticity: Manchukuo and the East Asian Modern*. Lanham, MD: Rowman and Littlefield.

Duara, Prasenjit. 2006. "Nationalism, Imperialism, Federalism, and the Example of Manchukuo: A Response to Anthony Pagden." *Common Knowledge* 12 (1): 47–65.

Duara, Prasenjit. 2012. "Hong Kong and the New Imperialism in East Asia, 1941–1966." In *Twentieth-Century Colonialism and China: Localities, the Everyday and the World*, edited by Bryna Goodman and David S. G. Goodman, 197–211. London: Routledge.

Duara, Prasenjit. 2019. "The Chinese World Order in Historical Perspective." *China and the World: Ancient and Modern Silk Road* 2 (4): 1–33.

Du Bois, W. E. B. 2005. *W. E. B. Du Bois on Asia: Crossing the Color Line*. Edited by Bill Mullen and Cathryn Watson. Jackson: University Press of Mississippi.

Dunbar-Ortiz, Roxanne. 2014. *An Indigenous Peoples' History of the United States*. Boston: Beacon.

Dun Kai-cheung 董啓章. 2014. *Menghualu* 夢華錄 [Dream of splendor] and *Fanshenglu* 繁勝錄 [Account of prosperity]. Taipei: Linking.

Dunn, Bill, and Hugo Radice, eds. 2006. *100 Years of Permanent Revolution*. London: Pluto.

Dupré, Louis. 1980. "Marx's Critique of Culture and Its Interpretations." *Review of Metaphysics* 34 (1): 91–121.

Duus, Peter. 1996. "Imperialism without Colonies: The Vision of a Greater East Asia Co-Prosperity Sphere." *Diplomacy and Statecraft* 7 (1): 54–72.

Economist. 2019. "Meet Me in Luneta." February 16, 2019, 34.

Economist. 2020. "No Cause to Stop: The Arab Spring at Ten." December 19, 2020, 79–80.

Economist. 2021a. "As in Xinjiang, China Is Tightening Its Grip in Tibet." February 13, 2021. https://www.economist.com/china/2021/02/13/as-in-xinjiang-china-is-tightening-its-grip-in-tibet.

Economist. 2021b. "The Chinese Communist Party's Model Emperor." September 18, 2021. https://www.economist.com/china/2021/09/18/the-chinese-communist-partys-model-emperor.

Editorial Departments of *Jen Min Jih Po* (People's Daily) and *Hung Ch'i* (Red Flag). 1964. *On Krushchov's Phoney Communism and Its Historical Lessons for the World—Comment on the Open Letter of the Central Committee of the CPUS (IX)*. July 14, 1964. Peking: Foreign Language Press.

Edwards, Louise. 2010. "Chinese Feminism in a Transnational Frame: Between Internationalism and Xenophobia." In *Women's Movement in Asia: Feminisms and Transnational Activism*, edited by Mina Races and Louise Edwards, 53–74. London: Routledge.

Eliaeson, Sven. 2000. "Max Weber's Methodology: An Ideal Type." *Journal of the History of the Behavioral Sciences* 36 (3): 241–63.

Ellison, Ralph. 1976. *Invisible Man*. Harmondsworth, UK: Penguin.

Elson, Anthony. 2013. *Globalization and Development: Why East Asia Surged Ahead and Latin America Fell Behind*. New York: Palgrave Macmillan.

Escalante, Rene. 2017. "Bonifacio and the Katipunan in the Cuerpo de Vigilancia Archival Collection." *Philippine Studies* 65 (4): 451–83.

Fallenbuchl, Z. M. 1970. "The Communist Pattern of Industrialization." *Soviet Studies* 21 (4): 458–84.

Fang Xiaoqian 方孝謙. 2001. *Zhimindi Taiwan de renting mosuo: Cong shanshu dao xiaoshuo de xushi fenxi, 1895-1945* 殖民地台灣的認同摸索：從善書到小說的敘事分析 [The identity-searching of Taiwan as a colony: Narrative analysis from morality books to fiction, 1895–1945]. Taipei: Juliu.

Fanon, Frantz. (1963) 2004. *The Wretched of the Earth*. Translated by Richard Philcox. New York: Grove.

Fanon, Frantz. (1967) 1986. *Black Skin, White Masks*. Translated by Charles Lam Markmann. London: Pluto.

Fennell, Vera Leigh. 2013. "Race: China's Question and Problem." *Review of Black Political Economy* 40 (3): 245–75.

Firchow, Peter Edgerly. 2002. *W. H. Auden: Contexts for Poetry*. Newark: University of Delaware Press.

Fitzgerald, John. 1995. "The Nationless State: The Search for a Nation in Modern Chinese Nationalism." *Australian Journal of Chinese Affairs*, no. 33, 75–104.

Flynn, Dennis, and Arturo Giráldez. 1995. "Born with a 'Silver Spoon': The Origin of World Trade in 1571." *Journal of World History* 6 (2): 201–21.

Fogel, Joshua A. 2012. "New Thoughts on an Old Controversy: *Shina* as a Toponym for China." *Sino-Platonic Papers*, no. 299, 1–25.

Fong, Brian C. H. 2015. *Hong Kong's Governance under Chinese Sovereignty*. London: Routledge.

Foucault, Michel. 2000. "Truth and Juridical Forms." In *Power*, vol. 3 of *Essential Works of Foucault, 1954–1984*, edited by James D. Faubion, 6–89. New York: New Press.

Foucault, Michel. 2008. *The Birth of Biopolitics: Lectures at the College de France, 1978-79*. Edited by Michel Senellart and translated by Graham Burchell. London: Palgrave Macmillan.

Fradera, Josep M. 1999. *Filipinas, la colonia más peculiar: La hacienda pública en la definición de la política colonial, 1762-1868* [The Philippines, the most peculiar colony: Public finance in the making of colonial politics, 1762–1868]. Madrid: Consejo Superior de Investigaciones Científicas.

Frank, Andre Gunder. 1998. *Re-ORIENT: Global Economy in the Asian Age*. Berkeley: University of California Press.

Frazier, Robeson Taj. 2014. *The East Is Black: Cold War China in the Black Radical Imagination*. Durham, NC: Duke University Press.
Friedman, Edward, and Mark Selden, eds. 1973. *America's Asia: Dissenting Essays on Asian-American Relations*. New York: Vintage.
Fröbel, Folker, Jürgen Heinrichs, and Otto Kreye. 1980. *The New International Division of Labor: Structural Unemployment in Industrialised Countries and Industrialization in Developing Countries*. Translated by Pete Burgess. Cambridge: Cambridge University Press.
Galison, Peter. 2003. *Einstein's Clocks, Poincaré's Maps: Empires of Time*. New York: W. W. Norton.
Gandhi, Leela. 1998. *Postcolonial Theory: A Critical Introduction*. New York: Columbia University Press.
Gann, Lewis H. 1984. "Western and Japanese Colonialism: Some Preliminary Comparisons." In *The Japanese Colonial Empire, 1895–1945*, edited by Ramon H. Myers and Mark R. Peattie, 497–525. Princeton, NJ: Princeton University Press.
Gaonkar, Dilip Parameshwar, ed. 2001. *Alternative Modernities*. Durham, NC: Duke University Press.
Garcia, Carlos, and Yew Lun Tian. 2021. "China's Xi Vows 'Reunification' with Taiwan." Reuters, October 9, 2021. https://www.reuters.com/world/china/chinas-xi-says-reunification-with-taiwan-must-will-be-realised-2021-10-09/.
Ghai, Yash. 1999. *Hong Kong's New Constitutional Order*. 2nd ed. Hong Kong: Hong Kong University Press.
Giaccaria, Paolo, and Claudio Minca. 2016. "Life in Space, Space in Life: Nazi Topographies, Geographical Imaginations, and *Lebensraum*." *Holocaust Studies* 22 (2–3): 151–71.
Giersch, C. Patterson. 2006. *Asian Borderlands: The Transformation of Qing China's Yunnan Frontier*. Cambridge, MA: Harvard University Press.
Gikandi, Simon. 1991. *Reading Chinua Achebe: Language and Ideology in Fiction*. London: James Currey.
Gilroy, Paul. 1993. *The Black Atlantic: Modernity and Double Consciousness*. Cambridge, MA: Harvard University Press.
Gilroy, Paul. 1997. "Diaspora and the Detours of Identity." In *Identity and Difference*, edited by Kathryn Woodward, 301–43. London: Sage in association with the Open University.
Gittings, Danny. 2013. *Introduction to the Hong Kong Basic Law*. Hong Kong: Hong Kong University Press.
Glissant, Édouard. 1997. *Poetics of Relation*. Translated by Betsy Wing. Ann Arbor: University of Michigan Press.
Goodman, Bryna, and David S. G. Goodman. 2012. "Introduction: Colonialism and China." In *Twentieth Century Colonialism and China: Localities, the Everyday and the World*, edited by Bryna Goodman and David S. G. Goodman, 1–22. Abingdon, UK: Routledge.
Goodstadt, Leo F. 2000. "China and the Selection of Hong Kong's Post-colonial Political Elite." *China Quarterly* 163:721–41.

Goodstadt, Leo F. 2013. *Poverty in the Midst of Affluence: How Hong Kong Mismanaged Its Prosperity*. Hong Kong: Hong Kong University Press.
Gorky, Maxim. 1939. "Soviet Intellectuals." In *Culture and the People*, 185–98. New York: International Publishers.
Gorky, Maxim. 1973a. *On Literature*. Seattle: University of Washington Press.
Gorky, Maxim. 1973b. "Soviet Literature: Address Delivered to the First All-Union Congress of Soviet Writers, August 17, 1934." In *On Literature*, 228–68.
Groppe, Alison. 2014. *Sinophone Malaysian Literature: Not Made in China*. Amherst, NY: Cambria.
Grosfoguel, Ramón. 2002. "Colonial Difference, Geopolitics of Knowledge, and Global Coloniality in the Modern/Colonial Capitalist World-System." *Review (Fernand Braudel Center)* 25 (3): 203–24.
Grossberg, Lawrence. 1996. "The Space of Culture, the Power of Space." In *The Post-colonial Question: Common Skies, Divided Horizons*, edited by Iain Chambers and Lidia Curti, 169–88. London: Routledge.
Grossberg, Lawrence. 2006. "Does Cultural Studies Have Futures? Should It? (Or What's the Matter with New York?): Cultural Studies, Contexts, and Conjunctures." *Cultural Studies* 20 (1): 1–32.
Grossberg, Lawrence, Cary Nelson, and Paula Treichler, eds. 1991. *Cultural Studies*. London: Routledge.
Guettel, Jens-Uwe. 2013. "The US Frontier as Rationale for the Nazi East? Settler Colonialism and Genocide in Nazi-Occupied Eastern Europe and the American West." *Journal of Genocide Research* 15 (4): 401–19.
Guillermo, Ramon. 2010. *Translation and Revolution: A Study of Jose Rizal's Guillermo Tell*. Quezon City: Ateneo de Manila University Press.
Habermas, Jürgen. 2001. "Conceptions of Modernity: A Look Back at Two Traditions." In *The Postnational Constellation: Political Essays*, translated by Max Pensky, 130–56. Cambridge, MA: MIT Press.
Hall, Stuart. 1997. "The Local and the Global: Globalization and Ethnicity." In *Dangerous Liaisons: Gender, Nation, and Post-colonial Perspectives*, edited by Anne McClintock, Aamir Mufti, and Ella Shohat, 173–87. Minneapolis: University of Minnesota Press.
Hamashita Takeshi 濱下武志. 1996. *Hon Kon* 香港 [Hong Kong]. Tokyo: Chikuma Shobō.
Hamashita Takeshi 濱下武志. 1997. 香港大視野—亞洲網絡中心 [Hong Kong macrovision : The center of the Asian network]. Translated by Ma Songzhi 馬宋芝. Hong Kong: Commercial Press.
Hamashita, Takeshi 濱下武志. 2008. *China, East Asia and the Global Economy: Regional and Historical Perspectives*. Edited by Linda Grove and Mark Selden. Abingdon, UK: Routledge.
Hamid, Mohsin. 2007. *The Reluctant Fundamentalist*. New York: Harcourt.
Han, Wing-Tak. 1981. "Bureaucracy and the Japanese Occupation of Hong Kong." In *Japan in Asia, 1942–1945*, edited by William H. Newell, 7–24. Singapore: Singapore University Press.

Hardt, Michael, and Antonio Negri. 2001. *Empire*. Cambridge, MA: Harvard University Press.

Harootunian, Harry. 2010. "'Modernity' and the Claims of Untimeliness." *Postcolonial Studies* 13 (4): 367–82.

Harper, Tim. 2020. *Underground Asia: Global Revolutionaries and the Assault on Empire*. Cambridge, MA: Harvard University Press.

Harrison, Sophie. 2006. "Fortunate Son." *New York Times*, April 9, 2006.

Harvey, David. 2003. *The New Imperialism*. Oxford: Oxford University Press.

Harvey, Robert. 2011. *The Fall of Apartheid: The Inside Story from Smuts to Mbeki*. London: Palgrave Macmillan.

Hau, Caroline S. 2000. "On Representing Others: Intellectuals, Pedagogy and the Uses of Error." In *Reclaiming Identity: Realist Theory and the Predicament of Postmodernism*, edited by Paula M. L. Moya and Michael R. Hames-García, 133–70. Berkeley: University of California Press.

Hau, Caroline S. 2013. "(Anglo-)Chinese." In *The Chinese Question: Ethnicity, Nation, and Region in and beyond the Philippines*, 283–320. Quezon City: Ateneo de Manila University Press.

Hau, Caroline S. 2014. "The True Story of Ah To." In *Recuerdos de Patay and Other Stories*, 25–34. Quezon City: Ateneo de Manila University Press.

Hau, Caroline S. 2017. *Elites and Ilustrados in Philippine Culture*. Quezon City: Ateneo de Manila University Press.

Hau, Caroline S., and Takashi Shiraishi. 2009. "Daydreaming about Rizal and Tetchō: On Asianism as Network and Fantasy." *Philippine Studies* 57 (3): 329–88.

Hau, Caroline S., and Kasian Tejapira, eds. 2011. *Traveling Nation Makers: Transnational Flows and Movements in the Making of Modern Southeast Asia*. Singapore: National University of Singapore Press; Kyoto: Kyoto University Press.

Hawes, Gary. 1987. *The Philippine State and the Marcos Regime*. Ithaca, NY: Cornell University Press.

He, Donghui. 2010. "Coming of Age in the Brave New World: The Changing Reception of the Soviet Novel, *How the Steel Was Tempered*, in the People's Republic of China." In *China Learns from the Soviet Union, 1949–Present*, edited by Thomas P. Bernstein and Hua-yu Li, 393–420. Lanham, MD: Lexington Books.

Hegel, G. W. F. 1955. *Vorlesungen über die Philosophie der Weltgeschichte*. Vol. 1, *Die Vernunft in der Geschichte*. Hamburg: Felix Meiner.

Hegel, G. W. F. 1980. *Lectures on the Philosophy of World History: Introduction, Reason in History*. Translated by H. B. Nisbet. Cambridge: Cambridge University Press.

Hegel, G. W. F. 1998. *Aesthetics: Lecture on Fine Arts*. Vol. 1. Translated by T. M. Knox. Oxford: Clarendon.

Heidegger, Martin. 1977. *Wozu Dichter?* [Why poets?]. In *Holzwege, Gesamtausgabe, I. Abteilung: Veröffentlichte Schriften 1914–1970* [Off the beaten track. Complete works, part one: Published writings], edited by

Friedrich-Wilhelm von Hermann, 5:248–95. Frankfurt am Main: Vittorio Klostermann.

Heidegger, Martin. 1979. *Heraklit: Der Anfang des abendländischen Denkens: Logik* [Heraclitus: The inception of occidental thinking and logic]. In *Heraklit: Freiburger Vorlesungen Sommersemester 1943 und Sommersemester 1944, Gesamtausgabe, II Abteilung: Vorlesungen 1923-1944* [Heraclitus: Freiburg lectures summer semester 1943 and summer semester 1944. Complete works, part two: Lectures], edited by Manfred S. Frings, 55:3–181. Frankfurt am Main: Vittorio Klostermann.

Heidegger, Martin. 2002. "Why Poets?" In *Off the Beaten Track*, edited and translated by Julian Young and Kenneth Haynes, 200–241. Cambridge: Cambridge University Press.

Heidegger, Martin. 2013. "The Provenance of Art and The Destination of Thought (1967)." *Journal of the British Society for Phenomenology* 44 (2): 119–28.

Heidegger, Martin. 2018. *Heraclitus: The Inception of Occidental Thinking and Logic; Heraclitus's Doctrine of the Logos*. Translated by Julia Goesser Assaiante and S. Montgomery Ewegen. London: Bloomsbury.

Hell, Julia. 2009. "*Katechon*: Carl Schmitt's Imperial Theology and the Ruins of the Future." *Germanic Review: Literature, Culture, Theory* 84 (4): 283–326.

Herzfeld, Michael. 2005. *Cultural Intimacy: Social Poetics in the Nation-State*. 2nd ed. New York: Routledge.

Hevia, James L. 1995. *Cherishing Men from Afar: Qing Guest Ritual and the Macartney Embassy of 1793*. Durham, NC: Duke University Press.

Hevia, James L. 2003. *English Lessons: The Pedagogy of Imperialism in Nineteenth-Century China*. Durham, NC: Duke University Press.

Hirschman, Charles. 1986. "The Making of Race in Colonial Malaya: Political Economy and Racial Ideology." *Sociological Forum* 1 (2): 330–61.

Ho, Elaine Yee Lin. 2006. "Imperial Globalization and Colonial Transactions: 'African Lugard' and the University of Hong Kong." In *Critical Zone 2: A Forum of Chinese and Western Knowledge*, 107–45. Hong Kong: Hong Kong University Press and Nanjing University Press.

Ho, Elaine Yee Lin. 2009a. "'Imagination's Commonwealth': Edmund Blunden's Hong Kong Dialogue." PMLA 124 (1): 76–91.

Ho, Elaine Yee Lin. 2009b. "Nationalism, Internationalism, the Cold War: Crossing Literary-Cultural Boundaries in 1950s Hong Kong." In *China Abroad: Travels, Subjects, Spaces*, edited by Elaine Yee Lin Ho and Julia Kuehn, 85–104. Hong Kong: Hong Kong University Press.

Ho, Elaine Yee Lin. 2010. "Language Policy, 'Asia's World City' and Anglophone Hong Kong Writing." *Interventions: International Journal of Postcolonial Studies* 12 (3): 428–41.

Ho, Elaine Yee Lin. 2019a. "Lei yingyu yuxi" 類英語語系 [Anglophonic]. Translated by Leung Ka Yan. In *Xianggang Guanjianqi* 香港關鍵詞 [Hong Kong keywords: Imagining the new future], edited by Yiu Wai Chu, 15–24. Hong Kong: Chinese University Press.

Ho, Elaine Yee Lin. 2019b. "The Novel of Hong Kong." In *The Novel in South and South East Asia since 1945. The Oxford History of the English Novel*, edited by Alex Tickell, 10:292–307. Oxford: Oxford University Press.

Ho, Louise. 2009. *Incense Tree: Collected Poems of Louise Ho*. Hong Kong: Hong Kong University Press.

Ho, Tammy Lai-ming. 2015. *Hula Hooping*. Hong Kong: Chameleon.

Hong Kong Exchanges and Clearing Ltd. 2020. HKEX *Fact Book 2019*. Accessed November 9, 2020. https://www.hkex.com.hk/-/media/HKEX-Market/Market-Data/Statistics/Consolidated-Reports/HKEX-Fact-Book/HKEX-Fact-Book-2019/FB_2019.pdf?la=en.

Hong Kong SAR Government. 2001. *Chief Executive's Policy Address 2001*. Hong Kong: Government Printer.

Horne, Gerald. 2004. *Race War: White Supremacy and the Japanese Attack on the British Empire*. New York: New York University Press.

Hostetler, Laura. 2001. *Qing Colonial Enterprise: Ethnography and Cartography in Early Modern China*. Chicago: University of Chicago Press.

Hou, Hsiao-hsien, dir. 1989. *A City of Sadness*. Taipei: 3-H Films.

Hsia, Joyce, and T. C. Lai, ed. 1977. *Hong Kong: Images on Shifting Waters*. Hong Kong: Kelly and Walsh.

Hsiau, A-Chin. 2013. "The Emergence of De-exile Cultural Politics and the Postwar Generation in Taiwan." *Oriens Extremus* 52:173–214.

Huang, C. Julia. 2009. *Charisma and Compassion: Cheng Yen and the Buddhist Tzu Chi Movement*. Cambridge, MA: Harvard University Press.

Huang Chunming 黃春明. 2000a. "Pingguo de ziwei" 蘋果的滋味 [The taste of the apples]. In *Erzi de da wan'ou* 兒子的大玩偶 [His son's big doll], 41–73. Taipei: Crown.

Huang, Chunming 黃春明. 2000b. "Xiaoqi de nayiding maozi" 小琪的那頂帽子 [Xiaoqi's cap]. In *Erzi de da wan'ou* 兒子的大玩偶 [*His son's big doll*], 75–112. Taipei: Crown.

Huang Deshi 黃得時. 1943. "Taiwan bungakushi josetsu" [An introduction to Taiwan's literary history]. *Taiwan bungaku* 台湾文学 [Taiwan literature] 3 (3): 2–11.

Huang, Hsin-yao dir. 2017a. *Great Buddha Plus*. A-Yao Film, Cream Film Production, Mandarin Vision, Ocean Deep Films, Triple Film House.

Huang, Hsin-yao. 2017b. "When People Pray, Are They Throwing Their Hopes into a Void? An Interview with Director Huang Hsin-yao." Translated by Harrison Chen. TW *Reporter*, October 7, 2017. https://www.twreporter.org/a/director-hsin-yao-huang.

Huang Wenfang 黃文放. 1997. *Zhongguo dui xianggang huifu xingshi zhuquan de juece lichen yu zhixing* 中國對香港恢復行使主權的決策歷程與執行 [The decision-making and execution of China's resumption of sovereignty over Hong Kong]. Hong Kong: David C. Lam Institute for East-West Studies, Baptist University.

Huggan, Graham. 2008. *Interdisciplinary Measures: Literature and the Future of Postcolonial Studies*. Liverpool: Liverpool University Press.

Hughes, Richard. 1976. *Borrowed Place, Borrowed Time*. Rev. ed. London: Andre Deutsch.

Idema, Wilt, Wai-yee Li, and Ellen Widmer, eds. 2006. *Trauma and Transcendence in Early Qing Literature*. Harvard East Asia Monograph Series. Cambridge, MA: Harvard University Asia Center, Harvard University Press.

Ileto, Reynaldo C. 1993. "The 'Unfinished Revolution' in Philippine Political Discourse." *Southeast Asian Studies* 31 (1): 62–82.

Ileto, Reynaldo C. 1999. "Orientalism and the Study of Philippine Politics." In *Knowing America's Colony: A Hundred Years from the Philippine War*, 41–65. Philippine Studies Occasional Papers Series 13. Manoa: Center for Philippine Studies, School of Hawaiian, Asian, and Pacific Studies, University of Hawai'i at Manoa.

Information Office of the State Council. 2014. *The Practice of the "One Country, Two Systems" Policy in the Hong Kong Special Administrative Region*. Beijing: Foreign Languages Press.

Isle Margin. 1993. "Alter-native Taiwanese" (special issue). *Isle Margin* 8 (July). http://intermargins.net/intermargins/IsleMargin/alter_native/index.htm.

Ivanov, Viacheslav Vs. 1994. "Why Did Stalin Kill Gorky?" *Russian Studies in Literature* 30 (4): 5–40.

Jameson, Fredric. 1986. "Third World Literature in the Era of Multinational Capitalism." *Social Text*, no. 15, 65–88.

Jameson, Fredric. 2002. *A Singular Modernity: Essay on the Ontology of the Present*. London: Verso.

Jay, Jennifer W. 1991. *A Change in Dynasties: Loyalism in Thirteenth-Century China*. Bellingham: Western Washington University Press.

Jayawickrama, Nihal. 1991. "Hong Kong: The Gathering Storm." *Bulletin of Peace Proposals* 22 (2): 157–74.

Jenco, Leigh K., and Jonathan Chappell. 2020. "Overlapping Histories, Co-produced Concepts: Imperialism in Chinese Eyes." *Journal of Asian Studies* 79 (3): 685–706.

Jensen, Lars, Julia Suárez-Krabbe, Christian Groes, and Zoran Lee Pecic, eds. 2017. *Postcolonial Europe: Comparative Reflections after the Empires*. London: Rowman and Littlefield.

Ji Xian 紀弦. 1956. "Xiandaipai xintiao shiyi" 現代派信條釋義 [Explicating the tenets of the modernist school]. *Xiandaishi* 現代詩 [Modern poetry quarterly] 13:4.

Jiang Weishui 蔣渭水. (1921) 1950. "Rinshō kōgi" 臨牀講義 [Clinical diagnosis]. In *Jiang Weishui yiji* 蔣渭水遺集 [The posthumous collection of Jiang Weishui], edited by Bai Chengzhi, 93–95. Taipei: Wenhua chubanshe.

JN. 2020. "Discrimination Isn't Helping to Contain the Coronavirus." *Nation*, February 7, 2020.

Joaquin, Nick. (1961) 1991. *The Woman Who Had Two Navels*. Manila: Bookmark.

Joaquin, Nick. (1988) 2004. *Culture and History*. Pasig City, Philippines: Anvil.

Joaquin, Nick. 1990. "Nick Joaquin w/ Jose F. ('Pete') Lacaba." Interview by Roger J. Bresnahan. In *Conversations with Filipino Writers*, 63–76. Quezon City: New Day.

Joaquin, Nick. (1997) 2005. *A Question of Heroes*. Mandaluyong City, Philippines: Anvil.

Johnson, Chalmers. 1982. MITI *and the Japanese Miracle: The Growth of Industrial Policy, 1925–1975*. Stanford, CA: Stanford University Press.

Jones, Robert A. 1990. *The Soviet Concept of "Limited Sovereignty" from Lenin to Gorbachev: The Brezhnev Doctrine*. New York: Palgrave Macmillan.

Kalinovsky, Artemy M. 2018. *Laboratory of Socialist Development: Cold War Politics and Decolonization in Soviet Tajikistan*. Ithaca, NY: Cornell University Press.

Kalyvas, Andreas. 2018. "Carl Schmitt's Postcolonial Imagination." *Constellations: An International Journal of Critical and Democratic Theory* 25 (1): 35–53.

Kamuf, Peggy. 1997. "Violence, Identity, Self-Determination, and the Question of Justice: On Specters of Marx." In *Violence, Identity, and Self-Determination*, edited by Hent DeVries and Samuel Weber, 271–83. Stanford, CA: Stanford University Press.

Karl, Rebecca. 2002. *Staging the World: Chinese Nationalism at the Turn of the Century*. Durham, NC: Duke University Press.

Keen, Ruth. 1988. "Information Is All That Counts: An Introduction to Chinese Women's Writing in German Translation." *Modern Chinese Literature* 4 (2): 225–34.

Kelliher, Daniel. 1994. "Chinese Communist Political Theory and the Rediscovery of the Peasantry." *Modern China* 20 (4): 287–415.

Kerr, Douglas. 2008. *Eastern Figures: Orient and Empire in British Writing*. Hong Kong: Hong Kong University Press.

Kerr, Douglas. 2009. Afterword to L. Ho 2009: 155–62.

Kervégan, J. F. 1999. "Schmitt and 'World Unity.'" In *The Challenge of Carl Schmitt*, edited by Chantal Mouffe, 54–74. London: Verso.

Khlebnikov, Boris, and Alexey Popogrebsky, dir. 2003. *Koktebel* (Коктебель). Koktebel Film Company, PBOUL Borisevich R.U.

Kinkley, Jeffrey. 1990. "Echoes of Maxim Gorky in the Works of Ding Ling and Shen Congwen." In *Interliterary and Intraliterary Aspects of the May Fourth Movement 1919 in China*, edited by Marian Galik, 179–88. Bratislava: Veda.

Kipling, Rudyard. 1889. "The Ballad of East and West." Kipling Society. Accessed April 2, 2022. https://www.kiplingsociety.co.uk/poem/poems_eastwest.htm.

Kistner, Ulrike. 2020. "In Search of a New Nomos: Post-colonially." *Constellations: An International Journal of Critical and Democratic Theory* 27 (2): 273–84.

Knight, Nick. 2005. *Marxist Philosophy in China: From Qu Qiubai to Mao Zedong, 1923–1945*, Dordrecht: Springer.

Koskenniemi, Martti. 2017. "Carl Schmitt and International Law." In *The Oxford Handbook of Carl Schmitt*, edited by Jens Meierhenrich and Oliver Simons, 592–611. Oxford: Oxford University Press.

Kramer, Paul A. 2002. "Empires, Exceptions, and Anglo-Saxons: Race and Rule between the British and United States Empires, 1880–1910." *Journal of American History* 88 (4): 1315–53.

Kramer, Paul A. 2006. *The Blood of Government: Race, Empire, the United States, and the Philippines*. Chapel Hill: University of North Carolina Press.

Kristeva, Julia. 1986. *About Chinese Women*. Translated by Anita Barrows. New York: Marion Boyars.

Krugman, Paul, James Alm, Susan M. Collins, and Eli M. Remolona. 1992. *Transforming the Philippine Economy*. Manila: United Nations Development Program.

Kureishi, Hanif. 1990. *The Buddha of Suburbia*. Harmondsworth, UK: Penguin.

Kureishi, Hanif. 1992. "The Rainbow Sign." In *London Kills Me: Three Screenplays and Four Essays*, 3–37. Harmondsworth, UK: Penguin.

Kusin, Vladimir V. 1971. *The Intellectual Origins of the Prague Spring: The Development of Reformist Ideas in Czechoslovakia, 1956–1967*. Cambridge: Cambridge University Press.

Kwong, Kin Ming, and Hong Yu. 2013. "Identity Politics." In *Hong Kong under Chinese Rule*, edited by Yongnian Zheng and Chiew Ping Yew, 125–49. Singapore: World Scientific Publishing.

Lahusen, Thomas. 2000. "Dr. Fu Manchu in Harbin: Cinema and Moviegoers of the 1930s." *South Atlantic Quarterly* 99 (1): 143–61.

Lai He 賴和 [Hui 灰]. 1935. *Taiwan xinwenxue* 台灣新文學 [Taiwanese new literature] 1 (1) (December): 67–69.

Lai He 賴和. 2000. *Lai He quanji hanshijuan xia* 賴和全集漢詩卷下 [Complete collection of Lai He, Han poetry, vol. 2], edited by Lin Ruiming. Taipei: Qianwei.

Landsberg, Alison. 2003. *Prosthetic Memory: The Transformation of American Remembrance in the Age of Mass Culture*. New York: Columbia University Press.

Lanot, Marra P. L. 1999. "The Trouble with Nick." In *The Trouble with Nick and Other Profiles*, 2–15. Quezon City: University of the Philippines Press.

Larson, Wendy. 2010. *From Ah Q to Lei Feng: Freud and Revolutionary Spirit in 20th Century China*. Stanford, CA: Stanford University Press.

Larson, Wendy. 2016. "Curing Unhappiness in Revolutionary China: Optimism under Socialism and Capitalism." In *Discourses of Disease: Writing Illness, the Body, and the Mind in Modern China*, edited by Howard F. Choy, 55–89. Leiden: Brill.

Latham, A. J. H. 1986. "Southeast Asia: A Preliminary Survey—1800–1914." In *Migration across Time and Nations*, edited by Ira Glazier and Luigi de Rosa, 11–29. New York: Holmes and Meier.

Law, Wing Sang. 2009. *Collaborative Colonial Power: The Making of the Hong Kong Chinese*. Hong Kong: Hong Kong University Press.

Lazarus, Neil. 1999. *Nationalism and Cultural Practice in the Postcolonial World*. Cambridge: Cambridge University Press.

Lazarus, Neil. 2011. *The Postcolonial Unconscious*. Cambridge: Cambridge University Press.

Lee, Francis L. F., Samson Yuen, Gary Tang, and Edmund W. Cheng. 2019. "Hong Kong's Summer of Uprising: From Anti-extradition to Anti-authoritarian Protests." *China Review* 19 (4): 1–32.

Leese, Daniel. 2011. *Mao Cult: Rhetoric and Ritual in China's Cultural Revolution*. Cambridge: Cambridge University Press.

Legarda, Benito J., Jr. 1999. *After the Galleons: Foreign Trade, Economic Change and Entrepreneurship in the Nineteenth-Century Philippines*. Quezon City: Ateneo de Manila University Press.

Legg, Stephen. 2011. "Inter-war Spatial Chaos? Imperialism, Internationalism and the League of Nations." In *Spatiality, Sovereignty and Carl Schmitt: Geographies of the Nomos*, edited by Stephen Legg, 106–23. Abingdon, UK: Routledge.

Lendvai, Paul. 2008. *One Day That Shook the Communist World: The 1956 Hungarian Uprising and Its Legacy*. Translated by Ann Major. Princeton, NJ: Princeton University Press.

Lenin, V. I. 1972. "The Right of Nations to Self-Determination." In *V. I. Lenin Collected Works*, translated by Bernard Isaacs and Joe Fineberg, 20:393–451. Moscow: Progress.

Lenin, V. I. 1987. "Imperialism, the Highest Stage of Capitalism." 1917. In *Essential Works of Lenin*, edited by Henry M. Christman, 177–270. New York: Dover.

Leung, Arthur Sai-cheong. 2008. "What the Pig Mama Says." Skyscraper City, September 3. Accessed April 1, 2022. https://www.skyscrapercity.com/threads/proud-of-arthur-leung-local-poet-wins-3rd-global-competition.702166/

Leung, Arthur Sai-cheong. 2012. "Poetic Statement." In "Hong Kong Poets under 40." Special issue, *Cha: An Asian Literary Journal*, no. 19. https://www.asiancha.com/content/view/1336/383/.

Leung, Ping-kwan. 1992. *City at the End of Time*. Translated by Gordon T. Osing and Leung Ping-kwan. Hong Kong: Twilight Books.

Leung, Ping-kwan. 1998. "The Story of Hong Kong." Translated by Martha P. Y. Cheung. In *Hong Kong Collage: Contemporary Stories and Writing*, edited by Martha P. Y. Cheung, 3–13. Hong Kong: Oxford University Press.

Levine, Caroline. 2006. "Strategic Formalism: Toward a New Method in Cultural Studies." *Victorian Studies* 48 (4): 625–57.

Levine, Caroline. 2015. *Forms: Whole, Rhythm, Hierarchy, Network*. Princeton, NJ: Princeton University Press.

Levitsky, Steven, and Daniel Ziblatt. 2018. *How Democracies Die*. New York: Broadway Books.

Li, David C. S. 2018. "Two Decades of Decolonization and Renationalization: The Evolutionary Dynamics of Hong Kong English and an Update of Its Functions and Status." *Asian Englishes* 20 (1): 2–14.

Li, Fu-Jen, and Shu-Tse Peng. 1974. *Revolutionaries in Mao's Prisons: Case of the Chinese Trotskyists*. London: Pathfinder.

Li Hou 李後. 1997. *Huigui de licheng* 回歸的歷程 [The path of Hong Kong's return to China]. Hong Kong: Joint Publishing.

Li Meng 李猛. 2015. "Limeng zhuanfang: Renwenjiauyu yao rang xuesheng mingbai, zuo yige haoren nanqiezhide" 李猛专访：人文教育要让学生明白，做一个好人难且值得 [Interview with Li Meng: Humanities education should get students to understand: It is difficult but worth it to be a good person]. Interview by Zhou Zhe 周哲. *Pengbai News* 澎拜新闻, May 29, 2015. https://www.thepaper.cn/newsDetail_forward_1335945.

Li, Mingjiang. 2012. *Mao's China and the Sino-Soviet Split: Ideological Dilemma*. London: Routledge.

Li Qiao 李喬. 1995. *Maiyuan yijiusiqi maiyuan* 埋冤 1947 埋冤 [Buried grievance of 1947]. Taipei: Haiyang Taiwan.

Li Qiao 李喬. 1998. "'Ererba' zai Taiwanren jingshenshi de yiyi" 「二二八」在台灣人精神史的意義 [The meanings of "2.28" in Taiwanese mental history]. In *Ererba shijian yanjiu lunwenji* 二二八事件研究論文集 [Collection of essays on the February 28 Incident], 397–408. Taipei: Wu Sanlian Taiwan Historical Material Foundation.

Li, Wai-yee. 2014. *Women and National Trauma in Late Imperial Chinese Literature*. Harvard East Asia Monograph Series. Cambridge, MA: Harvard University Asia Center, Harvard University Press.

Li Xiangping 黎湘萍. 2003. *Wenxue Taiwan: Taiwan zhishizhe de wenxue xushi yu lilun xiangxiang* 文學台灣：台灣知識者的文學敘事與理論想像 [Literary Taiwan: Taiwan intellectuals' literary discourse and theoretical imagination]. Beijing: Renmin wenxue chubanshe.

Li Xiaofeng 李筱峰. 1996. "Yibai nianlai Taiwan zhengzhi yundong zhong de guojia rentong" 一百年來台灣政治運動中的國家認同 [National identity in Taiwan's political movements over the past 100 years]. In *Taiwan jinbainianshi lunwenji* 台灣近百年史論文集 [Collection of essays on Taiwan's past 100-year history], edited by Zhang Yanxian, Chen Meirong, and Li Zhongguang, 275–301. Taipei: Wu Sanlian Taiwan Historical Foundation.

Li Yung-ping 李永平. 2006. *Haidong qing* 海東青 [Haidong blues]. Taipei: Lianhe Wenxue.

Liang Qichao 梁启超. 1999. "Zhongguo zhimin ba da weiren zhuan" 中国殖民八大伟人传 [Biographies of eight great Chinese colonialists]. 1904. In *Liang Qichao Quanji* 梁启超全集 [The complete works of Liang Qichao], 3:1366–68. Beijing: Beijing Chubanshe.

Liao Chaoyang 廖朝陽. 1992. "Shi sibuxiang haishi hubaoshixiang? Zaiyu Qiu Guifen tan Taiwan wenhua" 是四不像還是虎豹獅象?-再與邱貴芬談臺灣文化 [Not like any of the four or tiger-leopard-lion-elephant? Rediscussing Taiwanese culture with Chiu Kuei-fen]. *Zhongwai wenxue* 中外文學 [Chung-wai literary monthly] 21 (3): 48–58.

Liao Chaoyang 廖朝陽. 1994. "Guankan, rentong, moni: Cong *Xiangjiao tiantang* kan dianying jiqi" 觀看，認同，模擬：從《香蕉天堂》看電影機器 [The gaze, identification, and mimesis: Rereading "Xiangjiao tiantang" and the cinematic apparatus]. *Zhongwai wenxue* 中外文學 [Chung-wai literary monthly] 23 (6): 135–59.

Liao Xianhao 廖咸浩. 1995. "Chaoyue guozu: Weishenme yaotan rentong?" 超越國族：為什麼要談認同？" [Beyond nationalism: Why do we talk about identity?]. *Zhongwai wenxue* 中外文學 [Chung-wai literary monthly] 24 (4): 61–76.

Lide, Vanessa. 2019. "Why Are There Massive Protests in Hong Kong?" *Washington Post*, June 11, 2019.

Lih, Lars T. 2012. "Democratic Revolution *in Permanenz*." *Science and Society* 79 (4): 433–62.

Lin, Angel. 2015. "Egalitarian Bi/Multilingualism and Trans-semiotizing in a Global World." In *Handbook of Bilingual and Multilingual Education*, edited by W. E. Wright, S. Boun, and O. Garcia, 19–37. Hoboken, NJ: Wiley-Blackwell.

Lin Nansen 林楠森. 2015. "Taiwan gaozhong xuesheng chuanlian shiwei fan 'kegang weitiao'" 台灣高中學生串連示威反「課綱微調」 [Taiwanese high school students form a chain of demonstrations to oppose the "minor revision of curriculum"]. BBC News Chinese, July 5, 2015.

Lin Yaode 林燿德. 1990. *Yijiusiqi gaosha baihe 1947* 高砂百合 [*1947 Lilium formosanum*]. Taipei: Unitas.

Lindner, Kolja. 2010. "Marx's Eurocentrism: Postcolonial Studies and Marx Scholarship." *Radical Philosophy: Philosophical Journal of the Independent Left*, no. 161, 27–42.

Liu, Lydia H. 1995. *Translingual Practice: Literature, National Culture, and Translated Modernity—China, 1900–1937*. Stanford, CA: Stanford University Press.

Liu, Lydia H. 2004. *The Clash of Empires: The Invention of China in Modern World Making*. Cambridge, MA: Harvard University Press.

Liu Zhongwang 刘中望. 2012. "Yangban hua yu dazhonghua de heyi: Qu Qiuba de Gao Erji chongbai" 样板化与大众化的合一：瞿秋白的高尔基崇拜 [The unification of typicality and massification: Qu Qiubai's worship of Gorky]. *Journal of Hunan University (Social Sciences)* 26 (4): 100–105.

Lo Yi-chin. 2008. *Xixia lüguan* 西夏旅館 [Western Xia hotel]. Taipei: INK.

Loomba, Ania. 1998. *Colonialism/Postcolonialism*. London: Routledge.

López Jaena, Graciano. 1889. "Discurso pronunciado por D. Graciano López Jaena el 25 de Febrero de 1889 en el Ateneo Barcelonés. Tema: Filipinas en la Exposición Universal de Barcelona" [Speech delivered by Graciano López Jaena on February 25, 1889, at the Ateneo de Barcelona. Theme: The Philippines in the Universal Exposition at Barcelona]. *La Solidaridad* 1 (2) (February 28, 1889): 1–8.

Lossau, Julia. 2011. "Postcolonialism." In *Spatiality, Sovereignty and Carl Schmitt: Geographies of the Nomos*, edited by Stephen Legg, 251–59. Abingdon, UK: Routledge.

Louis, Wm. Roger. 1997. "Hong Kong: The Critical Phase, 1945–1949." *American Historical Review* 102 (4): 1052–84.

Lovell, Julia. 2019. *Maoism: A Global History*. London: The Bodley Head.

Löwy, Michael. 1981. *The Politics of Combined and Uneven Development: The Theory of Permanent Revolution*. London: Verso Editions and NLB.

Lu Xun. 1981a. "Guxiang" 故乡 [Hometown]. In *Lu Xun quanji* 鲁迅全集 [Complete works of Lu Xun], 1:476–86. Beijing: Renmin wenxue chubanshe.

Lu Xun. 1981b. "Lao diaozi yijing changwan" 老調子已經唱完 [Old tune is over]. In *Lu Xun quanji* 鲁迅全集 [Complete works of Lu Xun], 7:324–25. Beijing: Renmin wenxue chubanshe.

Lu Xun 鲁迅. (1921–22) 2008. "Ah Q zhengzhuan" 阿Q正传 [The true story of Ah Q]. In *Nahan* 呐喊 [Call to arms]. Project Gutenberg. Accessed April 2, 2021. https://www.gutenberg.org/cache/epub/27166/pg27166.html.

Lui, Tai-lok. 1999a. "Hong Kong Society: Anxiety in the Post-1997 Days." *Journal of Contemporary China* 8 (20): 89–101.

Lui, Tai-lok. 1999b. "Personal Trouble or Public Issue: The Service Class in the Process of Decolonization." In *East Asian Middle Classes in Comparative Perspective*, edited by Michael H. H. Hsiao, 225–42. Taipei: Institute of Ethnology, Academia Sinica.

Lui, Tai-lok. 2015. "A Missing Page in the Grand Plan of 'One Country, Two Systems.'" *Inter-Asia Cultural Studies* 16 (3): 396–409.

Lukianenko, Sergey. 2004. *Sumerenechniy dozor* Сумеречный Дозор [Twilight watch]. Moscow: ACT.

Luo Gongliu 罗工柳. 1999. *Luo Gongliu yishu duihua lu* 罗工柳艺术对话录 [Aesthetic conversations with Luo Gongliu]. With Liu Xiaochun 刘骁纯. Taiyuan: Shangxi jiaoyu chubanshe.

Ma, Ngok. 2015. "The Rise of 'Anti-China' Sentiments in Hong Kong and the 2012 Legislative Council Elections." *China Review* 15 (1): 39–66.

Macaulay, Thomas. (1835) 1995. "Minute on Indian Education." In *The Post-Colonial Studies Reader*, edited by Bill Ashcroft, Gareth Griffiths, and Helen Tiffin, 428–30. London: Routledge.

Macek, Steve. 2001. "Containing Cultural Studies: The Departmentalization of an Anti-disciplinary Project." *Janus Head* (Winter): 142–58.

Machcewicz, Pewel. 2009. *Rebellious Satellite: Poland, 1956*. Translated by Maya Latynski. Stanford, CA: Stanford University Press.

Madsen, Deborah L., ed. 1999. *Post-colonial Literatures: Expanding the Canon*. London: Pluto.

Maier, Charles S. 1978. "The Politics of Productivity: Foundations of American International Economic Policy after World War II." In *Between Power and Plenty: Foreign Economic Policies of Advanced Industrial States*, edited by Peter J. Katzenstein, 23–50. Madison: University of Wisconsin Press.

Mair, Victor H. 1991. "What Is a Chinese 'Dialect/Topolect'? Reflections on Some Key Sino-English Linguistic Terms." *Sino-Platonic Papers*, no. 29, 2–52.

Maniam, K. S. (1981) 1993. *The Return*. London: Skoob.

Mao Zedong 毛泽东. (1936) 1965a. "Problems of Strategy in China's Revolutionary War." In *Selected Works of Mao Tse-Tung*, 1:179–254. Peking: Foreign Languages Press.

Mao Zedong 毛泽东. (1939) 1965b. "The Chinese Revolution and the Chinese Communist Party." In *Selected Works of Mao Tse-Tung*, 2: 305–34. Peking: Foreign Languages Press.

Mao Zedong. (1940) 1967. *On New Democracy*. Beijing: Foreign Languages Press.

Mao Zedong 毛泽东. (1949) 1966. "Lun Renmin minzhu zhuanzheng" 论人民民主专政 [On the People's Democratic Dictatorship: In Commemoration of the Twenty-Eighth Anniversary of the Communist Party of China]. In *Selected Works of Mao Tse-tung*, 4: 1473–86. Peking: Foreign Languages Press.

Mao Zedong 毛泽东. (1956a) 1977. "Lun shida guanxi" 论十大关系 [On the ten major relationships]. April 25, 1956. In *Mao Zedong xuanji* 毛泽东选集 [Selected works of Mao Tse-Tung], 5: 267–68. Beijing: Renmin chubanshe

Mao Zedong 毛泽东. (1956b) 1994. "Yafei guojia yao tuanjie qilai, baozheng heping yu duli" 亚非国家要团结起来，保证和平与独立 [Asian and African countries should develop solidarity, to ensure peace and independence]. In *Mao Zedong waijiao wen xuan* 毛泽东外交文选 [Selected diplomatic writings of Mao Tse-tung], edited by PRC Ministry of Foreign Affairs and Party Literature Research Center, CPC Central Committee, 242–44. Beijing: Zhongyang wenxian chubanshe.

Mao Zedong 毛泽东. (1957) 1977. "Guanyu zhengque chuli renmin neibu maodun de wenti" 关于正确处理人民内部矛盾的问题 [On the correct handling of contradictions among the People]. In *Mao Zedong xuanji* 毛泽东选集 [Selected works of Mao Tse-Tung] 5: 363–402. Beijing: Renmin chubanshe.

Mao Zedong 毛泽东. 1960. *On the Correct Handling of Contradictions among the People*. Peking: Foreign Languages Press.

Mao Zedong 毛泽东. (1961–62) 1974. "Reading Notes on the Soviet Union's 'Political Economics.'" In *Miscellany of Mao Tse-Tung Thought (1949–1969)*, pt. 2, 247–313. Springfield, VA: Joint Publications Research Service.

Mao Zedong 毛泽东. (1963) 1994. "Zhongjian didai you liangge" 中间地带有两个 [There are two middle areas]. In *Mao Zedong waijiao wen xuan* 毛泽东外交文选 [Selected diplomatic writings of Mao Zedong], edited by PRC Ministry of Foreign Affairs and Party Literature Research Center, CPC Central Committee, 506–9. Beijing: Zhongyang wenxian chubanshe.

Mapp, Nigel. 1999. "Specter and Impurity: History and the Transcendental in Derrida and Adorno." In *Ghosts: Deconstruction, Psychoanalysis, History*, edited by Peter Buse and Andrew Stott, 92–124. Houndmills, UK: Palgrave Macmillan.

Mark, Chi-Kwan. 2004. *Hong Kong and the Cold War: Anglo-American Relations, 1949–1957*. Oxford: Oxford University Press.

Martin, Robert Montgomery. 1832. *British Relations with the Chinese Empire in 1832: Comparative Statement of the English and American Trade with India and Canton*. London: Parbury, Allen.

Marx, Karl. (1844) 1978. "On the Jewish Question." In *The Marx-Engels Reader*, edited by Robert C. Tucker, 26–46. New York: Norton.

Marx, Karl. 1990. *Capital: A Critique of Political Economy*. Vol. 1. Translated by Ben Fowkes. Harmondsworth, UK: Penguin.

Maslog, Crispin. 2000. "Philippines." In *Handbook of the Media in Asia*, edited by Shelton Gunaratne, 372–401. New Delhi: Sage.

Mbembe, Achille. 2017. *Critique of Black Reason*. Translated by Laurent du Bois. Durham, NC: Duke University Press.

Mbembe, Achille. 2019. *Necro-Politics*. Translated by Steven Corcoran. Durham, NC: Duke University Press.

McConaghy, Mark. 2013. "Whose China in Which World: Notes towards a Dialectical Conception of the Sinophone." In the *Conference Reader of the International Junior Scholar Conference on Sinophone Literature and Cinema*, 1:45–74. Taichung: National Chung-hsing University.

McCoy, Alfred W. 2009. *Policing America's Empire: The United States, the Philippines, and the Rise of the Surveillance State*. Madison: University of Wisconsin Press.

Meisner, Maurice. 1982. *Marxism, Maoism, and Utopianism: Eight Essays*. Madison: University of Wisconsin Press.

Meisner, Maurice. 1999. *Mao's China and After: A History of the People's Republic*. 3rd ed. New York: Free Press.

Mei Tsu-lin 梅祖麟. 2014. *Hanzang biiao ji lishi fangyan lunji* 漢藏比較及歷史方言論集 [Essays on a comparative and historical study of Sinitic-Tibetan local languages]. Shanghai: Zhongxi shuju.

Melville, Herman. 1851. *Moby-Dick, or The Whale*. New York: Harper and Brothers.

Mendelson, Edward, ed. 1996. *W. H. Auden: Prose and Travel Books in Prose and Verse*. Vol. 1. London: Faber and Faber.

Mendelson, Edward, ed. 1997. *The English Auden*. London: Faber and Faber.

Meng Yuanlao 孟元老. 1187. *Dongjing menghualu* 東京夢華錄 [East Capital: Dream of Splendor]. Art Education.com. Accessed April 15, 2022. https://www.arteducation.com.tw/guwen/book_171.html.

Mignolo, Walter D. 2000. *Local Histories/Global Designs: Coloniality, Subaltern Knowledges, and Border Thinking*. Princeton, NJ: Princeton University Press.

Mignolo, Walter D. 2007. "Delinking: The Rhetoric of Modernity, the Logic of Coloniality and the Grammar of De-coloniality." *Cultural Studies* 21 (2–3): 449–514.

Mignolo, Walter D. 2011. *The Darker Side of Western Modernity: Global Futures, Decolonial Options*. Durham, NC: Duke University Press.

Mignolo, Walter D., and Catherine E. Walsh. 2018. *On Decoloniality: Concepts, Analytics, Praxis*. Durham, NC: Duke University Press.

Miller, Robert J., Jacinta Ruru, Larissa Behrendt, and Tracey Lindberg. 2010. *Discovering Indigenous Lands: The Doctrine of Discovery in the English Colonies*. Oxford: Oxford University Press.

Minca, Claudio, and Rory Rowan. 2016. *On Schmitt and Space*. Abingdon, UK: Routledge.

Mitter, Rana. 2005. "Manchuria in Mind: Press, Propaganda, and Northeast China in the Age of Empire, 1930–1937." In *Crossed Histories: Manchuria in the Age of Empire*, edited by Mariko Asano Tamanoi, 25–52. Honolulu: University of Hawai'i Press.

Mojares, Resil B. 1983. *Origins and Rise of the Filipino Novel: A Generic Study of the Novel until 1940*. Quezon City: University of the Philippine Press.

Mojares, Resil B. 2006. *Brains of the Nation: Pedro Paterno, T. H. Pardo de Tavera, Isabelo de los Reyes and the Production of Modern Knowledge*. Quezon City: Ateneo de Manila University Press.

Moore-Gilbert, Bart. 1997. *Postcolonial Theory: Contexts, Practices, Politics*. London: Verso.

Moretti, Franco. 2000. "The Bildungsroman as Symbolic Form." In *The Way of the World: The Bildungsroman in European Culture*, translated by Albert Sbragia, 3–17. New ed. London: Verso.

Nagano, Yoshiko. 2015. *State and Finance in the Philippines, 1898–1941: The Mismanagement of an American Colony*. Quezon City: Ateneo de Manila University Press.

Nakajima Gakushō 中島楽章. 2013. "'Kōeki to funsō no jidai' no higashi ajia kaiiki"『交易と紛争の時代』の東アジア海域 [The East Asian maritime region in the 'Era of Trade and Conflict']. In *Nanban, kōmō, tōjin: 16, 17 seiki no higashi ajia kaiki* 南蛮、紅毛、唐人；１６、１７世紀の東アジア海域 [Southern barbarians, red-hairs, and Tang people: The East Asian maritime region in the sixteenth and seventeenth centuries], edited by Nakajima Gakushō, 3–33. Kyoto: Shibunkaku Shuppan.

Nakajima, Gakushō 中島楽. 2018. "The Structure and Transformation of the Ming Tribute Trade System." In *Global History and New Polycentric Approaches: Europe, Asia and the Americas in a World Network System*, edited by Manuel Perez Garcia and Lucio De Sousa, 137–62. Singapore: Palgrave Macmillan.

Natifix Asia Research. 2021. "Taiwan Outlook 2021: A Sweet Spot of Limited Covid Impact and Growing Demand in Tech Products." Email message, January 12, 2021.

Ng Kim Chew 黃錦樹. 2011–13. *Nanyang renmin gongheguo beiwanglu* 南洋人民共和國備忘錄 [The People's Republic of the South China Sea]. Taipei: Lianjing Chubangongsi.

Ng, Kim Chew 黃錦. 2016. *Slow Boat to China and Other Stories*. Edited and translated by Carlos Rojas. New York: Columbia University Press.

Ng, Stephanie Sooklyn. 2006. "Filipino Bands Performing in Hotels, Clubs and Restaurants in Asia: Purveyors of Transnational Culture in a Global Arena." PhD diss., University of Michigan.

Ngũgĩ wa Thiong'o. 1986. *Decolonising the Mind: The Politics of Language in African Literature*. Portsmouth, NH: Heinemann.

Ohana, David. 2019. "Carl Schmitt's Legal Fascism." *Politics, Religion and Ideology* 20 (3): 273–300.

Okamoto, Takashi. 2019a. "China's 'Territorial Sovereignty' and Its Origins." *Japan Review* 3 (2): 13–19.

Okamoto, Takashi. 2019b. "Internalizing 'Territory': How the 'Territory' Concept Became Part of China's Contemporary Conceptual Apparatus." In *A World History of Suzerainty: A Modern History of East and West Asia and Translated Concepts*, edited by Takashi Okamoto, 219–39. Tokyo: Tōyō Bunko.

One Country Two Systems Economic Research Institute. 1992. *The Basic Law of the Hong Kong Special Administrative Region of the People's Republic of China*. Hong Kong: One Country Two Systems Economic Research Institute.

Osterhammel, Jürgen. 1997. *Colonialism: A Theoretical Overview*. Princeton, NJ: Markus Weiner.

Owen, Norman G., ed. 2005. *The Emergence of Modern Southeast Asia: A New History*. Honolulu: University of Hawai'i Press.

Palaver, Wolfgang. 1996. "Carl Schmitt on Nomos and Space." *Telos*, no. 106, 105–27.

Pan Kuang-che 潘光哲. 2013. "'Zhimindi' de gainian shi: Cong 'xin mingci' dao 'guanjian ci'" 「殖民地」的概念史：從「新名詞」到「關鍵詞」 [The conceptual history of "colony": From "new term" to "essential term"]. *Zhongyang yanjiuyuan jindaishi yanjiusuo jikan* 中央研究院近代史研究所集刊 [Bulletin of the Institute of Modern History Academia Sinica], no. 82, 55–92.

Pang, Laikwan. 2017. *The Art of Cloning: Creative Production during China's Cultural Revolution*. New York: Verso.

Paredes, Ruby R., ed. 1989. *Philippine Colonial Democracy*. Quezon City: Ateneo de Manila University Press.

Park, Hyun Ok. 2000. "Korean Manchuria: The Racial Politics of Territorial Osmosis." *South Atlantic Quarterly* 99 (1): 193–217.

Parrini, Carl. 1993. "The Age of Ultraimperialism." *Radical History Review*, no. 57, 7–20.

Parry, Benita. 2004. *Postcolonial Studies: A Materialist Critique*. New York: Routledge.

Paul, Bappaditya. 2014. *The First Naxal: An Authorized Biography of Kanu Sanyal*. New Delhi: Sage.

Pazderic, Nikola. 2004. "Recovering True Selves in the Electro-Spiritual Field of Universal Love." *Cultural Anthropology* 19 (2): 196–225.

Peng, Shu-tse. 1980. *The Chinese Communist Party in Power*. Edited by Leslie Evans. New York: Monad.

Pepper, Suzanne. 1996. *Radicalism and Education Reform in 20th-Century China: The Search for an Ideal Development Model*. Cambridge: Cambridge University Press.

Perdue, Peter C. 1998. "Comparing Empires: Manchu Colonialism." *International History Review* 20 (2): 255–62.

Perdue, Peter C. 2005. *China Marches West: The Qing Conquest of Central Eurasia*. Cambridge, MA: Belknap Press of Harvard University Press.

Perdue, Peter C. 2009. "China and Other Colonial Empires." *Journal of American-East Asian Relations* 16 (1–2): 85–103.

Peterson, Carole J. 2020. "The Disappearing Firewall: International Consequences of Beijing's Decision to Impose a National Security Law and Operate National Security Institutions in Hong Kong." *Hong Kong Law Journal* 50, pt. 2: 633–56.

Polly, Matthew. 2018. *Bruce Lee: A Life*. New York: Simon and Schuster.

Postone, Moishe. 1993. *Time, Labour, and Social Domination: A Reinterpretation of Marx's Critical Theory*. Cambridge: Cambridge University Press.

Prendergast, Catherine. 2008. *Buying into English: Language and Investment in the New Capitalist World*. Pittsburgh: Pittsburgh University Press.

Purbrick, Martin. 2019. "A Report on the 2019 Hong Kong Protests." *Asian Affairs* 50 (4): 465–87.

Qi Xiangyan 齐向阳. 1969. "Fensui xin shahuang de 'youxiang zhuquan lun'" 粉碎新沙皇的"有限主权论" [Smash the new tsar's theory of "limited sovereignty"]. 红旗 *Hung Ch'I [Red Flag]*, no. 5. English translation in *Peking Review*, no. 21 (May 23, 1969): 21.

Qiu Yunhua 邱运华. 1997. "Xiandai Zhongguo wenlun jianshe guocheng zhong de Gao Erji dianxinglun—sanshi niandai Zhou Yang, Hu Feng yu dianxingshuo lunbian" 现代中国文论建设过程中的高尔基典型论—三十年代周扬、胡风与典型说论辩 [Gorky's theory of typicality in the development of modern Chinese literary theory: The 1930s debate on the theory of typicality by Zhou Yang and Hu Feng]. *Xiangtan daxue xuebao* 湘潭大学学报 [Journal of Xiangtan University (Philosophy and Social Sciences)] 6:72–77.

Rafael, Vicente L. 2000. "Introduction: Episodic Histories." In *White Love and Other Events in Philippine History*, 1–18, 229–32. Durham, NC: Duke University Press.

Rafael, Vicente L. 2005. *The Promise of the Foreign: Nationalism and the Technics of Translation in the Spanish Philippines*. Durham, NC: Duke University Press.

Ramasamy, P. 2001. "Politics of Indian Representation in Malaysia." *Economic and Political Weekly* 36 (45): 4312–18.

Ratzel, Friedrich. 1897. *Politische Geographie* [Political geography]. Munich: R. Oldenbourg.

Renan, Ernest. 1887. "Qu'est ce que une nation?" In *Discours et conferences*, 277–310. Paris: Calmann Lévy.

Republic of the Philippines Presidential Management Staff. 2002. *The Aquino Management of the Presidency: Her People's Emissary*. Manila: Office of the President of the Philippines.

Research Office, Legislative Council Secretariat. 2019. "Insurance Industry in Hong Kong." May 10, 2019. https://www.legco.gov.hk/research-publications/english/1819issh26-insurance-industry-in-hong-kong-20190510-e.pdf.

Reyes, Raquel A. G. 2008. *Love, Passion and Patriotism: Sexuality and the Philippine Propaganda Movement, 1882–1892*. Seattle: University of Washington Press.

Reyes, Soledad. 1982. *Ang Nobelang Tagalog (1905–1975): Tradisyon at Modernismo* [The Tagalog novel (1905–1975): Tradition and modernism]. Quezon City: Ateneo de Manila University Press.

Richardson, Jim. 2013. *The Light of Liberty: Documents and Studies on the Katipunan, 1892–1897*. Quezon City: Ateneo de Manila University Press.

Rivas, Ralf. 2020. "OFW Remittances Hit Record High of $33.5 Billion in 2019." *Rappler*, February 17, 2020. https://rappler.com/business/overseas-filipino-workers-remittances-2019.

Rizal, Jose. 1887. *Noli me tángere* [Touch me not]. Berlin: Berliner Buchdrukerei-Actien-Gesellschaft.

Rothwell, Matthew. 2013. *Transpacific Revolutionaries: The Chinese Revolution in Latin America*. London: Routledge.

Rowe, William T. 2001. *Saving the World: Chen Hongmou and Elite Consciousness in Eighteenth-Century China*. Palo Alto, CA: Stanford University Press.

Saaler, Sven. 2007. "Pan-Asianism in Modern Japanese History: Overcoming the Nation, Creating a Region, Forging an Empire." In *Pan-Asianism in Modern*

Japanese History: Colonialism, Regionalism and Borders, edited by Sven Saaler and J. Victor Koschmann, 1–18. New York: Routledge.

Safran, William. 1991. "Diasporas in Modern Societies: Myths of Homeland and Return." *Diaspora: A Journal of Transnational Studies* 1 (1): 83–99.

Said, Edward. 1978. *Orientalism*. New York: Vintage.

Sala, Illaria Maria. 2019. "To Understand Hong Kong, Don't Think about Tiananmen." *New York Times*, August 16, 2019.

Salaff, Janet, and Siu-lun Wong. 1994. "Exiting Hong Kong: Social Class Experiences and the Adjustment to 1997." In *Inequalities and Development: Social Stratification in Chinese Societies*, edited by Siu-kai Lau, Ming-kwan Lee, Po-san Wan, and Siu-lun Wong, 205–49. Hong Kong: Hong Kong Institute of Asia-Pacific Studies.

Schenk, Catherine R. 2004. "The Empire Strikes Back: Hong Kong and the Decline of Sterling in the 1960s." *Economic History Review* 57 (3): 551–80.

Schenk, Catherine R. 2010. *The Decline of Sterling: Managing the Retreat of an International Currency, 1945–1992*. Cambridge: Cambridge University Press.

Schmitt, Carl. 1950. *Der Nomos der Erde im Völkerrecht des Jus Publicum Europaeum* [The nomos of the earth, in the international law of the *Jus Publicum Europaeum*]. Cologne: Greven.

Schmitt, Carl. 1990. "The Plight of European Jurisprudence." Translated by G. L. Ulmen. *Telos*, no. 83:35–70.

Schmitt, Carl. 2003. *The Nomos of the Earth, in the International Law of the Jus Publicum Europaeum*. Translated by G. L. Ulmen. New York: Telos.

Schmitt, Carl. 2009. *Hamlet or Hecuba: The Intrusion of Time into the Play*. Translated by David Pan and Jennifer Rust. New York: Telos.

Schmitt, Carl. 2011. "*Großraum* versus Universalism: The International Legal Struggle over the Monroe Doctrine" (1939). Translated by Matthew Hannah. In *Spatiality, Sovereignty and Carl Schmitt: Geographies of the Nomos*, edited by Stephen Legg, 46–54. Abingdon, UK: Routledge.

Schneider, Julia C. 2020. "A Non-Western Colonial Power? The Qing Empire in Postcolonial Discourse." *Journal of Asian History* 54 (2): 311–41.

Schram, Stuart R. 1971. "Mao Tse-Tung and the Theory of Permanent Revolution, 1958–69." *China Quarterly* 46:221–44.

Schram, Stuart R. 1977. "Mao Tse-Tung and the Soviets." *Il Politico* 42 (3): 445–64.

Schram, Stuart R. 1989. *The Thought of Mao Tse-Tung*. Cambridge: Cambridge University Press.

Schumacher, John N. 1981. *Revolutionary Clergy: The Filipino Clergy and the Nationalist Movement, 1850–1903*. Quezon City: Ateneo de Manila University Press.

Schwab, George. 1994. "Contextualising Carl Schmitt's Concept of Grossraum." *History of European Ideas* 19 (1–3): 185–90.

Scott, Ian. 1989. *Political Change and The Crisis of Legitimacy in Hong Kong*. Hong Kong: Oxford University Press.

Sekyi-Otu, Aki. 2006. *Fanon's Dialectic of Experience*. Cambridge, MA: Harvard University Press.

Seow, Victor. 2014. "Socialist Drive: The First Auto Works and the Contradictions of Connectivity in the Early People's Republic of China." *Journal of Transport History* 35 (2): 145–61.

Sewell, Bill. 2004. "Reconsidering the Modern in Japanese History: Modernity in the Service of the Prewar Japanese Empire." *Japan Review*, no. 16, 213–58.

Shakespeare, William. (1597) 2017. *The Tragedy of King Richard the Second*. Edited by Frances E. Dolan. New York: Penguin.

Shapiro, Gary. 2012. "'Beyond the Line': Reading Nietzsche with Schmitt." Paper presented at the Telos Conference, "Space: Virtuality, Territoriality, Relationality," New York City, New York, January 14–15, 2012. Teloscope, http://www.telospress.com/beyond-the-line-reading-nietzsche-with-schmitt/.

Share, Michael B. 2007. *Where Empires Collided: Russia and Soviet Relations with Hong Kong, Taiwan, and Macao*. Hong Kong: Chinese University of Hong Kong.

Shen, Zhihua, and Yafeng Xia. 2011. "The Great Leap Forward, the People's Commune and the Sino-Soviet Split." *Journal of Contemporary China* 20 (72): 861–80.

Sheng Yan 聖嚴. 2003. *Guanyin famen* 觀音法門 [Lessons from Guanyin]. Taipei: Fagu Wenhua.

Sheng Yue 聖嚴. 2004. *Mosike Zhongshan daxue he Zhongguo geming* 莫斯科中山大学和中国革命 [Moscow's Sun Yat-sen University and China's revolution]. Beijing: Dongfang chubanshe.

Shi Fengzhen 石风珍. 2008. *Wenyi minzu xingshi lunzheng yanjiu* 文艺民族形式论争研究 [Debates of national form of arts and literature]. Beijing: Zhonghua shuju.

Shih, Shu-mei. 2003. "Globalization and Taiwan's (In)significance." *Post-colonial Studies* 6 (2): 143–53.

Shih, Shu-mei. 2004. "Global Literature and the Technologies of Recognition." *PMLA* 119 (1): 16–30.

Shih, Shu-mei. 2007. *Visuality and Identity: Sinophone Articulations across the Pacific*. Berkeley: University of California Press, 2007.

Shih, Shu-mei. 2008. "Hong Kong Literature as Sinophone Literature." *Journal of Modern Literature in Chinese* 8 (2): 12–18.

Shih, Shu-mei. 2010. "Theory, Asia and the Sinophone." *Postcolonial Studies* 13 (4): 465–84.

Shih, Shu-mei. 2011. "The Concept of the Sinophone." *PMLA* 126 (3): 709–18.

Shih, Shu-mei, Chien-hsin Tsai, and Brian Bernards, eds. 2013. *Sinophone Studies: A Critical Reader*. New York: Columbia University Press.

Shimada Kinji 島田謹二. (1941) 1995. "Taiwan no bungaku teki kagenmi" 台湾の文学的過現未 [The past, present, and future of Taiwan literature]. In *Kareitō bungakushi: Nihon shijin no Taiwan taiken* 華麗島文学志：日本詩人の台湾体験 [Record of Taiwan's literature: Japanese poets' Taiwan experience], 460–82. Tokyo: Meiji Shoin.

Shohat, Ella. 1992. "Notes on the 'Post-colonial.'" *Social Text*, no. 31/32, 99–113.

Simons, Oliver. 2017. "Carl Schmitt's Spatial Rhetoric." In *The Oxford Handbook of Carl Schmitt*, edited by Jens Meierhenrich and Oliver Simons, 776–802. Oxford: Oxford University Press.

Skeldon, Ronald. 1996. "Migration from China." *Journal of International Affairs* 49 (2): 434–55.

Skilling, Gordon. 1961. "Permanent or Uninterrupted Revolution: Lenin, Trotsky, and Their Successors on the Transition to Socialism." *Canadian Slavonic Papers/Revue Canadienne des Slavistes* 5 (1): 3–30.

Smeltzer, Joshua. 2018. "'Germany's Salvation': Carl Schmitt's Teleological History of the Second Reich." *History of European Ideas* 44 (5): 590–604.

Snow, Philip. 2003. *The Fall of Hong Kong: Britain, China, and the Japanese Occupation*. New Haven, CT: Yale University Press.

Spanier, John. 1983. *American Foreign Policy since World War II*. 9th ed. New York: Holt McDougal.

Spengler, Oswald. 1918–22. *Der Untergang des Abendlandes: Umrisse einer Morphologie der Weltgeschichte* [The decline of the West: Outline of a morphology in world history]. Munich: C. H. Beck.

Spivak, Gayatri Chakravorty. 1988. "Can the Subaltern Speak?" In *Marxism and the Interpretation of Culture*, edited by Cary Nelson and Lawrence Grossberg, 217–316. Urbana: University of Illinois Press.

Spivak, Gayatri Chakravorty. 1999. *A Critique of Postcolonial Reason*. Cambridge, MA: Harvard University Press.

Stalin, Joseph. 1954. "The National Question and Leninism." In *Works*, 11:348–72. Moscow: Foreign Languages Publication House.

Struve, Lynn. 1979. *From Ming to Ch'ing: Conquest, Region, and Continuity in Seventeenth-Century China*. New Haven, CT: Yale University Press.

Sugihara, Kaoru. 2019. "The Asian Path of Economic Development: Intraregional Trade, Industrialization and the Developmental State." In *Emerging States and Economies: Their Origins, Drivers and Challenges Ahead*, edited by Takashi Shiraishi and Tetsushi Sonobe, 73–98. Singapore: Springer.

Sun, Ge. 2000. "How Does Asia Mean? (Part 1)." Translated by Hui Shiu-Lun and Lau Kinchi. *Inter-Asia Cultural Studies* 1 (1): 13–47.

Sun Yat-sen 孫中山. 1924. "Sanmin zhuyi" 三民主義 [The three principles of the people]. http://chinese.larouchepub.com/wp-content/uploads/2017/05/sun_3_nationalism_zh.pdf.

Sun, Yat-sen 孫中山. (1924) 1975. *San Min Chu I: The Three Principles of the People*. Translated by Frank W. Price. New York: Da Capo.

Suuronen, Ville. 2020. "Mobilizing the Western Tradition for Present Politics: Carl Schmitt's Polemical Uses of Roman Law, 1923–1945." *History of European Ideas* 47 (5): 748–72.

Swedberg, Richard 2017. "How to Use Max Weber's Ideal Type in Sociological Analysis." *Journal of Classical Sociology* 18 (3): 181–96.

Tagangaeva, Maria. 2017. "'Socialist in Content, National in Form': The Making of Soviet National Art and the Case of Buryatia." *Nationalities Papers: The Journal of Nationalism and Ethnicity* 43 (5): 393–409.

Taiwanren 台灣人. 1993. "Jia Taiwanren: Taiwan de diwuda zuqun" 假台灣人: 台灣的第五大族群 [Alter-Taiwanese: Taiwan's fifth major ethnic group]. *Daoyu bianyuan* 島嶼邊緣 [Isle margin] 8:35–46.

Tam, Luisa. 2017. "Mandarin May Be the 'Common Language' But Here's Why Cantonese Reigns Supreme." *South China Morning Post*, November 20, 2017.

Tam, Winsome. 2010. "Miguel Syjuco—First an Expatriate, Then a Novelist." Asia Society, April 15, 2010. https://asiasociety.org/hong-kong/miguel-syjuco-first-expatriate-then-novelist.

Tan, E. K. 2013. *Rethinking Chineseness: Transnational Sinophone Identities in the Nanyang Literary World*. Amherst, NY: Cambria.

Tatad, Francisco. 2015. "The Andres Bonifacio Challenge." *Manila Times*, January 4, 2015. http://www.manilatimes.net/the-andres-bonifacio-challenge/153029/.

Tee Kim Tong. 2010. "(Remapping) Sinophone Literature." In *Global Chinese Literature*, edited by Jing Tsu and David Wang, 77–93. Leiden: Brill.

Teng, Emma Jinhua. 2004. *Taiwan's Imagined Geography: Chinese Colonial Travel Writing and Pictures, 1683–1895*. Cambridge, MA: Harvard University Asia Center.

Thomas, Megan C. 2012. *Orientalists, Propagandists, and Ilustrados: Filipino Scholarship and the End of Spanish Colonialism*. Minneapolis: University of Minnesota Press.

Thompson, E. P. 1967. "Time, Work-Discipline, and Industrial Capitalism." *Past and Present*, no. 38, 56–97.

Thornber, Karen Laura. 2009. *Empire of Texts in Motion: Chinese, Korean, and Taiwanese Transculturations of Japanese Literature*. Cambridge, MA: Harvard University Asia Center.

Tlostanova, Madina. 2012. "Postsocialist ≠ Postcolonial? On Post-Soviet Imaginary and Global Coloniality." *Journal of Postcolonial Writing* 48 (2): 130–42.

Tölölyan, Khachig. 1991. "The Nation-State and Its Others: In Lieu of a Preface." *Diaspora: A Journal of Transnational Studies* 1 (1): 3–7.

Tölölyan, Khachig. 1996. "Rethinking *Diaspora*(s): Stateless Power in the Transnational Moment." *Diaspora: A Journal of Transnational Studies* 5 (1): 3–36.

Travis, Peter, dir. 2009. *Endgame*. Daybreak Pictures.

Trotsky, Leon. 1970. *The Permanent Revolution and Results and Prospects*. New York: Pathfinder.

Tsang, Steve. 1997. *Hong Kong: An Appointment with China*. London: I. B. Tauris.

Tsang, Steve. 2004. *A Modern History of Hong Kong*. Hong Kong: Hong Kong University Press; New York: I. B. Tauris.

Tsu, Jing. 2010. *Sound and Script in Chinese Diaspora*. Cambridge, MA: Harvard University Press.

van Gelder, Sarah, ed. 2011. *This Changes Everything: Occupy Wall Street and the 99% Movement*. San Francisco: Berrett-Koehler.

Van Ree, Erik. 2013. "Marxism as Permanent Revolution." *History of Political Thought* 34 (3): 540–63.

Vines, Stephen. 1998. *Hong Kong: China's New Colony*. London: Aurum.

Wade, Geoff. 2005. "The Zheng He Voyages: A Reassessment." *Journal of the Malaysian Branch of the Royal Asiatic Society* 78 (1): 37–58.

Wade, Geoff. 2006. "Ming Chinese Colonial Armies in Southeast Asia." In *Colonial Armies in Southeast Asia*, edited by Karl Hack and Tobias Rettig, 68–98. New York: Routledge.

Wade, Geoff. 2008. "Engaging the South: Ming China and Southeast Asia in the Fifteenth Century." *Journal of the Economic and Social History of the Orient* 51 (4): 578–638.

Wallerstein, Immanuel. 1989. *The Modern World-System III: The Second Era of Great Expansion of the Capitalist World-Economy, 1730–1840s*. New York: Academic Press.

Wallerstein, Immanuel. 2004. *World Systems Analysis: An Introduction*. Durham, NC: Duke University Press.

Wallerstein, Immanuel. 2011. *The Modern World System*. Vols. 1–4. Berkeley: University of California Press.

Wang Changxiong 王昶雄. 1991. *Weng Nao, Wu Yongfu, Wang Changxiong heji* 翁鬧, 巫永福, 王昶雄合集 [A collection of works by Weng Nao, Wu Yongfu, and Wang Changxiong]. Taipei: Qianwei.

Wang, David Der-wei. 2004. *The Monster That Is History: History, Violence, and Fictional Writing in Twentieth-Century China*. Berkeley: University of California Press.

Wang David Der-wei 王德威. 2007. *Houyimin xiezuo: Shijian yu jiyi de zhengzhixue* 後遺民寫作：時間與記憶的政治學 [Postloyalist writing: The politics of time and memory]. Taipei: Ryefield.

Wang David Der-wei 王德威. 2013. "Qiannian huaxu zhimeng: Dung Kai-chueng, Meng Yuanlao, Menghuati xushi" 千年華胥之夢：董啟章、孟元老、華胥體敘事 [A thousand-year-old dream of the splendid kingdom of Huaxu: Dung Kai-cheung, Meng Yuanlao, and the Huaxu narrative style]. In *Kaifeng: Dushi jiyi yu wenhua xiangxiang* 開封：都市記憶與文化想像 [Kaifeng: Urban memory and cultural imaginary], edited by Chen Pingyuan, David Wang, and Guan Aihe, 11–18. Beijing: Peking University Press, 2013.

Wang, David Der-wei, and Jing Tsu, eds. 2010. *Global Chinese Literature: Critical Essays*. Leiden: Brill.

Wang, Fan-hsi. 1980. *Chinese Revolutionary: Memoirs, 1919–1949*. Translated by Gregor Benton. Oxford: Oxford University Press.

Wang Jiezhi 汪介之. 2005. "Gao Erji de wenxue lilun yu pipan zai Zhongguo de jieshou" 高爾基的文學理論與批評在中國的接受 [The reception of Gorky's literary theories and criticism in China]. *Jilin University Journal Social Sciences Edition* 45 (4): 202–7.

Wang Shilang 王詩琅. 1979. "Lai Lanyun lun" 賴懶雲論 [On Lai Lanyun]. In *Lai He xiansheng quanji* 賴和先生全集 [Complete works of Lai He], edited by Li Nanheng, 399–406. Taipei: Mingtan.

Wang Xiaoshuai, dir. 2014. *Red Amnesia*. Chongqing Film Group, 21st Century Media, Chinese Shadows.

Wang Zhenhe 王禎和. 1982. *Meiren tu* [The beauty trap]. Taipei: Hongfan.

Wang Zhenhe 王禎和. 1984. *Meigui meigui wo ai ni* [Rose rose I love you]. Taipei: Yuanjing.
Wei Desheng 魏德聖. 2008. *Haijiao qihao* 海角七號 [Cape no. 7]. ARS Film Production.
Wei Desheng 魏德盛. 2011. *Saideke balai* 賽德克巴萊 [Seediq bale]. Vie Vision Pictures.
West, Michael O. 2014. "China, Africa and the Bandung Idea, Then and Now." *Agrarian South: Journal of Political Economy* 3 (1): 111–23.
Weston, T. B. 2010. "China, Professional Journalism, and Liberal Internationalism in the Era of the First World War." *Pacific Affairs* 83 (2): 327–47.
Wickberg, Edgar. 1965. *The Chinese in Philippine Life, 1850–1898*. New Haven, CT: Yale University Press.
Wong, David T. K. 1990. *Lost River and Other Stories*. Hong Kong: Asia2000.
Wong, Kevin, Victor Zheng, and Po-san Wan. 2016. "The Impact of Cross-Border Integration with Mainland China on Hong Kong's Local Politics." *China Quarterly* 228:1081–104.
Wong, Man. 1956. *Between Two Worlds*. Hong Kong: Student Book Store.
Wright, Richard. 1956. *The Colour Curtain: A Report on the Bandung Conference*. London: Dennis Dobson.
Wu Rwei-ren 吳叡人. 2006. "Fuermosha yishixingtai: Shilun Riben zhimin tongzhi xia Taiwan minzu yundong 'minzu wenhua' lunshu de xingcheng" 福爾摩沙意識形態：試論日本殖民統治下台灣民族運動「民族文化」論述的形成 [The Formosan ideology: Preliminary reflections on the formation of the discourse of national culture of the Taiwanese national movement under Japanese colonial rule]. *Xinshixue* 新史學 [New history] 17 (2): 127–218.
Wu Zhuoliu 吳濁流. (1956) 1973. *Ajia no koji* アジアの孤児 [Orphan of Asia]. Tokyo: Shin Jinbutsu Oraisha.
Xihu laoren 西湖老人 (pseud.). n.d. *Xihu laoren fanshenglu* 西湖老人繁勝錄 [Account of prosperity by a senior gentleman on the West Lake]. Chinese Text Project, Wikipedia. Accessed April 15, 2022. https://ctext.org/wiki.pl?if=en&chapter=350750.
Xie Yongguang 謝永光. 1995. 香港淪陷：日軍攻港十八日戰爭紀實 [The fall of Hong Kong: The war record of the eighteen-day Japanese invasion]. Hong Kong: Commercial Press.
Xu Jiatun 許家屯. 1993. *Xu Jiatun Xianggang huiyilu shangce* 許家屯香港回憶錄上冊 [Xu Jiatun's Hong Kong Memoire, vol. 1]. Taipei: Lianjing Publishing.
Xu Jielin 許介鱗. 2008. "Haijiao qihao . . . zhimindi ciwenhua yinying" 海角七號 . . . 殖民地次文化陰影 [*Cape no. 7*: The shadow of colonial subculture]. *Lianhe bao* 聯合報 [United Daily News], September 25, 2008.
Xue Hanwei 薛汉伟, Xin Zhongqin 辛仲勤, and Pan Guohua 潘国华. 1984. *Geming yu buduan geming yanjiu* 革命与不断革命研究 [Research on revolution and permanent revolution]. Lanzhou: Gansu renmin chubanshe.
Yahuda, Michael. 1997. "Hong Kong and China's Integration into the International Community." In *Hong Kong under Chinese Rule*, edited by Warren Cohen and Li Zhao, 198–212. Cambridge: Cambridge University Press.

Yamamuro, Shin'ichi. 2006. *Manchuria under Japanese Dominion*. Translated by Joshua A. Fogel. Philadelphia: University of Pennsylvania Press.

Yang, Edward, dir. 1986. *Terrorizers*. Central Motion Pictures.

Yang Kui 楊逵. (1932) 1979. *Song bao fu* 送報伕 [Newspaper boy]. Taipei: Yuanjing Chunabshe.

Yang, Lan. 1996. "'Socialist Realism' versus 'Revolutionary Realism plus Revolutionary Romanticism.'" In *In the Party Spirit: Socialist Realism and Literary Practice in the Soviet Union, East Germany and China*, edited by Hilary Chung with Michael Falchikov, Bonnie S. McDougall, and Karin McPherson, 88–105. Amsterdam: Rodopi.

Yang, Ya-che, dir. 2017. *The Bold, the Corrupt, and the Beautiful*. Atom Films, CMC Entertainment, CS Productions, Kaohsiung Film Fund.

Ye Dewei 葉德偉. 1982. *Xianggang lunxian shi* 香港淪陷史 [History of the fall of Hong Kong]. Hong Kong: Guangjiaojing chubanshe.

Yi Qun 以群, ed. 1963–64. *Wenxue de jiben yuanli* 文学的基本原理 [The basic principles of literature]. Shanghai: Shanghai wenyi chubanshe.

Young, Louise. 1998. *Japan's Total Empire: Manchuria and the Culture of Wartime Imperialism*. Berkeley: University of California Press.

Young, Robert J. C. 2001. *Postcolonialism: An Historical Introduction*. Oxford: Blackwell.

Young, Robert J. C. 2004. *White Mythologies: Writing History and the West*. 2nd ed. London: Routledge.

Young, Robert J. C. 2016. *Postcolonialism: An Historical Introduction*. 15th-anniv. ed. Oxford: Blackwell.

Yu Guangzhong 余光中. 1977. "Lang laile" 狼來了 [The wolves are here]. *Lianhe fukan* 聯合副刊 [United Daily News supplement], August 20, 1977: 12.

Yu Zhaoping 俞兆平. 2011. *Langman zhuyi zai Zhongguo de sizhong fanshi: Lu Xun, Shen Congwen, Guo Moruo, Lin Yutang* 浪漫主义的四种范式：鲁迅，沈从文，郭沫若，林语堂 [Four kinds of romanticism in China: Lu Xun, Shen Congwen, Guo Moruo, Lin Yutang]. Guilin: Guangxi Normal University Press.

Zeitlin, Judith. 2007. *The Phantom Heroine: Ghosts and Gender in Seventeenth-Century Chinese Literature*. Honolulu: University of Hawai'i Press.

Zhang, Kun, and Xiaoxiao Xie. 2019. "'Call Me Comrade Not Mister': Vicente Rovetta and the Spread of Maoism in Latin America's Global Sixties." *The Sixties: A Journal of History, Politics and Culture* 12 (2): 205–37.

Zhang Meng, dir. 2011. *The Piano in a Factory*. Étoile Pictures.

Zhang Tiexian 张铁弦. 1958. "Gao Erji yu wenxue sixiang douzheng" 高尔基与文学思想斗争 [Gorky and the debate on literary thought]. *The People's Literature* 3:7–8.

Zhi Ning 支宁. 2008. Dui Yi Qun zhubian *Wenxue de jiben yuanli* [1964 nian ban] de shehuixue fansi 对以群主编《文学的基本原理》[1964 年版] 的社会学反思 [Sociological reflections on *The Basic Principles of Literature* (1964 edition), edited by Yi Qun]. *Wenyi yanjiu* 文艺研究 [Literary studies] 9:41–49.

Zhou Yang 周扬. 1936. "Xianshi zhuyi shilun" 现实主义史论 [Thoughts on realism]. *Wenxue* 文学 [Literature] 6 (1).

Zhou Yang. 1996. "Thoughts on Realism." Translated by Catherine Pease Campbell. In *Modern Chinese Literary Thought: Writings on Literature, 1893–1945*, edited by Kirk A. Denton, 335–44. Stanford, CA: Stanford University Press.

Zhu Yunhan 朱雲漢. 2001. "Guomindang yu Taiwan de minzhu zhuanxing" 國民黨與台灣的民主轉型 [The KMT and the democratic transition in Taiwan]. *Ershiyi shiji pinglun* 二十一世紀評論 [The twenty-first-century review] 65:4–13.

Ziegler, Dominic. 2020. "China Wants to Put Itself Back at the Center of the World." *Economist*, February 6, 2020.

Žižek, Slavoj. 2009. *The Parallax View*. Cambridge, MA: MIT Press.

Contributors

PHENG CHEAH is professor of rhetoric and geography at the University of California, Berkeley. He is the author of *Spectral Nationality: Passages of Freedom from Kant to Postcolonial Literatures of Liberation* (2003), *Inhuman Conditions: On Cosmopolitanism and Human Rights* (2006), and, most recently, *What Is a World? On Postcolonial Literature as World Literature* (2016).

DAI JINHUA is professor in the Department of Chinese Literature and Language, Institute of Comparative Literature and Culture, Peking University. She is a leading critic and researcher in the fields of Chinese culture, popular mass culture, film studies, and gender studies.

CAROLINE S. HAU is professor in the Center for Southeast Asian Studies, Kyoto University. Her books include *The Chinese Question: Ethnicity, Nation, and Region in and beyond the Philippines* (2014) and *Intsik: An Anthology of Chinese Filipino Writing* (2000).

ELAINE YEE LIN HO is honorary professor in the School of English, University of Hong Kong. Until her early retirement in 2016, she was full professor in the School of English, the first Hong Kong Chinese in that position. She is the author of books on Timothy Mo and Anita Desai; the coeditor of a volume of essays, *China Abroad*; and the author of many articles on the English Renaissance and anglophone literatures, Hong Kong writing, film and culture, law, and literature.

WENDY LARSON is emeritus professor in East Asian languages and literatures at the University of Oregon. Her most recent monograph is *Zhang Yimou: Globalization and the Subject of Culture* (2017), and she is presently working on a comparative project on progress and optimism under socialist and capitalist cultures.

LIAO PING-HUI is currently the Chuan Lyu Endowed Chair Professor in Taiwan studies and the founding director of the Taiwan Studies Center at the University of California, San Diego. He has published critical essays on postcolonial theory, music and culture, and modern Taiwan literature and film, among other topics. Among the books he has coedited with friends and colleagues are *Comparatizing Taiwan* (2015) and *Taiwan under Japanese Colonial Rule* (2006). He is now completing a book manuscript on travels in modern East Asia.

LIN PEI-YIN is associate professor in the School of Chinese, University of Hong Kong. She is the author of *Gender and Ethnicity in Taiwanese Literature: Japanese Colonial Era to Present Day* (2021) and *Colonial Taiwan: Negotiating Identities and Modernity through Literature* (2017).

LO KWAI-CHEUNG is the head of the Department of Humanities and Creative Writing at Hong Kong Baptist University. Currently he is completing a book manuscript on China's ethnic-minority cinema.

LUI TAI-LOK is chair professor of Hong Kong studies at the Education University of Hong Kong. He is the coeditor of the *Routledge Handbook of Contemporary Hong Kong* (2019).

PANG LAIKWAN teaches cultural studies at the Chinese University of Hong Kong and is the author of a few books, including, most recently, *The Appearing Demos: Hong Kong during and after the Umbrella Movement* (2020).

LISA ROFEL is research professor and professor emerita of the Department of Anthropology, University of California, Santa Cruz. Her recent publications include (with coauthor Sylvia Yanagisako) *Fabrication Transnational Capitalism: A Collaborative Ethnography of Italian-Chinese Global Fashion* (2019), (as editor) *After the Post-Cold War: The Future of Chinese History, Essays by Dai Jinhua*, and (with coauthor Carlos Rojas) *New World Orderings: China and the Global South* (2022).

DAVID DER-WEI WANG is Edward C. Henderson Professor of Chinese Literature and Comparative Literature at Harvard University. His recent publications include *Why Fiction Matters in Contemporary China* (2020) and the edited volume *A New Literary History of Modern China* (2017).

EREBUS WONG is a researcher at Lingnan University, Hong Kong.

ROBERT J. C. YOUNG, FBA, is Julius Silver Professor of English and Comparative Literature at New York University. His most recent book is an edition of writings by Frantz Fanon, edited with Jean Khalfa, *Alienation and Freedom* (2018). He is editor of the journal *Interventions: International Journal of Postcolonial Studies*.

Index

135th meridian, 39
1492, 37–41
1942, 37–42
1947 Lilium Formosanum (Lin), 185
2.28 (February 28 incident, 1947), viii, 184–85
9/11 terrorist attack, 65

Abel, Lionel, 34
acceleration, 79
Africa, 55, 56, 100; and China relations, 98, 101; Maoist groups, 99; nation-states, 56; Netherlands territorial holdings, 110; Soviet Union military intervention, 56
African National Congress, 54, 68n1
Afrocentrism, 252–53
Age of Discovery, 49
agents, 84, 85
agrarian commune, 113
Aguinaldo, Emilio, 237
Ahmad, Aijaz, 72
Alexander VI, Pope: *Inter caetera divinae* (Edict), 38
Altaic: school (historiography), 9; system, 9, 10. *See also* Qing empire
amah, 166n12
America, 40; European discovery of, 38
American patronage, 123
American satire, 183
American society: racism, 100
Americans, 117; maritime powers, 110
Amin, Samir: dependency theory, 58
amity lines, 39
An Kyong-su, 237

Anderson, Benedict, 232, 250
Anderson, Sherwood, 61
Anghie, Anthony: *Imperialism, Sovereignty and the Making of International Law*, 48
Anglo-Chinese, 240, 269
Anglo-Japanese alliance, 119
anglophone, 215, 272; ecumene, 165n5; inventions, 161; usage, 160, 165n; writers, 34; writing, 149, 150, 151, 153–54, 158, 165n5
Anglo-Saxon global order, 40
anticolonial ideologies, 115
anticolonial revolution, 234, 236
anti-colonialism, 73
Anti-Extradition Bill Movement, 145–46
anti-imperialism, 73
Antilles, 51n1
antiquarian history, 37
anti-Semitism, 51
Aoki Masaru, 13
Apollonian (Classical) civilization, 37
Arendt, Hannah: *The Origins of Totalitarianism*, 34–35
Argentina: British invasion, 50
Armenians, 117
Asia, 55, 100; and China relations, 98; border wars, 56; colonialism, 153; community, 114; cultures and values, 114; decided by Asians, 113; intra-Asian trade system, 236; Manchukuo most industrialized region, 117; maritime powers, 110; nation-states, 56; Netherlands territorial holdings, 110; reviving, 113; solidarity, 113

Asian Financial Crisis (1997–98), 234
Asian Infrastructure Investment Bank, 66
Asianism, 112. *See* Pan-Asianism
Atlantic Ocean, 39
atrocity, imperialist, 65
Auden, W. H., 163; "Hongkong" (sonnet), 153–54; *Journey to a War* (book), 154; poem revision, 166n9; silent native, 164
Auerbach, Erich: *Mimesis*, 48–49, 50
Auslandsdeutsche Volksdeutsche, 44
Australia, 135, 39
Austria, 44, 117
author-speakers' movement, 156
Autonomy, 24, 85
Aw, Tash, 251, 269, 272, 274
Axial Age, 182
axis powers, 45
Azores, 38

Bai Suxiang, 93
Bandung Conference, 56, 98, 156
Baojia system (Chinese), 122
Barcelona, 237
Baudelaire, Charles, 36, 1850 characterization, 37
Baudrillard, Jean, 55
Beauty Trap, The (Wang), 183
Beijing: and Hong Kong relations, 136; as center, 98; "overall jurisdiction" over Hong Kong SAR, 145; student movement, 142
Beijing Consensus, 268
Belgians, 117
Belgium, 44
Belt and Road Initiative, ix, 6, 18, 68n5, 192, 268. *See also* One Belt, One Road
Bendersky, Joseph, 43
Bengali: psychological orientation, 84
Berlin Conference, 40, 42
Berlin Wall, 71
Berlin, Isaiah, 150
Between Two Worlds (Wong), 156
Bhabha, Homi, 206, 254–55
Bildung, 251, 252, 259
bildungsroman, 89n5, 251, 258, 268

binary: East and West, 22, 112; Cold War, 57; colonial/postcolonial, 55, 60; colonizer versus colonized, 7, 27, 55; exclusion of the third world, 56; West and rest, 5
Black Atlantic, 252–53, 262
Black Atlantic, The (Gilroy), 252, 256
black music, 253, 254
Blanco, John, 43
Blunden, Edmund: "*The Sleeping Amah*" (poem), 155; Orientalized silent native, 156
Bold, the Corrupt, and the Beautiful, The (film), 195, 197–200, 205–6, 208
Booth, Joyce: "*The Old Boat Woman*" (poem), 155; "*The Letter Writer*" (poem), 155
Booth, Martin: *Gweilo* (book), 156
Bosteels, Bruno, 42, 49
bourgeois liberalization, 138
bourgeois nations, 97
Bretton Woods, 45
BRICS (Brazil, Russia, India, China, South Africa), 63, 67, 268
Britain, 39, 43, 47, 117; and China over Hong Kong, 127, 129–30; China relations, 137; colonial-capitalist master, 154; Hong Kong status, 146n1; maritime powers, 110; negotiations with China, 132
British colonial period: anglophone writing, 153; and Japanese occupation compared, 122; benevolent/enlightened colonizer, 125; bureaucrats, 123; decolonization, 149; Hong Kong's socioeconomic institutions, 133
British Empire, 43, 155
Buddha of Suburbia, The (Kureishi), 259, 260–61, 265
Buddhism, 194, 196–98, 200; medicine, 204; movies, 195–200, 205, 206–7; organizations, 201
Buddhist, 118; organizations, 201, 205, 208
Buduan geming. See Permanent Revolution

Buried Grievance of 1947 (Li), 185
Button, Peter, 89n5
Byzantine Empire, 46

Cabrera, Lydia, *Retorno al país natal* (1943), 34
Cahier d'un retour au pays natal (pamphlet, Césaire), 33–34
Cai Peihuo, 174, 175
Campbell, Catherine Pease, 88n4
Canada: emigration from Hong Kong, 135
Canary Islands, 39
Cantonese, 158, 159
Cantonese-Chinese language, 151; sinophonism, 159
Cape Verde, 38
capital, 63, 84; accumulation, 62, 104; universalization of, 85, 86
capitalism, 59, 61, 67, 71, 76, 85, 87, 139, 146; colonial, 158; global, 64, 67, 257, 265, 268, 272, 274; versus socialism, 59
capitalization, 66, 85
caravela, 38
cash crops, 57
Catholicism, 39, 196, 233
Central America, 111
Césaire, Aimé: *Cahier d'un retour au pays natal* (book), 33–34; versions, 35; French edition, 34; "Poésie et connaissance" (poetry and knowledge), 36; postcoloniality, 37
Chakrabarty, Dipesh, 105; modernity in the East, 83
Chan, Koonchung, 152
change, 79; revolutionary, 76
Chatterjee, Partha: modernity in the East, 83
Chen Duxiu, 78
Chen Fangming, 184
Chen Yingzhen, 181, 184
Chen Zhaoying, 184
Cheung, Martha, 151
Chiang Kai-shek, 129, 181, 199, 228: sovereignty over Hong Kong, 129
Chibber, Vivek, 72, 73; class conflict, 84; cultural difference, 84, 85; "On the Decline of Class Analysis in South Asian Studies," 88n2; parochialism of Western theories, 84–85; postcolonial studies, 86, 87; *Postcolonial Theory and the Specter of Capitalism*, 83, 88n2
Chile: socialist regime, 56
China proper: Japanese colonization, 114
China, 66, 113; and Britain over Hong Kong, 129–30, 132–33, 135, 137; as hypocolony, 14, 25; capitalism, 62; civil war, 129; closed currency policy, 66; colonialism/imperialism: theory of, 66; de-Sovietization, 101, 103, 105; economic development, 65–66, 67, 102, 128, 144; Five-Year Plan, 144; Four Modernizations, 133; Gorky as foreign influential literary theorist, 80; Hong Kong development, 131, 140–41; Hong Kong sovereignty, 124, 128, 132, 144; intellectuals in Soviet Union, 93; Marxism engagement, 74; nationalism/internationalism, 96, 98–99, 100, 103; "One Country, Two Systems," 138; peasant workers, 62, 78; politics and art, 95; rule of law, 142; "Sick Man of Asia," 7; socialism, 101; socialist economy liberation, 138; Soviet Union relations, 78, 91, 93, 97–98; third world leader, 98; United States relations, 66–67. *See also* People's Republic of China
China-Hong Kong relations, 139–42
Chinese Communist Party (CCP), 74, 91, 94, 124–25; end of Cultural Revolution, 128; Great Leap Forward, 102; internal nation building, 129; limited-sovereignty idea, 98; "Long March," 106n2; permanent revolution, 77; Second National Congress, 77; socialist internationalism, 96; victory, 78
Chinese emperor, 126n3
Chinese Gorky, 82, 85, 86; literature and literary studies, 75; subjectivity, 80; theory of typicality, 80–83. *See also* Gorky, Maxim
Chinese imperialism, 66

Index 317

Chinese language, 213, 214, 215, 221–22, 226, 230. *See also* Chinese literature
Chinese literature, 165n5, 214–15, 217, 226, 230. *See also* Chinese language
Chinese Marxists, 97
Chinese nationalization, 125; Manchukuo is puppet of Japan, 117–19
Chinese People's Political Consultative Conference, 137
Chinese revolution, 67, 78, 99; success, 55
Chinese Revolutionary Alliance, 175
Chinese revolutionary romanticism, 83
Chinese writers: Gorky's influence, 82
Chou, David, 186
Chou, Michael, 201–3
Chow, Rey: on the Joint Declaration, 152–53
Chrysanthemum and the Sword, The (Benedict), 58
Chu Tien-hsin, 224
Chun, Allen: postcolonial theories, 95
City of Sadness (film), 193–94
class, 88; and capitalism, 65; conflict, 84; universalizing theories, 84
Clementi, Cecil, 226
Closer Economic Partnership Arrangement, 140
code-mixing, 166n16
Cold War, 119, 216, 237, 244; age of ultraimperialism, 123, 124; alliance, 66; East/West confrontation, 57; global flow, 59; laissez-faire free economy, 123; North/South wealth inequality, 57; political culture, 58, 59; postcolonial narrative, 58; superpower, 55–58
colonialism, 34, 36, 41–45, 51, 55, 60–62, 65, 105, 134, 258, 272; racist, 53, 54; new, 55–58, 124
coloniality, 156; followed by emancipation, 152; in nation building, 125
colonization, 62, 63, 64, 65
Columbus, Christopher, 45, 46
communism, 67, 74, 76, 85, 102, 123
Communist Party of the Soviet Union (CPSU), 91, 92; revolutionary activities, 97

community, virtues of, 113
complacency, 79
compromise, political, 133–34
Congress of Vienna, 46
Conrad, Joseph: *The Heart of Darkness*, 271
cosmopolitanism, 250, 252, 256, 265, 266, 272
counterculture movement, 58
Cradock, Percy, 130
critical theory, 72
Cuban Revolution: United States military intervention, 56
cultural politics. *See* Cultural Revolution
Cultural Revolution, 58, 73, 96, 129, 131
cultural studies, 58, 71, 73, 83, 86–87
cultural theory, 59
cultural-racial unity, 114
culture, 84, 87; diaspora, 60; importance, 84, 85; intimacy, 159; local 61; norms, 85; pedagogy, 85–86; and politics, 95; source of agency, 85; traditional, 61–62
Czechoslovak Republic, 44
Czechs, 117

Dai Jinhua, 72, 73
Danes, 117
Daoist, 118
Darwinism, 115
Das Schwarze Korps (journal), 42
Decline of the West, The (Spengler), 36–37
decolonial thinking, 249
decoloniality, 36
decolonization, 55; global, 122–23, 151
Del Valle, Ivonne, 43
Delmas, Candice: on 2009 protest, 166n8
democracy, 142, 192
Democratic Progressive Party, 193
Deng Xiaoping, 102; on New Territories lease, 131; on One Country, Two Systems, 138
Denmark, 44

Denton, Kirk: on Zhou Yang and Hu Feng, 82
dependency theory, 58, 110
de-Sovietization, 90, 91–96, 99, 101, 103, 105
Derrida, Jacques, 220
Deutsche Juristen-Zeitung (journal), 42
diaspora, 216, 251, 252; Black, 251–54; Chinese diaspora, 214, 216, 218, 251; cosmopolitanism, 250, 252; Filipinos, 235, 245–47; literature, 250, 252, 258; Malaysia, 259, 263; migration, 261, 265; South Asia, 251, 258–60; temporality, 253–56, 258, 268, 272
dictatorship versus democracy, 58
difference, principle, of, 56
Dikötter, Frank, 101
Ding Ling, 80
Dionysian (Universal) civilization, 37
Dirlik, Arif, 72
Discours sur le colonialism (pamphlet, Césaire), 34, 37
discoveries, 45
disequilibrium, 79
District Affairs Bureau, 121, 122
doctrine of discovery, 49
domination, 112
Du Bois, W. E. B., 99
Drang nach Osten ("Drive to the East") plan, 44
Duara, Prasenjit: Belt and Road Initiative, 19; Japanese imperialism and Manchukuo, 11, 12, 23; new imperialism, 109
Dung Kai-cheung, 226, 227
Dutch Republic, 39, 46, 47, 117

East: civilization, 112; religious orientation, 84
East and West, 155, 156
East Asia: colonial/postcolonial, 65, 109; intra-cultural/intellectual network, 116; solidarity, 113
East/West coordinate, 57, 58
East-Central European studies, 101
economic liberalization, 128, 138, 141

economism, 128, 139, 144–46
Edo Period: Japan in Hong Kong, 119
Edwin Morgan International Poetry Competition, 166–67n19
electro-spiritual, 196, 200, 201–2
elite culture: to popular culture, 86
emerging countries, 63
emigration, 134
Emperor system, 126n3
"*En guise de manifeste littéraire*" (Césaire), 33
Endgame (film), 54
Engels, Friedrich, 75, 76
England. *See* Britain
English language, 136, 158; and Cantonese-Chinese, 150; official language of post-1997 Hong Kong, 149
enthusiasm, 79
equilibrium, 79
ethnic studies, 87
Euro-America: (New) Left and Right, 59; classical literature: the Other, 60, 61; imperialist: as subject, 60
Eurocentrism, 41, 47, 73, 103; world map, 58
Europe: center of global power, 39, 45–46; civility and state border, 47; cultural politics, 58; geography, 38; imperialism, 35, 37; integration, 65, 66; legal system, 41–42 46–47; mode of colonization, 40–41, 51, 45, 114; mutual enmity, 39; nationalism, 111; state system, 44
European *Großraum*, 49
European New Order, 44
European orientalism, 241–42
European Union, 60
exploitation, global, 62
expropriation: during 1995–97, 63

Fagu (Dharma Drum), 201, 204
Fall of Apartheid: The Inside Story from Smuts to Mbeki, The (Harvey), 54
familism, 113
Fanon, Frantz, 34, 37, 149: critical theory, 60

Fanshenglu (Account of Prosperity), 226–27
farmerism, 162, 164
fascism, 34, 35, 102, 154
Faustian (Western European) civilization, 37
feminist studies, 87
fictional writing, 150, 185
financial crisis (2008), 65
Fitzgerald, John, 94
Five Star Billionaire (Aw), 251, 269–74
folk deities, 118
formalism, 74
Formosa Incident, 200
Foucault, Michel, 21, 257
Fourth National Congress, 78
France, 39, 43, 44, 46, 117; maritime powers, 110; prose to poetry, 36
Frank, Hans, 42
francophone, 215
Frankfurt School, 71
free Asia, 244
free trade, 154; forced, 240
free-market capitalism, 124, 133, 136
French poetry: protosurrealist, 36
Fugitive Offenders Ordinance, 146

galleon trade, 236, 245, 248
Gandhi, Mahatma, 53
Gansu (China), 106n2
gender, 87
General Agreement on Tariffs and Trade, 123
Geopolitik of National Socialism, 43
German *Mitteleuropa*, 44, 47
Germany, 40, 44, 117; Czechoslovakia invasion, 42; land imperialism, 51; Nazi expansion, 49
Gikandi, Simon, 149
Gilroy, Paul, 252–54
globalization, 38, 57, 60, 63, 67, 154; capitalist, 59–65, 110, 115; postcolonial, 265; space, 40
Golden Boy (book), 156
Goll, Yvan, 34
Göring, Hermann, 42

Gorky, Maxim: "blood and tears," 75; humanistic perspective, 80; literature and physical labor, 81; *On Literature* ("How I Studied"), 81; on typicality in China, 83; political-romantic model, 81; proper subjectivity, 74; romanticism and realism, 83; transformation, 80; work in literary textbooks, 83
governmentality, 244
Gramsci, Antonio, 71
Great Britain. *See also* Britain
Great Buddha Plus (film), 195–97, 206–8
Great Leap Forward, 102, 106n3
Greater East Asia Co-Prosperity Sphere, 112, 114, 119
Greater German Reich, 43, 44
Greece, 43, 44, 117
Green Revolution, 57
Grossberg, Lawrence, 86
Großdeutsches Reich. *See* Greater German Reich
Grossraum (*Großraum*) of *Mitteleuropa*, 42
Guandong Lease, 114
Guangzhou, 271
Guevara, Che: "fomenting revolution elsewhere," 57
Guo Moruo, 80, 95
Gweilo (Booth), 156

Haidong qing (Li), 228
Hamid, Mohsin, 251, 259, 265
Han Chinese, 25, 101, 116–18, 126, 214, 221
Han culture, 94
Han Guoyu, 196
Hangzhou, 226–27
Harbin (Manchukuo): ethnic diversity, 117
Harootunian, Harry: alternative modernities, 103–4
Harvey, Robert. *The Fall of Apartheid: The Inside Story from Smuts to Mbeki* (2011), 54
Haushofer, Karl, 43; *Raumtheorie*, 42
He Donghui: Chinese cultural world, 93
He Qifang, 95

hegemony, 88
Heidegger, Martin, 49, 255; concept of worldliness, 273–74
Heqi Tao, 201–4
Herzfeld, Michael: cultural intimacy, 159
Hirohito (Japanese Emperor), 118
hispanophone, 215
history, 86, 35, 36; colonial, 35, 65; by definition, 50; pivot points, 36–37; postcolonial, 35
Hitler, Adolf, 42; *Drang nach Osten* ("Drive to the East") plan, 44; European New Order, 44
Ho Chi Minh, 237
Ho, Louise: anglophone writing, 160; *Jamming* (Poem), 160; *Well-Spoken Cantonese* (poem), 159
Ho, Tammy Lai-ming, 159; Cantonese idioms, 161; insular and cosmopolitan, 163
Holy Roman Empire, 46
"Hongkong" (Auden), 153–54
Hong Kong, 119–25, 234–35, 237; anglophone writing, 149, 150, 151, 154–55, 164, 165n5; anomaly of colonialism, 153; autonomy, 125, 133, 146, 149; and Beijing relations, 136, 139–42; British colonial rule, 119, 121, 129; capitalist economic system, 131, 134, 135, 139, 141–42; colonial-capitalist identity, 149, 155; colonialism, 119, 142, 152, 159; decolonizing story, 148; democratization, 145; District Affairs Bureau head, 121–22; domestic product, 141; economic growth, 123–24, 137; film, 150; freedom of expression, 151; handover of, 24, 166n7, 223, 225, 226, 227; haven for Filipino activism, 237; identity, 158, 160; Japanese occupation, 119, 120–22; literary history and culture, 152, 226; local administrative region of China, 143–44; and London balance of power, 124; loyalism, 226; middle-class professionals, 133, 134; modernity, 151, 157–58; native subjects, 124, 155; One Country, Two Systems (OCTS), 128, 132–37, 139, 142–46, 149; political hub, 237, 245; political status, 129, 134, 135–39, 143, 144, 145; postcolonial, 227–28; "postcolonizing" project, 110, 125, 149; post-1997, 128, 134, 137–39; protests, 134, 148, 153, 165n1; push and pull containment, 124; removal from list of colonies, 127, 129; "retrocession" to China, 128, 132, 152; rule of law, 151, 158; sinophone, 155, 226; stock market capitalization, 141; trade hub, 236; transit for migrants, 119; university student activists, 134
Hong Kong National Security Law (NSL), 24, 146, 149, 152, 223
Hong Kong Special Administrative Region (SAR), 128, 133, 135, 149; Basic Law, 134, 136, 137, 139, 143, 144; flows of people and money, 141; political structure, 142
"Hong Kong story," 148, 149, 151, 152; *longue durée*, 153, 161
Horne, Gerald: Japanese propaganda, 100
Hou Hsiao-hsien, 193
Hu Feng, 75, 82, 95
Huang Chunming, 182
Huang Deshi, 178–79
Huang Hsin-yao, 195, 197, 207, 208
Huang Hua, 127, 129–30
Huggan, Graham, 72, 88n1
Hui Muslims, 118
human nature, 85
human subjectivity, 79
humanitarian intervention, wars of, 40
humanities, 58, 83–88
Hungary, 44, 117; anti-Stalinist revolt, 92
hybridity (Bhabha), 184
hybridization, 3, 19, 158–59, 161, 166n16, 178–79

identity, 46, 100
imperialism, 43, 51, 53, 54, 97, 105, 115; cultural, 61, 93; developmental, 120; informal, 40; of free trade, 109; new, 109–10; old, 109–10

Index   321

Imperialism, Sovereignty and the Making of International Law (Anghie), 48
India, 113, 117; anglophone writing, 150; Japanese colonization, 114
Indian peasants. See Bengali
indigenous culture, 150
Indochina: border war, 56; industrialization, 61; Japanese colonization, 114
industrialization, 68n2, 76, 85
inequality, 64, 65, 100
institutional continuity, 136, 137
Inter caetera divinae (Alexander VI, Pope), 38
internal colonization, 62, 63, 193
International Bank for Reconstruction and Development, 123
International division of labor (IDL), 251, 258, 259, 261, 265
international law, 42, 43, 46, 47, 50; concept of war, 40; Eurocentric order, 38
International Monetary Fund, 123
international society, 59
internationalism, 98; political ideology, 102; sovereignty in, 97
intra-European rebellion, 47
Inukai Tsuyoshi, 237
Isherwood, Christopher, 154
Itagaki Taisuke, 174
Italians (People), 117

Jameson, Fredric, 61, 103, 104
Jamming (Ho), 160
Janszoon, Willem, 39
Japan, 39; Asian Monroe Doctrine, 113; bureaucracy: censuses, 122; colonialism: literature, 178–80; domination in Manchukuo, 115; economic development in conquered islands, 117, 123; foreign investment: China, 117; governing Taiwan, 119; Manchuria, 117; mandate principle, 115; modernizing East Asia, 113–14; new imperialism, 109; "Overcoming Modernity," 103–4; pan-Asianism, 112–13, 237; pan-nationalism, 115; post-colonial project in Manchukuo, 116; racism propaganda, 100, 120; Taiwan, 174–79, 182–83, 185–88, 224; "territorial osmosis," 114
Japanese (from Japan proper, *naichi*, or inner land), 117
Japanese Army: on Hong Kong, 120
Japanese Empire: foreign governance, 119
Japanese military government: Chinese presence in bureaucracy, 12
Japanophilia, 188
Japan-Qing cooperation, 113
Jews, 117
Ji Xian, 180
Jiandao (Manchuria): Japanese colonization, 114
Jiang Weishui, 174, 175
Jiang Zuhui, 93
Jin Shangyi: *Our Friends All Over the World* (Painting), 106n4
Jin Zhimang, 229
Joaquin, Nick, 234–35, 236, 238, 242–43, 245, 248
Johnson v. M'Intosh case, 49
Joint Declaration: between the People's Republic of China and Britain, 132, 142, 151–52, 157, 158
Journey to a War (Auden), 154
judicial system: Hong Kong, 136

Kalyvas, Andreas, 41, 51
Kangxi emperor, 7, 14
Kant, Immanuel, 244
Kautsky, Karl, 76
Keen, Ruth, 230n1
Kerr, Douglas, 166n14
Khrushchev, Nikita: de-Stalinization process, 92
King, Martin Luther, 53
kinship, racial, 113
Kipling, Rudyard, 155
Kistner Ulrike, 41
Koktebel (film), 68n3
Korea: border war, 56; Japanese occupation, 113, 114; people, 117, 118

Korean War, 129
Kowloon: ceded to Britain, 129; District Affairs Bureau head, 121–22
Kristeva, Julia, 99
Kuomintang (KMT), 91, 94, 118, 172, 173, 193; literature, 180, 181, 187; party system, 182
Kwantung Army (Manchukuo), 115, 118, 126n3

"L'impossible contact" (Césaire), 34
La revanche de Dionysos sur Apollon (Césaire), 36
La Solidaridad (journal), 237
labor, 65, 81, 88
Lai He, 176
laid-off workers, 63
laissez-faire free economy, 123, 134
land appropriation, 41–45
landownership, 38
language mixing, 164
language, 213
Lao (PDR), 98
Larson, Wendy, 90
Latin America, 55, 100; and China relations, 98; Maoist groups, 99; resistance movements, 56; United Sates military intervention, 56
Latvians, 117
law: common-, 136; European, 38; mythic origin, 47
Lazarus, Neil, 72
Le grand saut dans le vide poétique (Césaire), 36
League for Local Self-Rule, 175, 176
League of Nations, 111
Lebensraum, 44
Lee Teng-hui, 193, 204
Left, 64, 65, 99; literary studies, 88
legacy, 88
legend: mythmaking in history, 48–51
Lenin, Vladimir, 74, 94; peasants, 78; proletariat as leader, 77; right of nations to self-determination, 97
"Letter Writer, The" (Booth), 155

Leung, Arthur Sai-cheong, 164; award, 166n19; *What the Pig Mama Says* (poem), 163–64
Leung, C. Y., 145
Leung, Ping-kwan (Yarsi), 150, 151, 153
Levine, Caroline, 74
Li, David C. S.: on Hong Kong English, 166n6
Li Meng, 64
Li Qiao, 185
Li, Ruihuan, 137
Li, Yung-ping, 228
Lian Wenqing, 175
Liao Chaoyang, 184
Liao Xianhao, 184
Liaodong Peninsula (Manchuria): Japanese colonization, 114
liberalization, 144; economic, 138, 141
limited sovereignty, theory of, 98
Lima, 236
linguistic hybridization, 158, 161
literary pedagogy, 75, 83, 85–86
literary theory, 75
literature, 75, 150; fictional character, 86; revolutionary, 80; sinophone, 213, 214, 220
Lithuania, 44
Liu, Lydia, 13
Liu Shaoqi, 102
Liu Zhongwang, 80
Lo Yi-chin, 225
local people/foreigners, 65
local resistance, 62
López Jaena, Graciano, 245
Löwy, Michael, 75–76
loyalism, 217–20
Lu Ling, 82
Lu Xun, 80, 226; "Hometown," 275; *The True Story of Ah Q*, 89n5
Lu Xun Academy: Maxim Gorky's works, 91
Lukács, Georg, 82
Lukianenko, Sergey: *Twilight Watch*, 68n4
Luo Gongliu, 93
Luther, Martin: *Ninety-Five Theses*, 46

Index   323

Luxembourg, 44
Luxemburg, Rosa, 77

Macau: removal from list of colonies, 127, 129
Mackinder, Halford J., 3
MacLehose, Murray: China invitation, 130–31; on socialist sociopolitical system, 137–38
Magian (Semitic) civilization, 37
Mak, Old (Protagonist): "Hong Kong story," 157–58
Malayan Federation, 229
Malayan People's Republic, 229–30
Malaysia, 265; diaspora, 259, 263; literature, 259; Maoist groups, 99; pan-Asianism, 113; postloyalist, 228; sinophone, 228–29
Manchu (people), 117, 118, 126n4
Manchukuo, viii, ix, 12, 18, 20, 23, 115–19; banking system, 117; created as modern state, 117; currency, 117; economic development, 118; Han Chinese population, 126n4; Japanese "family state," 118; Japanese governance, 118, 120; migration, 117; "postcolonizing" project, 110; social religious movements, 118. *See also* Manchuria
Manchukuo model, 120
Manchuria: Japanese colonization, 114; Japanese population, 126n4; melting pot, 117. *See also* Manchukuo
Mandarin Chinese, 161, 221
mandate, 111
Mandela, Nelson, 53–54, 68n1
Mandela: Long Walk to Freedom (film), 53
Maniam, K. S., 259, 261–62, 263–64
Manilamen (seafarers), 236, 245, 246–47. *See* Moby-Dick
Mao Zedong (1893–1976), 54, 88n3, 128, 92; "About the People's Democratic Dictatorship," 91; "continuous revolution," 74; importance of national style, 95; "On the Ten Major Relationships,"

93; permanent revolution, 75; praxis and mastery, 99–100; revolutionary theory, 78–79; socialism vision, 79; Soviet Union relations, 79, 93, 96, 102; US imperialism, 98
Maoism, 74, 90, 91, 95, 99, 100, 101, 103
Maoist Naxalite movement (India), 99
market capitalism, 141, 142
marketization, 128, 138, 139, 140, 144
Marshall, John, 49–50
Marcos, Ferdinand: era, 244; family, 237
Marx, Karl, 74; peasants, 78; permanent revolution, 75, 76
Marxism, 34, 72, 87, 88n2
Marxist theory, 71, 73–74, 75
mass mobilization, 79
materialism, dialectical, 85
materialism, historical, 76
May Fourth movement: humanistic traditions, 74; writers, 80, 81
Mbembe, Achille, 41
Mehring, Franz, 77
Meiji era, 13; Asianist discourse, 113
Meisner, Maurice, 93
Memorandum on My Martinique (*Cahier d'un retour au pays natal*, 1943), 34
memory, historical, 64
Menghualu (Dream of Splendor) (Dun), 226–27
Messianism, 195
Mexico, 50, 235–36
Miao Chan, 205
Miao Tian, 205
Micronesia: Japanese mandate, 111
middle-class youth, 64
Mignolo, Walter, 41
migration, 250, 251, 261, 265; labor, 247
Ming dynasty, 7, 9, 14, 28, 218, 223
Miyazaki, Tōten, 237
mobilization, 65
Moby-Dick (Melville), 245
Modern Standard Chinese (Mandarin/Putonghua), 156, 158, 159; and Cantonese intermixing, 165n5
Modern Standard English, 156, 159
modern world-systems theory, 58

modernity, 36, 63, 83, 84, 91, 101, 105, 113, 151, 173, 174, 183, 219, 235, 247; alternative, 23, 86, 87, 101–5; capitalist, 27, 157, 158, 187, 251, 255–58; Chinese, 230; colonial, 174, 196; Japanese, 173, 179, 190n6; linear time of, 250–51; literary, 214, 229; Maoist, 95; overcoming, 104, 113, 114; Taiwanese, 180; Western, 3, 19, 21, 63, 203, 253, 254, 255
modernization, 63, 68n2, 103, 119, 138; Eurocentric, 114; political, 84
Molotov-Ribbentrop Pact, 44
Mongols (people), 117, 118
Monroe Doctrine, 40, 42
Monthly Review (journal); 1955 French edition of Cahier, 34
Moscow: as supreme power, 97
Moscow Sun Yat-sen University, 91
motherland imagery, 158
multinationalism, 115
Munich Agreement, 44
myth versus history, 48, 50

Nagasaki, 236
Names Disappearing from the Map (film), 68n3
Nanyang renmin gongheguo (The People's Republic of the South China Sea, Ng), 229–30
narrative: nationalist, 158
National Character. *See* National Forum
National Forum campaign, 93–94
National People's Congress, Standing Committee, 145, 146
national self-determination, 61
nationalism, 65, 92, 111, 115, 158
Nationalist Party (Koumintang [KMT]), 77–78, 172, 173
nation-state, 46, 59, 115; Hong Kong model, 153; modern, 61
Native soil (Taiwan), 187, 247
nativism, 73
Naumann, Friedrich, 43
Nazi colonialism, 44, 45, 49
Nazi Germany, 43; race ideology, 51
Nazi *Kronjurist*, 42

Nazi political ideology, 51
neocolonialism, 61, 258
neoliberalism, 200
Netherlands, The, 44
New Qing History, 9–10, 28n10
New Territories: District Affairs Bureau head, 121–22; ninety-nine-year lease, 129, 130, 131
New World, 38, 39, 40, 45. *See also* United States
"Newspaper Boy, The" (Yang), 177
Ng Kim Chew, 228–30
Nicaraguan Revolution: United States military intervention, 56
Nietzsche, Friedrich, 36
Nigeria: postcolonial writing, 149
Ninety-Five Theses (Luther), 46
Ningxia (China), 106n2
Ninth People's Congress of the People's Republic of China, 96
Nishikawa Mitsuru, 178
Nomos of the Earth, The (Schmitt), 39, 40, 42, 43, 45, 47–49; mythmaking, 46; race, 51
Non-Aligned Movement, 56, 57, 59
noncooperation, 53
nongovernmental organization, 56
nonviolence, 53
norms, role of, 84
North-South opposition, 38, 57
Norway, 44
Nusinov, Isaac, 82

Occupy Hong Kong (2014), 148
Occupy Wall Street movement, 59
"Odysseus' Scar" (Auerbach), 48
Off-duty (*Xiagang*) workers. *See* laid-off workers
"Old Boat Woman, The" (Booth), 155
Old World, 39
On New Democracy, 78
"On the Decline of Class Analysis in South Asian Studies" (Chibber), 88n2
"On the Jewish Question" (Marx), 75
One Belt, One Road, 66. *See* Belt and Road Initiative

One Country, Two Systems (OCTS), 24, 128, 132–37, 139, 142–46, 149, 208
opium: addiction, 157, 176; smoking, 174
Opium Wars, 5, 7, 10, 11
orientalism, 73, 86, 88n2, 226
origins, notion of, 153
Origins of Totalitarianism, The (Arendt), 34–35
Orphan of Asia (Wu), 179, 223
Ostarbeiter (slave labor), 44
outsourcing industry, 63

Pacific Islands: Japanese colonization, 114
Pacific Ocean, 39
Pacific War, 119
Pact of Biak-na-Bato, 237
Pak Yong-hyo, 237
pan-African movement, 56, 59
pan-Asianism, 114, 115, 117, 121. *See* Asianism
Pang Laikwan, 88n3; "overcoming," 114
pan-Germanic Europe, 51
pan-Latin American movement, 59
pan-nationalism, 111–12
Paris Commune, 63–64
Parry, Benita, 72
Parti Communiste Française (PCF), 34
participation, political, 134
particularism, cultural, 62
"Partition del mar océano" (An ocean sea partition), 39
"Party's Construction," 105n1
Parvus, Alexander, 77
Peace of Westphalia, 46
Pearl River Delta: Hong Kong's manufacturing industries, 139
peasant revolution, 78
peasant society: "semifeudal" status, 78
Peng Shuzhi, 78
People's Liberation Army: in Hong Kong, 144
People's Republic of China (PRC), 132–33, 268, 272; agricultural collectivism, 92; biology and politics, 100; capital accumulation, 102; civilization discourse, 112; colonizing power, 125; de-Sovietization, 23, 90, 91–92, 95, 96, 98; economic ascendancy, 148; First Five-Year Plan, 102; internationalism, 101; material aid to armed struggle, 101; national-cultures policies, 94; nationalism/internationalism, 90, 91; new world order, 104; permanent revolution, 91; political instability, 157; propaganda, 95–96; Second Five-Year Plan, 102; sovereignty over Hong Kong, 148; Soviet Union relations, 90–91, 92, 96; supremacy of national sovereignty, 97; Taiwan, 193; United States racism, 100. *See also* China
permanent revolution, 74–80, 85, 91
personal freedom: guarantee, 144
perspectivalism, 155
persuasion, 79
Philippine Propaganda Movement, 233, 237, 240, 245, 268
Philippines, 99, 113, 153; colonialism, 232, 233, 234; crony capitalism, 233–34, 244; European orientalism, 241; Hong Kong, 237–38; *ilustrados*, 233, 234, 235, 240–43; Japan, 232, 234; language, 249; Mexico, 235–36; Overseas Filipino Worker (OFW), 245, 246–47; People Power, 233, 234, 244; postcolonial, 233; revolution, 1896, 242–43, 248; seafarers, 244–45; Spain, 232, 233, 240, 248; trade, 240, 243; United States, 232, 243–44, 248
"Poésie et connaissance" (Césaire), 36
"phonic" literature, 165n5
Piano in a Factory, The (film), 63
pirates, 39
place-making, 160, 247, 272, 274
Poland, 44, 117; anti-Stalinist revolt, 92
Political Consultative Conference, 137
political ideology, Nazi, 42
political system: Hong Kong, 136
politics: and art, 95
Politische Geographie (Ratzel), 44
poor: global oppression/exploitation, 62
popular culture, 73

Portugal, 39, 43, 47, 110, 117; colonies, 127
post-1997 Hong Kong. *See* Hong Kong
post–Cold War, 55; dictatorship versus democracy, 58
postcolonial, 172, 191–92; Europe, 192; literature, 215; Philippines, 233; Taiwan, 171–73, 184, 187–88, 194, 208–9
postcolonial studies, vii, 1, 3, 4, 5, 8, 10, 22, 23, 25, 26–27, 28, 71–73, 74, 75, 83, 85, 87, 88, 172, 184, 189
postcolonial theory, 54, 58–65, 73, 75, 95, 109
Postcolonial Theory and the Specter of Capitalism (Chibber), 83, 88n2
postcolonialism, 35, 58, 60, 72, 83–88, 101, 103; contribution, 95, 104; nomos of, 50–51; process, 110; race, 61
postloyalism, 217, 218, 220, 221, 247; Malaysia, 228
posttruth, 194
power relations: in nation-states, 116
powers: mandatory, 111; Western, 13, 114, 116, 120, 189n2
Practice of the "One Country, Two Systems" Policy in the Hong Kong Special Administrative Region, The, 145
pragmatism, 129
Prague Spring in Czechoslovakia, the, 92
Présence Africaine (publisher), 34
private property, protection of, 144
propaganda, 92; domestic, 100
Propaganda Movement (Philippine), 233, 241, 245
Protestantism, 46
proto-Foucauldian epistemic shift, 36
Pu Yi, 118
public wealth, 62

Qianlong emperor, 14, 19
Qing empire, 6, 7, 8, 10, 11, 14, 15, 16, 18, 28n7, 215, 216, 219, 223, 245
Qu Qiubai, 78, 80
Quanzhou, 236

race, 35, 51, 65, 87, 101
racism, 65, 100, 101

radicalism, 64, 65
Ratzel, Friedrich, 43; *Politische Geographie*, 44
Rayas, 39
realism, socialist, 86
realist causality, 158
realist literature: theory of typicality, 82
Red Amnesia (film), 63
"Red, Amber, Green" (Wong), 157, 158
redemptive societies, 118
regionalized movements, 56
religious fundamentalism, 65
religious tolerance, 46
Reluctant Fundamentalist, The (Hamid), 251, 259, 265–67, 268
Renan, Ernest, 50
research, 85–86
resistance movements, 59, 88, 236
retail sales: Hong Kong, 141
Retorno al país natal (Cabrera), 34
retrocession, 166n7
Return, The (Maniam), 259, 261–64, 265, 268
revolution, proletarian, 76, 77
right-wing populisms, 65
Roman Church: power structure, 39
Roman Empire, 43
Romanians, 117
romanticism, 81, 83, 86
Rose Rose I Love You (Wang), 183
Rothwell, Matthew, 99
Rousseau, Jean-Jacques: aesthetic romanticism, 81–82
Rozental, Mark, 82
rural youths, 62
Russia, 63, 77, 268. *See also* Soviet Union
Russian Revolution: success, 55
Russo-Japanese War (1904–5), 113
Rwandan genocide, 65
Ryazanov, David, 77

Said, Edward, vii, 1–2, 41
Sanya Declaration, 268
Sanyal, Kanu, 99

Schmitt, Carl: *Der Nomos der Erde im Völkerrecht des Jus Publicum Europaeum* (*The Nomos of the Earth, in the International Law of the Jus Publicum Europaeum*), 37, 38; account of European history, 50–51; "das Erde," 42; European coloniality, 41
Schram, Stuart, 95
Scott, Ian: autonomous Hong Kong, 130
Seattle antiglobalization protest, 59
sedentary spatiality, 41
self-cultivation, 118
self-determination, 85, 97, 111
self-orientalism, 61
self-regulating market, 124
self-satisfaction, 79
self-surveillance system, 118
self-transformation, moral, 118
separatism, 60
Serbs, 117
Seven Years' War (1756–63), 240
Seville, 236
settler colonialism, 43, 44, 216, 221
Shaanxi, 106n2
Shanghai free-trade-zone initiative, 66
Shen Congwen, 80
Sheng Yue, 105n1
Shih Shu-mei, 28n9, 165n5, 213–17
Shimada Kinji, 178
Shina (China), 13
Shum Chum (Shum Chun, Shenzhen), 131
Siberia, 39
Simons, Oliver, 42
Singapore: economic growth, 123; Maoist groups, 99; state-owned literary writing, 150
Sinic East Asia: "center" of pan-Asianism, 113
Sino-American rivalry, 146
Sino-British Joint Declaration, 158
Sino-Japanese War: First (1894–1895), viii, 7, 28n4; Second (1937–1945), 94, 178
sinophone, 213, 214, 215, 217, 221, 225, 230n1; diaspora, 216, 221; hybridization, 159; Hong Kong, 226, loyalism, 220; Malaysia, 228; migration, 216; narratives, 153; studies, 165n5; Taiwan, 223
Skipping, 79
Sleeping Amah, The (Blunden), 155
Slovenia, 44
social bottom, 64
social change, 75–80, 85
social difference, 85
social justice, 75, 83–88; humanistic study, 87, 88; importance, 71; leftist focus, 87; Marxist context, 72; promotion, 73
social movements, 64–65, 149
social sciences: scholarly inquiry, 87
socialism, 74, 77, 146, 154, 157; versus capitalism, 58, 59
socialist interference, 144
socialist internationalism, 97
socialist realism, 80, 82, 92; theory of, 81
Socialist Revolution, 76
Song dynasty, 218
Song Qili, 205
South Africa Communist Party, 54
South Africa: limited independence, 53–55; white rule, 53, 54, 62
South Korea, 123, 124
Southeast Asia, viii, ix, 4, 5, 6, 9, 11, 12, 19, 22, 25, 27, 113, 213; Chinese migration to, 7, 8, 221, 228, 269; communist networks in, 237; Hong Kong's networks with, 119; hybrid cultures and societies, 9, 206; Indian migration to, 261; industrializing, 265; leftist insurgencies in, 230; solidarity, 113
"South-South Cooperation," 98
sovereignty, 98; monetary, 61; political, 61
Soviet bloc, 71
"Soviet Construction," 105n1
Soviet debate (1933–34), 82
Soviet Union (USSR), 43, 44, 55; antiracism, 35; champion of self-

determination, 97; China relations, 91; control over client states, 97, 119–20; curriculum, 92; economic class, 96–97; films, 92; intellectuals, 81; "international division of labor," 68n2; multinational culture, 94; new imperialism, 90, 94, 109; Political Economy textbook, 93; socialist realism template, 80; socialist revolution, 77; versus United States, 59; Western modernity, 103

space theory, 38, 42

Spain, 39, 43, 46, 47, 110

spatiality, 41, 42

spatiotemporal: boundaries, 213; configurations from below, 23; imagination, 43; matrix, 5; postcolonial theory's limits, 4

Spengler, Oswald, *The Decline of the West*, 36–37

Spice Islands of the Moluccas, 39

Spivak, Gayatri Chakravorty, 3

spiritual civilization, 118

stability, 79

Stalin, Joseph (1878–1953), 74; death, 92; dogma of orthodoxy, 77; "national in form, socialist in content," 94; notion of the "socialist nation," 97; peasants, 78; sovereignty to Eastern European countries, 97

Stalinism, 99, 100

Standard English communication, 163

state intervention, 124

state land grabs: juridical legitimation, 41–48

state sovereignty, doctrine of, 98

state-owned enterprises, 62

student movement (1989), 138, 142

Subaltern Studies Group, 73

subject: as abject, 158

subject-object theory, 56, 60, 61

subjectivity, 74, 86, 88, 95

Supreme State Conference, 78

surface reconnaissance, 244

Sweden, 46, 117

Switzerland, 46, 117

Taiwan: aborigines, 185–86, American culture, 182–83; American imperialism, 182, 186; assimilation, 174, 184; Buddhism, 194–95, 196; colonialism, 153; economic growth, 123; egalitarian society, 124; identity, 172–73, 178, 179, 180, 182–83, 186, 190; language, 177; literature, 178–80, 223, 224; Martial Law, 199–200; migration, 223–24; modernism, 180; political status, 131; postcolonial, 171–73, 184, 187–88, 194, 208–9; provincialism, 181; sinophone, 223; United States, 181, 189

Taiwan Assembly, 175, 189n7

Taiwan Assimilation Society, 174, 175

Taiwanese (people), 117

Taiwanese Cultural Association, 174, 175, 176; language, 177

Taiwanese People's Party, 175, 176, 189n7

Taoism, 202

Taste of the Apples, The (Huang), 182

Tea Party to ISIS, 65

telescoping, 79

temporality: capitalist, 104, 251, 256–57, 261, 264–66, 268, 272; diasporic, 250–51, 252, 253, 254, 255–56, 258, 259, 261, 267, 270, 274; difference, 50, 103, 232, 234; disjunctive, 256, 258, 262; linear, 27, 105, 253; multiple (including alternative), 26, 35, 36, 50, 104, 114, 225, 229, 258, 268, 272; of nation, 254–55; ontological sense, 255; politics of, 214; postcolonial, 153, 172; spatialization of, 91, 104

territorial law, 42

Terrorizers, The (film), 193–94

Thailand: Maoist groups, 99

Thatcher, Margaret: visit to Beijing, 132

Third World countries: political and economic modernization, 61

Third World, 63; alliances, 98; Cold War structure, 57; nonalignment, 55–58; as Object, 60; political elites, 62

Thirty Years' War, 46

Thought: literary research focus, 88

Tibet, 9, 18, 19, 215

Index 329

time, 26, 27, 36, 37, 38, 48, 50, 79, 83, 103, 130, 138, 217, 218, 220, 225, 227, 233, 253–55, 256, 257, 268, 269–70, 274; diasporic cosmopolitanism, 250, 251, 252; distinct from temporality, 255; "The East Has All the Time, the West has none," 155; gift of, 255, 269; homogeneous empty time, 252, 256, 257, 261, 268; Hong Kong's "borrowed time," 129, 132; as independent framework for all events and actions, 268; "in fold," 217; labor time, 256, 257, 275n5; linear, 251, 252, 253–54, 255, 258, 274; "masterless," 63; "monumental," 37; narrative, 36; socialist realism, 82; space-time, 35, 36, 104, 257; teleological, 257, 268, 271; "time-deep," 155; time-out-of-joint, 233, 242; "untimely whispers," 54
Tokyo, 118, 179, 237, 246
Tokyo War Cabinet, 120
tonarigumi (neighborhood associations), 122
Torrent, The (Wang), 179
totalitarianism, 35
tourism: Hong Kong, 141
transformation, 79; after Cold War, 66
transnational spiritualism, 118
Treaties of Westphalia, 47
Treaty of Lausanne, 49
Treaty of Saragossa, 39
Treaty of Sevres, 49
Treaty of Tordesillas, 39, 46, 47
Treaty of Versailles, 40, 42, 49
Tributary system (China-centered), 7, 14, 15, 19, 28n4, 28n8; end of, 28n4; tribute and trade system, 6, 7, 236; world-system, 14
Tropiques (journal), 33
Trotsky, Leon, 74; proletariat, 78; socialist revolution, 77
True Story of Ah Q, The (Lu), 89n5
Tsai Ing-wen, 195–96, 199
Tsang, Donald, 145
Tsang, Steve: freedom of expression, 151
Tung Chee-hwa: on Chinese economy, 140; resignation, 145
Tungusic tribes, 117

Turks (people), 117
Twilight Watch (film), 68n4
typicality, theory of, 82, 85, 86, 89n5
Tzu Chi (Mercy Charity), 201, 204, 208

Umbrella Movement, 24, 145
Umkhonto we Sizwe, 68n1
uninterrupted revolution. *See* Permanent revolution
United Kingdom. *See* Britain
United Nations, 45; China as third world leader, 98
United Soviet Socialist Republic (USSR). *See* Soviet Union (USSR)
United States, 40, 45, 98, 181, 189, 232, 243, 244; China relations, 65–67, 127; control over client states, 119–20; cultural politics, 58; emigration from Hong Kong, 135; on Hong Kong, 124, 127; international institutions, 123; military intervention, 56; new imperialism, 109; nongovernmental organization, 56; objectification process, 56; open-door policy, 123; peacekeeping forces, 56; versus Soviet Union (USSR), 58, 59. *See also* New World
universal literature, 83
universal values, 61
universalism, 43, 118
University of Hong Kong students: acts of language violence, 162
Untergang, 37
Untermenschen ("subhuman" inferior races), 44
Urban Council, 121
urban-rural dyadic system, 62

Van Ree, Erik, 76
verisimilitude, 166n10
Versailles Conference, 44
Vienna, 47
Vietnam: border war, 56; pan-Asianism, 113
Vietnamese Communist Party, 237
Vines, Stephen: "Hong Kong: China's New Colony," 166n8

Volksgemeinschaft (racial community), 2
Volontés (journal), 33
voluntarism, 79

Wall Street financial crisis, 66
Wallerstein, Immanuel: modern world-system theory, 58
Wang Changxiong, 179
Wang Di, 93
Wang Minchuan, 175
Wang Tuo, 181
Wang Zhaowen, 95
Wang Zhenhe, 183
Wang Xiaoshuai: *Red Amnesia* (film), 63
war, conduct of, 46
ward system, 122
wartime propaganda, 121
wealth: unequal distribution, 64
Weber, Max, 88n4
Weil, Simone, 51
Well-Spoken Cantonese (Ho), 159
Wenxue de jiben yuanli (The basic principles of literature, Yi), 83
Wenxue gailun (Introduction to literature, Cai), 83
West/East Indies: maritime powers, 110
West: political psychology, 84
Western countries: and China relations, 13, 98, 114, 116, 120, 189n2
Western Xia dynasty, 225
Westerners: "bourgeois consciousness," 84
Westphalian state, 39
What the Pig Mama Says (Leung), 163–64
Wilson, Woodrow, 110–11, 125n1
Wing Sang Law: Hong Kong Chinese elites, 165n3
Woman Who Had Two Navels, The (Joaquin), 234–35, 236, 238–40, 245, 246, 247–48
Wong, Man: on Blunden, 156; *Between Two Worlds* (poem), 156
Wong, T. K.: *Red Amber Green* (short story), 157
working-class subjects, 155
World Social Forum, 59

World War I, 113
World War II, 58, 100; in Europe, 55;
world order, 57
Wu Birui: *Our Friends All Over the World* (Painting), 106n4
Wu Zhuoliu, 179
Wu Zujiang, 93
Wuhan Plenum (1958), 78

Xie Fei, 93
Xinjiang, 9, 18, 19, 215
Xixia lüguan (Lo), 237

Ya-fei-la figures, 100
Yamamuro Shin'ichi: Manchuria a "chimera," 115, 125–26n3
Yan'an: Soviet influences, 91
Yang Kui, 177
Yang Ya-che, 195, 205
Yang, Edward, 193
Ye Shitao, 181
yellow race, 113
yimin, 217, 218
Yin Chengzong, 93
Yokohama, 237
Yoshimi Takeuchi: Asianism is a mood, 125n2
Yu Dengfa, 199–200
Yu Guangzhong, 181
Yu Kil-chun, 237
Yu Zhaoping: on Gorky, 80–81; on Zhou Yang, 81–82
Yuan Shikai, 175
Yuhai (Fish bones, Ng), 229
Yunnan, 9, 10, 28n8

Zhang Meng: *The Piano in a Factory* (film), 63
Zhang Tiexian: on Gorky, 83
Zhou dynasty, 218
Zhou Yang, 75; article published in *Wenxue* (journal), 88n4; on Gorky, 81; and Hu Feng debate, 82; "Thoughts on Realism," 82; works as textbooks, 83; Zhu Xining, 181
Žižek, Slavoj, 102

www.ingramcontent.com/pod-product-compliance
Lightning Source LLC
Chambersburg PA
CBHW051048230426
43666CB00012B/2605